T0271397

PRICE AND QUANTITY INDEX NUMBERS

Price and quantity indices are important, much-used measuring instruments, and it is therefore necessary to have a good understanding of their properties. This book is the first comprehensive text on index number theory since Irving Fisher's 1922 *The Making of Index Numbers*. The book covers intertemporal and interspatial comparisons, ratio- and difference-type measures, discrete and continuous time environments, and upper- and lower-level indices. Guided by economic insights, this book develops the instrumental or axiomatic approach. There is no role for behavioral assumptions. In addition to subject matter chapters, two entire chapters are devoted to the rich history of the subject.

Bert M. Balk is Professor of Economic Measurement and Economic-Statistical Research at the Rotterdam School of Management, Erasmus University, and Senior Researcher at Statistics Netherlands. Other positions that Professor Balk held at Statistics Netherlands include Chief of the Research Section in the Department for Price Statistics, Deputy Head of the Department for Price Statistics, Senior Researcher in the Department of Statistical Methods/Methods and Informatics Department, Director of the Center for Research of Economic Micro-Data (CEREM), and Researcher/Consultant in the Division of Macro-Economic Statistics and Dissemination. He is the author of *Industrial Price, Quantity, and Productivity Indices: The Micro-Economic Theory and an Application* (1998). Professor Balk is Associate Editor of *Statistica Neerlandica* and the *Journal of Productivity Analysis* and author of a large number of papers in learned journals.

Price and Quantity Index Numbers

Models for Measuring Aggregate Change and Difference

BERT M. BALK

Rotterdam School of Management
Erasmus University
and
Statistics Netherlands

CAMBRIDGE
UNIVERSITY PRESS

CAMBRIDGE
UNIVERSITY PRESS

32 Avenue of the Americas, New York NY 10013-2473, USA

Cambridge University Press is part of the University of Cambridge.

It furthers the University's mission by disseminating knowledge in the pursuit of education, learning and research at the highest international levels of excellence.

www.cambridge.org
Information on this title: www.cambridge.org/9780521889070

© Bert M. Balk 2008

First published 2008

A catalogue record for this publication is available from the British Library

Library of Congress Cataloguing in Publication data

Balk, B. M.
Price and quantity index numbers: models for measuring aggregate change and difference / Bert M. Balk.
p. cm.
Includes bibliographical references and index.
ISBN 978-0-521-88907-0 (hardback)
1. Price indexes. 2. Index numbers (Economics) I. Title.
HB225.B354 2008
338.528 – dc22 2008014567

ISBN 978-0-521-88907-0 Hardback
ISBN 978-1-107-40496-0 Paperback

Contents

List of Tables

Preface

Basically, this book is the result of my curiosity. Let me try to explain this.

Equipped with a mathematics degree and having completed my military service, I found myself, more or less accidentally, employed at the Netherlands' Central Bureau of Statistics (now called Statistics Netherlands). Though not very explicitly formulated, the aim was that I should set up research in price statistics, because this was somehow found to be necessary – inflation was high in those years. After a while I had, I think, a fair idea of what all those price statisticians were doing, individually and collectively. But, though Mudgett's 1951 book, *Index Numbers*, was given to me as a sort of welcome present (in 1973!), there was no research tradition at the office to continue. So I started looking at the then-current literature for clues – there was no Internet in those days, but, fortunately, the office had an excellent library – and, driven by internally and externally motivated research questions, gradually the field of theory opened up for me.

I learned that there were several approaches, going by names such as the "test approach," "economic approach," and "stochastic approach." There was the rather arcane "Divisia approach," and the even more obscure "factorial approach." I traced back the history of ideas by looking at source materials. Meanwhile, a number of concrete problems came along for which practical solutions had to be found, such as the treatment of seasonal commodities, the choice between direct or chained indices, and the best way of making international price and volume comparisons.

The central questions that, in the background, kept me occupied through all those years are questions such as: What, exactly, is a price or quantity index? Alternatively, which question is this or that index supposed to be the answer to? Are the actual indices as compiled and published by statistical agencies theoretically justified, and, if not, can something be said about their "biases"? This book more or less summarizes what I have learned and what I want to leave as a legacy to the coming generation(s). If anything, this book wants to convey the message that there is no single question and, hence, no single answer, but this does not mean that anything goes.

What to Expect?

This book is about measurement in economics, in particular the measurement of aggregate price and quantity change (through time) or difference (across regions or countries). The approach chosen is the instrumental one, rooted in the second half of the 19th century and brought to maturity by Irving Fisher. Alternative names are "axiomatic approach" or "test approach." Thus, there is no formal economic theory involved, and data are taken as given. Though no use is made of behavioural assumptions, the treatment of the various subjects is of course based on economic insights, more or less of the common-sense variety.

The mathematical prerequisites for reading this book are very modest. Any official index, such as a CPI or a PPI, is just a big machine that eats a lot of data and crunches out a small number of results, called index numbers. Mathematics is a way of describing efficiently what one wants such a machine to do, and of exploring the relations between all those requirements. The level of mathematics is, I guess, that of undergraduate economics.

Having had this book at the start of my career would have made my journey much easier. However, this book could not have been written in 1973, because many important developments took place during the last quarter of the 20th century; moreover, I was involved in most of these developments. As a result, the organisation of the materials in this book is tainted by my prejudices and idiosyncrasies.

The Readers

Though index numbers are everywhere in the media and occasionally surface in political debates, not everyone needs to read this book to obtain a proper understanding of what can and cannot be concluded from those numbers, though some parts might be helpful. This book is primarily intended for those who would go a step further. In particular, I am thinking of the following groups:

- Those who are interested in measurement in economics, beyond the basics taught in undergraduate economics courses.
- Those working in national accounts and price statistics departments of official statistical agencies or central banks.

- Those working with indices or indicators in other fields (because the mathematics does not depend on the particular interpretation of certain variables as representing prices and other variables as representing quantities).
- Graduate and Ph.D. students, and academic researchers who want to develop this area further.

A Reader's Guide

The core of this book is formed by chapter 3, which is by far the longest. It is a survey of the axiomatic approach to the measurement of price or quantity change through time, and thereby concentrates on bilateral comparisons. Change can be measured as a ratio or as a difference, which leads to indices and indicators, respectively. Both are measurement devices, intended to summarize in a single number thousands of individual changes. What, precisely, are the requirements that such devices must satisfy? Which devices satisfy which requirements? Are all such requirements compatible with each other, and what if they are not? These are some of the questions answered in chapter 3.

Chapters 4 and 5 are connected in the sense that they treat special topics from the same viewpoint. The first part of chapter 4 is concerned with the question of whether an index can always be written as a weighted mean of subindices for (groups of) commodities. If yes, that would be of great help for the interpretation of outcomes. The second part of chapter 4 is concerned with a similar problem, but in the time domain. In practice one usually deals with periods (say, years) consisting of subperiods (say, months). It would be very helpful if for any index formula there was a clear relation between outcomes for periods and those for subperiods.

Chapter 5 is also concerned with an important practical issue. The structure of a CPI or a PPI usually consists of multiple layers of aggregates. At the lowest, so-called elementary aggregate, level cost- and response-burden-related considerations dictate the use of relatively small samples of price and quantity data. Elementary aggregate price indices must then be estimated. From a theoretical perspective, this chapter looks into the interplay of estimators, sampling designs, and estimation targets.

Chapter 6 reviews the theory of line-integral indices, of which the Divisia indices are the best known species. The distinguishing feature of this approach is that time is conceived as a continuous variable. The theory of Divisia indices is usually seen as providing the conceptual framework for chained indices. The path-(in)dependency issue, which has been a source of much confusion, here gets a serious treatment.

Price and quantity indices are used not only for intertemporal comparisons but also for making comparisons between countries or regions. International comparisons, under the aegis of some international organisation executed by national agencies, have gained in (political) importance over the past decades. Chapter 7 spells out the progress that has been made in understanding the nature of the many comparison methods that have been developed.

Last but not least, chapters 1 and 2 are about the history of the subject. Chapter 1 paints, in broad strokes, the development of index number theory through history. Being aware of the sometimes very colorful historical developments is not only interesting as such but can also help to prevent rediscoveries, as I have seen happen repeatedly. Chapter 2 recounts the many controversies about the methodology of international comparisons that made the last quarter of the 20th century so lively. The perspective here is decidedly the author's; reader be warned!

All the chapters can be read independently. To make this possible, some repetition, especially of notational issues, had to be retained. Also, some topics are seemingly treated twice: for example, direct and chained indices. In chapter 3 this subject is treated from the viewpoint of bilateral indices, whereas in chapter 6 the viewpoint is that of continuous time.

Provenance

This book[1] draws upon a number of formally and informally published articles and reports. Here follows an overview of its main sources.

Chapter 1 is the revised and expanded version of a 1984 report, entitled "A Brief Review of the Development of Price Index Theory" (Statistics Netherlands, Voorburg).

Chapter 2 is a revised version of the second half of my 1999 article "Contributions from Statistics Netherlands to the Axiomatic Theory of Price Indices," in *A Century of Statistics*, edited by J. G. S. J. van Maarseveen and M. B. G. Gircour (Statistics Netherlands, Voorburg; Stichting Beheer IISG, Amsterdam).

Chapter 3 is a thoroughly revised and expanded version of my 1995 article "Axiomatic Price Index Theory: A Survey," *International Statistical Review* 63, 69–93. It also contains results from my 2003 article "Ideal Indices and Indicators for Two or More Factors," *Journal of Economic and Social Measurement* 28, 203–17.

---

[1] The views expressed in this book are those of the author and do not necessarily reflect any policy of Statistics Netherlands.

The first part of chapter 4 is an extended version of my 2004 article "Decompositions of Fisher Indexes," *Economics Letters* 82, 107–13.

Chapter 5 is a reorganised version of an article, entitled "Price Indexes for Elementary Aggregates: The Sampling Approach," that appeared in 2005 in the *Journal of Official Statistics* 21, 675–99.

Chapter 6 has a long publication history. The first version was written in 1983 and has been circulating under the title "Line-Integral Price and Quantity Indices: A Survey." An expanded second version, bearing the title "Divisia Price and Quantity Indices: 75 Years After," was informally released in 2000 and has since then been frequently cited. The current version comprises the main part of an article, entitled "Divisia Price and Quantity Indices: 80 Years After," *Statistica Neerlandica* 59 (2005), 119–58.

Chapter 7 is an abridged and updated version of the 2001 report "Aggregation Methods in International Comparisons: What Have We Learned?" (Erasmus Research Institute of Management, Erasmus University Rotterdam).

Acknowledgments

Over the years many people have crossed my way and I have crossed the ways of many people. Sometimes our ways coincided, sometimes our ways parted. To draw up a list of all those fine professionals would be impossible – and quite a number of them are no longer with us – so here is one big thank-you for all the inspiration they gave to me. But a special word of thanks goes to Erwin Diewert, who fed me with detailed comments on one of the last drafts.

1

Price Indices through History

1.1 Introduction

Where people trade with each other, there are prices involved – either explicitly, when for the provision of goods or services has to be paid with money, or implicitly, when there is payment in kind. Over the course of history people have expressed concerns about fluctuations of prices, especially of daily necessities such as bread. Also, though to a lesser extent, regional price differences were a source of concern. Since sharp price fluctuations easily led to social unrest, authorities considered it their task to regulate prices. And price regulation presupposes price measurement. Though the systematic measurement of price changes and price differences had to wait until the emergence of official (national) statistical agencies around the turn of the 20th century, there are numerous examples of individuals and authorities who were engaged in price measurement and/or regulation.

A rather famous example is the *Edict on Maximum Prices* (Edictum de Pretiis Rerum Venalium), issued by the Roman emperor Diocletianus in the year 301. Along with a coinage reform, the Edict declared maximum prices for more than a thousand commodities, including food, clothing, freight charges, and wages. This turned out to be not very helpful, because the continued money supply increased inflation, and the maximum prices were apparently set too low.

An interesting case is the regulation on bread prices that was issued by the municipal council of Gdańsk in 1433 (see Kula 1986, chapter 8). Here the price of bread was fixed through time, while fluctuations in the supply of corn were to some extent accommodated by letting the weight of a loaf

1

vary. Technically speaking, the unit of measurement was allowed to vary. Kula remarks that

The system of a constant price for bread coupled with a variable weight for the loaf must have accorded well with the pre-industrial mentality as well as with the social situation that obtained in urban markets, or else it would hardly have been found throughout Europe.

He goes on to observe that

Its ideological basis was St. Thomas's theory of the just price – just in the sense of being invariable, its invariability being dictated above all by its usefulness to man. The practice thus constituted a tolerable compromise between the theory of invariable price and the requirements of the commodity market, while preserving as constant the quantity of money paid. Technically, it would seem this method was favored by the frequent lack of small change and the limited divisibility of coinage.

In our view, however, the paramount importance of this system lay in the political sphere. For it made it possible to alter the price of the most basic article of diet in a manner that was not obvious, and therefore less offensive, to the urban plebs, whose wrath was often feared by the bakers' guild as well as by the municipal authorities and their feudal overlords.... It is thus reasonable to look upon the whole process, within limits, as a safety-valve or a buffer against social reaction to market developments.

In his historic overview entitled "Digressions concerning the variations in the value of silver during the course of the four last centuries," which is part of chapter 11 of book one of *An Enquiry into the Nature and Causes of the Wealth of Nations*, Adam Smith (1776) quotes numerous individuals and authorities who were engaged in price measurement and/or regulation. Among those Bishop Fleetwood figures as one of "the two authors who seem to have collected, with the greatest diligence and fidelity, the prices of things in ancient times."

Indeed, according to Edgeworth (1925a), "the earliest treatise on index numbers and one of the best" is Bishop William Fleetwood's *Chronicon Preciosum; Or an Account of English Money, the Price of Corn and Other Commodities for the Last 600 Years*, the first edition of which was published in 1704. Edgeworth (1925a), Ferger (1946), and Kendall (1969) all provide the relevant details. Based on their accounts the story can be summarized as follows. A certain Oxford college was founded between 1440 and 1460, and one of its original statutes required a person, when admitted to fellowship, to swear to vacate it if coming into possession of a personal estate of more than £5 per annum. The question was whether, in the year 1700, a man might conscientiously take his oath even if he possessed a larger estate, seeing that the value of money had fallen in the meantime.

Fleetwood rightly decided that "the Founder intended the same ease, and favour to those who should live in his college 260 years after his decease, as to those who lived in his own time." To answer the question, Fleetwood executed an extensive inquiry into the course of prices over the past 600 (!) years. In particular he considered how much money would be required to buy £5 worth (at 1440/60 prices) of four commodities – corn, meat, drink, and cloth, these being then, apparently, the necessities of academic life. He came to the conclusion that for these four, respectively, the present value of £5 was £30, £30, "somewhat above £25," and "somewhat less than £25." "And therefore I can see no cause, why £28, or £30 per annum should now be accounted, a greater estate, than £5 was heretofore, betwixt 1440, and 1460." The inference was that an income of £30 or less "may be enjoyed, with the same innocence and honesty, together with a Fellowship, according to the Founder's will."

Fleetwood thus had four items in his basket-of-goods. As he found, in each case, the decrease in the purchasing power of money to be of more or less the same magnitude, he was relieved of the necessity of averaging his four price relatives, or of considering their weights. His formulation of the problem, however, is strikingly modern. Fleetwood tried to determine the amount of money that would guarantee "the same ease and favour" as could be obtained with £5 in 1440/1460.

Similar concerns led the government of the State of Massachusetts in 1780 to issue bonds whose value was indexed by means of a so-called Tabular Standard (see Fisher 1913). The goal here was to terminate unrest among the soldiers fighting in the independence war. Apart from incidents like this, however, it took about 200 years before Fleetwood's problem was rediscovered and its central importance recognized.

Although there has not yet been written a complete history of the development of price measurement, it is not the purpose of this chapter to remedy this. Such a project would require one or more separate volumes.[1] The more modest purpose of this chapter is to give an impression of the genesis of the main types of price index theory as well as the various formulas that will be discussed in more detail in the remainder of this book.

There exist a number of (short) surveys about the history of the subject. Fisher's (1922) *The Making of Index Numbers* contains a separate historical

---

[1] Interesting material can be found in a number of recent reviews, such as Reinsdorf and Triplett (2008). The Boskin Commission Report (1996) gave rise to a lot of (historical) research. See the Spring 2006 issue of the *International Productivity Monitor* on this report's impact on price measurement.

appendix, entitled "Landmarks in the History of Index Numbers" and has historical remarks scattered throughout the book. Walsh (1932) reviews the history up to 1920. The *Bibliography on Index Numbers* (compiled by R. G. D. Allen and W. R. Buckland), issued in 1956 by the International Statistical Institute, contains a brief but useful general survey of the literature up to 1954. Also, the paper by Ruggles (1967), though focussed on international price comparisons, contains a lot of information about the historical development. Kendall's (1969) essay on the early history of index numbers reviews the progress of the subject up to 1900. There is an interesting note on the origins of index numbers by Chance (1966). Diewert (1988) surveyed the (early) history of price index research under five distinct headings: the fixed basket approach, the statistical approach, the test approach, the Divisia approach, and the economic approach. More recently, a brief review of the history was provided by Persky (1998).

This chapter will highlight the main events in a more or less chronological order.[2] The notation used therefore deviates from the notation systems in the various sources and complies with modern standards.

In line with most of the literature it is assumed that there are N commodities, labelled as $1, \ldots, N$, which are available through a number of consecutive time periods t (usually but not necessarily of equal length). The period t vector of prices will be denoted by $p^t \equiv (p_1^t, \ldots, p_N^t)$, and the associated vector of quantities by $x^t \equiv (x_1^t, \ldots, x_N^t)$. All the prices and quantities are assumed to be positive real numbers.[3]

A bilateral comparison concerns two periods, which may or may not be adjacent, and is carried out by means of a price and/or quantity index. In its most general form, a *bilateral price index* is a certain positive function $P(p, x, p', x')$ of $4N$ variables, two price vectors and two quantity vectors, which shows "appropriate behavior" with respect to the prices that are the subject of comparison. Likewise, a *bilateral quantity index* is another positive function $Q(p, x, p', x')$ of the same $4N$ variables, that shows "appropriate behavior" with respect to the quantities.

Let the periods to be compared be denoted by 0, called the *base period*, and 1, called the *comparison period*. Then $P(p^1, x^1, p^0, x^0)$ and

----

[2] More detailed discussions and biographies of the people involved can be accessed via the references.

[3] The term *commodity* serves as a primitive term that can refer to goods as well as services, tightly or loosely defined. It is assumed that there are no new or disappearing commodities. It is also (tacitly) assumed that the commodities do not exhibit quality change, or that quality change has been accounted for by making appropriate adjustments to the prices or quantities. For the history of quality adjustment, see Banzhaf (2001).

$Q(p^1, x^1, p^0, x^0)$ are price and quantity index numbers, respectively, for period 1 relative to period 0. Put otherwise, an index number (outcome) is a particular realisation of an index (function). In literature and daily talk the distinction between index and index number is often blurred. Although it is important to keep this distinction in mind, in the interest of readability an index is usually presented in the form of an index number for a certain period 1 relative to another period 0. The suggestion therefore is that period 0 precedes period 1.

1.2 The Fathers

All historians agree that the first genuine price index was constructed by the French economist Dutot (1738).[4] His computation can be formalized as

$$P^D(p^1, p^0) \equiv \frac{\sum_{n=1}^N p_n^1}{\sum_{n=1}^N p_n^0} = \frac{(1/N)\sum_{n=1}^N p_n^1}{(1/N)\sum_{n=1}^N p_n^0}, \tag{1.1}$$

Dutot's price index can, according to the rightmost part of (1.1), be conceived as a ratio of arithmetic averages of prices coming from the two periods. Either average could be viewed as measuring the price level of a period. Hence, Dutot's price index can also be conceived as a ratio of price levels.

Next comes the Italian, more precisely Istrian, economist Carli (1764).[5] The price index he computed was a simple arithmetic average of price relatives,

$$P^C(p^1, p^0) \equiv (1/N)\sum_{n=1}^N \frac{p_n^1}{p_n^0}. \tag{1.2}$$

Young (1812) appears to be one of the first who recognized, although rather implicitly, the necessity of introducing weights into a price index, to reflect the fact that not all the commodities are equally important. His proposal could be interpreted as a generalization of the Dutot index, namely $\sum_{n=1}^N a_n p_n^1 / \sum_{n=1}^N a_n p_n^0$, where a_n is some (positive, real-valued) measure of the importance of commodity n ($n = 1, \ldots, N$). Walsh (1932), however, interpreted Young as proposing the following price index,

$$P^Y(p^1, p^0; a) \equiv \frac{\sum_{n=1}^N a_n(p_n^1/p_n^0)}{\sum_{n=1}^N a_n}, \tag{1.3}$$

---

[4] On Dutot and his work see Mann (1936).
[5] Details on Carli's life can be found at the website www.istrianet.org.

which can be considered a generalization of the Carli index.[6] A rather realistic system of weights was proposed by Lowe (1823). He suggested

$$P^{Lo}(p^1, p^0; x^b) \equiv \frac{\sum_{n=1}^{N} p_n^1 x_n^b}{\sum_{n=1}^{N} p_n^0 x_n^b}, \tag{1.4}$$

where x_n^b was a (rough) estimate of the quantity of commodity n ($n = 1, \ldots, N$) consumed during a certain period of time b. Such a system of weights was called a Tabular Standard. Lowe's index, then, compares the cost of the commodity basket $(x_1^b, \ldots, x_N^b)$ at the two periods 0 and 1.[7] The Tabular Standard employed by the State of Massachusetts during 1780–6 had a simple structure and used only four commodities, namely "Five Bushels of Corn, Sixty-eight Pounds and four-seventh Parts of a Pound of Beef, Ten Pounds of Sheeps Wool, and Sixteen Pounds of Sole Leather" (see Fisher 1913).

In the second half of the 19th century the interest in the construction of price indices increased gradually. Jevons (1863) was a sort of pioneer.[8] He introduced what later came to be called the geometric mean price index,

$$P^J(p^1, p^0) \equiv \prod_{n=1}^{N} \left(\frac{p_n^1}{p_n^0}\right)^{1/N}, \tag{1.5}$$

and argued why this mean should be preferred to other kinds of mean.

Jevons, like other authors of the decades to come, was primarily concerned with the measurement of a concept called "the value of money," "the purchasing power of money," "the general price level," and all this in connection with fluctuations in the quantity of gold. Since he was of the opinion that a change on the part of gold affected the prices of all commodities equiproportionately, he thought the geometric mean of the price relatives to be the appropriate measure (see also Jevons 1865). Laspeyres (1864) opposed this view and advocated instead the Carli index (1.2).

[6] But note that by choosing $a_n = p_n^0$ ($n = 1, \ldots, N$) one gets the Dutot index.
[7] Essentially the same idea was proposed in 1828 by Phillips, though Jastram (1951) interprets Phillips's idea as being identical to Paasche's index. In the context of producing annual index numbers, Lowe suggested keeping the quantities fixed during five years.
[8] On Jevons see Fitzpatrick (1960), Aldrich (1992), and Maas (2001). Jevons was regarded by Fisher (1922, p. 459) as "the father of index numbers." According to Walsh (1932) he "opened the theory of the subject." Edgeworth (1925c), Kendall (1969), and Diewert (1988), however, regarded Lowe as "father." Actually, Fleetwood could be considered as the real "father."

In 1871, Drobisch discussed a number of alternatives, among which was the formula

$$P^U(p^1, x^1, p^0, x^0) \equiv \frac{\sum_{n=1}^{N} p_n^1 x_n^1 / \sum_{n=1}^{N} x_n^1}{\sum_{n=1}^{N} p_n^0 x_n^0 / \sum_{n=1}^{N} x_n^0}. \tag{1.6}$$

This formula has since then become known as the "unit value" index (hence the superscript U). It admits two interpretations: first, as a ratio of weighted arithmetic averages of prices, and, second, as a value index divided by a Dutot-type quantity index.

Laspeyres (1871) took up the issue again.[9] He showed the inadequacy of the unit value index to measure price change – if prices do not change, that is, $p_n^1 = p_n^0$ for $n = 1, \ldots, N$, then formula (1.6) can nevertheless deliver an outcome different from 1[10] – and again strongly advocated the use of the Carli index (1.2). In the course of his argument, however, he proposed the formula[11]

$$P^L(p^1, x^1, p^0, x^0) \equiv \frac{\sum_{n=1}^{N} p_n^1 x_n^0}{\sum_{n=1}^{N} p_n^0 x_n^0} \tag{1.7}$$

as being superior to the Carli index. However, since Laspeyres thought that the quantities that are necessary for the computation could not be determined accurately enough, he rejected formula (1.7) for practical purposes. Obviously he failed to notice the identity

$$\frac{\sum_{n=1}^{N} p_n^1 x_n^0}{\sum_{n=1}^{N} p_n^0 x_n^0} = \sum_{n=1}^{N} \frac{p_n^0 x_n^0}{\sum_{n'=1}^{N} p_{n'}^0 x_{n'}^0} \frac{p_n^1}{p_n^0}; \tag{1.8}$$

that is, Laspeyres' price index can be written as a weighted arithmetic mean of price relatives, with the base period value shares as weights. Thus knowledge of the base period quantities is not necessary. Only the value shares do matter. Irving Fisher was the first to recognize the operational significance of the identity (1.8). It is mainly because of this identity that the Laspeyres price index (1.7) gained such a widespread acceptance in later years.[12]

---

[9] For biographical details about Laspeyres one should consult Rinne (1981). This paper is accompanied by a reprint of Laspeyres' 1871 publication. See also Diewert (1987b) and Roberts (2000).

[10] We see here the birth of the (strong) identity test.

[11] Actually, this formula was among the alternatives discussed by Drobisch (1871).

[12] See Fisher (1922, p. 60). In practice, however, value shares and price relatives usually come from different sources (for example, from a household expenditure survey and a price survey respectively). The problem whether the resulting statistic can still be interpreted as

Three years later, Paasche (1874) argued that aggregate price change should be measured neither by the Carli index nor by the value ratio, $\sum_{n=1}^{N} p_n^1 x_n^1 / \sum_{n=1}^{N} p_n^0 x_n^0$, as suggested by Drobisch, but by

$$P^P(p^1, x^1, p^0, x^0) \equiv \frac{\sum_{n=1}^{N} p_n^1 x_n^1}{\sum_{n=1}^{N} p_n^0 x_n^1}. \qquad (1.9)$$

Though Paasche was aware of Laspeyres' 1871 paper, because he refers to it, he did not provide reasons why formula $(1.9)^{13}$ should be preferred to Laspeyres' formula (1.7). In turn, Laspeyres (1883) took notice of Paasche's proposal, but, rather than discussing their difference, considered Paasche as an ally in his battle against a geometric mean price index.

Like Laspeyres, however, Paasche was apparently unaware of the fact that the index he favored, expression (1.9), can be written as a weighted mean of price relatives, the type of mean now being harmonic and the weights being the value shares of the comparison period. The recognition of the operational significance of this identity had also to wait for Fisher.

A very complicated formula was derived by Lehr (1885). Recast in modern notation, this formula reads

$$P^{Le}(p^1, x^1, p^0, x^0) \equiv \frac{\sum_{n=1}^{N} p_n^1 x_n^1 / \sum_{n=1}^{N} p_n^0 x_n^0}{\sum_{n=1}^{N} \bar{p}_n x_n^1 / \sum_{n=1}^{N} \bar{p}_n x_n^0}, \qquad (1.10)$$

where

$$\bar{p}_n \equiv \frac{p_n^0 x_n^0 + p_n^1 x_n^1}{x_n^0 + x_n^1} \ (n = 1, \ldots, N).$$

There are two interesting features here. The first is that Lehr's price index is defined as value index divided by a Lowe-type quantity index. Thus expression (1.10) defines what is now called an *implicit* price index. Of course, Lehr himself did not see it this way. Central to his derivation is the argument that $\sum_{n=1}^{N} p_n^t x_n^t / \sum_{n=1}^{N} \bar{p}_n x_n^t$ must be seen as the average price of the "pleasure-units" of period t ($t = 0, 1$).

The second interesting feature is that in Lehr's quantity index $\bar{p}_n$ is defined as the unit value of commodity n ($n = 1, \ldots, N$) over the two periods 0 and 1. This is one of the earliest occurrences of weights that are averages over the two periods considered.

---

a Laspeyres index was discussed by Ruderman (1954) and Banerjee (1956). Walsh (1901, pp. 349–50) noticed already that the Lowe price index (1.4) can be written as a weighted arithmetic or harmonic mean of price relatives.

13 Actually, this formula was also among the alternatives discussed by Drobisch (1871).

Palgrave (1886) proposed what later would appear to be an obvious variant to the right-hand side of equation (1.8), namely

$$P^{Pa}(p^1, x^1, p^0, x^0) \equiv \sum_{n=1}^{N} \frac{p_n^1 x_n^1}{\sum_{n'=1}^{N} p_{n'}^1 x_{n'}^1} \frac{p_n^1}{p_n^0}, \qquad (1.11)$$

that is, a weighted arithmetic mean of price relatives, where the weights are the comparison period value shares.

Also in 1886, in a note contributed to the first volume of *The Quarterly Journal of Economics*, a certain Coggeshall returned to Jevons' discussion of the type of mean to be used for averaging price changes. He expressed a preference for the (unweighted) harmonic mean of price relatives,[14]

$$P^{Co}(p^1, p^0) \equiv \left[(1/N) \sum_{n=1}^{N} \left(\frac{p_n^1}{p_n^0} \right)^{-1} \right]^{-1}. \qquad (1.12)$$

However, he added immediately that "This is a very awkward mean to calculate, which renders it undesirable for general use." Therefore his advice was to use the geometric mean, that is, Jevons' index as defined in expression (1.5).

1.3 Early Price Statistics

As said, most of the authors in the second half of the 19th century were interested in price index numbers as measures of changes in "the value of money." However, there were no statistical offices to provide (reliable) price statistics. Thus all these authors had to search for suitable price data. Such data usually came from import, export, or trade authorities. Using such data, the London-based journal *The Economist* started in 1869 with the annual publication of a table with price index numbers for 22 commodities, four of which were varieties of cotton, which led Pierson (1894) to the conclusion that such index numbers were meaningless.

German authors, such as Laspeyres and Paasche, could use price (= unit value) and quantity data for more than 300 commodities as collected and published by the Chamber of Commerce at Hamburg. This rich database,

---

[14] When he comes to discuss the harmonic mean, Walsh (1932) refers to Messedaglia, and the bibliography of Walsh (1901) refers to an article by Messedaglia (1880). Angelo Messedaglia (1820–1901) is considered as one of the fathers of statistical methodology in Italy (according to Zalin 2002), though Gini (1926) does not mention his name. Messedaglia (1880) discusses the calculation of averages in various situations, but there appears to be no particular mention of index number issues in this article.

going back to 1847, had been founded by the German economist Soetbeer, who worked there from 1840 to 1872, first as librarian and later as secretary. Using this material, Soetbeer published in the second edition (Berlin, 1886) of his book *Materialien zur Erläuterung und Beurteilung der wirtschaftlichen Edelmetallverhältnisse und der Währungsfrage* price index numbers for 114 commodities. Using the same material, the German economist Kral published in his book *Geldwert und Preisbewegung im Deutschen Reiche* (1887) price index numbers for 265 commodities.

All these price index numbers were calculated according to what came later to be known as the Carli formula (1.2).

In 1886 the London wool merchant Sauerbeck published an article entitled "Prices of Commodities and the Precious Metals" in the September issue of the *Journal of the Statistical Society of London*. Sauerbeck was primarily concerned with the causes behind the unprecedented price decline in the United Kingdom that had occurred during the previous 12 years. Basically, Sauerbeck considered the supply side of the economy. His database was therefore "confined to the prices of general commodities, almost entirely raw produce. Of articles not comprised in my statistics, wine is the only important one which has risen" (p. 599). From various sources he could obtain annual prices (= unit values) for 45 produced and imported commodities that had a trade value larger than one million pounds; the more important of these commodities were represented by more than one variety. The tables show three groups of food commodities and three groups of materials commodities, respectively consisting of 19 and 26 items. The data cover the years 1848–85. Price index numbers for groups and the grand total were computed according to the Carli formula (though without referring to this or other names – Jevons and Newmarch, the architect of *The Economist* index numbers,[15] were mentioned only in the data construction appendix), whereby 1867–77 was used as the base period and each of the years 1848–85 acted as comparison period.

Though for Sauerbeck "the price index" appeared to be identical to the Carli index, and alternatives were not considered, he was aware of the weighting issue:

It may be argued that index numbers do not in the aggregate give a correct illustration of the actual course of prices, as they take no notice of quantities, and estimate all articles as of equal importance. This is true to some extent, particularly if a comparison is made with very remote times, and if in the interval a radical change

[15] On Newmarch, see Fitzpatrick (1960).

in the supply and demand of a certain article has taken place. To calculate each year separately according to quantities would be an undertaking of very great labour, and besides the statistical data would not be fully available, but I have worked out the three most important years for our comparison, viz., 1849, 1873, and 1885, according to the importance of each article in the United Kingdom, on the average during the three years 1848–50, 1872–74, and 1883–85 respectively. (pp. 594–5)

It then appears that for these three years Sauerbeck was able to compute (or estimate) what are now called Paasche price index numbers. He concluded that, for these years, the differences between the Carli and Paasche price index numbers were not material.

It is also interesting to notice that, in his search for an explanation of the spectacular, general price decline during the 1873–85 period, Sauerbeck looked at quantity developments of the supply side. In this context we then encounter what can be called a Lowe-type quantity index $\sum_{n=1}^{N} p_n^b x_n^1 / \sum_{n=1}^{N} p_n^b x_n^0$, with period b being 1867–77, and period 0 being 1872–4 (pp. 609–10). Sauerbeck's conclusion appears to be

Independent of the reasons which brought the unusually high prices of 1872–73 to a more moderate level, the causes of the present decline may be described as follows:

1. Reduction of the cost of production and conveyance of some large articles of consumption by the opening of the Suez Canal, by the increase of steamers, and by the enormous extension of railways and telegraph lines, especially in extra-European countries. The opening of new sources of supply. In consequence of these causes, great increase in production.

2. Alterations in currencies, demonetisation of silver, and insufficient supply of gold.

It is impossible to decide which of these causes had the greater influence upon prices, but I am inclined to ascribe it to the second; the average decline on all the 45 descriptions of commodities combined, not in comparison with 1873, but with the average of twenty-five years, is too great to be simply explained away by the reduction of cost. It would be difficult to prove such a reduction in the case of a few articles, but it is out of the question if all commodities are considered combined. (pp. 618–9)

The article concludes with a wonderful graph picturing the grand total index numbers and moving averages thereof over the period 1820–85 with all the "principal political and commercial events" (p. 594) added, from the opening of the first public railway in England in 1825 to the American railway collapse in 1884.

Starting in 1887, each March issue of the journal, in the meantime renamed *Journal of the Royal Statistical Society*, contained an update of the

1886 statistics. The final update appeared in the March 1913 issue, where Sauerbeck announced that

I find it necessary for various reasons to relinquish the collection of Prices and Index-Numbers, which I have given regularly in the Society's *Journal* since 1886, retracing the matter till 1818. Sir George Paish has, however, arranged to have the same continued in the *Statist* under his supervision as nearly as possible on the same lines as hitherto, and I am convinced that in his able and experienced hands most reliable data will be collected, and that the comparison with my figures will be fully maintained.

The only exception occurred in the year 1893. Instead of the March issue, the June issue of this year contained an article entitled "Prices of Commodities During the Last Seven Years" that had been read at a meeting of the *Society*. Sauerbeck's conclusion here was that "During the last seven years . . . the first cause [of the 1886 article] . . . was again at work" (p. 231), but "The second cause . . . has apparently not had any *additional* influence on prices since 1887" (p. 234).

   This meeting was attended by Edgeworth, who made some observations about the index number formula employed by Sauerbeck. In particular, Edgeworth suggested as alternatives the formulas of Laspeyres and Paasche, without mentioning their names. The report of the meeting continued,

Theoretically one method was as good as the other; perhaps, ideally, a mixture of the two would be best. Another method was to take, not the arithmetic average, but the median, *i.e.* the figure which was just in the intermediate position when all the given comparative prices were arranged in quantitative order. (p. 248)

As we will see in the next section, Edgeworth was already heavily involved in the problems of price index construction.

1.4 Edgeworth's Investigations

Extensive methodological investigations into the subject of price index construction were carried out by Edgeworth. As secretary of a committee "appointed for the purpose of investigating the best methods of ascertaining and measuring Variations in the Value of the Monetary Standard," he presented in the years 1887/89 three extensive memoranda to the British Association for the Advancement of Science.[16] They have been reprinted in his *Papers*

---

[16] According to his own words, Edgeworth's (1925c) article in *Palgrave's Dictionary* can be considered as an abridgement of this "voluminous disquisition."

Relating to Political Economy, Volume 1 (1925b). The opening paragraphs of the first memorandum clearly describe the problem involved:

The object of this paper is to define the meaning, and measure the magnitude, of variations in the value of money. It is supposed that the prices of commodities (including services), and also the quantities purchased, at two epochs are given. It is required to combine these data into a formula representing the appreciation or depreciation of money. It will appear that beneath the apparent unity of a single question there is discoverable upon a close view a plurality of distinct problems.

In fact, Edgeworth succeeded in distinguishing among six[17] principal definitions of the problem, or "Standards" as he called them: the capital standard, the consumption standard, the currency standard, the income standard, the indefinite standard, and the production standard.[18] The consumption standard was proposed as the principal standard:

[It] takes for the measure of appreciation or depreciation the change in the monetary value on a certain set of articles. This set of articles consists of all the commodities consumed yearly by the community either at the earlier or the later epoch, or some mean between those sets.

When discussing the appropriate formula for the consumption standard, Edgeworth distinguished between two cases. The first case occurs when the interval of time between the periods 0 and 1 is small, such that $x_n^0 \approx x_n^1$ ($n = 1, \ldots, N$). In this case it does not matter very much which one of the hitherto proposed formulas is used. Edgeworth himself preferred

$$P^{ME}(p^1, x^1, p^0, x^0) \equiv \frac{\sum_{n=1}^{N} p_n^1(x_n^0 + x_n^1)/2}{\sum_{n=1}^{N} p_n^0(x_n^0 + x_n^1)/2}, \qquad (1.13)$$

which nowadays is known as the Marshall-Edgeworth price index.[19] The second case occurs when the time interval is large and the quantities consumed, x_n^0 and x_n^1, differ appreciably from each other. Here Edgeworth suggested to use the *chaining principle*, proposed by Marshall in 1887. This principle says that if we have, say, three consecutive time periods 0, 1, and 2, then the price index number for period 1 relative to period 0 multiplied by the price index number for period 2 relative to period 1 should be taken

---

[17] Kendall (1969) is not entirely correct on this point, as he lists seven standards.
[18] Returning to this topic in his 1925 article, typically called "The Plurality of Index-Numbers," Edgeworth distinguished between three concepts, namely index-numbers representing welfare, unweighted index-numbers, and the labour standard.
[19] Marshall proposed this index in an 1887 article. Walsh (1932), however, attributed this index to Drobisch (1871).

as a price index number for period 2 relative to period 0. Put otherwise, Edgeworth's suggestion was that

$$P^{ME}(p^1, x^1, p^0, x^0) P^{ME}(p^2, x^2, p^1, x^1) \qquad (1.14)$$

should be used as the appropriate price index number for period 2 relative to period 0.[20]

Edgeworth's "indefinite standard" followed a line of reasoning that had been initiated by Jevons and after Frisch (1936) came to be called the *stochastic approach*.[21] With hindsight one could say that Edgeworth's approach here was based on a model for the individual price relatives of the form

$$p_n^1 / p_n^0 = f(\mu^{01}, \varepsilon_n^{01}) \ (n = 1, \dots, N). \qquad (1.15)$$

In such a model the price change of any individual commodity is considered as being composed of a common (scalar) component μ^{01} and an idiosyncratic component ε_n^{01}. The common component was, according to Edgeworth, supposed to measure variations in the "intrinsic value of money," whereas the consumption standard, discussed earlier, would measure variations in the "power of money." Edgeworth considered the idiosyncratic components as random variables. He was well aware of the fact that different specifications of the model (1.15) as well as different assumptions concerning the probability distribution of the random components naturally lead to different estimators of the common component. In Edgeworth's second memorandum (1888) a preference was expressed for the median of the price relatives p_n^1 / p_n^0 as an estimator of the common component μ^{01}.

1.5 The Birth of the Test Approach

In 1896, an important article was published by the Dutch economist Pierson.[22] In fact, this article was the final and culminating one of a series of three articles devoted to price indices. In the first article, Pierson (1894) discussed the use of price index numbers for measuring changes in the purchasing power of gold. In particular he discussed issues concerning the choice of

---

[20] It must be remarked that Marshall was primarily concerned with the practical problem of allowing for the introduction of *new commodities* into an index of prices, which he thought would be greatly facilitated if the weights were changed every year and the successive yearly indices linked or chained together by simple multiplication. Walsh (1932) attributed the chaining system to Lehr (1885).

[21] On the history of the stochastic approach, see Aldrich (1992). Aldrich remarks that some of Cournot's ideas preceded Jevons' by 25 years.

[22] For background material on Pierson, see Fase (1992), in Dutch, and Fase (1998).

the mean (arithmetic or geometric); the weighting of the commodity price relatives; the proper choice of the base year; and the relative merits of the then available price statistics (those of *The Economist*, Sauerbeck, Soetbeer, and Kral).

In 1895, Pierson returned to the question of whether in the composite price index the commodity price relatives should be weighted. In his opinion a great *number* of commodities is required rather than a smaller number of *important* commodities.[23] In his 1896 article, however, Pierson arrived at the conclusion "that the system of index-numbers is . . . to be abandoned altogether, because it is faulty in principle." His argument was threefold. In the first place he noticed – recast in modern language – that the Carli price index does not satisfy the *time reversal test*; that is,

$$P^C(p^1, p^0) = (1/N) \sum_{n=1}^{N} \frac{p_n^1}{p_n^0} \neq \left[(1/N) \sum_{n=1}^{N} \frac{p_n^0}{p_n^1} \right]^{-1} = (P^C(p^0, p^1))^{-1}.$$

(1.16)

Put otherwise, the price index number for period 1 relative to period 0 is not equal to the reciprocal of the price index number for period 0 relative to period 1. In the second place he noticed that, when applied to the same price material, the Dutot index, the Carli index and the Jevons index can yield substantially different outcomes. In the third place he showed that the Dutot price index is not *dimensionally invariant*: changing the units of measurement can change the price index number dramatically. His overall conclusion was that "all attempts to calculate and represent average movements of prices, either by index-numbers or otherwise, ought to be abandoned." Indeed, Pierson never again wrote about index numbers. His negative conclusion, however, was not accepted generally.[24] Edgeworth (1896) replied with

---

[23] This article was basically a response to Sauerbeck (1895), which in turn was a reaction to Pierson (1894). Sauerbeck (1895) gives a detailed comparison of his and Soetbeer's price statistics, thereby concentrating on the issue of the number of commodities in the index. Sauerbeck's conclusion was that "although it is desirable to include as many articles as possible, small articles should not be taken account of in an index number constructed like Soetbeer's. If they agree generally with the larger articles they are not required at all, but if their fluctuations differ widely from the general course they will upset the system of index numbers in an unwarrantable degree."

[24] Though concerns similar to Pierson's were raised by others. For instance, Oker (1896) from Washington, DC, argued for measuring the purchasing power of gold by a Lowe price index (1.4) but showed that, with the same price data, different systems of quantities $x_1^b, \ldots, x_N^b$ can lead to very different outcomes. His conclusion was therefore "inasmuch as it is impossible to construct a table which will hold good of more than one of an infinite number of quantity relations, and inasmuch as in commerce quantities as well

"a defence of index-numbers." He mainly attacked Pierson on his use of artificial instead of real-life examples and on his tacit assumption about the Dutot index as being the proper method.

Today, Pierson's name seems to be forgotten. He must be credited, however, for the invention of two rather important tests for price indices: the time reversal test and the test of dimensional invariance.

Some years earlier, Westergaard (1890) had stipulated that a price index, supposed to measure the change of the purchasing power of money, should satisfy the *circularity test*; that is, $P(p^1, x^1, p^0, x^0)P(p^2, x^2, p^1, x^1) = P(p^2, x^2, p^0, x^0)$. In his own words, such a measure

muss, um rationell zu sein, die Bedingung erfüllen, für eine gegebene Periode zu denselben Ergebnissen zu führen, ob man dieselbe ungeteilt betrachtet oder sie in zwei zerlegt, welche nachher zusammengefasst werden. (pp. 218–9)

He noticed that of all till then proposed formulas, Jevons' price index (1.5) was the only formula that satisfied this condition.

The debate about the proper price index formula to be used for measuring changes in the purchasing power of money continued. At the turn of the century, Bowley (1899) suggested to use the geometric mean of the Laspeyres price index (1.7) and the Paasche price index (1.9); that is, the formula which later came to be known as the Fisher price index. But two years later Bowley (1901) preferred the arithmetic mean of the Laspeyres and the Paasche index, a construct that had already been suggested by Drobisch (1871).

In 1901, out of the blue, *The Measurement of General Exchange-Value* by an, until then, unknown author named Correa Moylan Walsh appeared.[25] This monumental, but long-winded, book reviewed the literature on the measurement of the value of money from Fleetwood to 1900 and tried to

---

as proportions are constantly varying, it appears that tables and methods such as we have examined have no practical utility whatever, unless it be to furnish employment to some statistician in producing bogies to frighten 'good honest folk' into the limbo called bimetallism in this country."

[25] There appears to be not much known about Walsh. He was born in 1862 in Newburgh, N.Y. In 1884 he obtained an undergraduate arts degree from Harvard and studied further in Berlin, Paris, Rome, and Oxford. After 1890 he lived in Bellport (Long Island), until his death in 1936. Without academic or other known affiliation, he published *The Measurement of General Exchange-Value* in 1901. The book does not contain a preface. In December 1920 he acted as discussant at the meeting of the American Statistical Association where Fisher presented an outline of his then forthcoming book (see Fisher 1921). In the following year he published *The Problem of Estimation*, whereas Fisher's book was published in 1922. The last book was dedicated to Edgeworth and Walsh. Walsh published a number of books in various fields, such as political science and religion, was an editor of Shakespeare's sonnets, and contributed to the literature about Fermat's last theorem.

make a contribution. Walsh appeared to have a strong preference for geometric means and stressed the importance of weighting prices or price relatives. His direct legacy to index number theory consists of two formulas.

The formula he recommended is the geometric analogue of the Marshall-Edgeworth index (1.13), namely

$$P^{W1}(p^1, x^1, p^0, x^0) \equiv \frac{\sum_{n=1}^{N} p_n^1 (x_n^0 x_n^1)^{1/2}}{\sum_{n=1}^{N} p_n^0 (x_n^0 x_n^1)^{1/2}}. \tag{1.17}$$

As one sees, instead of arithmetic means of base and comparison period quantities, this formula employs geometric means. Walsh (1901, p. 373) called (1.17) "Scrope's emended method,"[26] though he later (in 1932) replaced "Scrope" by "Lowe." Indeed, expression (1.17) is a special case of expression (1.4).

Next best is what Walsh (1901, p. 373) called "the geometric method." This is a weighted version of Jevons' price index (1.5),

$$P^{W2}(p^1, x^1, p^0, x^0) \equiv \prod_{n=1}^{N} \left(\frac{p_n^1}{p_n^0} \right)^{\bar{s}_n}, \tag{1.18}$$

where the weights are defined by

$$\bar{s}_n \equiv \frac{(p_n^0 x_n^0 p_n^1 x_n^1)^{1/2}}{\sum_{n'=1}^{N} (p_{n'}^0 x_{n'}^0 p_{n'}^1 x_{n'}^1)^{1/2}} \quad (n = 1, \dots, N).$$

Thus, to start with, the weight of each commodity is given by the geometric mean of its base period value, $p_n^0 x_n^0$, and its comparison period value, $p_n^1 x_n^1$; and these weights must then be normalized such that they add up to 1.[27]

All these authors pursued a line of reasoning that had started with Pierson and would culminate in Irving Fisher's monumental *The Making of Index Numbers*.[28] They assessed the large number of then available formulas with help of criteria such as the time reversal test and the circularity test.[29]

---

[26] After Scrope (1833).

[27] Notice that $\bar{s}_n$ is unequal to the geometric mean of the base period value share, $s_n^0 \equiv p_n^0 x_n^0 / \sum_{n'=1}^{N} p_{n'}^0 x_{n'}^0$, and the comparison period value share, $s_n^1 \equiv p_n^1 x_n^1 / \sum_{n'=1}^{N} p_{n'}^1 x_{n'}^1$. But $\bar{s}_n = (s_n^0 s_n^1)^{1/2} / \sum_{n'=1}^{N} (s_{n'}^0 s_{n'}^1)^{1/2}$.

[28] On Fisher, see the biography by Allen (1993). See also Dimand and Geanakoplos (2005) for a collection of papers that "celebrate the life, contributions, and legacy of Irving Fisher, a great scientific economist and outspoken social crusader, a man of brilliance, integrity, and eccentricity who did much to advance theoretical and empirical economics."

[29] Boumans (2001) described Fisher's instrumental approach as "finding the best balance between theoretical and empirical requirements, even if these requirements are incompatible."

The novel feature introduced by Fisher (1911) is the separate attention paid to the construction of a quantity index alongside a price index. In the Appendix to chapter X, he reviewed 44 price and quantity indices with respect to their satisfaction of five tests. In addition to the circularity test (here called changing-of-base test) and the test of dimensional invariance, Fisher proposed three other tests, namely the proportionality test, the determinateness test, and the withdrawal or entry test. He concluded with the following recommendation for practice:

The final *practical* conclusion, therefore, is that the weighted median serves the purpose of a practical barometer of prices, and also of quantities as well as, if not better than, formulae theoretically superior. (p. 427)

In the body of Chapter X itself this was expressed as follows:

For practical purposes the *median* is one of the best index numbers. It may be computed in a small fraction of the time required for computing the more theoretically exact index numbers, and it meets many of the tests of a good index number remarkably well. (p. 230)

In addition to codifying and systematizing much existing wisdom, Fisher's (1921, 1922) most important contribution to the theory of price and quantity indices was the formulation of the *factor reversal test*, which

hitherto been entirely overlooked, presumably because index numbers of *quantities* have so seldom been computed and, almost never, side by side with the index number of the prices to which they relate. (1922, p. 82)

The test runs as follows. Let $P(p^1, x^1, p^0, x^0)$ be a price index formula for period 1 relative to period 0. Interchange in this formula the prices and the quantities. Then the resulting formula, $P(x^1, p^1, x^0, p^0)$, is a quantity index for period 1 relative to period 0. Now the factor reversal test requires that

$$P(p^1, x^1, p^0, x^0)P(x^1, p^1, x^0, p^0) = \frac{\sum_{n=1}^{N} p_n^1 x_n^1}{\sum_{n=1}^{N} p_n^0 x_n^0}; \qquad (1.19)$$

that is, the product of the price index and the structurally similar quantity index must be equal to the value index.[30]

[30] Naturally the test can also be formulated departing from a quantity index. When it comes to sampling, Fisher (1927) added the "total value criterion": "For securing the best *sampling* the analogous Total Value Criterion is our guide. It prescribes that our samples are to be so chosen that their *price index* multiplied by their *quantity index* shall give the *true value index* for the *whole field* represented by those samples."

Fisher considered the factor reversal test and the time reversal test as the two supreme tests, "the two legs on which index numbers can be made to walk" (1922, p. xii). Out of the multitude of formulas he examined, only a few satisfied both tests. The simplest of these is the geometric mean of the Laspeyres and the Paasche price index,

$$P^F(p^1, x^1, p^0, x^0) \equiv [P^L(p^1, x^1, p^0, x^0) P^P(p^1, x^1, p^0, x^0)]^{1/2},$$
(1.20)

which had been suggested already by Bowley (1899) but since 1921 has been known as Fisher's "ideal" price index.

Fisher considered the circularity test to be theoretically mistaken. A quote from his 1921 paper:

I have come to three conclusions: first, a *complete* fulfillment of that test by a formula for a weighted index number is impossible; second, it is not desirable; and third, the "ideal" index number comes closer to fulfilling this test than any other. (1921, p. 549)

Fisher also concluded that "The chain system is of little or no real use" (1922, p. 308). This was a major departure from his earlier opinion because in his 1911 book, *The Purchasing Power of Money*, he did advocate the principle of chaining price index numbers.

Fisher is often quoted as having said that "the purpose to which an index number is put does not affect the choice of formula." Indeed, this statement can be found as the heading of Section 11 of Chapter XI of his 1922 book. Taken in isolation, however, it tends to give a somewhat too crude picture of Fisher's opinion. Of relevance in this context is Fisher's rejoinder to the discussion following the presentation of his 1921 paper. In this discussion, Mitchell and Persons had remarked that the specific purpose to which an index is put must determine the formula used.[31] Fisher agreed with them that

the purpose of an index number is a very important factor in determining what is the best index number. This is certainly true as to the elements of an index number other than the formula – the character and number of commodities, for instance. But as to the mathematical formula itself, I take a different view. . . . As to an index number, I would hold that an index number is itself a purpose. It is a purpose . . . sufficiently homogeneous within its own realm to require certain definite general criteria of its own, whatever the sub-purpose within the domain of index numbers may be.

---

[31] On the differing views of Mitchell and Fisher, see Banzhaf (2004).

Moreover, as Fisher remarked, neither of his opponents

has pointed out a single specific case in which the sub-purpose would require that either of the two tests which I have indicated as the supreme tests should be disregarded.

On page 232 of his 1922 book, Fisher made a similar remark. His conclusion was that

an index number formula is merely a statistical mechanism like a coefficient of correlation. It is as absurd to vary the mechanism with the subject matter to which it is applied as it would be to vary the method of calculating the coefficient of correlation. (1922, p. 234)

There are, however, indications that Fisher was not completely consistent in his rigid view that an index number is itself a purpose. Fisher did have some general purpose in mind, as is corroborated by the closing sentences of his book. Meditating about the future he remarked that

the original purpose of index numbers – to measure the purchasing power of money – will remain a principal, if not the principal, use of index numbers. It is through index numbers that we measure, and thereby realize, changes in the value of money. (1922, p. 369)

Meanwhile, Fisher's conclusion that his "ideal" price index is the "best" one or "probably the king of all index number formulae" (1922, p. 366) was endorsed by others, notably by Walsh.[32] Walsh had published a book – actually a lengthy pamphlet – entitled *The Problem of Estimation. A Seventeenth-Century Controversy and its Bearing on Modern Statistical Questions, Especially Index-Numbers* (1921), in the preface of which he expressed his surprise that

one economist after another takes up the subject of index-numbers, potters over it for a while, differs from the rest if he can, and then drops it. And so nearly sixty years have gone by since Jevons first brought mathematics to bear upon this question, and still economists are at loggerheads over it. Yet index-numbers involve the use of means and averages, and these being a purely mathematical element, demonstration ought soon to be reached, and the agreement should speedily follow.

The same optimism prevailed with Fisher: "I think we may be confident that the end is being reached of the long controversy over the proper formula for an index number" (1922, p. 242).

---

[32] A dissenting view was voiced by von Bortkiewicz (1923, p. 393), who concluded, "Vom theoretischen Gesichtspunkte aus gesehen, rechtfertigt sich die Charakterisierung von [(1.20)] als 'ideale Preisindexziffer' keinesfalls."

As an illustration of the influence of Fisher's work it is interesting to consider the various editions of Pigou's main publication. In 1912, the economist Pigou published *Wealth and Welfare*. According to the book reviewer of *The American Economic Review*,

The book is a general treatise with a special point of view and method of attack which put the author's personal mark on everything he touches, from index numbers to outdoor relief. The point of view is the constant inquiry how society can get the maximum satisfaction-income from economic goods and services, and the method is an unusually keen and exacting deductive analysis, fortified with citations of fact which show remarkably wide and varied knowledge.[33]

Indeed, the topic of index numbers appears in Part I, Chapter III, which is on what we would today call the measurement of welfare change. Pigou considers the situation where the average consumer (whose tastes are supposed to be unchanging) experiences an income (= expenditure) change from $\sum_{n=1}^{N} p_n^0 x_n^0$ to $\sum_{n=1}^{N} p_n^1 x_n^1$. What can be said about welfare change?

Basically Pigou considers two measures, namely the value ratio divided by the Laspeyres price index (1.7), and the value ratio divided by the Paasche price index (1.9), though these names are not mentioned. We would say that he considers the Paasche and Laspeyres quantity index respectively. If in a certain situation both quantity indices exhibit an outcome greater than 1, Pigou would conclude that welfare has increased, whereas if both indices exhibit an outcome less than 1, Pigou's conclusion would be that welfare has decreased. In these two cases any mean of the two quantity indices could also be used as measuring rod. The remaining problem is what to do when one quantity index exhibits an outcome less than 1 and the other an outcome greater than 1.

Based on an intricate and almost irreproducible reasoning, in such a case Pigou proposes to use the product of the two index numbers; that is,

$$\frac{\sum_{n=1}^{N} p_n^1 x_n^1 / \sum_{n=1}^{N} p_n^0 x_n^0}{P^L(p^1, x^1, p^0, x^0)} \times \frac{\sum_{n=1}^{N} p_n^1 x_n^1 / \sum_{n=1}^{N} p_n^0 x_n^0}{P^P(p^1, x^1, p^0, x^0)}. \tag{1.21}$$

With today's knowledge it is easy to see that this formula is identical to the square of Fisher's quantity index. Under the assumption that income does not change Pigou shows that his welfare measure reduces to the ratio $\sum_{n=1}^{N} p_n^0 x_n^1 / \sum_{n=1}^{N} p_n^1 x_n^0$.

In 1920 the first edition of *The Economics of Welfare* appeared, apparently a revision and expansion of the 1912 work. The welfare measurement issue

---

[33] Book review by J. M. Clark in Volume 3 (1913), pp. 623–5.

is here treated in Part I, Chapter VI. Though the reasoning is somewhat modernized, Pigou basically retains his former position. Between the third and the fourth edition (1932), however, something must have happened (presumably some criticism by Keynes). In paragraph 12 Pigou now informs his readers that he considers the line of reasoning leading to expression (1.21) as being not correct, but leaves it at that. In the case where one quantity index number is greater and the other less than 1, nothing definite can be said about (the direction of) welfare change.

When both quantity index numbers are on the same side of 1, says Pigou in paragraph 13, "it is practically much more convenient to write down some single expression intermediate between the two limiting expressions rather than both of these. There are an infinite number of intermediate expressions available." Referring to Fisher (1922), Pigou requires that the price index, by which the expenditure ratio must be divided, satisfies the time reversal test as well as the factor-reversal test. This, then, leads Pigou to Fisher's ideal price index (1.20).

The 1912 as well as the later texts are noteworthy for the fact that in all these texts there appears to be an embryonic form of what today is called the *Laspeyres-Paasche bounds test*: any bilateral price index should lie between the Laspeyres and the Paasche index. At the background one discerns revealed-preference type arguments. The 1920 and later texts add to this feature the distinction between indices based on population data and indices based on sample data, and a discussion of the reliability of sample indices.

1.6 The Weakness of the Test Approach Revealed

The optimism of Fisher and Walsh, however, appeared to be unwarranted. One of the weaknesses of Fisher's approach was his all too easy dismissal of the circularity test. This dismissal was not particularly convincing for those economists who were – like Fisher himself! – concerned with measuring the development of the general purchasing power or value of money.[34] For these people fulfilment of the circularity test seemed to be indispensable. But at the same time it was common knowledge that all known bilateral indices violated this test. How to cope with this situation? This was the central theme of the discussion between Edgeworth and Walsh in the years 1923/24.

---

[34] It is interesting to notice that most of Fisher's arguments against the circularity test came from the field of interspatial price comparisons (where the circularity test is more appropriately called the transitivity test).

Edgeworth reviewed Walsh's (1921) book in two lengthy, interrelated articles (Edgeworth 1923a, 1923b). In these articles he basically returned to the stochastic approach as providing a conceptual solution for the problem of the (violation of the) circularity test. The stochastic approach is, according to Edgeworth, characterized by "the hypothesis that the change in general prices is connected with a common cause . . . apart from the proper fluctuation of each due to sporadic independent causes" (1923a, p. 350). Let us return to expression (1.15). It is clear that the "common cause" μ^{01}, being a scalar, satisfies the circularity test. Any price relative p_n^1 / p_n^0 can be considered as a, necessarily imprecise, observation of μ^{01}. Any price index, being some sort of average of the price relatives, can then be considered as an estimator of μ^{01}. But such an estimator is by nature necessarily imprecise, and cannot be expected to satisfy the circularity test precisely. One thus has to search for an index that, in reasonable circumstances, comes as closely as possible to fulfilment of this test. The conditions under which formulas like those of Fisher and Marshall-Edgeworth appear to attain approximate cicularity are: (1) the time interval over which the index is to be computed must be small, and/or (2) the dispersion of the price relatives must be small. In the second of the two articles Edgeworth again expressed his preference for the median of the price relatives as an estimator of the "common cause." Walsh (1924) characterized Edgeworth's position by concluding that

Professor Edgeworth accepts the circular test, but swallows the small non-fulfilment of it in ordinary cases, and tries to cast out the glaring non-fulfilment in violent suppositions, by alleging that these are unallowable. (p. 510)

Walsh then proceeds by attacking Edgeworth's stochastic approach. The analogy of price relatives to observations

is purely fanciful. The true altitude of the sun is independent of the errors we make in observing it. The true variation of the general exchange-value of money is dependent on the variations of the prices of commodities. The variations of the prices of commodities are the inverse variations of the particular exchange-values of money in those commodities, which particular exchange-values make up the general exchange-value of money. Two observations become less trustworthy the more widely they diverge, because then the more erroneous they become, until they lose all influence on our opinion. Not so a wide divergence of the prices of two commodities: each of them affects the general exchange-value of money all the more, the more it varies, and so much the more they are needed in our calculation. They never deserve to be thrown out as worthless, as absurdly divergent observations must be. (pp. 515–6)

How, then, should one attack the problem according to Walsh? The target being "to measure the constancy or variation of the general exchange-value of money," the problem is to find the proper weighted average of price relatives. The guiding principles are given by the various tests, and the solution is to be expected from mathematical ingenuity:

[T]he perfect method is a *desideratum*; and I only wish I could induce Professor Edgeworth to turn his great mathematical talents to the search for the perfect formula. (p. 505)

[T]he fault for our not attaining perfection in averaging price-variations lies in the nature of the (geometric) average that is properly to be applied. Here mathematics itself fails us, unless there is another, as yet unknown, average that is the proper one to use. (p. 516)

The article of Walsh (1932) in the *Encyclopaedia of the Social Sciences* concisely surveyed the state of the art from Walsh's point of view. He viewed the problem of constructing price indices as that of averaging and weighting price relatives. That led to the following conditions: (1) if all the relatives are equal, the average must be equal to them; (2) if a relative equal to the average is added or withdrawn, the average must be unaffected; (3) if a relative unequal to the average is added or withdrawn, the average must change. With respect to weighting, (4) the weighting of both periods should be used and of these only. Walsh listed as number (5) the criterion that changes of the physical units must not affect the result. Finally, he discussed the factor reversal test (6), the time reversal test (7), and the circularity test (8). Walsh was well aware of the fact that, at least at the moment of his writing, "There is no perfect formula satisfying all the tests."

Quite remarkably, Walsh's (1932) article made no mention of the publications by the French statistician Divisia. In a certain sense, Divisia's (1925) approach can be regarded as a response to the challenge put by Walsh to Edgeworth.

The essence of this novel approach consists in considering all the prices and quantities as continuous functions of continuous time. A time period is considered as being of infinitesimal short length, represented by the real variable t.

The price index, called by Divisia "indice monétaire," for period t relative to a certain base period 0, is then defined by the line integral

$$P^{Div}(t, 0) \equiv \exp \left\{ \int_0^t \sum_{n=1}^{N} s_n(\tau) d \ln p_n(\tau) \right\}, \qquad (1.22)$$

where

$$s_n(\tau) \equiv \frac{p_n(\tau)x_n(\tau)}{\sum_{n'=1}^{N} p_{n'}(\tau)x_{n'}(\tau)} \quad (n = 1, \ldots, N)$$

is the value-share of commodity n at time period τ. Interchanging prices and quantities at the right-hand side of expression (1.22) delivers the Divisia quantity index for period t relative to period 0,

$$Q^{Div}(t, 0) \equiv \exp\left\{ \int_0^t \sum_{n=1}^{N} s_n(\tau)d\ln x_n(\tau) \right\}, \qquad (1.23)$$

and it is not difficult to check that these two indices satisfy the factor reversal relation.

It is also readily seen that, along the path followed by prices and quantities through time, both indices satisfy the circularity test. This, for example, means that, given intermediate time periods $1, \ldots, t-1$, one can decompose the price index for period t relative to period 0 as a product of price indices for adjacent periods,

$$P^{Div}(t, 0) = \prod_{\tau=1}^{t} P^{Div}(\tau, \tau - 1). \qquad (1.24)$$

But these nice theoretical features are counterbalanced by some practical disadvantages. The line integral (1.22) generally depends on the particular path that prices and quantities have followed between the two periods compared, but, because of the discreteness of real-life economic data, this path will as a rule not be known precisely. Given observations at intermediate time periods $1, \ldots, t-1$, one has to use a suitable approximation for each $P^{Div}(\tau, \tau - 1)$.

There are essentially two ways to proceed. One way is to specify a reasonable but hypothetical path connecting the observable pairs $(p^{\tau-1}, x^{\tau-1})$ and (p^τ, x^τ) and evaluate the line integral along this path; the alternative is to look for a good approximation according to numerical mathematics.

The approximation generally considered to be the best is

$$\ln P^{Div}(\tau, \tau - 1) \approx \sum_{n=1}^{N} \frac{1}{2}(s_n(\tau - 1) + s_n(\tau))\ln(p_n(\tau)/p_n(\tau - 1)).$$

$$(1.25)$$

The price index obtained by exponentiating the right-hand side is customarily called after the Finnish economist Törnqvist, but had been classified already by Fisher (1922) – in his system the index was numbered as formula 123. Because of the approximation property stated by expression (1.25) the Törnqvist price index is also frequently called Divisia or Divisia-Törnqvist price index. The term *Divisia price index* will be reserved, however, for the original line integral definition (1.22).

Folklore has it that the Törnqvist price index was proposed in a 1936 article by this author. This, however, is not true. Guided by Divisia's theory, Törnqvist (1936) constructed a weekly consumption price index of the form (1.24), where $P^{Div}(\tau, \tau - 1)$ was approximated by $\prod_{n=1}^{N}(p_n(\tau)/p_n(\tau - 1))^{\alpha_n(\tau)}$ and the weights $\alpha_n(\tau)$ $(n = 1, \ldots, N)$, adding up to 1, were kept constant as long as possible. As Törnqvist explains,

As soon as it is established that the weighting system employed no longer constitutes a good approximation for the per unit rates of the consumers' total expenditure that falls to the share of the respective class of goods, an adjustment of the weights is undertaken and the adjusted weighting system is applied in calculating the changes from week to week.

The so-called Törnqvist price index did, however, materialize in a later article (Törnqvist and Törnqvist 1937). But in this article the authors were concerned with estimating the purchasing power parity between the Finnish mark (1933) and the Swedish kronor (1931), and there is only a passing reference to Divisia. Among a number of alternative measures (Palgrave, Paasche, Geometric Paasche, Laspeyres, Geometric Laspeyres, Harmonic Laspeyres, and symmetric means thereof) the "geometric ideal index" emerges, which is the Törnqvist index. The authors show that this index is, on their data, numerically close to Fisher's "ideal" index, but do not express a clear preference for either index.

According to established practice, however, we will continue to call the bilateral price index

$$P^T(p^1, x^1, p^0, x^0) \equiv \exp\left\{\sum_{n=1}^{N}\frac{1}{2}(s_n^0 + s_n^1)\ln(p_n^1/p_n^0)\right\} \quad (1.26)$$

and the kindred quantity index after Törnqvist. As one easily checks, this price index does not satisfy the factor reversal test. In later years, this has led some authors to search for a so-called log-change price index, that is, a formula of the form

$$\ln P(p^1, x^1, p^0, x^0) \equiv \sum_{n=1}^{N}\alpha_n(p^1, x^1, p^0, x^0)\ln(p_n^1/p_n^0), \quad (1.27)$$

that would satisfy this test to a better degree of approximation than the Törnqvist price index does. Theil (1973), Sato (1974), and again Theil (1974) developed and compared several interesting formulas.[35] In 1974, however, Vartia succeeded in developing two log-change price indices that meet the factor reversal test exactly (see also Vartia 1976). The Montgomery-Vartia price index was defined by

$$\ln P^{MV}(p^1, x^1, p^0, x^0) \equiv \frac{\sum_{n=1}^{N} L(p_n^0 x_n^0, p_n^1 x_n^1) \ln(p_n^1/p_n^0)}{L(\sum_{n=1}^{N} p_n^0 x_n^0, \sum_{n=1}^{N} p_n^1 x_n^1)}, \quad (1.28)$$

and the Sato-Vartia price index was defined by

$$\ln P^{SV}(p^1, x^1, p^0, x^0) \equiv \frac{\sum_{n=1}^{N} L(s_n^0, s_n^1) \ln(p_n^1/p_n^0)}{\sum_{n=1}^{N} L(s_n^0, s_n^1)}, \quad (1.29)$$

where the logarithmic mean of two positive real numbers a and b is defined by $L(a, b) \equiv (a - b)/\ln(a/b)$ if $a \neq b$ and $L(a, a) \equiv a$. The Sato-Vartia price index was independently discovered by Sato (1976) around the same time; hence its double name. The Montgomery-Vartia price index, however, had been proposed already by Montgomery (1929, 1937) – an almost completely forgotten author – who derived this index as a special case of a second type of line integral index.[36]

It is clear, however, that in the process of approximating a Divisia price index (1.22) the circularity property gets lost. Neither the Törnqvist nor the two Vartia price indices satisfy this property. This suggests that it is not possible for a price index formula to satisfy both the factor reversal and the circular test. Indeed, Frisch (1930) and Wald (1937) revealed a number of inconsistencies in Fisher's system of tests. Hence, the test, or axiomatic approach, so vigorously defended by Fisher and Walsh, faced a

---

[35] See also a later contribution by Banerjee (1983).

[36] Montgomery's (1937) book was reviewed by E. C. R(amsbottom) in the *Journal of the Royal Statistical Society*, volume CI (1938), p. 211. The review is very brief, but captures the essence, for right in the middle of it, there they are in full glory: the price index (1.28) and the corresponding quantity index. The reviewer concluded by saying that "The book is severely mathematical in character, and it is difficult to trace the argument, but it should be read by all those interested in the making of index numbers." Fisher reviewed the book in the *Journal of the American Statistical Association*, volume 32 (1937), pp. 805–7. He misstated formula (1.28) but concluded that "Mr. Montgomery has definitely contributed to the [theory] but not the [practice]." The rediscovery of Montgomery's contribution was documented in the 1983 predecessor of chapter 6. Subsequent references to Montgomery (1929) and (1937) are to be found in Diewert (1993) and Balk (1995). A more extensive discussion was provided by Diewert (2005a), the discussion paper version of which appeared in 1998.

severe dilemma. On the one hand, maintaining the whole system of tests is inconsistent: it can be *proven* that there does not exist a formula satisfying all the tests. On the other hand, when one deletes one or more of the tests, the circularity test for example, the remaining system does not have a unique solution anymore. Moreover, there are no clear guidelines as to which tests must be rejected and which must be retained.

1.7 The Birth of the Economic Approach

Fisher's program did not meet with general approval, not only because of its mathematical inconsistency, but also because the background concepts such as "general price level," "general purchasing power of money," "(intrinsic) value of money" – all of them associated with the (naive) quantity theory of money[37] – gradually lost their appeal. All these concepts were given up as too vague and sweeping, and the attention was – again!, see the earlier work of Edgeworth – directed toward the particular purposes, uses, and interpretations of price indices. Illustrative is the analysis of Keynes in his *A Treatise on Money, Volume I* (1930):

Since the Purchasing Power of Money in a given context depends on the quantity of goods and services which a unit of money will purchase, it follows that it can be measured by the price of a *composite commodity*, made up of the various individual goods and services in proportions corresponding to their importance as objects of expenditure. Moreover, there are many types and purposes of expenditure, in which we may be interested at one time or another, corresponding to each of which there is an appropriate composite commodity. The price of a composite commodity which is representative of some type of expenditure, we shall call a *Price-level*; and the series of numbers indicative of changes in a given price-level we shall call *Index numbers. . . .*

Is there any one of these Price-levels, and if so which, corresponding *par excellence* to what we mean by the Purchasing Power of Money? . . . We mean by the Purchasing Power of Money the power of money to buy the goods and services on the purchase of which for purpose of consumption a given community of individuals expend their money income. (pp. 53–4)

This corresponds to Edgeworth's consumption standard. In addition to this fundamental price-level there is a plurality of secondary price-levels, and according to Keynes

---

[37] It should be kept in mind that Fisher's work on price indices emerged from his attempts to measure P in the equation of exchange $MV = PT$. Here M denotes the quantity of money (stock), V its velocity, P the general price level, and T the volume of trade. See Fisher (1911). On the history of the measurement of V see Morgan (2007).

The duty of official Statistical Departments should be, I think, firstly to prepare a really good Index of the Purchasing Power of Money, and secondly to multiply the number and variety of the specialised secondary and sub-Indexes which they compile and publish . . . so as to render it as easy as possible to build up by various combinations of these sub-indexes more complex indexes appropriate to the particular purpose or inquiry on hand. (p. 75)

But Keynes rejected the "indefinite standard" of Edgeworth – see expression (1.15) – as "root-and-branch erroneous":

there is no moving but unique centre, to be called the general price-level or the objective mean variation of general prices, round which are scattered the moving price-levels of individual things. There are all the various, quite definite, conceptions of price-levels of composite commodities appropriate for various purposes and inquires which have been scheduled above, and many others too. There is nothing else. Jevons was pursuing a mirage. (p. 85–6)

This view was supported by other writers (such as Leontief 1936) and became gradually accepted by the various statistical agencies. Nowadays almost every official price or quantity index corresponds to a well-defined "composite commodity," or, as we now call it, an aggregate or economic flow in the sense of the National Accounts. The practical elaboration of these ideas, however, took a long time and is still not yet finished.[38] Conceptually, the oldest part of any system of indices appears to be a consumer price index (CPI) or a set of consumer price indices for different socio-economic groups of private consumers. Considerations concerning simplicity, of calculation as well as understanding, and timeliness by and large led statistical agencies to adopt the Laspeyres or Lowe price index as model for their CPI. The value or quantity weights are thereby usually kept fixed during a number of years.[39]

Keynes (1930, p. 95), however, also noticed that there is a problem with this approach, caused by the empirical fact that "the composite commodities representative of the actual expenditure of money incomes are not stable in their constitution as between different places, times or groups." This

[38] Zieschang (2004) provides a complete description of the systems view. On the closely related and equally interesting history of national accounting see, for a start, Vanoli (2005). A Netherlands perspective was provided by Bos (2006): here bilateral price and quantity indices, as a breakdown of value changes, were for the first time used in the 1954 accounts and chained indices in the 1984 accounts. See also den Butter (2007).

[39] Official guidelines, such as United Nations (1975), or the various ILO resolutions, respectively issued in 1925, 1947, 1962, 1987 and 2003, suggested that the weights be revised every five or ten years. Important for practitioners turned out to be the manual written by Turvey (1989).

subsequently led to the problem of decomposing any change of (aggregate) expenditure of a certain group of consumers or a single consumer into two parts, a part due to the change of prices and a part due to the change of quantities consumed: in other words, a part corresponding to changes in cost of living and a part corresponding to changes in standard of living (Bennet 1920). The practical relevance of this question was reinforced by the already established practice of regulation of wages and pensions. As Fisher (1922, p. 368) had already remarked, "In Great Britain alone, three million laborers have their wages regulated annually by an index number of retail prices." What should be the purpose of regulating, or, as we are now used to call it, indexing of wages? At this point the old answer of Fleetwood was picked up again: the purpose should be to maintain a constant satisfaction, "the same ease and favour." The appropriate index was to be a cost-of-living index, or, as Frisch (1936) called it, a functional price index. He provided a clear definition:

Suppose that we dispose of some criterion by which it is possible to ascertain objectively whether or not a person who in 0 spends an amount ρ_0, is just "as well off" as a person who in 1 spends an amount ρ_1. If they are equally "well off", the two amounts may be called *equivalent*. In symbols, ρ_0 equiv. ρ_1. If such a criterion exists, we take the ratio

$$P_{01}^{Func} = \rho_1/\rho_0 \text{ (when } \rho_0 \text{ equiv. } \rho_1),$$

as the definition of the functional price index number between 0 and 1. (p. 11)

The crucial question is, of course, where do we find an objective criterion for being equally "well off"? And, second, if we have such a criterion, will it be possible to derive a formula for the cost-of-living index that is applicable in practice?

Although Bowley (1920) still suggested relying on the judgment of "representative working-class women," the first question soon came to be answered, at least in principle, by calling in utility theory.

In this approach, each consumer (person or household) is assumed to be equipped with a well-behaved preference ordering over the space of all (positive) quantity vectors $x \equiv (x_1, \ldots, x_N)$. Under appropriate regularity conditions, such a preference ordering can be represented by a so-called utility function that associates any quantity vector with a scalar utility level, $U(x)$. Given commodity prices $p \equiv (p_1, \ldots, p_N)$ and a certain amount of money (budget) e, the consumer is supposed to spend this budget such that it yields the highest utility level. Formally stated, the consumer is supposed to solve the following maximization problem:

$$\max U(x) \text{ subject to } \sum_{n=1}^{N} p_n x_n \leq e. \qquad (1.30)$$

If all consumers act rational in this sense, then observed expenditures could be used to retrieve the essential parameters of the underlying utility function. Suitable econometric techniques would then guarantee the required objectivity.

Now, referring back to Frisch's definition, in different price situations two amounts of money are defined equivalent if they enable the consumer to precisely attain the same utility level. Therefore the cost-of-living index is also frequently called a constant-utility price index.

The elaboration of the second question led to the economic theory of price indices, in particular with respect to private consumers. The foundations of this theory were laid down in the years 1920–30, with Bennet (1920), Haberler (1927),[40] Bowley (1928), and Konüs (1924, translated in 1939)[41] among the founding fathers. The whole "state of the art" at the eve of the second world war was described in a still important review article by Frisch (1936).

The economic theory of index numbers soon became the dominant theory. Quite a number of economists contributed to its expansion, as can be learned from more recent reviews by Pollak (1971), Afriat[42] (1972, 1977), Samuelson and Swamy (1974), and Diewert (1981).[43] Especially W. Erwin Diewert[44] had a great share in advancing the theory. Very important was the development and application of duality theory (which is concerned with the various representations of a preference ordering) and Diewert's (1976) introduction of the concept of a "superlative price index." A classical price index is called "superlative" when the index can be conceived as a cost-of-living index that is consistent with a fairly general representation of a consumer's preference ordering.

---

[40] On Haberler, see Samuelson (1996). Haberler was the first one to establish the Laspeyres and Paasche bounds on cost-of-living indices. The first guesstimate of the substitution bias of Laspeyres and Paasche price indices was provided by Ulmer (1946): for the United States he came to 1.5% per year over the period 1929–40.

[41] On Konüs, see Diewert (1987c).

[42] Afriat's complete bibliography as well as a collection of his publications is contained in Afriat (2005).

[43] See also the relevant chapters written by Diewert in *CPI Manual* and *PPI Manual*, both published in 2004.

[44] On Diewert, see Harris, Laidler, and Nakamura (1996).

Over the course of time it also became clear that by a modification of some basic concepts the theory can be made to cover not only the consumer but also the producer case. And from there it is a small step to the area of productivity measurement.[45]

The characteristic feature of the economic approach is the use of formal optimization models (for utility in the consumer case, or for cost, revenue, or profit in the producer case). Such models imply that prices and quantities are interdependent variables. Though the axiomatic (or test) approach as well as the stochastic approach are guided by economic experience, these two approaches do not wish to formally impose relations between prices and quantities, and thus remain closer to the actual data.

1.8 The Revival of the Stochastic Approach

Though Walsh and Keynes seemed to have delivered almost deadly blows to the stochastic approach as advocated by Jevons and Edgeworth, its revival started in the 1980s by Balk (1980b) and Clements and Izan (1981, 1987).

Basically, the stochastic approach considers the price change of any commodity between two periods, measured as a ratio, as a function of a common component, which is usually called "inflation," and a specific component. The principal aim is to estimate the common component. Recalling expression (1.15), one of the generic models is

$$p_n^1 / p_n^0 = f(\mu^{01}, \varepsilon_n^{01}) \ (n = 1, \ldots, N), \tag{1.31}$$

and the various developments can best be viewed from there. A number of directions will be briefly indicated.

First, the function $f(.)$ can be chosen as additive or as multiplicative. In the last case the model can be reformulated as an additive model for logarithmic price changes.

Second, the specific component, which in general depends both on the commodity and the time periods involved, can be conceived as a zero-mean random variable or as composed of a commodity-specific component (independent of time) *plus* a zero-mean random variable. For example, Clements and Izan's (1987) model reads

$$\ln(p_n^t / p_n^{t-1}) = \alpha^t + \beta_n + \varepsilon_n^t \ (n = 1, \ldots, N), \tag{1.32}$$

---

[45] See Balk (1998b) for a synthesis.

with the assumption that $E(\varepsilon_n^t) = 0$ $(n = 1, \ldots, N)$. Of course, the commodity-specific parameters β_n are not identified, which raises a number of identification and estimation issues.

Third, if there are more than two time periods under consideration there are a number of possibilities. The model (1.31) can be applied to consecutive time periods separately; this delivers estimates of the common components that can be chained together to obtain results for longer time spans. Alternatively, the model can be used to compare any given period to a fixed base period. But since there are overlapping time spans, another alternative is to combine the various two-period models into one (seemingly unrelated) system of equations.

Fourth, one can impose various assumptions on the random variables, in particular with respect to their variances and covariances.

With obvious modifications the stochastic approach can also be used for international comparisons. The common components are then interpreted as purchasing power parities. In this case it is particularly interesting to impose transitivity on the common components.

It has been shown that certain simple specifications of the model (1.31) deliver classical price index formulas as estimators of the common component. More intricate specifications, however, often result in estimators for which no explicit expression can be derived. In any case, each estimator is accompanied by an estimable standard error, which can best be considered as a measure of the strength of the signal (that is, the common component) relative to the concomitant noise.

The factor-analytic approach of Balk, Van Driel, and van Ravenzwaaij (1978) can be regarded as a generalization of the model (1.31) with respect to both the number of time periods and the number of common components simultaneously included. Kindred models were developed by Meinlschmidt (1985).[46]

In addition to models for price relatives there have been developed models for prices. Balk (1980b) modified Summers' (1973) Country-Product-Dummy method, which was developed to deal with missing observations in international comparisons, for application in the temporal context on seasonal commodities. The multiplicative model used by Balk (1980b) was

$$p_n^t = \pi^t \alpha_n \varepsilon_n^t \ (n = 1, \ldots, N; t = 0, 1, \ldots, T); \tag{1.33}$$

that is, the price of commodity n in period t is composed of a common component π^t, a commodity-specific component α_n, and a random

---

[46] An early contribution in this direction was by Chardon (1962).

component ε_n^t. The common component, normalized such that $\pi^0 = 1$, is called the price level of period t and is the primary target of estimation. Of course, a suitable identification constraint on the commodity-specific components must be added, as well as specifications for the random components, before estimation can proceed.

Suppose now that each commodity n can be exhaustively described by its scores z_{nk} on a number of so-called quality characteristics which are labelled as $k = 1, \ldots, K$. Then expression (1.33) transforms into

$$p_n^t = \pi^t \phi(z_{n1}, \ldots, z_{nK}) \varepsilon_n^t \ (n = 1, \ldots, N; t = 0, 1, \ldots, T) \quad (1.34)$$

for some function $\phi(.)$. If logarithms are applied, and the function $\ln \phi(.)$ is assumed to be linear, then expression (1.34) transforms into

$$\ln p_n^t = \ln \pi^t + \sum_{k=1}^K \beta_k z_{nk} + \ln \varepsilon_n^t \ (n = 1, \ldots, N; t = 0, 1, \ldots, T).$$

$$(1.35)$$

Finally, in order to deal with quality *change* the scores z_{nk} are allowed to vary through time, so that we get

$$\ln p_n^t = \ln \pi^t + \sum_{k=1}^K \beta_k z_{nk}^t + \ln \varepsilon_n^t \ (n = 1, \ldots, N; t = 0, 1, \ldots, T)$$

$$(1.36)$$

as our final model. This, then, is a so-called hedonic regression model. This model dates back to Court (1939) and was revitalized by Griliches (1961). Though in the course of time various other specifications have been developed, it appears that all those models, intended for the estimation of aggregate price change when there is simultaneously quality change, are stochastic by nature.[47]

Other signs that the interest in the stochastic approach is reviving are the attempts to measure so-called core inflation. Although the precise meaning of this term is generally left somewhat in the dark – in some way it seems to be related to money growth – Bryan and Cecchetti (1994) proposed the weighted median of the price changes as a suitable measure of core inflation. However, this appears to be old wine in a new bottle. The weighted median had already been proposed by Edgeworth in 1888, based on his study of the characteristics of the distribution of price changes.

---

[47] Expression (1.36) can be reformulated as a so-called time-dummy model by setting $\ln \pi^t = \ln \pi^0 + \sum_{t'=0}^T D^{t't} \ln(\pi^{t'}/\pi^0)$ with $D^{t't} = 1$ if $t' = t$ and $D^{t't} = 0$ otherwise. On the relation with other models, see Silver and Heravi (2007a).

New, however, is Bryan and Cecchetti's (1993) introduction of a dynamic factor model to measure (core) inflation. Recall the primary model (1.31). Here all the individual price changes are considered as, although noisy, concurrent indicators of inflation. More generality obtains when one allows for some price changes to be leading and other price changes to be lagging. This seems to be a fruitful area for further research.[48]

All these developments have been documented in a monograph by Selvanathan and Rao (1994), a rather critical discussion paper by Diewert (1995b), and a review article by Clements, Izan, and Selvanathan (2006). It appears that, despite Walsh and Keynes, the stochastic approach is still alive and well.

We finally consider two related approaches to the construction of price and quantity indices. These approaches share with the axiomatic approach the nonimposition of optimization. Their starting point is the want to decompose values or value changes into price and quantity components, but this is executed by means of a formal stochastic model.

The first is the "best linear" approach, developed by Theil (1960) and others. The basic model for two time periods is

$$\begin{pmatrix} \sum_{n=1}^{N} p_n^0 x_n^0 & \sum_{n=1}^{N} p_n^0 x_n^1 \\ \sum_{n=1}^{N} p_n^1 x_n^0 & \sum_{n=1}^{N} p_n^1 x_n^1 \end{pmatrix} = \begin{pmatrix} P^0 \\ P^1 \end{pmatrix} (Q^0 \ Q^1) + E, \qquad (1.37)$$

where P^0 and P^1 are positive scalars, to be interpreted as the price levels of periods 0 and 1 respectively, whereas the positive scalars Q^0 and Q^1 are to be interpreted as the corresponding quantity levels. Finally, the matrix E is regarded as a matrix of disturbances. The price index of period 1 relative to period 0 is then defined as P^1/P^0 and the quantity index as Q^1/Q^0.

The price and quantity levels are obtained by solving the least squares problem, that is, by minimizing the trace of the matrix (EE'). The generalization to more than two periods is obvious. It is clear that in case of more than two periods the indices $P^t/P^{t'}$ and $Q^t/Q^{t'}$ depend on all the data of all the periods involved. These indices are therefore called *multilateral*. Other authors developed variants, among others by solving the minimization problem under additional constraints on the elements of the matrix E.[49]

---

[48] See BIS (1999) and the recent survey by Silver (2006).
[49] See Kloek and de Wit (1961), Kloek and van Rees (1962), Kloek (1966), Jazairi (1971, 1973), and Fisk (1977). A closely related approach was developed by Bamberg and Spremann (1985).

Of kindred spirit is the "factorial approach," which since 1961 has been developed by Banerjee. This approach can be conceived as a generalization of an earlier idea of Stuvel (1957). In this approach the elements of the left-hand side matrix in (1.37) are considered as outcomes of a 2^2 factorial experiment (two factors at two levels), which can be modeled linearly by

$$\sum_{n=1}^{N} p_n^t x_n^{t'} = \mu + \alpha^t + \beta^{t'} + (\alpha\beta)^{tt'} + \varepsilon^{tt'} \ (t, t' = 0, 1), \quad (1.38)$$

where $\sum_{t=0}^{1} \alpha^t = \sum_{t'=0}^{1} \beta^{t'} = \sum_{t=0}^{1} (\alpha\beta)^{tt'} = \sum_{t'=0}^{1} (\alpha\beta)^{tt'} = 0$. The main price effect is defined by $P \equiv \alpha^1 - \alpha^0$ and the main quantity effect by $Q \equiv \beta^1 - \beta^0$.

OLS estimation delivers as estimators of these main effects

$$\hat{P} = (1/2) \sum_{n=1}^{N} (p_n^1 - p_n^0)(x_n^1 + x_n^0) \quad (1.39)$$

$$\hat{Q} = (1/2) \sum_{n=1}^{N} (p_n^1 + p_n^0)(x_n^1 - x_n^0), \quad (1.40)$$

which are identical to the price and quantity indicators derived by Bennet (1920).

The generalization to more than two periods proceeds along the same lines, but does not deliver such neat closed-form solutions. The reader is referred to the comprehensive monograph by Banerjee (1980). A number of extensions of this method are discussed in Banerjee (1989).

In the field of intertemporal price and quantity comparisons these multilateral approaches have not found many applications because of the fact that with any addition of a new time period all the previous index numbers have to be recomputed.

1.9 Conclusion: Recurrent Themes

Looking back over some 150 years it is possible to see a number of recurrent themes.

First, there is the quest for a measure that reflects changes in the "value" or, more specifically, the "purchasing power" of money through time.

This is one of the oldest themes, going back to the days of Jevons. Traditionally, "money" is seen as "currency": the purchasing power of, say, a U.S. dollar is different from the purchasing power of, say, a euro. However, upon further reflection one soon realizes that regional differentiation is necessary: the purchasing power of a euro in, say, The Netherlands is different from the purchasing power of the same euro in, say, Italy. Further, in terms of purchasing power, a euro given to a private consumer differs from a euro given to a producer. And finally, consumers and producers are all but homogeneous groups, which asks for further differentiation. The baseline here is that one cannot talk about the purchasing power of money without taking into account the specific conditions and purposes of purchasing.

We owe here much to the pioneering insights of Edgeworth. Interestingly, however, though one might suspect that the reflection on the meaning of "purchasing power" would lead to calling off the search for some "general" price index, this theme is still vivid. It occurs in more or less disguised form in the search for a measure of "(core) inflation" that could figure in monetary-economic theory and/or could be used in monetary policy.

Second, there is the quest for measures that enable one to decompose nominal value changes of economic flows into their price and quantity components. A profit change for a producer or an income change for a consumer is as such not very interesting. The really interesting figures are those concerning the underlying quantity- or so-called real developments, and price indices are instrumental in this sort of decomposition exercises. This theme is relatively new, inspired by Keynes and Leontief, but has gradually gained in importance because of the increased complexity of national accounts systems operated by statistical agencies. Yet, even the most sophisticated system contains flows for which no natural decomposition seems to exist and one has to fall back on some "general" price index.

Third, the oldest theme, going all the way back to Bishop Fleetwood, is the quest for a measure or a number of measures that can be used to "compensate" private consumers for the effect of price level changes on their incomes. This theme is, of course, related to the previous two, but has exhibited its own dynamics through time. Income is used for purchasing a basket of goods and services, which reflects a certain standard of living. Increasing prices make it, *ceteris paribus*, impossible to maintain such a standard of living, unless the income is compensated. One of the interesting questions here is how good a cost-of-living index, which does the compensation job, can be approximated by some classical formula.

Though these three themes time and again resurface, and it thus seems that no progress has been made, there are a couple of important developments to note:

- We have learned to be more precise with respect to the concepts and targets of measurement. For instance, what is to be understood by "inflation," "purchasing power," "cost of living," "being equally well off"? The downside, of course, is that there appears to be no single, universally applicable "solution," but that one has to live up to a number of different instruments that are to be used for a number of different purposes.

• Price measurement has by and large been institutionalized. The regular publication of consumer and producer price indices nowadays belongs to the core program of any national statistical agency and is governed by international guidelines and resolutions from institutions such as United Nations, the OECD, and the IMF. There is a lot of public and political interest in these figures. But users have to *trust* that all those guidelines are well founded and that the rules are well-implemented by the agencies.

• Data have become more easily available. From sparse data gathered by isolated academics or editorial offices of newspapers, we proceeded to survey data obtained at regular time intervals by national statistical agencies or other institutions, and further to electronic transaction data (so-called scanner data). The progress here is remarkable, as are the challenges. There is a downside here, too. The national economies have become increasingly complex and interrelated, and this translates into complexity of data capture and processing. A simple, independent checking of statistical outcomes is beyond any user's reach. Here, again, *trust* is essential.

After 150 years there is still a role for scientific research. First, because trust requires (regular) verification. Second, because there are still a number of challenging problems to solve.

For seeing these problems at a glance it is helpful to return to the assumptions mentioned toward the end of the introductory section. As stated there, theory treats "commodity" as a primitive term that obtains its precise meaning in operational use. Until recently, the emphasis was on commodities of the "goods" type, for which it is relatively simple to define units of measurement, quantities, and prices. In all the expenditure patterns of the developed countries, however, the emphasis has gradually shifted toward commodities of the "services" type, for which it is much harder to define units of measurement, quantities, and prices. Further, theory treats the set of commodities as fixed, but in reality consumer and producer markets exhibit much turbulence from disappearing and new commodities. Finally, commodities themselves suffer from quality change, for which price indices must be adjusted.

Much research is channeled via the so-called Ottawa Group (International Working Group on Price Indices), acting under the auspices of the United Nations Statistical Commission. The Ottawa Group came into being in 1994 and had its 10th meeting in 2007. During its existence topics for discussion included price indices for durable goods (such as computers), for owner-occupied housing, and for "hard-to-measure" areas such as health services, financial services, and telecom services. Most papers can be downloaded from the Group's website, www.ottawagroup.org. The Ottawa Group also acted as cradle of the *CPI Manual* and *PPI Manual*, which cover both theory and practice.

The Quest for International Comparisons

2.1 Introduction

Price and quantity indices are not only used for intertemporal comparisons but also for interspatial – that is, international or interregional – comparisons; the price index numbers are then called "purchasing power parities." The purpose could be to have an instrument for salary compensation of expatriates; or to answer the question whether a particular exchange rate is set too high or too low; or to obtain an ordering of countries with respect to their level of welfare.

The simplest approach is to make such comparions pairwise: that is, to base them on the price and quantity data of two countries in turn. The methodology of bilateral intertemporal comparisons can then simply be translated; all that is needed is to replace time periods by spatial designations.

Thus, modifying the notation introduced in the previous chapter, it is assumed that there are N commodities, labelled as $1, \ldots, N$, which are available in I countries, labelled as $1, \ldots, I$. The country i vector of prices will be denoted by $p^i \equiv (p^i_1, \ldots, p^i_N)$, and the associated vector of quantities by $x^i \equiv (x^i_1, \ldots, x^i_N)$ $(i = 1, \ldots, I)$. All the prices and quantities are assumed to be positive real numbers, referring to some well-defined time period. This period is usually, but not necessarily, the same for all the countries involved in a comparison. Any bilateral price index $P(p^j, x^j, p^i, x^i)$ compares the prices of country j to those of country i, conditional on the quantities of the two countries. Likewise, any bilateral quantity index $Q(p^j, x^j, p^i, x^i)$ compares the quantities of country j to those of country i, conditional on the prices of the two countries. In this chapter, which surveys the history of ideas, we sidestep the enormous operational difficulties which come with measuring all those prices and quantities.

An early example of the simple, bilateral approach is provided by the article by Törnqvist and Törnqvist (1937), to which we have already referred in the previous chapter. This study was concerned with the comparison of but two countries, Finland and Sweden. Similar work, on more than two countries, was executed by Gilbert and Kravis (1954). Using a National Accounts framework, the team headed by these authors compared four European countries to the United States, by means of Laspeyres, Paasche and Fisher indices. In 1958, Gilbert and his associates extended this study by four more European countries.[1]

These two studies, however, also mention the problem of nontransitivity. Given I countries and a particular bilateral price or quantity index, there are $I(I - 1)$ possible comparisons. How to create a unique ordering out of this? The intertemporal method of chaining cannot be carried over unconditionally, because there is no such thing as a "natural" ordering of countries.

In order to obtain a unique ranking, price and quantity indices must be transitive. Transitivity, however, easily conflicts with other desired features of a comparison method. Consider, for instance, the following interspatial variant of the Lowe price index,

$$P^{Lo}(p^j, p^i; \bar{x}) \equiv \frac{\sum_{n=1}^{N} p_n^j \bar{x}_n}{\sum_{n=1}^{N} p_n^i \bar{x}_n} \ (i, j = 1, \ldots, I), \qquad (2.1)$$

where the vector $\bar{x}$ is the unweighted mean of the quantity vectors x^i ($i = 1, \ldots, I$); that is, $\bar{x} \equiv (1/I) \sum_{i=1}^{I} x^i$. It is easily checked that this index leads to a unique ordering of the countries with respect to their purchasing power parity.[2] However, the quantity vector that figures in the Lowe price index (2.1) is naturally dominated by the larger countries that are participating in the comparison project, which is considered a disadvantage.

This is one of the reasons why, from the early 1950s onwards, researchers have been searching for the "best" system of multilateral indices: that is, indices that by definition are functions of the price and quantity data of all the countries involved in a comparison project.

The task of making international comparisons naturally fell into the hands of international organisations, usually working together with national

---

[1] Such an approach is not obsolete, as the example of Fukao, Ma, and Yuan (2006) demonstrates. These authors calculated Fisher price indices comparing Japan, Korea, and Taiwan, based on 1935–6 expenditure and price data.

[2] This method was used in the comparison projects carried out by the United Nations Economic Commission for Latin America and the Caribbean. See Ruggles (1967) and ECLAC (1978).

statistical agencies. Most important with respect to the development of methodology were Eurostat (and its predecessors), the OECD, the United Nations Statistical Office, and the various (commissions of) experts appointed by these organisations. Because of this institutional loading, the methodological debate at times exhibited the features of a battle. This chapter reviews the rather turbulent history.

2.2 The Demand for European Purchasing Power Parities

As part of its mission, the European Coal and Steel Community (ECSC) – predecessor of the European Union, founded in 1952 – wanted to be able to compare the real wages of miners and steelworkers within Western Europe. A "real wage" comparison is a comparison between the nominal wages, adjusted for differences in the price levels between the various regions (countries). It was clear that the bilateral purchasing power parities of Laspeyres, Paasche, and Fisher would not produce unambiguous results because of major differences on the one hand and lack of transitivity on the other hand. So in 1954 the Statistical Bureau of the European Communities (later called Eurostat) commissioned an expert committee to study the issue. One of the representatives of Statistics Netherlands in this committee was the mathematician Jan van IJzeren.[3]

He developed the first set of genuinely multilateral methods. Departing from what he called a "tourist" model, he developed three methods: (1) the heterogeneous group method (in later publications called the basket combining method); (2) the homogeneous group method (later called the price combining method); and (3) the balanced method. The first method generates a set of transitive purchasing power parities P^i ($i = 1, \ldots, I$) as a solution of the following system of equations:

$$\sum_{i=1}^{I} g_i P^L(p^j, x^j, p^i, x^i) P^i / P^j = \alpha \; (j = 1, \ldots, I), \qquad (2.2)$$

where the g_i ($i = 1, \ldots, I$) are given, positive, scalar country weights and α is some positive scalar. The second method employs a slightly different system of equations,

$$\sum_{i=1}^{I} g_i P^L(p^i, x^i, p^j, x^j) P^j / P^i = \alpha \; (j = 1, \ldots, I). \qquad (2.3)$$

---

[3] Jan van IJzeren, 1914–98, was employed by Statistics Netherlands from 1947 to 1958. From 1958 to 1979 he worked at the Technical University Eindhoven.

The third method appears to combine these two equation systems into one,

$$\sum_{i=1}^{I} g_i P^L(p^j, x^j, p^i, x^i) P^i / P^j$$

$$= \sum_{i=1}^{I} g_i P^L(p^i, x^i, p^j, x^j) P^j / P^i \quad (j = 1, \ldots, I). \qquad (2.4)$$

The first publication in which these methods were described, in the Dutch language, was Van IJzeren (1955). The methods gained wider attention through the publication of Van IJzeren (1956), which was in the English language.[4]

Under the direction of Rolf Wagenführ, then head of the statistical office of the ECSC, the first method of Van IJzeren was applied to the data of the price survey that was held in 1954. The purchasing power parities were published in ECSC (1956). It was a primer, not only for Europe but for the world. The methodological description can be found in ECSC (1957). The next price survey took place in 1958. The results were published in BSEC (1960). This elaborate publication also describes the three methods of Van IJzeren. The third method was applied to the surveys of 1954 and 1958. The purchasing power parities for the years in between were calculated by interpolation with help of the national price index numbers.

The next price survey took place in 1963. Again the method of Van IJzeren was used, but the purchasing power parities were never published. The next survey was that of 1970. At a conference held in Mexico in 1971, officials Silvio Ronchetti and Guy Bertaud gave a presentation on the calculation of purchasing power parities by the Bureau of Statistics of the EC. They said the following about the method used:

A method devised by an expert from the Statistical Office, Professor Van IJzeren, has many advantages. It has been described at length both in the publications of the Central Statistical Office at The Hague and by those of the Statistical Office in Luxembourg. It is worth recalling that this is a calculation by iteration of a non-linear system of I equations with I unknown factors, in which the parameters are shown by the Laspeyres indexes. The system is based on a very concrete tourist-type model and has a number of qualities: in particular, its lack of sophistication. This method will again be applied by the Statistical Office of the European Communities to the results of the November 1970 survey. (Ronchetti and Bertaud 1974, p. 326)

---

[4] This publication is sometimes dated as 1957 because the cover contains two dates. The mathematics of the methods will be discussed in section 7.3.2.

The results were never published, however, because of their poor quality (see Diehl 1976). There was a new survey in 1972, followed in 1973 by a rather informal publication of purchasing power parities calculated according to the formula of Fisher (BSEC 1973). Here we find the following promise:

For the final publication we will use a more refined calculation method, named after its spiritual father, Van IJzeren. This method, with results that maintain their transitive character, makes the interpretation and presentation of the data a great deal easier.

It seems that such a final publication never materialized. In the meantime the focus had shifted away from real wage comparisons towards purchasing power parities for the comparison of aggregates defined in the framework of the national accounts, such as Gross Domestic Product, national income, household consumption, and industrial production. Moreover, because the EC was expanding, there had been a shift in the price survey method, so that there was no longer a price for every commodity on the list for each country available. This led to a reconsideration of the calculation methods used. Diehl (1976) lets us in on some of the considerations. The impression was that the Van IJzeren method had two problems: the method could not be applied when the information about prices was incomplete, and the method could not supply a corresponding quantity index satisfying the product relation. Although both of these allegations were unwarranted, people started looking for different methods.

There were two candidates, the GK and the EKS methods, to be discussed in the next section. The GK method was preferred at first, and it was applied to the 1974 survey results; however, there has not been a publication of the outcomes. There appeared an informal publication of the results of the 1975 survey (Eurostat 1976), but with purchasing power parities calculated according to the EKS method. However, the final publication, Eurostat (1977), contained purchasing power parities calculated according to the Gerardi method, which will also be discussed below.

2.3 The GK Method and the EKS Method

In 1958, the Irish statistician R. C. Geary, following up on a discussion he had in the Netherlands in 1957 with Van IJzeren,[5] published his famous three-page-long article "A Note on the Comparison of Exchange Rates and Purchasing Power between Countries." In this article he developed

---

[5] According to a statement by Van IJzeren in a letter to Drechsler dated 14 December 1970.

the method which, due to Khamis (1972), has become known later as the Geary-Khamis (GK) method.[6] The purchasing power parities according to this method are generated by a system of equations:

$$\pi_n = \frac{\sum_{i=1}^{I} p_n^i x_n^i / P^i}{\sum_{i=1}^{I} x_n^i} \quad (n = 1, \ldots, N)$$

$$P^i = \frac{\sum_{n=1}^{N} p_n^i x_n^i}{\sum_{n=1}^{N} \pi_n x_n^i} \quad (i = 1, \ldots, I).$$

(2.5)

The first set of equations, one for each commodity, defines what one could call the "international" price of a commodity: its total value, made additive by dividing national prices through purchasing power parities, divided through its total quantity. The second set of equations, one for each country, defines the purchasing power parity of a country as its Paasche price index relative to the country with "international prices."

The article by Geary referred to Van IJzeren (1956) and employed his numerical example (two commodities, four countries) to show that the parities according to Van IJzeren's methods are almost always higher than those according to Geary's method, and that the outcomes of Geary's method resemble most those of Van IJzeren's second method. The methods as such, however, were not compared to each other. Finally, Geary noticed that his contribution should be seen against the backdrop of the problem how to calculate quantity indices for the regional and worldwide agricultural output that are consistent with the national indices.

After balancing several alternatives, the Geary-Khamis method was chosen as the privileged method in the International Comparison Project, a joint venture of the United Nations Statistical Office, the World Bank, and the International Comparison Unit of the University of Pennsylvania. The report on the first phase appeared in 1975, written by Irving B. Kravis, Zoltan Kenessey, Alan Heston, and Robert Summers.[7] On page 67–8 one finds a brief description of the third method of Van IJzeren.

The choice for the GK method was motivated from the additive structure of the defining system of equations and the transitivity of the purchasing power parities. Because of these features, according to these authors, the

---

[6] According to Khamis (1972), Geary, as a consultant of the United Nations Food and Agriculture Organization, had developed his method already in 1952. More information about Geary can be found in Neary (1997).

[7] The GK method still underlies the construction of the Penn World Table, an important source for international comparisons; see Summers and Heston (1991).

method had a "clear economic rationale." On Van IJzeren's method they observed that "The Van Yzeren method's complicated interpretation puts it at a substantial disadvantage relative to Geary-Khamis." The interpretation was also the key subject of an exchange of letters in the years 1970–1 between the Hungarian Lázló Drechsler, at that time employed by the United Nations Economic Commission for Europe, and Van IJzeren. By virtue of his function, Drechsler was engaged with a comparative study of a number of methods for the international comparison of purchasing power. Via Statistics Netherlands he called on Van IJzeren's help with respect to the difference between his third method and a method that had been developed some years earlier by the Hungarians Ödön Eltetö and Pál Köves (1964) and the Polish Bohdan Szulc (1964), independent of each other. What these authors did not know at that time was that their method – which through Drechsler (1973) came to be known in the West as the EKS method – had already been proposed by Gini (1924), and therefore appeared to be a rediscovery.

The two methods, the EKS method as well as Van IJzeren's third method, can be conceived as solutions to minimization problems. Van IJzeren's system of equations (2.4) is nothing but the set of first-order conditions for the minimization problem

$$\min_{P^1,\dots,P^I} \sum_{i=1}^{I} \sum_{j=1}^{I} g_i g_j P^L(p^j, x^j, p^i, x^i) P^i/P^j, \qquad (2.6)$$

whereas the EKS method was defined by

$$\min_{P^1,\dots,P^I} \sum_{i=1}^{I} \sum_{j=1}^{I} (1/I)^2 [\ln P^F(p^j, x^j, p^i, x^i) - \ln(P^j/P^i)]^2. \quad (2.7)$$

The discussion between Drechsler and Van IJzeren concerned the interpretation of the function to minimize, and the use of country weights. The question of interpretation could not be solved adequately, however. This is apparent from the following paragraph in the final article of Drechsler (1973), originally presented at the 1971 conference of the International Association for Research in Income and Wealth (IARIW):

The Dutchman Van Yzeren, almost a decade before Eltetö, Köves and Szulc, proposed three sets of inter-country indices, which all satisfy the circularity requirement [here called transitivity]. There is a striking similarity between the EKS and van Yzeren methods: in all cases the Fisher formula plays the central role. However, van Yzeren sets requirements for his indices other than minimising deviation from the characteristic indices [that is, the bilateral Fisher indices]. His interest focuses on price indices (currency ratios) and he determines his indices with the aim of minimising the total increase in costs due to ill-adapted currency ratios. All three methods he proposes have their strict economic meaning and may be very useful in special inter-country comparisons. In general purpose comparisons, however, where the main objective is to determine differences in levels between the countries compared, the EKS requirement of minimising deviation from characteristic indices seems to be more important than the requirements of the van Yzeren methods.

This quote makes clear which method was preferred by Drechsler. However, one cannot call his conclusion well founded.

2.4 Van IJzeren's Return on the Scene

In 1977 Van IJzeren and the Italian Dino Gerardi got in touch. Gerardi had started work at Eurostat's Price Comparison Unit, managed by the former Statistics Netherlands statistician Hugo Krijnse Locker. Gerardi was familiar with Van IJzeren's work, because as a student at the University of Padova he had written a paper in which he developed variants of the three methods of Van IJzeren. Where Van IJzeren (1956) derived three sets of equations from a model based on groups of tourists, Gerardi (1974) came up with a model based on groups of immigrants. This led him to three different sets of equations.

A number of visits between Van IJzeren and Gerardi led to the idea of writing a joint article about the matter of purchasing power parities (letter of Van IJzeren to Gerardi, dated 2 February 1978). The contents is sketched, and after a few months there is mention of a concept written by Van IJzeren. In a letter dated 19 July 1978 Gerardi writes to Van IJzeren that it might be better to compose two separate papers, one by Van IJzeren and the other by Gerardi. Van IJzeren agrees and sends his first draft, entitled "Modèles pour Comparer le Pouvoir d'Achat," to Gerardi on 6 September 1978. Gerardi delivered his comments, which led to a second draft on 11 January 1979. It discussed the original Van IJzeren tourist model and Gerardi's immigrant model, and compared them with the Gini (EKS) and the GK methods. In 1979, Van IJzeren made an effort to get this paper published by Eurostat as a contribution to the methodological debate. However, his letters to Eurostat director Guy Bertaud, whom Van IJzeren knew from their work back in the 1950s, did not produce the desired result. In the end, on 23 October 1980, he sent his paper to his former Statistics Netherlands colleague C. A. Oomens, who was then director of Economic Statistics, and asked what he should do next. This is how the paper got to me.

What followed were several meetings in person which led to a close co-operation and finally in 1983 to the publication of "Index Numbers for Binary and Multilateral Comparison; Algebraical and Numerical Aspects" as number 34 of the series Statistical Studies. In the meantime the original manuscript had grown into a 60-page report. The first and second methods of Van IJzeren were now derived by employing the notion of an "artificial base country" with (weighted or unweighted) international quantities and international prices, respectively (basket combining and price combining, respectively). Starting with international quantities led to the first method, characterized by purchasing power parities with an additive structure and quantity indices that are nonadditive. Starting with international prices led to the second method, characterized by quantity indices with an additive structure and purchasing power parities that are nonadditive. The third method can be seen as a synthesis through the balancing principle. Here purchasing power parities and quantity indices both have a nonadditive structure, which is made explicit in the so-called correction factors. In other words, additivity is replaced by a sort of nonlinear aggregation.

This publication can be considered as the preliminary study for Van IJzeren's Ph.D. thesis. Van IJzeren had formally retired from academia in 1979. His contacts with Köves, which had come about several years earlier via Drechsler, gave rise to the idea to write a thesis about this material. The thesis was printed in September 1987 and defended by Van IJzeren on 2 November 1987 in front of the Committee of Scientific Qualifications of the Hungarian Academy of Sciences in Budapest. Because bureaucracy took its time, he received the degree of "Candidate of Sciences," the equivalent of a doctorate, somewhere in 1988. The thesis is rather difficult to read because of the wealth of mathematical detail and the many numerical results. However, the essence can be found in a lengthy review by Balk (1989a); see also Balk (1996c). A new aspect introduced in the thesis was the detailed analysis of the issue of nonlinear aggregation in connection with the problem of consistency-in-aggregation.

2.5 International Discussion

We now return to Gerardi and the contribution he had promised. It is not clear what actually became of it. One could suppose that the paper "Selected Problems of Inter-Country Comparisons on the Basis of the Experiences of the EEC," presented in 1981 during the conference of the IARIW, and later published in revised form in *The Review of Income and Wealth* (1982a), may be considered as the final product. Here Gerardi used a classification of indices inspired by Van IJzeren's original work. He distinguished six groups: weighted and unweighted homogeneous, heterogeneous, and balanced indices. Distinctions were also made within these groups. The matter was further complicated by the use of generalized averages. Various considerations then brought Gerardi to the proposal to calculate purchasing power parities according to a set of equations that can be considered as a variant of the GK system:

$$\pi_n = \left(\prod_{i=1}^{I} p_n^i / P^i \right)^{1/I} \quad (n = 1, \ldots, N)$$

$$P^i = \frac{\sum_{n=1}^{N} p_n^i x_n^i}{\sum_{n=1}^{N} \pi_n x_n^i} \quad (i = 1, \ldots, I).$$

(2.8)

This system became known as the Gerardi method. It had been used already by Eurostat (1977) for comparing National Accounts aggregates for the year 1975. It is useful to note the differences and similarities with the GK method. In both methods international prices form the point of departure. The GK method employs an arithmetic average, weighted with quantities, whereas the Gerardi method employs an unweighted geometric average. The GK method is a set of equations that has to be solved by means of a numerical method, whereas the Gerardi method turns out to reduce to an explicit formula for the purchasing power parities. The detailed methodological account in Eurostat (1977) runs partly parallel with the story in Gerardi (1982a), thereby revealing its author.

The difference of opinion about the preferred method between Eurostat and the United Nations Statistical Office, co-ordinator of the International Comparison Programme, which was several steps ahead by that time, was on the agenda of an Expert Group Meeting in December 1980 in Bellagio. The discussion was based on a draft report written by Peter Hill, later published by Eurostat (1982). He says the following about the differences between the methods:

The main difference between the Geary-Khamis and Gerardi methods stems not from the fact that one is an arithmetic average and the other a geometric average, but from the fact that one is weighted average of the national prices whereas the other is unweighted.

He concluded in favour of the GK method:

Geary's method is preferred, therefore, because his international price is simple, meaningful, objective and characteristic of the group of countries as a whole.

As a consequence we see that the comparison made by Eurostat for the year 1980 used the GK method as the official one (Eurostat 1983). This publication, however, also contains results produced by a number of other methods, including those of Gerardi and EKS.

The result of the international discussion clearly did not please everyone, as is shown in a paper presented by Gerardi in 1982 at the Luxembourg IARIW Special Conference on PPPs. He goes for the direct attack:

As I will show you in this note, the proposals made for both the basic headings and the aggregate level are far from being the best in view of the attainment of the methodological harmonisation in the framework of the ICP.

The considerations in this paper (Gerardi 1982b) led to the suggestion of yet another new method, the Ideal Prices or Implicit Prices (IP) method. The results of this method can also be found in the publication by Eurostat (1983). However, the method was never adequately documented, so that this was a lone exercise. The results published for the year 1985 were exclusively based on the GK method (Eurostat 1988).

However, the debate continued under the surface so to speak, and did not deal just with the methods described above. Eurostat became increasingly critical because of the alleged fact that the GK method suffered from the so-called Gerschenkron effect. This effect would be caused by a phenomenon that also occurs in intertemporal comparisons, namely negative or positive correlation (depending on the type of market considered) between relative price differences and relative quantity differences. The organisations involved, Eurostat, OECD, and UNSO, called a new Expert Group, which met in June 1988 in Luxembourg and in June 1989 in Paris.

In the meantime, however, there had been some progress in methodology. Until the mid-eighties the debates had mainly consisted of verbal arguments. Of course, the use of some formulas had been indispensable, but for the most part the reasoning was not terribly exact. The Hill (1982) report is a good example of this: a small number of formulas are used as illustration, but there is a lot of verbal text.

An important step in the right direction was set by Diewert (1986). Here we see a set of criteria (called tests), formulated with mathematical precision, that purchasing power parities and quantity indices should satisfy. The various methods should be judged against each other with help of these criteria. Diewert demonstrated, for example, that the quantity indices implied by the GK method do not satisfy one of the key criteria. Diewert, who was a member of the Expert Group, presented a slightly revised version of his paper there. Balk, also a member of this group, presented there the first draft of Balk (1989a), in which Diewert's criteria were reformulated by introducing country weights. The "performance" of Van IJzeren's balanced method was also tested. It was found that this method satisfied all criteria except one, the one the GK method violated as well. However, it was shown that the violation was "worse" in the case of GK than in the case of Van IJzeren.

Balk also demonstrated why the purchasing power parities according to the EKS method are a good approximation of those resulting from Van IJzeren's balanced method, something that had attracted the attention on the basis of empirical work for quite some time. Balk's conclusion was that

The time is ripe for a reconsideration of the GK method. As demonstrated in this paper, the Van IJzeren method is a better alternative. At the same time the foregoing can be seen as a defence of the EKS method, which provides a close approximation of the Van IJzeren method but is much easier to calculate. In the light of the growing number of countries participating in the International Comparison Programme and the growing complexity of the work involved (regionalisation etc.) this is also a worthwhile alternative to contemplate.

During the second meeting of the Expert Group, the IP method was judged "not appropriate," because of a number of major drawbacks. The Expert Group recommended to present two sets of results in the future: for comparisons between countries the EKS (or a similar) method, and for more analytical purposes the GK (or a similar) method.[8] In accordance with this we see that Eurostat only published the results according to the EKS method for the years 1990 and 1991 (Eurostat 1994).

2.6 Conclusion

Balk (1996a) compared a dozen methods for multilateral purchasing power parities and quantity indices, including the balanced method of Van IJzeren, the EKS method, the GK method, and Gerardi's method, using the criteria just mentioned. The conclusion was that none of the methods satisfies all criteria. The best-scoring methods, however, were those of Van IJzeren and GK.

The choice between the two depends on the importance the user attaches to additivity. The price one has to pay for additivity is a certain risk of suffering from the Gerschenkron effect. After all, economic reality seems not to be additive. That is why Balk preferred the method of Van IJzeren,

---

[8] During the joint meeting of Price Statistics and National Accounts experts on 15 November 1989, Eurostat nevertheless attempted to salvage the IP method, but this was stopped thanks to various, including Dutch, interventions (see Balk 1989b).

with the (weighted) EKS method as a second best. As Van IJzeren (1987) demonstrated himself, the two methods are relatively insensitive to the country weights used, which is a practical advantage. Balk's preference was supported by Hill (1997) and Diewert (1999).

Newer research is mainly directed to the solution of a number of more or less practical problems that arise in international comparisons. As one can imagine, international comparisons are expensive projects, and the larger the number of countries involved becomes, the more expensive these projects become. Thus, because of funding problems, large-scale international comparisons are usually restricted to so-called benchmark years. However, since there is also demand for yearly international comparisons, it is necessary to obtain estimates for the intervening years by combining intertemporal and interspatial indices in an intelligent way. As Hill (2004 and 2007) has shown, there is no unique way of doing this.

Also, the larger the number of countries, the more difficult it becomes to draw up a list of commodities that is at the same time universally applicable and representative for the individual countries. This necessitates regionalization as well as the use of two-stage methods for linking the regional comparisons to obtain global results. Again, there is no unique method here, and research is directed to finding optimal solutions.

3

Axioms, Tests, and Indices

3.1 Introduction

Since the beginning of the 19th century a large number of price and quantity indices have been invented. Every statistician knows at least the most famous names: Laspeyres, Paasche, Fisher. But there are many more indices, mostly named after their inventors.

Parallel with the invention of new indices went the development of criteria for distinguishing between them. This was a rather natural process. Inventing a new formula is not enough. One should also provide evidence that the newborn index is "better" than all existing ones. In the beginning of the 20th century this line of research culminated in the still impressive book *The Making of Index Numbers* by Irving Fisher (1922).[1] In this book Fisher evaluated in a systematic manner a very large number of indices with respect to a number of criteria. These criteria were called *tests*.

Most of these tests were of older date. For instance, the identity test (saying that, if the prices of period 1 are the same as those of period 0, then the price index number should be equal to 1) is due to Laspeyres (1871). The time reversal test (saying that the price index number for period 1 relative to period 0 should be the reciprocal of the price index number for period 0 relative to period 1) and the dimensional invariance or commensurability test (saying that the price index should not be dependent on the units of measurement) have been proposed by Pierson (1896). Westergaard (1890) required that a price index should satisfy the circularity test (that is, the price index number for period 1 relative to period 0 times the price index number for period 2 relative to period 1 must be equal to the price index number for period 2 relative to period 0). Fisher (1911, 1921, 1922) himself contributed

---

[1] The Appendix to chapter X of Fisher (1911) can be regarded as a preparatory study.

the product test (saying that the price index number times the quantity index number must be equal to the ratio of the values of the two periods) and the factor reversal test (which is a stronger version of the product test: price index and quantity index should have the same mathematical form, with prices and quantities interchanged). He considered the factor reversal test and the time reversal test as the two supreme tests, "the two legs on which index numbers can be made to walk" (1922, p. XIII).

Fisher's system of tests has been challenged with regard to its consistency. Frisch (1930) and Wald (1937) proved the impossibility of maintaining certain tests simultaneously.[2] Swamy (1965) derived a similar result. Pfouts (1966) discussed a number of tests separately. All of these results, however, are partial by nature. The first, and final, integral attack on Fisher's system was provided by Eichhorn (1973, 1976) and his Karlsruhe colleague Voeller (1974). Their joint work was summarized in a still-important monograph (Eichhorn and Voeller 1976).[3]

The axiomatic theory must be distinguished from a number of other approaches. First, in the axiomatic theory the prices and the quantities of commodities are considered as independent variables. In particular, no assumption is made concerning some underlying optimizing behaviour. Such an assumption forms the core of the *economic* theory of price and quantity indices. Second, it is not assumed that price (or quantity) changes of individual commodities originate from an underlying probability distribution. That assumption is characteristic for the *stochastic* theory of price and quantity indices. Finally, price and quantity indices are considered as measures relating discrete time periods to each other. This feature distinguishes the present theory from the *Divisia* index theory, where time is treated as a continuous variable.

This chapter is organized as follows. In section 3.2 the concepts of price index and quantity index are introduced. Following Eichhorn and Voeller (1976) a distinction is made between axioms – which are considered to be more or less self-evident requirements – and tests – about which more debate is possible. The axioms will be discussed in section 3.2 and the four most important tests in section 3.4. In between, in section 3.3, the main (classes of) price and quantity indices will be reviewed. A small numerical example serves to illustrate the differences between the formulas.

---

[2] Eichhorn (1973) showed that Frisch's proof is not completely satisfactory. Wald's proof will be replicated below.

[3] Additional historical details are given by Boumans (2001).

Both axioms and tests can be formalized as functional equations. For some combinations of these functional equations it can be shown that the solution space is empty. Section 3.5 presents the main inconsistency theorems. This section could be kept rather short because Eichhorn and Voeller's (1976) monograph still serves as the ultimate source.

Section 3.6 gives a survey of all characterization theorems the author is aware of. A price index (usually in combination with a quantity index) is said to be characterized by a set of functional equations if it is the unique solution of these functional equations. In order to make this survey as self-contained as possible, not only the theorems but also the proofs are given, except for a few very technical ones. At first reading these may be skipped.

Section 3.7 introduces two newer tests, namely the consistency-in-aggregation test and the equality test. These tests are important in situations where the economic aggregate under consideration is, or can be, partitioned into subaggregates. This section discusses a characterization theorem that has far-reaching consequences for the possibility of additivity in economic-statistical accounting systems.

Section 3.8 contains a brief evaluation of the insights provided by the axiomatic theory of price and quantity indices.

Section 3.9 turns to the case where the number of periods exceeds two. Then one has the choice between using direct or chained indices. The advantages and disadvantages of the two index number strategies will be discussed.

Indices are ratio-type measures. It is natural, but less usual, to consider difference-type measures as well. These are called indicators and will be discussed in the final section, 3.10. In particular, the relation between indices and indicators throws new light on the requirement of consistency-in-aggregation.

Some limitations of this chapter must be mentioned. First, we concentrate on the mathematical rather than the numerical viewpoint. An index that (mathematically) does not satisfy a certain test can nevertheless in practice satisfy it (numerically) almost always. In fact, it has been shown that the more important indices are first- or second-order approximations of each other.[4] However, numerical considerations are necessarily of limited value. One can easily devise examples or encounter situations where such approximations appear to be invalid. The mathematical theory then provides insight into the cause of such breakdowns. Readers who are interested

---

[4] See Diewert (1978) and Hill (2006b) for a number of results.

in more numerical details than provided in this chapter could consult Fisher (1922) or, more recently, the *CPI Manual* and *PPI Manual* (2004).

Second, we concentrate on intertemporal indices rather than interspatial indices. Although intertemporal and interspatial comparisons share a lot of structural features, there are also important differences. For instance, unlike time periods, countries or regions are usually considered as being not equally important in an economic sense. Further, time proceeds indefinitely, whereas interspatial comparisons are usually restricted to a given number of entities.

3.2 The Axioms

We consider a certain economic aggregate; that is, production or consumption of a set of well-defined commodities. Let these commodities be labelled (in an arbitrary way) from 1 to N, and let t and t' be generic variables denoting well-defined time periods. For each commodity, x_n^t denotes its quantity and p_n^t its price at period t ($n = 1, \ldots, N$). The product of price and quantity, $v_n^t \equiv p_n^t x_n^t$ ($n = 1, \ldots, N$), is the (transaction) value.[5] The complete quantity, price, and value vectors are denoted by $x^t \equiv (x_1^t, \ldots, x_N^t)$, $p^t \equiv (p_1^t, \ldots, p_N^t)$, and $v^t \equiv (v_1^t, \ldots, v_N^t)$ respectively. It is assumed that $p^t, x^t \in \Re_{++}^N$; that is, prices and quantities are positive. Generic N-dimensional price, quantity, and value vectors will be denoted by p, x, and v, respectively (sometimes with a prime).

For any two periods t and t' the inner product of a price vector p^t and a quantity vector $x^{t'}$ is defined by $p^t \cdot x^{t'} \equiv \sum_{n=1}^N p_n^t x_n^{t'}$. This is called the value of the period t' quantity vector at period t prices. When $t = t'$, $V^t \equiv p^t \cdot x^t = \sum_{n=1}^N v_n^t$ is called the value (of the aggregate) at period t.

We want to track the aggregate behaviour of all the prices and quantities through time. In this chapter we consider the comparison of two distinct time periods, which may or may not be adjacent, by means of functions that use only price and quantity data of these two periods; that is, the attention will be restricted to *bilateral indices*. For convenience' sake the two (arbitrary) periods to be compared will mostly be denoted by 0, which is

---

[5] The term *commodity* serves as a primitive term, encompassing goods and services, tightly or loosely defined. Formally, a commodity is a set of economic transactions, according to some classification criterium. It is assumed that for each commodity a unit of measurement has been selected, such that its quantity can be measured. Transaction values are expressed in a certain currency. It is assumed that the length of the time period is such that it is considered meaningful to add up transaction values. The price, then, is the unit value: that is, the total transaction value of the period divided by the total quantity.

called the base period, and 1, which is called the comparison period. The suggestion thereby is that period 0 precedes period 1.

The (at least potentially) available information consists of the vectors of prices and quantities (p^0, x^0) and (p^1, x^1). The individual price and quantity changes are given by p_n^1/p_n^0 and x_n^1/x_n^0 $(n = 1, \ldots, N)$, respectively. Usually this is a huge amount of information. Price and quantity indices are developed to summarize all the individual changes between the two periods in the form of two positive numbers.

Any comparison of two periods is carried out by a price and/or quantity index. A *price index* is a positive, continuously differentiable function $P(p, x, p', x') : \mathfrak{R}_{++}^{4N} \to \mathfrak{R}_{++}$ that correctly indicates any increase or decrease of the elements of the vector p and/or the vector p', conditional on the quantity vectors x and x'.[6] The minimal requirements on such a function are that

$$\partial P(p, x, p', x')/\partial p_n > 0 \text{ and } \partial P(p, x, p', x')/\partial p_n' < 0 \ (n = 1, \ldots, N) \tag{3.1}$$

for all $(p, x, p', x') \in S$, where S is a sufficiently large, simply connected, compact subset of $\mathfrak{R}_{++}^{4N}$.

Similarly, a *quantity index* is a positive, continuously differentiable function $Q(p, x, p', x') : \mathfrak{R}_{++}^{4N} \to \mathfrak{R}_{++}$ that correctly indicates any increase or decrease of the elements of the vector x and/or the vector x', conditional on the price vectors p and p'. The minimal requirements on such a function are that

$$\partial Q(p, x, p', x')/\partial x_n > 0 \text{ and } \partial Q(p, x, p', x')/\partial x_n' < 0 \ (n = 1, \ldots, N) \tag{3.2}$$

for all $(p, x, p', x') \in S$. The two functions are supposed to satisfy certain further requirements, which will be discussed below.[7]

Any particular realization of $P(p, x, p', x')$ or $Q(p, x, p', x')$ will be called an *index number*. The distinction between index and index number is important. According to our definition, $P(p^1, x^1, p^0, x^0)$ as well as $P(p^1, x^0, p^0, x^0)$ are price index numbers for period 1 relative to period 0. Though the price index is the same, the price index numbers are likely

---

[6] The requirement of continuous differentiability rules out certain functions, such as $\min\{p_1^1/p_1^0, \ldots, p_N^1/p_N^0\}$ or $\max\{p_1^1/p_1^0, \ldots, p_N^1/p_N^0\}$, which are of no practical value as summary measures of price change.

[7] Eichhorn and Voeller (1976) and Eichhorn (1978) considered also functions $P(p, p')$ and $Q(x, x')$. Krtscha (1988) considered functions $P(p, p', x')$ and $Q(x, p', x')$. Diewert (2004a) considered functions $P(p, v, p', v')$ and $Q(p, v, p', v')$.

to be different. Reversely, we might have two different price indices, say
$P(.)$ and $P'(.)$, delivering for period 1 relative to period 0 the same index
numbers, $P(p^1, x^1, p^0, x^0) = P'(p^1, x^1, p^0, x^0)$. However, if this equality
holds for all $(p^1, x^1, p^0, x^0) \in \mathfrak{R}^{4N}_{++}$, then the price indices must be equal;
that is, $P(.) = P'(.)$.

The requirements to be discussed in this chapter concern structural
properties of the functions $P(.)$ and $Q(.)$. In the interest of readability,
however, price and quantity indices are mostly presented in the form of
index numbers for a certain period 1 relative to a certain period 0. It will
not be stated explicitly that all the requirements are supposed to hold for all
$(p^1, x^1, p^0, x^0) \in \mathfrak{R}^{4N}_{++}$.

The following axioms, originally formulated by Eichhorn and Voeller (1976)
and Eichhorn (1978), seem rather natural.[8]

A1. Monotonicity in prices. $P(p, x^1, p^0, x^0)$ is increasing in comparison
period prices p_n and $P(p^1, x^1, p, x^0)$ is decreasing in base period prices p_n
$(n = 1, \ldots, N)$.

A1′. Monotonicity in quantities. $Q(p^1, x, p^0, x^0)$ is increasing in comparison period quantities x_n and $Q(p^1, x^1, p^0, x)$ is decreasing in base period
quantities x_n $(n = 1, \ldots, N)$.

A2. Linear homogeneity in comparison period prices. Multiplication of
all comparison period prices by a common factor leads to multiplication
of the price index number by this factor; that is, $P(\lambda p^1, x^1, p^0, x^0) = \lambda P(p^1, x^1, p^0, x^0)$ $(\lambda > 0)$.

A2′. Linear homogeneity in comparison period quantities. Multiplication
of all comparison period quantities by a common factor leads to multiplication of the quantity index number by this factor; that is, $Q(p^1, \lambda x^1, p^0, x^0) = \lambda Q(p^1, x^1, p^0, x^0)$ $(\lambda > 0)$.

A3. Identity property. If all the comparison period prices are equal to the
corresponding base period prices, then the price index number must be
equal to 1: $P(p^0, x^1, p^0, x^0) = 1$. Put otherwise, changing quantities as
such do not affect the price index.

A3′. Identity property. If all the comparison period quantities are equal to
the corresponding base period quantities, then the quantity index number
must be equal to 1: $Q(p^1, x^0, p^0, x^0) = 1$. Put otherwise, changing prices
as such do not affect the quantity index.

---

[8] A proof of the independence of these axioms can be found in these references.

A4. Homogeneity of degree 0 in prices. Multiplication of all comparison and base period prices by the same factor does not change the price index number; that is, $P(\lambda p^1, x^1, \lambda p^0, x^0) = P(p^1, x^1, p^0, x^0)$ $(\lambda > 0)$.

A4'. Homogeneity of degree 0 in quantities. Multiplication of all comparison period and base period quantities by the same factor does not change the quantity index number; that is, $Q(p^1, \lambda x^1, p^0, \lambda x^0) = Q(p^1, x^1, p^0, x^0)$ $(\lambda > 0)$.

A5. Dimensional invariance (or commensurability). The price index is invariant to changes in the units of measurement of the commodities: let Λ be a diagonal matrix with elements of $\mathfrak{R}_{++}$, then it is required that $P(p^1 \Lambda, x^1 \Lambda^{-1}, p^0 \Lambda, x^0 \Lambda^{-1}) = P(p^1, x^1, p^0, x^0)$.

A5'. Dimensional invariance (or commensurability). The quantity index is invariant to changes in the units of measurement of the commodities: let Λ be a diagonal matrix with elements of $\mathfrak{R}_{++}$, then $Q(p^1 \Lambda, x^1 \Lambda^{-1}, p^0 \Lambda, x^0 \Lambda^{-1}) = Q(p^1, x^1, p^0, x^0)$.

It is clear that axioms **A1** and **A1'** extend the minimal requirements (3.1) and (3.2) respectively to the entire $4N$-dimensional positive orthant. Axioms **A5** and **A5'** are vital invariance requirements. Axioms **A2–A4** and **A2'–A4'**, respectively, serve to give $P(.)$ and $Q(.)$ the character of a ratio-type measure of change.

To ease the reading of tables of index numbers, statistical agencies usually present price and quantity index numbers as $100 P(p^1, x^1, p^0, x^0)$ and $100 Q(p^1, x^1, p^0, x^0)$. Notice that, if $P(.)$ satisfies the axioms **A1–A5**, then $\alpha P(.)$ (for all $\alpha > 0$) satisfies **A1, A2, A4**, and **A5**. But $\alpha P(p^0, x^1, p^0, x^0) = \alpha$. Similarly, if $Q(.)$ satisfies the axioms **A1'–A5'**, then $\alpha Q(.)$ (for all $\alpha > 0$) satisfies **A1', A2', A4'**, and **A5'**. But $\alpha Q(p^1, x^0, p^0, x^0) = \alpha$.

Some consequences of this system of axioms are also worthy of mention. One immediately sees that the axioms **A2** and **A3** (**A2'** and **A3'**, respectively) imply the proportionality axiom.

A6. Proportionality with respect to prices. If all the individual price relatives are the same, then the price index number must be equal to these relatives, that is, $P(\lambda p^0, x^1, p^0, x^0) = \lambda$ $(\lambda > 0)$.

A6'. Proportionality with respect to quantities. If all the individual quantity relatives are the same, then the quantity index number must be equal to these relatives, that is, $Q(p^1, \lambda x^0, p^0, x^0) = \lambda$ $(\lambda > 0)$.

Reversely, **A3** (**A3'**) is a particular instance of **A6** (**A6'**), namely for $\lambda = 1$.

The system of axioms $\{\textbf{A1}, \textbf{A4}, \textbf{A5}, \textbf{A6}\}$ was proposed by Eichhorn and Voeller (1983). It is somewhat weaker than $\{\textbf{A1}, \textbf{A2}, \textbf{A3}, \textbf{A4}, \textbf{A5}\}$.[9] Gleissner (1990) provided a characterization of all the positive functions satisfying $\{\textbf{A1}, \textbf{a generalized form of A2}, \textbf{A3}, \textbf{A4}, \textbf{A5}\}$; and Gleissner (1992) did the same for all the positive functions satisfying $\{\textbf{A1}, \textbf{A4}, \textbf{A5}, \textbf{a generalized form of A6}\}$. These results, however, appear to be not very helpful from an economic-statistical point of view.

Axiom **A5** appears to be very powerful. This can be seen as follows. Let $\hat{p}^t$ be the diagonal matrix obtained from p^t and recall that the vector of period t commodity values is given by $v^t \equiv (p_1^t x_1^t, \ldots, p_N^t x_N^t)$. Then, by definition,

$$P(p^1, x^1, p^0, x^0) = P(p^1, v^1(\hat{p}^1)^{-1}, p^0, v^0(\hat{p}^0)^{-1}).$$

Now, using **A5** with $\Lambda = (\hat{p}^0)^{-1}$, defining p^1/p^0 as the vector of price relatives $(p_1^1/p_1^0, \ldots, p_N^1/p_N^0)$ and 1_N as the vector consisting of N ones, we obtain

$$P(p^1, x^1, p^0, x^0) = P(p^1/p^0, v^1(p^1/p^0)^{-1}, 1_N, v^0) \equiv \tilde{P}(p^1/p^0, v^1, v^0).$$

Thus any function $P(p, x, p', x')$ satisfying axiom **A5** can be written as a function of only $3N$ variables, namely price relatives p_n/p_n', comparison period values $p_n x_n$, and base period values $p_n' x_n'$ ($n = 1, \ldots, N$). Reversely, any such function $\tilde{P}(.)$ satisfies **A5**.

Similarly, any function $Q(.)$ that satisfies axiom **A5′** can be written as a function of only $3N$ variables, namely quantity relatives x_n/x_n', comparison period values $p_n x_n$, and base period values $p_n' x_n'$ ($n = 1, \ldots, N$); any such function satisfies **A5′**.

If $P(p, x, p', x')$ satisfies axioms **A4** and **A2**, then $P(p, x, p', x')$ is homogeneous of degree -1 in base period prices. This is easy to check: Using **A4** and **A2**, respectively, for any $\lambda > 0$ it follows that

$$P(p^1, x^1, \lambda p^0, x^0) = P(\lambda^{-1} p^1, x^1, p^0, x^0) = \lambda^{-1} P(p^1, x^1, p^0, x^0).$$

Likewise, if $Q(p, x, p', x')$ satisfies **A4′** and **A2′**, then $Q(p, x, p', x')$ is homogeneous of degree -1 in base period quantities.

If $P(p, x, p', x')$ satisfies axioms **A4** and **A5**, then $P(p, x, p', x')$ is homogeneous of degree 0 in quantities. This is also easy to check: Using **A5**

[9] The Stuvel price index, see (3.145) below, is an example of an index satisfying the weaker but not the stronger system. The Montgomery-Vartia price index, see (3.86) below, is an example of an index not satisfying the weaker system. An even more liberal system of axioms was developed by Vartia (1985).

and **A4**, respectively, for any $\lambda > 0$ it follows that

$$P(p^1, \lambda x^1, p^0, \lambda x^0) = P(\lambda^{-1} p^1, x^1, \lambda^{-1} p^0, x^0) = P(p^1, x^1, p^0, x^0).$$

Likewise, if $Q(p, x, p', x')$ satisfies **A4′** and **A5′**, then $Q(p, x, p', x')$ is homogeneous of degree 0 in prices.

Finally, **A1** and **A6** (**A1′** and **A6′**, respectively) imply the mean value axiom:

A7. Mean value with respect to prices. A price index number lies between the smallest and the largest of the individual price relatives; that is, $\min_{n=1}^{N}\{p_n^1/p_n^0\} \leq P(p^1, x^1, p^0, x^0) \leq \max_{n=1}^{N}\{p_n^1/p_n^0\}$. For $N = 1$, this reduces to $P(p^1, x^1, p^0, x^0) = p^1/p^0$.

A7′. Mean value with respect to quantities. A quantity index number lies between the smallest and the largest of the individual quantity relatives; that is, $\min_{n=1}^{N}\{x_n^1/x_n^0\} \leq Q(p^1, x^1, p^0, x^0) \leq \max_{n=1}^{N}\{x_n^1/x_n^0\}$. For $N = 1$, this reduces to $Q(p^1, x^1, p^0, x^0) = x^1/x^0$.

Reinsdorf (2007) suggests the system $\{$**A7, A2, A4, A5**$\}$ as fundamental, since a number of much-used price indices appear to violate axiom **A1**.

Notice that if a function $P(p, x, p', x')$ satisfies $\{$**A1**,..., **A5**$\}$, then the function obtained by interchanging prices and quantities, $P(x, p, x', p')$, satisfies $\{$**A1′**,..., **A5′**$\}$. Reversely, if a function $Q(p, x, p', x')$ satisfies the system $\{$**A1′**,..., **A5′**$\}$, then the function obtained by interchanging prices and quantities, $Q(x, p, x', p')$, satisfies $\{$**A1**,..., **A5**$\}$.

Some authors argue that the proportionality axioms **A6** and **A6′** are too strong, since economic theory precludes situations where comparison period prices are proportional to base period prices but comparison period quantities are not proportional to base period quantities. These authors would replace axiom **A6** by the weaker requirement that $P(\lambda p^0, \mu x^0, p^0, x^0) = \lambda$, and **A6′** by $Q(\lambda p^0, \mu x^0, p^0, x^0) = \mu$ $(\lambda > 0, \mu > 0)$. However, we do not want to impose *a priori* conditions on the price and quantity data.

3.3 The Main Indices

This section reviews in a systematic way most of the price and quantity indices that were introduced in chapter 1. We start with the class of basket-type indices, proceed with geometric mean indices, and close with the unit value index.

3.3.1 Basket-Type Indices

3.3.1.1 Asymmetric Indices

The first and most famous of the basket-type indices is the Laspeyres price index. This index is defined by[10]

$$P^L(p^1, x^1, p^0, x^0) \equiv p^1 \cdot x^0 / p^0 \cdot x^0. \tag{3.3}$$

This is a ratio of two values: the numerator is the value of the base period quantity vector (also called the base period basket) at comparison period prices, and the denominator is the value of this quantity vector at base period prices. In other words, the Laspeyres price index compares two price vectors on the base period basket.

The Laspeyres price index can also be expressed as a weighted arithmetic average of price relatives,

$$P^L(p^1, x^1, p^0, x^0) = \sum_{n=1}^{N} s_n^0(p_n^1 / p_n^0), \tag{3.4}$$

where the weights are the base period value shares. Value shares are in general defined by $s_n^t \equiv p_n^t x_n^t / p^t \cdot x^t$ $(n = 1, \ldots, N)$. Notice that value shares add up to 1; that is, $\sum_{n=1}^{N} s_n^t = 1$.

By interchanging prices and quantities in expression (3.3) we obtain the Laspeyres quantity index

$$Q^L(p^1, x^1, p^0, x^0) \equiv p^0 \cdot x^1 / p^0 \cdot x^0. \tag{3.5}$$

This is also a ratio of two values: the numerator is the value of the comparison period quantity vector (the comparison period basket) at base period prices, and the denominator is the value of the base period quantity vector at base period prices. In other words, the Laspeyres quantity index compares two baskets on the base period price vector.

The Laspeyres quantity index can also be expressed as a weighted arithmetic average of quantity relatives,

$$Q^L(p^1, x^1, p^0, x^0) = \sum_{n=1}^{N} s_n^0(x_n^1 / x_n^0). \tag{3.6}$$

Instead of comparing prices on the base period basket or comparing baskets on the base period price vector, one could use the comparison

---

[10] Although this is not a function of comparison period quantities, the general notation is retained.

period basket and price vector. This leads to the Paasche price and quantity indices. The Paasche price index is defined by

$$P^P(p^1, x^1, p^0, x^0) \equiv p^1 \cdot x^1 / p^0 \cdot x^1, \tag{3.7}$$

and the Paasche quantity index by

$$Q^P(p^1, x^1, p^0, x^0) \equiv p^1 \cdot x^1 / p^1 \cdot x^0. \tag{3.8}$$

It is straightforward to verify that expression (3.7) can be written as a weighted harmonic average of price relatives,

$$P^P(p^1, x^1, p^0, x^0) = \left(\sum_{n=1}^{N} s_n^1 (p_n^1/p_n^0)^{-1} \right)^{-1}, \tag{3.9}$$

and expression (3.8) as a weighted harmonic average of quantity relatives,

$$Q^P(p^1, x^1, p^0, x^0) = \left(\sum_{n=1}^{N} s_n^1 (x_n^1/x_n^0)^{-1} \right)^{-1}. \tag{3.10}$$

It is important to notice that in these two expressions the weights are given by the comparison period value shares. It is of course possible to write the Paasche price index as a weighted arithmetic average of price relatives,

$$P^P(p^1, x^1, p^0, x^0) = \sum_{n=1}^{N} s_n^{01} (p_n^1/p_n^0), \tag{3.11}$$

but notice that the weights are now given by $s_n^{01} \equiv p_n^0 x_n^1 / p^0 \cdot x^1$ ($n = 1, \ldots, N$). These weights are so-called hybrid value shares, composed of prices of period 0 and quantities of period 1. Notice further that, if these hybrid value shares were replaced by comparison period value shares, then the Palgrave price index would be obtained; that is,

$$P^{Pa}(p^1, x^1, p^0, x^0) \equiv \sum_{n=1}^{N} s_n^1 (p_n^1/p_n^0). \tag{3.12}$$

By a fundamental property of (weighted) means, it follows that

$$P^{Pa}(p^1, x^1, p^0, x^0) \geq P^P(p^1, x^1, p^0, x^0). \tag{3.13}$$

It is left to the reader to check that the Paasche quantity index also can be written as a weighted arithmetic average of quantity relatives, where the weights are hybrid value shares (but now composed of period 1 prices and period 0 quantities). Replacing these hybrid value shares by comparison period value shares would lead to the Palgrave quantity index.

Also, the Laspeyres price index (3.3) can be written as a weighted harmonic average of price relatives,

$$P^L(p^1, x^1, p^0, x^0) = \left(\sum_{n=1}^{N} s_n^{10} (p_n^1/p_n^0)^{-1} \right)^{-1}, \qquad (3.14)$$

where the weights are defined by $s_n^{10} \equiv p_n^1 x_n^0 / p^1 \cdot x^0$ ($n = 1, \ldots, N$). Replacing these hybrid value shares by base period value shares delivers a different price index,

$$P^{HL}(p^1, x^1, p^0, x^0) = \left(\sum_{n=1}^{N} s_n^0 (p_n^1/p_n^0)^{-1} \right)^{-1}, \qquad (3.15)$$

which goes by the name "Harmonic Laspeyres" price index. Again, by a fundamental property of (weighted) means we find that

$$P^{HL}(p^1, x^1, p^0, x^0) \leq P^L(p^1, x^1, p^0, x^0). \qquad (3.16)$$

There is of course also a Harmonic Laspeyres quantity index.[11]

It is interesting to consider the relationship between the Laspeyres and Paasche indices. Let us economize on notation by using the abbreviation $(p^1, x^1, p^0, x^0) = (1, 0)$. It is easy to check that the following relation, which was for the first time derived by von Bortkiewicz (1923), holds:

$$P^P(1, 0) - P^L(1, 0) = \frac{\sum_{n=1}^{N} s_n^0 \left(\frac{p_n^1}{p_n^0} - P^L(1, 0) \right) \left(\frac{x_n^1}{x_n^0} - Q^L(1, 0) \right)}{Q^L(1, 0)}. \qquad (3.17)$$

Dividing both sides of this equation by $P^L(1, 0)$, and using the fact that $V^1/V^0 = P^L(1, 0)Q^P(1, 0) = P^P(1, 0)Q^L(1, 0)$, we obtain

$$\frac{P^P(1, 0)}{P^L(1, 0)} - 1 = \frac{Q^P(1, 0)}{Q^L(1, 0)} - 1 = \sum_{n=1}^{N} s_n^0 \left(\frac{p_n^1/p_n^0}{P^L(1, 0)} - 1 \right) \left(\frac{x_n^1/x_n^0}{Q^L(1, 0)} - 1 \right). \qquad (3.18)$$

The right-hand side of this expression is the (base period value share weighted) covariance of relative price changes, $\frac{p_n^1/p_n^0}{P^L(1,0)}$, and relative quantity changes, $\frac{x_n^1/x_n^0}{Q^L(1,0)}$. If this covariance is negative, which is usually the case at the consumer or producer input side of a market, then $P^P(1, 0) < P^L(1, 0)$ and $Q^P(1, 0) < Q^L(1, 0)$. If this covariance is positive, which might happen

---

[11] Notice that the Palgrave price (quantity) index can be called the "Harmonic Paasche" price (quantity) index.

at the producer output side of a market, then $P^P(1, 0) > P^L(1, 0)$ and $Q^P(1, 0) > Q^L(1, 0)$.

3.3.1.2 Symmetric Indices

As we have seen, the Laspeyres indices use the base period orientation, whereas the Paasche indices use the comparison period orientation. It is tempting to consider some sort of symmetric orientation. The first alternative is to use an average basket for the price index or an average price vector for the quantity index. Dependent on the type of average, there are several options. Chosing the *arithmetic* mean of the base and comparison period baskets leads us to the Marshall-Edgeworth price index,

$$P^{ME}(p^1, x^1, p^0, x^0) \equiv \frac{p^1 \cdot (x^0 + x^1)/2}{p^0 \cdot (x^0 + x^1)/2}. \tag{3.19}$$

Similarly, the arithmetic mean of the base and comparison period price vector leads us to the Marshall-Edgeworth quantity index,

$$Q^{ME}(p^1, x^1, p^0, x^0) \equiv \frac{(1/2)(p^0 + p^1) \cdot x^1}{(1/2)(p^0 + p^1) \cdot x^0}. \tag{3.20}$$

Instead of arithmetic means one could employ *geometric* means. This leads to the Walsh-1 indices. The Walsh-1 price index is based on the basket of geometric mean quantities,

$$P^{W1}(p^1, x^1, p^0, x^0) \equiv \frac{p^1 \cdot (x^0 x^1)^{1/2}}{p^0 \cdot (x^0 x^1)^{1/2}} \tag{3.21}$$

where $(x^0 x^1)^{1/2} \equiv ((x_1^0 x_1^1)^{1/2}, \ldots, (x_N^0 x_N^1)^{1/2})$. Similarly, the Walsh-1 quantity index is defined by

$$Q^{W1}(p^1, x^1, p^0, x^0) \equiv \frac{(p^0 p^1)^{1/2} \cdot x^1}{(p^0 p^1)^{1/2} \cdot x^0} \tag{3.22}$$

where $(p^0 p^1)^{1/2} \equiv ((p_1^0 p_1^1)^{1/2}, \ldots, (p_N^0 p_N^1)^{1/2})$ is the vector of geometric mean prices. Finally, one could employ *harmonic* means of base and comparison period prices or quantities. Let $1/\bar{p}_n \equiv (1/p_n^0 + 1/p_n^1)/2$ and $1/\bar{x}_n \equiv (1/x_n^0 + 1/x_n^1)/2$ $(n = 1, \ldots, N)$. Then

$$P^{GK}(p^1, x^1, p^0, x^0) \equiv \frac{p^1 \cdot \bar{x}}{p^0 \cdot \bar{x}} \tag{3.23}$$

and

$$Q^{GK}(p^1, x^1, p^0, x^0) \equiv \frac{\bar{p} \cdot x^1}{\bar{p} \cdot x^0}. \tag{3.24}$$

The label "GK" is chosen for these two indices because they appear to be identical to the two-country solution of the Geary-Khamis system of equations, which will be discussed in a later chapter. But, of course, these indices had already figured in Fisher's (1922) catalog as no. 3153 and 3154.

It is simple to check that the Marshall-Edgeworth, Walsh-1, and Geary-Khamis indices can be expressed in the form of a weighted mean of price or quantity relatives.

The second alternative is to take some mean of the Laspeyres and Paasche indices. The first type of mean that comes to mind is the *arithmetic* mean. This leads to

$$P^{LP}(p^1, x^1, p^0, x^0) \equiv [P^L(p^1, x^1, p^0, x^0) + P^P(p^1, x^1, p^0, x^0)]/2$$

$$= (1/2) \sum_{n=1}^{N} (s_n^0 + s_n^{01})(p_n^1/p_n^0) \qquad (3.25)$$

and

$$Q^{LP}(p^1, x^1, p^0, x^0) \equiv [Q^L(p^1, x^1, p^0, x^0) + Q^P(p^1, x^1, p^0, x^0)]/2$$

$$= (1/2) \sum_{n=1}^{N} (s_n^0 + s_n^{10})(x_n^1/x_n^0). \qquad (3.26)$$

Of this pair, the price index was advocated by Bowley (1901) but had been mentioned already by Drobisch (1871). Fisher (1922) numbered $P^{LP}(.)$ as 8053.

Using instead the *geometric* mean of Laspeyres and Paasche indices leads to the Fisher price and quantity indices,

$$P^F(p^1, x^1, p^0, x^0) \equiv [P^L(p^1, x^1, p^0, x^0) P^P(p^1, x^1, p^0, x^0)]^{1/2}$$

$$= \left[\frac{p^1 \cdot x^0}{p^0 \cdot x^0} \frac{p^1 \cdot x^1}{p^0 \cdot x^1} \right]^{1/2} \qquad (3.27)$$

$$Q^F(p^1, x^1, p^0, x^0) \equiv [Q^L(p^1, x^1, p^0, x^0) Q^P(p^1, x^1, p^0, x^0)]^{1/2}$$

$$= \left[\frac{p^0 \cdot x^1}{p^0 \cdot x^0} \frac{p^1 \cdot x^1}{p^1 \cdot x^0} \right]^{1/2}. \qquad (3.28)$$

The question whether these indices can be expressed as weighted means of price or quantity relatives will be considered in the next chapter. Interesting equations materialize by applying the Bortkiewicz relation (3.18) to definitions (3.27) and (3.28). One obtains, respectively,

$$P^F(1,0) = P^L(1,0)[P^P(1,0)/P^L(1,0)]^{1/2}$$

$$= P^L(1,0)\left[1 + \sum_{n=1}^{N} s_n^0 \left(\frac{p_n^1/p_n^0}{P^L(1,0)} - 1\right)\left(\frac{x_n^1/x_n^0}{Q^L(1,0)} - 1\right)\right]^{1/2}$$

(3.29)

and

$$Q^F(1,0) = Q^L(1,0)[Q^P(1,0)/Q^L(1,0)]^{1/2}$$

$$= Q^L(1,0)\left[1 + \sum_{n=1}^{N} s_n^0 \left(\frac{p_n^1/p_n^0}{P^L(1,0)} - 1\right)\left(\frac{x_n^1/x_n^0}{Q^L(1,0)} - 1\right)\right]^{1/2}.$$

(3.30)

By combining these two relations, one obtains

$$V^1/V^0 = P^F(1,0)Q^F(1,0)$$

$$= P^L(1,0)Q^L(1,0)\left[1 + \sum_{n=1}^{N} s_n^0 \left(\frac{p_n^1/p_n^0}{P^L(1,0)} - 1\right)\left(\frac{x_n^1/x_n^0}{Q^L(1,0)} - 1\right)\right].$$

(3.31)

The value ratio is here decomposed into three parts. Sometimes it is said that $P^L(1,0)$ measures the magnitude of aggregate price change, that $Q^L(1,0)$ measures the magnitude of aggregate quantity change, and that the (residual) part between brackets is a measure of structural change. This would suggest a specific role for the two Laspeyres indices.

Finally, one could opt for the *harmonic* mean of Laspeyres and Paasche indices, which leads to[12]

$$P^{HLP}(p^1, x^1, p^0, x^0)$$

$$\equiv \left[[1/P^L(p^1, x^1, p^0, x^0) + 1/P^P(p^1, x^1, p^0, x^0)]/2\right]^{-1}$$

$$= \left[(1/2)\sum_{n=1}^{N}(s_n^{10} + s_n^1)(p_n^1/p_n^0)^{-1}\right]^{-1}$$

(3.32)

$$Q^{HLP}(p^1, x^1, p^0, x^0)$$

$$\equiv \left[[1/Q^L(p^1, x^1, p^0, x^0) + 1/Q^P(p^1, x^1, p^0, x^0)]/2\right]^{-1}$$

$$= \left[(1/2)\sum_{n=1}^{N}(s_n^{01} + s_n^1)(x_n^1/x_n^0)^{-1}\right]^{-1}.$$

(3.33)

---

[12] In Fisher's (1922) system $P^{HLP}(.)$ got number 8054.

It is left to the reader to check that all the asymmetric and symmetric price indices discussed in this subsection satisfy the axioms $\{A1, \ldots, A5\}$, and that all the quantity indices satisfy the axioms $\{A1', \ldots, A5'\}$. Thus all these indices are measuring the magnitude of aggregate change, and the ratio (or difference) of any two of these indices can be used as a measure of structural change (whatever that precisely may mean).

3.3.2 Lowe and Young Indices

When comparing the prices of period 1 to those of period 0, one could use the basket of some third period b. This leads to the class of Lowe price indices,

$$P^{Lo}(p^1, p^0; x^b) \equiv p^1 \cdot x^b / p^0 \cdot x^b. \tag{3.34}$$

Notice that such an index does not depend on base and comparison period quantities, which is the reason why a different notation is introduced. Likewise, the class of Lowe quantity indices is defined as

$$Q^{Lo}(x^1, x^0; p^b) \equiv p^b \cdot x^1 / p^b \cdot x^0, \tag{3.35}$$

where p^b is the price vector of some third period b. Such an index does not depend on base and comparison period prices.

Notice that Lowe indices can be considered as ratios of Laspeyres or Paasche indices. Specifically, one easily checks that

$$P^{Lo}(p^1, p^0; x^b) = \frac{P^L(p^1, x^1, p^b, x^b)}{P^L(p^0, x^0, p^b, x^b)} = \frac{P^P(p^b, x^b, p^0, x^0)}{P^P(p^b, x^b, p^1, x^1)}. \tag{3.36}$$

Lowe indices can also be expressed as weighted arithmetic or harmonic means of price or quantity relatives, as observed already by Walsh (1901). The weights, however, are neither base period nor comparison period value shares. They are hybrid value shares, composed of prices and quantities of different periods. For the price index one obtains

$$P^{Lo}(p^1, p^0; x^b) = \sum_{n=1}^{N} s_n^{0b}(p_n^1/p_n^0)$$

$$= \left(\sum_{n=1}^{N} s_n^{1b}(p_n^1/p_n^0)^{-1} \right)^{-1}, \tag{3.37}$$

with $s_n^{0b} \equiv p_n^0 x_n^b / p^0 \cdot x^b$ and $s_n^{1b} \equiv p_n^1 x_n^b / p^1 \cdot x^b$ $(n = 1, \ldots, N)$. When the hybrid value shares s_n^{0b} are replaced by period b value shares

$s_n^b \equiv p_n^b x_n^b / p^b \cdot x^b$ $(n = 1, \ldots, N)$, one obtains the class of Young price indices

$$P^Y(p^1/p^0; s^b) \equiv \sum_{n=1}^{N} s_n^b (p_n^1 / p_n^0). \tag{3.38}$$

The corresponding Young quantity indices are defined by

$$Q^Y(x^1/x^0; s^b) \equiv \sum_{n=1}^{N} s_n^b (x_n^1 / x_n^0). \tag{3.39}$$

The Laspeyres and Paasche indices can be conceived as special cases of Lowe indices, namely by setting $b = 0$ or 1 in (3.34) and (3.35). The Marshall-Edgeworth and Walsh-1 indices could also be conceived as special cases. The midyear price indices as defined by Szulc (1998) and Okamoto (2001) also belong to the class of Lowe indices. The Laspeyres price (quantity) index is also a special case of a Young price (quantity) index; the Paasche price (quantity) index, however, is not.

3.3.3 Geometric Mean Indices

As we have seen in a previous subsection, the Laspeyres and Paasche price and quantity indices can be expressed as weighted arithmetic or harmonic means of price or quantity relatives. Natural alternatives emerge by considering instead indices defined as geometric means of price or quantity relatives. Thus, the natural counterpart to the Laspeyres price index, given by expression (3.4), is the Geometric Laspeyres price index

$$P^{GL}(p^1, x^1, p^0, x^0) \equiv \prod_{n=1}^{N} (p_n^1 / p_n^0)^{s_n^0}, \tag{3.40}$$

where the weights are the base period value shares. Similarly, the Geometric Laspeyres quantity index is defined by

$$Q^{GL}(p^1, x^1, p^0, x^0) \equiv \prod_{n=1}^{N} (x_n^1 / x_n^0)^{s_n^0}. \tag{3.41}$$

The natural counterpart to the Paasche price index, given by expression (3.9), is the Geometric Paasche price index

$$P^{GP}(p^1, x^1, p^0, x^0) \equiv \prod_{n=1}^{N} (p_n^1 / p_n^0)^{s_n^1}, \tag{3.42}$$

where the weights are the comparison period value shares. Similarly, the Geometric Paasche quantity index is defined by

$$Q^{GP}(p^1, x^1, p^0, x^0) \equiv \prod_{n=1}^{N}(x_n^1/x_n^0)^{s_n^1}. \qquad (3.43)$$

Based on the well-known fact that an harmonic mean is less than or equal to a geometric mean, which in turn is less than or equal to an arithmetic mean, we obtain the following inequalities, thereby extending expressions (3.13) and (3.16):

$$P^{HL}(p^1, x^1, p^0, x^0) \leq P^{GL}(p^1, x^1, p^0, x^0) \leq P^L(p^1, x^1, p^0, x^0) \quad (3.44)$$

$$Q^{HL}(p^1, x^1, p^0, x^0) \leq Q^{GL}(p^1, x^1, p^0, x^0) \leq Q^L(p^1, x^1, p^0, x^0) \quad (3.45)$$

$$P^P(p^1, x^1, p^0, x^0) \leq P^{GP}(p^1, x^1, p^0, x^0) \leq P^{Pa}(p^1, x^1, p^0, x^0) \quad (3.46)$$

$$Q^P(p^1, x^1, p^0, x^0) \leq Q^{GP}(p^1, x^1, p^0, x^0) \leq Q^{Pa}(p^1, x^1, p^0, x^0). \quad (3.47)$$

These inequalities are strict, unless all price or quantity relatives are equal to each other.

It is interesting to consider the relationship between the Geometric Laspeyres and Paasche indices. Let us consider, for example, the price indices. Based on their definitions – see expressions (3.40) and (3.42) – one immediately obtains

$$\ln(P^{GP}(1,0)/P^{GL}(1,0)) = \sum_{n=1}^{N}(s_n^1 - s_n^0)\ln(p_n^1/p_n^0)$$

$$= \sum_{n=1}^{N}(s_n^1 - s_n^0)\ln\left(\frac{p_n^1/p_n^0}{P^{GL}(1,0)}\right)$$

$$= \sum_{n=1}^{N} s_n^0\left(\frac{s_n^1}{s_n^0} - 1\right)\ln\left(\frac{p_n^1/p_n^0}{P^{GL}(1,0)}\right), \qquad (3.48)$$

where in the third line use was made of the fact that value shares add up to 1. The last line of this chain of expressions is the (base period value share weighted) covariance between value share changes, s_n^1/s_n^0, and (logarithmic) relative price changes, $\ln(\frac{p_n^1/p_n^0}{P^{GL}(1,0)})$.[13] Hence, when relative price changes are positively (negatively) correlated with value share changes, then the Geometric Paasche price index will be larger (smaller) than the Geometric Laspeyres price index.

---

[13] Recall that $\ln z \approx z - 1$ if $z \approx 1$.

Additional insight is obtained by following up some hints given by Vartia (1978).[14] Consider the third line of (3.48), and notice that $P^{GL}(1, 0)$ can be replaced by any other price index. In particular, we replace $P^{GL}(1, 0)$ by the Sato-Vartia price index $P^{SV}(1, 0)$ as defined in expression (3.84). Then the logarithmic mean (see Appendix 1, in section 3.11, for its definition) is applied to obtain

$$\ln(P^{GP}(1, 0)/P^{GL}(1, 0)) = \sum_{n=1}^{N} L(s_n^1, s_n^0) \ln(s_n^1/s_n^0) \ln\left(\frac{p_n^1/p_n^0}{P^{SV}(1, 0)}\right).$$

(3.49)

Expression (3.84) also tells us that $V^1/V^0 = P^{SV}(1, 0)Q^{SV}(1, 0)$. By using the definition of the value shares, it is straightforward to verify that

$$\ln(s_n^1/s_n^0) = \ln\left(\frac{p_n^1/p_n^0}{P^{SV}(1, 0)}\right) + \ln\left(\frac{x_n^1/x_n^0}{Q^{SV}(1, 0)}\right).$$

(3.50)

After substituting (3.50) into (3.49) we obtain

$$\ln(P^{GP}(1, 0)/P^{GL}(1, 0)) = \sum_{n=1}^{N} L(s_n^1, s_n^0) \left[\ln\left(\frac{p_n^1/p_n^0}{P^{SV}(1, 0)}\right)\right]^2$$
$$+ \sum_{n=1}^{N} L(s_n^1, s_n^0) \ln\left(\frac{p_n^1/p_n^0}{P^{SV}(1, 0)}\right) \ln\left(\frac{x_n^1/x_n^0}{Q^{SV}(1, 0)}\right).$$

(3.51)

Both sides of this equation are then divided by $\sum_{n=1}^{N} L(s_n^1, s_n^0)$ to finally obtain

$$\frac{\ln(P^{GP}(1, 0)/P^{GL}(1, 0))}{\sum_{n=1}^{N} L(s_n^1, s_n^0)} = \frac{\sum_{n=1}^{N} L(s_n^1, s_n^0)\left[\ln\left(\frac{p_n^1/p_n^0}{P^{SV}(1,0)}\right)\right]^2}{\sum_{n=1}^{N} L(s_n^1, s_n^0)}$$
$$+ \frac{\sum_{n=1}^{N} L(s_n^1, s_n^0) \ln\left(\frac{p_n^1/p_n^0}{P^{SV}(1,0)}\right) \ln\left(\frac{x_n^1/x_n^0}{Q^{SV}(1,0)}\right)}{\sum_{n=1}^{N} L(s_n^1, s_n^0)}.$$

(3.52)

The first term at the right-hand side is a weighted variance of (logarithmic) relative price changes, which is always positive, whereas the second term is a weighted covariance of (logarithmic) relative price and quantity changes, which can be positive or negative. It can be shown that, to the second order in

[14] See Vartia and Vartia (1984) for a related result.

relative changes, this term can be approximated by $\ln(P^P(1,0)/P^L(1,0))$. The entire equation supports the empirical fact that, if a Paasche price index number is smaller than a Laspeyres price index number, then the difference between the Geometric Paasche and Laspeyres price index numbers is usually smaller in absolute magnitude than the difference between the Paasche and Laspeyres index numbers.

The Törnqvist price index is defined as the geometric mean of the Geometric Laspeyres and Paasche indices,

$$P^T(p^1, x^1, p^0, x^0) \equiv [P^{GL}(p^1, x^1, p^0, x^0) P^{GP}(p^1, x^1, p^0, x^0)]^{1/2}$$

$$= \prod_{n=1}^{N} (p_n^1/p_n^0)^{(s_n^0 + s_n^1)/2}. \tag{3.53}$$

Similarly, the Törnqvist quantity index is defined by

$$Q^T(p^1, x^1, p^0, x^0) \equiv [Q^{GL}(p^1, x^1, p^0, x^0) Q^{GP}(p^1, x^1, p^0, x^0)]^{1/2}$$

$$= \prod_{n=1}^{N} (x_n^1/x_n^0)^{(s_n^0 + s_n^1)/2}. \tag{3.54}$$

Both indices are geometric means of price or quantity relatives, whereby the commodity weights are given by the arithmetic means of the value shares of the two periods. Geometric means of these value shares, normalized such that they add up to 1, $(s_n^0 s_n^1)^{1/2} / \sum_{n'=1}^{N} (s_{n'}^0 s_{n'}^1)^{1/2}$, lead to Walsh-2 indices, which are also called Geometric Walsh indices.

The geometric mean price indices discussed in this subsection satisfy the axioms $\{A1, \ldots, A5\}$, and the quantity indices satisfy the axioms $\{A1', \ldots, A5'\}$, except that under extreme circumstances their monotonicity breaks down. Olt (1996) and Reinsdorf and Dorfman (1999) provide an extensive discussion of this issue. By way of example the case of the Geometric Paasche price index is considered in appendix 2 (in section 3.12). The indices, however, do satisfy the weaker axiom system suggested by Reinsdorf (2007).

3.3.4 The Unit Value Index

Referring back to footnote 5 one might say that any price relative p_n^1/p_n^0 is a unit value index. However, the name *unit value index* will be reserved for the construct introduced by Drobisch that reads

$$P^U(p^1, x^1, p^0, x^0) \equiv \frac{p^1 \cdot x^1/1_N \cdot x^1}{p^0 \cdot x^0/1_N \cdot x^0}, \tag{3.55}$$

where $1_N \equiv (1, \ldots, 1)$. It is clear that the unit value index compares values divided by sums of quantities; that is, average prices. The foregoing expression can be rewritten as

$$P^U(p^1, x^1, p^0, x^0) = \frac{V^1/V^0}{1_N \cdot x^1/1_N \cdot x^0}, \tag{3.56}$$

which is the value ratio divided by the simple sum or Dutot quantity index,

$$Q^D(p^1, x^1, p^0, x^0) \equiv \frac{1_N \cdot x^1}{1_N \cdot x^0}. \tag{3.57}$$

One easily checks that the unit value index violates the proportionality axiom **A6**. It is simple to see that

$$P^U(\lambda p^0, x^1, p^0, x^0) = \lambda \text{ if and only if } x^1/1_N \cdot x^1 = x^0/1_N \cdot x^0 \ (\lambda > 0); \tag{3.58}$$

that is, relative quantities (or, the quantity mix) must be the same in the two periods. The unit value index also violates the dimensional invariance axiom **A5**, which implies that the index is sensitive to the units of measurement. The reason for this violation is that the Dutot quantity index violates axiom **A5′**.

Though the unit value index violates two vital axioms it continues to be used in the price statistics of certain areas. It is therefore interesting to consider the relation of the unit value index to a genuine price index; that is, an index that does satisfy the basic axioms. Thus, consider the (relative) bias of the unit value index relative to the Laspeyres price index, $P^U(1, 0)/P^L(1, 0) - 1$, where we are again using the shorthand notation introduced earlier. Recall the Bortkiewicz relation (3.17). Using the fact that $P^P(1, 0)Q^L(1, 0) = V^1/V^0$, this relation can be restated as

$$V^1/V^0 - P^L(1, 0)Q^L(1, 0) = \sum_{n=1}^N s_n^0 \left(\frac{p_n^1}{p_n^0} - P^L(1, 0) \right) \left(\frac{x_n^1}{x_n^0} - Q^L(1, 0) \right)$$
$$\equiv \text{cov}_0(p_n^1/p_n^0, x_n^1/x_n^0). \tag{3.59}$$

Now, using relation (3.56) and definition (3.57), one obtains for the unit-value bias

$$\frac{P^U(1, 0)}{P^L(1, 0)} - 1 = \frac{V^1/V^0}{P^L(1, 0)Q^D(1, 0)} - 1, \tag{3.60}$$

which, by substituting the Bortkiewicz relation (3.59), reduces to

$$\frac{P^U(1,0)}{P^L(1,0)} - 1 = \frac{\text{cov}_0(p_n^1/p_n^0, x_n^1/x_n^0)}{P^L(1,0)Q^D(1,0)} + \left(\frac{Q^L(1,0)}{Q^D(1,0)} - 1\right). \quad (3.61)$$

This helpful relation was derived by von der Lippe (2006). The unit-value bias appears to be the sum of two terms, each of which can be positive or negative. Even when the covariance of price and quantity relatives, $\text{cov}_0(p_n^1/p_n^0, x_n^1/x_n^0)$, is negative, which is usually the case, then the unit-value bias might be positive. It all depends on the size of the ratio $Q^L(1,0)/Q^D(1,0)$ relative to 1; and this ratio reflects whether quantity changes are skewly distributed towards lower or higher (base period) priced commodities.

Some decades earlier Párniczky (1974) considered the unit-value bias relative to the Paasche price index, and Balk (1998a) developed an expression for the unit-value bias relative to the Fisher price index. Straightforward algebraic manipulations deliver the expression

$$\frac{P^U(1,0)}{P^F(1,0)} = \left[(1 + \text{relcov}_0(p_n^1, x_n^1/x_n^0))(1 + \text{relcov}_0(p_n^0, x_n^1/x_n^0))\right]^{1/2},$$

$$(3.62)$$

where the relative (weighted) covariances are defined by

$$\text{relcov}_0(p_n^t, x_n^1/x_n^0) \equiv \frac{\sum_{n=1}^{N} x_n^0(p_n^t - p^t \cdot x^0/1_N \cdot x^0)(x_n^1/x_n^0 - Q^D(1,0))}{\left(\sum_{n=1}^{N} x_n^0\right)(p^t \cdot x^0/1_N \cdot x^0)Q^D(1,0)}$$

for $t = 0, 1$. The following conclusions can be drawn from this expression. The unit-value bias will be equal to zero if one or more of the following situations occur:

- all base period prices p_n^0 are equal to each other and all comparison period prices p_n^1 are equal to each other;
- all quantity relatives x_n^1/x_n^0 are equal to each other;
- in the two periods there is no correlation between prices and quantity relatives.

It might be clear that in real-life situations it is highly unlikely that the unit-value bias disappears.[15] For empirical evidence on the unit-value bias the reader is referred to Silver (2007).

---

[15] See Bradley (2005) for the implications of this for the estimation of cost-of-living indices and parameters of consumer demand systems.

Table 3.1. *Prices for Six Commodities*

Period t	p_1^t	p_2^t	p_3^t	p_4^t	p_5^t	p_6^t
1	1.0	1.0	1.0	1.0	1.0	1.0
2	1.2	3.0	1.3	0.7	1.4	0.8
3	1.0	1.0	1.5	0.5	1.7	0.6
4	0.8	0.5	1.6	0.3	1.9	0.4
5	1.0	1.0	1.6	0.1	2.0	0.2

3.3.5 A Numerical Example

It is useful to illustrate the foregoing with a small example in order to see whether the differences between the various price and quantity indices indeed matter. The example has been constructed by Diewert (2004c) and concerns prices and quantities for six commodities over five periods. A period can here be thought of as somewhere between a year and 5 years. The trends in the data are generally more pronounced than would be seen in the course of a year. The price and quantity data p_n^t and x_n^t are listed in Tables 3.1 and 3.2, respectively. The period t values $V^t \equiv p^t \cdot x^t$ are listed along with the value shares $s_n^t \equiv p_n^t x_n^t / p^t \cdot x^t$ in Table 3.3.

According to Diewert's explanation, one can think of the first four commodities as the consumption of various classes of goods in some economy, whereas the last two commodities are the consumption of two classes of services. Think of the first good as agricultural consumption; its quantity fluctuates around 1 and its price also fluctuates around 1. The second good is energy consumption; its quantity shows a gently upward trend during the five periods with some minor fluctuations. Note, however, that the price of energy fluctuates wildly from period to period. The third good is traditional manufactures. Rather high rates of price inflation are assumed for this commodity for periods 2 and 3, which diminish to a very low inflation rate by the end of the sample period. The consumption of traditional manufactured goods is more or less static in the data set. The fourth

Table 3.2. *Quantities for Six Commodities*

Period t	x_1^t	x_2^t	x_3^t	x_4^t	x_5^t	x_6^t
1	1.0	1.0	2.0	1.0	4.5	0.5
2	0.8	0.9	1.9	1.3	4.7	0.6
3	1.0	1.1	1.8	3.0	5.0	0.8
4	1.2	1.2	1.9	6.0	5.6	1.3
5	0.9	1.2	2.0	12.0	6.5	2.5

Table 3.3. *Values and Value Shares for Six Commodities*

Period t	V^t	s_1^t	s_2^t	s_3^t	s_4^t	s_5^t	s_6^t
1	10.00	0.1000	0.1000	0.2000	0.1000	0.4500	0.0500
2	14.10	0.0681	0.1915	0.1752	0.0645	0.4667	0.0340
3	15.28	0.0654	0.0720	0.1767	0.0982	0.5563	0.0314
4	17.56	0.0547	0.0342	0.1731	0.1025	0.6059	0.0296
5	20.00	0.0450	0.0600	0.1600	0.0600	0.6500	0.0250

commodity is high-technology manfactured goods, for example computers, video cameras, and compact discs. The demand for these high-technology commodities grows 12 times over the sample period, whereas the final period price is only one-tenth of the first period price. The fifth commodity is traditional services. The price trends for this commodity are similar to those of traditional manufactures, except that the period-to-period inflation rates are a little higher. The demand for traditional services, however, grows much more strongly than for traditional manufactures. The final commoditiy is high-technology services, for example telecommunications, wireless phones, Internet services, and stock market trading. For this final commodity, the price shows a very strong downward trend to end up at 20 percent of the starting level, while demand increases fivefold.

Table 3.4 contains the asymmetrically weighted (direct) price index numbers $P(p^t, x^t, p^1, x^1)$ for $t = 1, \ldots, 5$ that were introduced in the previous subsections. The indices $P^{HL}(.)$, $P^{GL}(.)$, $P^L(.)$, $P^P(.)$, $P^{GP}(.)$, and $P^{Pa}(.)$ are called *asymmetrically weighted* because their weights (value shares) refer to only one of the two periods compared. The dispersion between the various numbers in a row is remarkable; this, however, is an empirical issue. Of mathematical origin is the fact that the numbers in column HL are less than those in column GL which in turn are less than those in column L. The same relation is seen to exist between columns P, GP, and Pa. These numbers reflect the mathematical relation between a harmonic, a geometric, and an arithmetic mean. Of empirical nature, again, is the fact

Table 3.4. *Asymmetrically Weighted Price Index Numbers*

Period t	HL	GL	L	P	GP	Pa
1	1.0000	1.0000	1.0000	1.0000	1.0000	1.0000
2	1.2542	1.3300	1.4200	1.3823	1.4846	1.6096
3	1.1346	1.2523	1.3450	1.2031	1.3268	1.4161
4	0.8732	1.1331	1.3550	1.0209	1.3282	1.5317
5	0.5556	1.0999	1.4400	0.7968	1.4153	1.6720

Table 3.5. *Asymmetrically Weighted Quantity Index Numbers*

Period t	HL	GL	L	P	GP	Pa
1	1.0000	1.0000	1.0000	1.0000	1.0000	1.0000
2	1.0039	1.0119	1.0200	0.9930	0.9991	1.0054
3	1.1329	1.1844	1.2700	1.1361	1.1847	1.2665
4	1.2908	1.4213	1.7200	1.2959	1.4216	1.7171
5	1.3806	1.6522	2.5100	1.3889	1.5443	2.0564

that rowwise the Laspeyres price index numbers in column 4 are greater than the Paasche price index numbers in column 5. Notice, however, that the Geometric Laspeyres price index numbers (column 3) are less than the Geometric Paasche price index numbers (column 6). Notice also that the absolute difference between the GP and GL index numbers is smaller than the absolute difference between the P and L index numbers.

Table 3.5 contains the asymmetrically weighted (direct) quantity index numbers $Q(p^t, x^t, p^1, x^1)$ for $t = 1, \ldots, 5$ that were introduced in the previous subsections. Similar observations as before could be made. Though rowwise the Laspeyres quantity index numbers are greater than the Paasche quantity index numbers, there appears to be no systematic relationship between the GL and GP index numbers in columns 3 and 6. The absolute differences between these index numbers, however, appear to be systematically smaller than those between the L and P index numbers.

Table 3.6 contains the symmetric (direct) price index numbers of Fisher, Törnqvist, Marshall-Edgeworth, and Walsh-1. These indices are called *symmetric* because they employ value shares or quantities of the two periods compared. Recall that the Fisher index is the (simple) geometric mean of the Laspeyres and Paasche indices, and that the Törnqvist index is the (simple) geometric mean of the Geometric Laspeyres and Geometric Paasche indices. The rowwise dispersion in Table 3.6 is less than in Table 3.4, but still remarkable.

Table 3.6. *Symmetric Price Index Numbers*

Period t	F	T	ME	W1
1	1.0000	1.0000	1.0000	1.0000
2	1.4011	1.4052	1.4010	1.4017
3	1.2721	1.2890	1.2656	1.2850
4	1.1762	1.2268	1.1438	1.2193
5	1.0712	1.2477	0.9801	1.1850

Table 3.7. *Symmetric Quantity Index Numbers*

Period t	F	T	ME	W1
1	1.0000	1.0000	1.0000	1.0000
2	1.0064	1.0055	1.0041	1.0060
3	1.2012	1.1845	1.1932	1.1887
4	1.4930	1.4214	1.4760	1.4425
5	1.8671	1.5973	1.8484	1.6386

Table 3.7 contains the symmetric (direct) quantity index numbers of Fisher, Törnqvist, Marshall-Edgeworth, and Walsh-1. This table must be compared to Table 3.5.

3.4 Four Tests

In addition to the axioms several other requirements have been proposed in the literature. Following Fisher (1922), these requirements are usually called tests. In this section the most important of these tests will be discussed: the circularity test, the time reversal test, the product test, and the factor reversal test.

Additional material on axioms and tests can be found in Martini (1992a, 1992b) and Olt (1996). At the occasion of the fiftieth anniversary of Fishers death, Vogt and Barta (1997) provided an in-depth study of Fisher's system of tests. The most recent survey was provided by Diewert (2004a).

3.4.1 The Circularity Test and the Time Reversal Test

For the circularity test we must consider more than two time periods, let us say 0, 1, and 2. Suppose that we have decided on a price index $P(p, x, p', x')$ and a quantity index $Q(p, x, p', x'.)$. Then we can compute $P(p^1, x^1, p^0, x^0)$, $P(p^2, x^2, p^0, x^0)$, and $P(p^2, x^2, p^1, x^1)$, as well as the corresponding quantity index numbers. What is the relation between these index numbers? It seems natural to require that $P(p, x, p', x')$ and $Q(p, x, p', x')$ satisfy the following tests, respectively.

T1. Circularity (transitivity) test. The price index number for period 2 relative to period 1 times the price index number for period 1 relative to period 0 is equal to the price index number for period 2 relative to period 0; that is, the following relation holds: $P(p^2, x^2, p^1, x^1) \times P(p^1, x^1, p^0, x^0) = P(p^2, x^2, p^0, x^0)$.

T1′. Circularity (transitivity) test. The quantity index number for period 2 relative to period 1 times the quantity index number for period 1 relative to period 0 is equal to the quantity index number for period 2 relative to period 0; that is, the following relation holds: $Q(p^2, x^2, p^1, x^1) \times Q(p^1, x^1, p^0, x^0) = Q(p^2, x^2, p^0, x^0)$.

The product $P(p^2, x^2, p^1, x^1) \times P(p^1, x^1, p^0, x^0)$ is called a *chained* price index number for period 2 relative to period 0. Similarly, the product $Q(p^2, x^2, p^1, x^1) \times Q(p^1, x^1, p^0, x^0)$ is called a *chained* quantity index number for period 2 relative to period 0. The difference between $P(p^2, x^2, p^1, x^1) \times P(p^1, x^1, p^0, x^0)$ and $P(p^2, x^2, p^0, x^0)$ (or between $Q(p^2, x^2, p^1, x^1) \times Q(p^1, x^1, p^0, x^0)$ and $Q(p^2, x^2, p^0, x^0)$), expressed as a ratio or percentage or whatever, is called the "chain drift." Schoch and Wagener (1984) showed that when a price index satisfies the circularity test, then the possibility of inflationary or deflationary cycles is ruled out.

The reader easily checks that of all the indices discussed in the previous section, only the Lowe price and quantity indices, the unit value index, and the Dutot quantity index satisfy the circularity test. In other words, maintaining this test would rule out many indices. We will repeatedly return to this issue in the next sections.

It is easy to see that **T1** (**T1′**) together with the identity axiom **A3** (**A3′**) imply the time reversal test (let $(p^2, x^2) = (p^0, x^0)$).

T2. Time reversal test. The price index number for period 1 relative to period 0 is equal to the reciprocal of the price index number for period 0 relative to period 1; that is, $P(p^1, x^1, p^0, x^0) = 1/P(p^0, x^0, p^1, x^1)$.

T2′. Time reversal test. The quantity index number for period 1 relative to period 0 is equal to the reciprocal of the quantity index number for period 0 relative to period 1; that is, $Q(p^1, x^1, p^0, x^0) = 1/Q(p^0, x^0, p^1, x^1)$.

It is easy to verify that the Laspeyres price (quantity) index does not satisfy **T2** (**T2′**), and that the same holds for the Paasche indices. It appears that

$$1/P^L(p^0, x^0, p^1, x^1) = P^P(p^1, x^1, p^0, x^0), \tag{3.63}$$

and

$$1/P^P(p^0, x^0, p^1, x^1) = P^L(p^1, x^1, p^0, x^0). \tag{3.64}$$

Similar relations hold for the quantity indices. However, the Fisher price (quantity) index, the Walsh-1 price (quantity) index, and the Törnqvist price (quantity) index do all satisfy **T2** (**T2′**).

3.4.2 The Product Test

The next test is concerned with the decomposition of any value ratio into a price index number and a quantity index number. This is frequently called "the index number problem" and can be stated as follows.

T3 = T3′. Product test. $P(p^1, x^1, p^0, x^0)Q(p^1, x^1, p^0, x^0) = p^1 \cdot x^1/p^0 \cdot x^0.$

Notice that, taken in isolation, the product test **T3** is a rather meaningless statement. Given a function $P(.)$, one can always define a function $Q(.)$ by $p \cdot x/p' \cdot x' P(p, x, p', x')$, such that **T3** is trivially satisfied. Such a function is called an *implicit quantity index*. Similarly, starting with a function $Q(.)$, one can always define a function $P(.)$ by $p \cdot x/p' \cdot x'Q(p, x, p', x')$, such that **T3** is trivially satisfied. Such a function is then called an *implicit price index*.

The power of **T3** appears when this test is combined with other requirements. For instance, **T3** implies that, for any $\lambda > 0$,

$$P(p^1, \lambda x^0, p^0, x^0)Q(p^1, \lambda x^0, p^0, x^0) = \lambda \frac{p^1 \cdot x^0}{p^0 \cdot x^0}. \qquad (3.65)$$

Now, if $Q(.)$ is required to satisfy the proportionality axiom **A6′**, then expression (3.65) reduces to

$$P(p^1, \lambda x^0, p^0, x^0) = \frac{p^1 \cdot x^0}{p^0 \cdot x^0}. \qquad (3.66)$$

Vogt (1978, 1979) called this the "value-index preserving test" ("Wertindex-treue-Test"), and Vogt (1992) showed that it is a simple reformulation of Fisher's (1911) "test of proportionality as to trade." For $\lambda = 1$, expression (3.66) reduces to

$$P(p^1, x^0, p^0, x^0) = \frac{p^1 \cdot x^0}{p^0 \cdot x^0}; \qquad (3.67)$$

that is, if the comparison period quantities are equal to the base period quantities, then the price index must be equal to the ratio of comparison period and base period values of this constant basket. Diewert (1992) called this the "tabular standard, [fixed] basket or constant quantities test."

Another example. Axiom **T3** implies also that, for any $\lambda > 0$,

$$P(p^1, \lambda x^1, p^0, x^0)Q(p^1, \lambda x^1, p^0, x^0) = \lambda \frac{p^1 \cdot x^1}{p^0 \cdot x^0}. \qquad (3.68)$$

Now, if $Q(.)$ is required to satisfy the linear homogeneity axiom **A2′**, then expression (3.68) reduces to

$$P(p^1, \lambda x^1, p^0, x^0)Q(p^1, x^1, p^0, x^0) = \frac{p^1 \cdot x^1}{p^0 \cdot x^0}. \qquad (3.69)$$

Applying again the product test **T3**, one finds that

$$P(p^1, \lambda x^1, p^0, x^0) = P(p^1, x^1, p^0, x^0); \qquad (3.70)$$

that is, the price index must be invariant to proportional changes of the comparison period quantities. This was proposed as a test by Vogt (1980a).

The general meaning of the product test can be expressed as follows. Given a price index $P(.)$ that satisfies the axioms **A1**, ..., **A5**, one wants the implicit quantity index $p \cdot x / p' \cdot x' P(.)$ to satisfy the axioms **A1′**, ..., **A5′**. Reversely, given a quantity index $Q(.)$ that satisfies the axioms **A1′**, ..., **A5′**, one wants the implicit price index $p \cdot x / p' \cdot x' Q(.)$ to satisfy the axioms **A1**, ..., **A5**.

It is easy to see that in this sense the Laspeyres and the Paasche indices satisfy **T3**. For example, the implicit Laspeyres quantity index appears to be equal to the Paasche quantity index:

$$\begin{aligned}
p^1 \cdot x^1 / p^0 \cdot x^0 P^L(p^1, x^1, p^0, x^0) &= (p^1 \cdot x^1 / p^0 \cdot x^0)(p^0 \cdot x^0 / p^1 \cdot x^0) \\
&= p^1 \cdot x^1 / p^1 \cdot x^0 \\
&= Q^P(p^1, x^1, p^0, x^0). \qquad (3.71)
\end{aligned}$$

Put otherwise, the Laspeyres price index multiplied by the Paasche quantity index is equal to the value ratio. In the same way one can show that the Paasche price index multiplied by the Laspeyres quantity index is equal to the value ratio. Or, the implicit Paasche quantity index is equal to the Laspeyres quantity index. The following expression combines the two results:

$$\begin{aligned}
\frac{p^1 \cdot x^1}{p^0 \cdot x^0} &= P^L(p^1, x^1, p^0, x^0)Q^P(p^1, x^1, p^0, x^0) \\
&= P^P(p^1, x^1, p^0, x^0)Q^L(p^1, x^1, p^0, x^0). \qquad (3.72)
\end{aligned}$$

Not surprisingly, one also obtains that

$$\frac{p^1 \cdot x^1}{p^0 \cdot x^0} = P^{LP}(p^1, x^1, p^0, x^0) Q^{HLP}(p^1, x^1, p^0, x^0)$$

$$= P^{HLP}(p^1, x^1, p^0, x^0) Q^{LP}(p^1, x^1, p^0, x^0), \qquad (3.73)$$

where the arithmetic mean of the Laspeyres and Paasche price index, $P^{LP}(.)$, was defined by expression (3.25); the harmonic mean of the Laspeyres and Paasche quantity index, $Q^{HLP}(.)$, was defined by expression (3.33); the harmonic mean of the Laspeyres and Paasche price index, $P^{HLP}(.)$, was defined by expression (3.32); and the arithmetic mean of the Laspeyres and Paasche quantity index, $Q^{LP}(.)$, was defined by expression (3.26).

For the Fisher indices one verifies easily that

$$\frac{p^1 \cdot x^1}{p^0 \cdot x^0} = P^F(p^1, x^1, p^0, x^0) Q^F(p^1, x^1, p^0, x^0); \qquad (3.74)$$

that is, the Fisher indices satisfy the product test.

The value ratio divided by the Walsh-1 price index (3.21) yields

$$\frac{p^1 \cdot x^1}{p^0 \cdot x^0} \Big/ P^{W1}(p^1, x^1, p^0, x^0) = \frac{\sum_{n=1}^N s_n^0 (x_n^1/x_n^0)^{1/2}}{\sum_{n=1}^N s_n^1 (x_n^1/x_n^0)^{-1/2}}, \qquad (3.75)$$

which is a quadratic mean of order 1 quantity index. Likewise, the value ratio divided by the Walsh-1 quantity index (3.22) yields a quadratic mean of order 1 price index. Thus, we have two expressions for the value ratio, namely

$$\frac{p^1 \cdot x^1}{p^0 \cdot x^0} = P^{W1}(p^1, x^1, p^0, x^0) \frac{\sum_{n=1}^N s_n^0 (x_n^1/x_n^0)^{1/2}}{\sum_{n=1}^N s_n^1 (x_n^1/x_n^0)^{-1/2}}$$

$$= \frac{\sum_{n=1}^N s_n^0 (p_n^1/p_n^0)^{1/2}}{\sum_{n=1}^N s_n^1 (p_n^1/p_n^0)^{-1/2}} Q^{W1}(p^1, x^1, p^0, x^0). \qquad (3.76)$$

The quadratic mean of order r $(r \geq 0)$ price and quantity indices were introduced by Diewert (1976). They satisfy the axioms **A1**, ..., **A5** and **A1'**, ..., **A5'**, respectively.

Most indices, however, do not satisfy the product test in the general sense expressed above. Consider, for example, an implicit Lowe quantity index, given by

$$p^1 \cdot x^1/p^0 \cdot x^0 P^{Lo}(p^1, p^0; x^b) = (p^1 \cdot x^1/p^0 \cdot x^0)(p^0 \cdot x^b/p^1 \cdot x^b).$$
$$(3.77)$$

Table 3.8. *Asymmetrically Weighted Implicit Price Index Numbers*

Period t	HL	GL	L	P	GP	Pa
1	1.0000	1.0000	1.0000	1.0000	1.0000	1.0000
2	1.4045	1.3934	1.3823	1.4200	1.4113	1.4024
3	1.3488	1.2901	1.2031	1.3450	1.2898	1.2065
4	1.3604	1.2355	1.0209	1.3550	1.2352	1.0226
5	1.4486	1.2105	0.7968	1.4400	1.2951	0.9726

One easily checks that in general this function violates the proportionality axiom **A6'**, and thus cannot be regarded as a genuine quantity index. The same applies to the implicit Harmonic Laspeyres, Geometric Laspeyres, Geometric Paasche, and Palgrave quantity indices. Also, it is instructive to consider the implicit Törnqvist quantity index, given by

$$p^1 \cdot x^1 / p^0 \cdot x^0 P^T(p^1, x^1, p^0, x^0) = (p^1 \cdot x^1 / p^0 \cdot x^0) \prod_{n=1}^{N} (p_n^0 / p_n^1)^{\bar{s}_n},$$
(3.78)

where $\bar{s}_n \equiv (s_n^0 + s_n^1)/2$ $(n = 1, \ldots, N)$. In general this function violates the proportionality axiom **A6'**. Hence, the right-hand side of expression (3.78) cannot be regarded as a genuine quantity index.

An interesting case is the implicit Marshall-Edgeworth quantity index. It is easy to check that

$$p^1 \cdot x^1 / p^0 \cdot x^0 P^{ME}(p^1, x^1, p^0, x^0) = \frac{1 + Q^L(p^1, x^1, p^0, x^0)}{1 + 1/Q^P(p^1, x^1, p^0, x^0)}.$$
(3.79)

This function[16] satisfies the proportionality axiom **A6'**, but violates the linear homogeneity axiom **A2'**.

Finally, the GK price index was defined by expression (3.23). It is straightforward to check that the implicit GK quantity index violates the proportionality axiom **A6'**.

Let us return to our numerical example. Table 3.8 contains the main asymmetrically weighted (direct) implicit price index numbers. The generic form of these index numbers is $V^t / V^1 Q(p^t, x^t, p^1, x^1)$ for $t = 1, \ldots, 5$. Notice

[16] Its dual, $p^1 \cdot x^1 / p^0 \cdot x^0 Q^{ME}(.) = (1 + P^L(.))/(1 + 1/P^P(.))$, is known as the true factorial price index (see Banerjee 1980 and Balk 1983). In Fisher's (1922) system this index got number 2154.

Table 3.9. *Asymmetrically Weighted Implicit Quantity Index Numbers*

Period t	HL	GL	L	P	GP	Pa
1	1.0000	1.0000	1.0000	1.0000	1.0000	1.0000
2	1.1242	1.0602	0.9930	1.0200	0.9497	0.8760
3	1.3467	1.2201	1.1361	1.2700	1.1517	1.0790
4	2.0109	1.5497	1.2959	1.7200	1.3221	1.1456
5	3.6000	1.8184	1.3889	2.5100	1.4131	1.1961

that, as should be, columns 4 and 5 of Table 3.8 coincide with columns 5 and 4 respectively of Table 3.4.

Likewise, Table 3.9 contains the main asymmetrically weighted (direct) implicit quantity index numbers, defined as $V^t/V^1 P(p^t, x^t, p^1, x^1)$ for $t = 1, \ldots, 5$. Notice that, as should be, columns 4 and 5 of Table 3.9 coincide with columns 5 and 4 respectively of Table 3.5.

Table 3.10 contains the symmetric (direct) implicit price index numbers of Fisher, Törnqvist, Marshall-Edgeworth, and Walsh-1. As should be, column 2 of this table coincides with column 2 of Table 3.6. Likewise, Table 3.11 contains the symmetric (direct) implicit quantity index numbers of Fisher, Törnqvist, Marshall-Edgeworth, and Walsh-1. Notice that column 2 of this table coincides with column 2 of Table 3.7.

3.4.3 The Factor Reversal Test

From the definitions of the Fisher indices (3.27), (3.28) we see that if we interchange the prices and quantities in $P^F(p^1, x^1, p^0, x^0)$, then we obtain $Q^F(p^1, x^1, p^0, x^0)$. In the same way, by interchanging prices and quantities, we obtain $P^F(p^1, x^1, p^0, x^0)$ from $Q^F(p^1, x^1, p^0, x^0)$. Thus equation (3.74) tells us that the Fisher indices satisfy a test much stronger than the product test, namely the so-called factor reversal test.

Table 3.10. *Symmetric Implicit Price Index Numbers*

Period t	F	T	ME	W1
1	1.0000	1.0000	1.0000	1.0000
2	1.4011	1.4023	1.4042	1.4015
3	1.2721	1.2900	1.2806	1.2854
4	1.1762	1.2354	1.1897	1.2173
5	1.0712	1.2521	1.0820	1.2206

Table 3.11. *Symmetric Implicit Quantity Index Numbers*

Period t	F	T	ME	W1
1	1.0000	1.0000	1.0000	1.0000
2	1.0064	1.0034	1.0064	1.0059
3	1.2012	1.1854	1.2073	1.1891
4	1.4930	1.4313	1.5353	1.4402
5	1.8671	1.6030	2.0407	1.6878

Recall that interchanging prices and quantities transforms any price index into a quantity index and *vice versa*. Thus, the factor reversal test can be formulated in two equivalent ways, namely as **T4** or **T4'**.

T4. Factor reversal test. $P(p^1, x^1, p^0, x^0) P(x^1, p^1, x^0, p^0) = p^1 \cdot x^1 / p^0 \cdot x^0$.

T4'. Factor reversal test. $Q(x^1, p^1, x^0, p^0) Q(p^1, x^1, p^0, x^0) = p^1 \cdot x^1 / p^0 \cdot x^0$.

A price or quantity index is called *ideal* if it satisfies **T4** or **T4'**. Thus the Fisher price and quantity indices are ideal indices. They are, however, not unique.

Sato (1976) and Vartia (1974, 1976) independently discovered a new pair of ideal price and quantity indices. A simple derivation runs as follows. Consider the following identity for the value shares

$$\sum_{n=1}^{N}(s_n^1 - s_n^0) = 0. \tag{3.80}$$

Applying the logarithmic mean (see appendix 1 for details), this can be written as

$$\sum_{n=1}^{N} L(s_n^1, s_n^0) \ln(s_n^1/s_n^0) = 0. \tag{3.81}$$

Employing the fact that $s_n^t = v_n^t / V^t$ ($n = 1, \ldots, N; t = 0, 1$), expression (3.81) can be written as

$$\sum_{n=1}^{N} L(s_n^1, s_n^0)(\ln(v_n^1/v_n^0) - \ln(V^1/V^0)) = 0. \tag{3.82}$$

Rearranging this equality, one obtains

$$\ln\left(\frac{V^1}{V^0}\right) = \frac{\sum_{n=1}^{N} L(s_n^1, s_n^0)\ln(v_n^1/v_n^0)}{\sum_{n=1}^{N} L(s_n^1, s_n^0)}$$

$$= \frac{\sum_{n=1}^{N} L(s_n^1, s_n^0)\ln(p_n^1/p_n^0)}{\sum_{n=1}^{N} L(s_n^1, s_n^0)} + \frac{\sum_{n=1}^{N} L(s_n^1, s_n^0)\ln(x_n^1/x_n^0)}{\sum_{n=1}^{N} L(s_n^1, s_n^0)}.$$

$$(3.83)$$

By exponentiation one finally obtains

$$\frac{V^1}{V^0} = \prod_{n=1}^{N}\left(\frac{p_n^1}{p_n^0}\right)^{L(s_n^1,s_n^0)/\sum_{n=1}^{N} L(s_n^1,s_n^0)} \prod_{n=1}^{N}\left(\frac{x_n^1}{x_n^0}\right)^{L(s_n^1,s_n^0)/\sum_{n=1}^{N} L(s_n^1,s_n^0)}$$

$$\equiv P^{SV}(p^1, x^1, p^0, x^0)Q^{SV}(p^1, x^1, p^0, x^0).$$

$$(3.84)$$

Each index has the form of a weighted geometric mean of price (quantity) relatives, whereby the weights are given as the normalized logarithmic means of base and comparison period value shares.

The Sato-Vartia price and quantity indices[17] satisfy the axioms **A1,...,** **A5** and **A1',..., A5'**, respectively, except that, like the Törnqvist indices, they do not satisfy the monotonicity axioms globally (as noticed by Olt 1996 and Reinsdorf and Dorfman 1999). Appendix 2 (drawn from Balk 2003) provides the details. It appears that the failure of monotonicity will only materialize in rather exceptional circumstances. The indices also satisfy the time reversal tests, as can be checked easily.

Montgomery (1929, 1937) obtained an interesting solution to the index number problem. By applying the logarithmic mean two times, the logarithm of the value ratio can be decomposed as follows:

$$\ln\left(\frac{V^1}{V^0}\right) = \frac{V^1 - V^0}{L(V^1, V^0)} = \frac{\sum_{n=1}^{N}(v_n^1 - v_n^0)}{L(V^1, V^0)}$$

$$= \frac{\sum_{n=1}^{N} L(v_n^1, v_n^0)\ln(v_n^1/v_n^0)}{L(V^1, V^0)}$$

$$= \sum_{n=1}^{N}\frac{L(v_n^1, v_n^0)}{L(V^1, V^0)}\ln(p_n^1/p_n^0) + \sum_{n=1}^{N}\frac{L(v_n^1, v_n^0)}{L(V^1, V^0)}\ln(x_n^1/x_n^0).$$

$$(3.85)$$

[17] These indices are sometimes referred to as Vartia-II indices.

By exponentiating both sides one obtains a decomposition of the value ratio itself,

$$\frac{V^1}{V^0} = \prod_{n=1}^{N} \left(\frac{p_n^1}{p_n^0}\right)^{L(v_n^1, v_n^0)/L(V^1, V^0)} \prod_{n=1}^{N} \left(\frac{x_n^1}{x_n^0}\right)^{L(v_n^1, v_n^0)/L(V^1, V^0)}$$

$$\equiv P^{MV}(p^1, x^1, p^0, x^0) Q^{MV}(p^1, x^1, p^0, x^0). \tag{3.86}$$

Each index has the form of a weighted product of price (quantity) relatives. Each weight is equal to the logarithmic mean of a commodity's value in base and comparison period divided by the logarithmic mean of the aggregate value in base and comparison period. Thus, each weight has the structure of a mean value share. These weights, however, do not add up to 1. This can be seen as follows. Since $L(a, 1)$ is concave, the application of Jensen's Inequality yields

$$\sum_{n=1}^{N} L(v_n^1, v_n^0) = \sum_{n=1}^{N} v_n^0 L(v_n^1/v_n^0, 1)$$

$$= V^0 \sum_{n=1}^{N} s_n^0 L(v_n^1/v_n^0, 1)$$

$$< V^0 L\left(\sum_{n=1}^{N} s_n^0 v_n^1/v_n^0, 1\right)$$

$$= V^0 L(V^1/V^0, 1)$$

$$= L(V^1, V^0), \tag{3.87}$$

in which sequence of expressions the linear homogeneity of the logarithmic mean was used repeatedly.

Because Vartia (1974, 1976) independently rediscovered this solution to the index number problem, the functions $P^{MV}(.)$ and $Q^{MV}(.)$ will be called Montgomery-Vartia indices.[18] The last line of expression (3.85) corresponds to the result actually obtained by Montgomery (1929, p. 15). Although Montgomery (1937, p. 32) obtained expression (3.86), the result was expressed in a less intelligible form, due to the fact that the logarithmic mean had not yet been discovered.

The Montgomery-Vartia indices are ideal and satisfy the time reversal test, as one can easily check. With respect to the basic axioms it must be noticed that these indices are not globally monotonic. However, as shown in

---

[18] These indices are sometimes referred to as Vartia-I indices.

Table 3.12. *Ideal Price Index Numbers*

Period t	F	SV	MV	S(a,a)
1	1.0000	1.0000	1.0000	1.0000
2	1.4011	1.4018	1.4024	1.4042
3	1.2721	1.2897	1.2907	1.2742
4	1.1762	1.2335	1.2392	1.1552
5	1.0712	1.2540	1.2678	0.9770

appendix 2, such a failure can hardly be expected to occur in practice. More important is the fact that these indices fail to satisfy the basic proportionality axioms **A6** and **A6′**, because of the fact that the weights do not add up to 1.

It is interesting to compare the three pairs of ideal indices on our numerical example. The results are to be found in Tables 3.12 and 3.13. The final columns of these two tables contain price and quantity index numbers according to the formula of Stuvel (1957). This fourth pair of ideal indices will be introduced in section 3.6.3.

Though the weights of the Montgomery-Vartia indices do not add up to 1, the discrepancy appears to be small. In the four comparisons considered in our example the sums of the weights appear to be 0.9919, 0.9952, 0.9870, and 0.9849, respectively.

3.5 Some Inconsistency Results

Frisch (1930) and Wald (1937) were the first who discovered inconsistencies if one requires some of the functional equations to hold simultaneously. In the course of time there have been proved more of these so-called inconsistency theorems. The reader is referred to Eichhorn and Voeller (1976) for a complete treatment of this topic. In this section the most important results will be presented. The proof of the first theorem proceeds by the construction of a counterexample, whereas the proof of the second theorem is more deductive. It will be assumed that $N \geq 2$.

Table 3.13. *Ideal Quantity Index Numbers*

Period t	F	SV	MV	S(a,a)
1	1.0000	1.0000	1.0000	1.0000
2	1.0064	1.0058	1.0054	1.0042
3	1.2012	1.1848	1.1839	1.1992
4	1.4930	1.4236	1.4170	1.5202
5	1.8671	1.5949	1.5776	2.0470

Theorem 3.1 *There do not exist functions $P(.)$, $Q(.)$ that satisfy simultaneously the identity axioms* **A3**, **A3'**, *the circularity test* **T1**, *and the product test* **T3**.

Proof: (Wald 1937) Four time periods are considered, with prices and quantities subsequently (p^0, x^0), (p^1, x^1), (p^2, x^2), and (p^3, x^3). We assume that $p^0 = p^2$, $p^1 = p^3$, $x^0 = x^1$, and $x^2 = x^3$. If **A3** and **A3'** are satisfied we get

$$P(p^2, x^2, p^0, x^0) = P(p^3, x^3, p^1, x^1) = 1 \qquad (3.88)$$

$$Q(p^1, x^1, p^0, x^0) = Q(p^3, x^3, p^2, x^2) = 1. \qquad (3.89)$$

If **T3** is satisfied we derive from expression (3.89) that

$$P(p^1, x^1, p^0, x^0) = p^1 \cdot x^1 / p^0 \cdot x^0 = p^3 \cdot x^0 / p^0 \cdot x^0 \qquad (3.90)$$

and

$$P(p^3, x^3, p^2, x^2) = p^3 \cdot x^3 / p^2 \cdot x^2 = p^3 \cdot x^3 / p^0 \cdot x^3. \qquad (3.91)$$

From **T1** we get

$$P(p^3, x^3, p^1, x^1) P(p^1, x^1, p^0, x^0) = P(p^3, x^3, p^2, x^2) P(p^2, x^2, p^0, x^0) \qquad (3.92)$$

and substituting expressions (3.88), (3.90), and (3.91) into (3.92) we obtain

$$p^3 \cdot x^0 / p^0 \cdot x^0 = p^3 \cdot x^3 / p^0 \cdot x^3. \qquad (3.93)$$

Since the vectors p^0, x^0, p^3, x^3 can be chosen in such a way that (3.93) is not satisfied, a contradiction is established. QED

Theorem 3.2 *There does not exist a function $P(.)$ that satisfies simultaneously the identity axiom* **A3**, *the circularity test* **T1**, *and the factor reversal test* **T4**.

Proof[19]: Let **T1** hold. Then for all (p^0, x^0), (p^1, x^1), (p^2, x^2) we have the relation

$$P(p^1, x^1, p^0, x^0) = P(p^1, x^1, p^2, x^2) / P(p^0, x^0, p^2, x^2). \qquad (3.94)$$

Since the left-hand side is independent of (p^2, x^2), one can fix these variables and define $g(p, x) \equiv P(p, x, p^2, x^2)$. Thus (3.94) can be expressed as

$$P(p^1, x^1, p^0, x^0) = g(p^1, x^1) / g(p^0, x^0). \qquad (3.95)$$

---

[19] This proof was inspired by Samuelson (1974) and makes use of Theorem 4.3.3 of Eichhorn and Voeller (1976).

The satisfaction of **A3** implies that

$$P(p^0, x^1, p^0, x^0) = g(p^0, x^1)/g(p^0, x^0) = 1; \qquad (3.96)$$

that is, $g(p, x)$ is independent of x and can be expressed as $g(p, x) \equiv h(p)$. Thus

$$P(p^1, x^1, p^0, x^0) = h(p^1)/h(p^0). \qquad (3.97)$$

Now if **T4** is satisfied, then

$$\frac{h(p^1)h(x^1)}{h(p^0)h(x^0)} = \frac{p^1 \cdot x^1}{p^0 \cdot x^0}, \qquad (3.98)$$

or

$$h(p)h(x) = bp \cdot x \qquad (3.99)$$

for an arbitrary constant $b > 0$. Let $h(1_N) = a$. By inserting $p = 1_N$ and $x = 1_N$, respectively, into expression (3.99) we see that

$$h(p) = bp \cdot 1_N/a \text{ and } h(x) = b1_N \cdot x/a. \qquad (3.100)$$

Inserting these expressions into (3.99) yields

$$b \left(\sum_{n=1}^{N} p_n \right) \left(\sum_{n=1}^{N} x_n \right) \Big/ a^2 = \sum_{n=1}^{N} p_n x_n. \qquad (3.101)$$

However, for $N \geq 2$ this equation cannot be valid for all p and x.   QED

Notice that it is trivial to satisfy the identity axiom **A3**, the circularity test **T1**, and the product test **T3** simultaneously. We simply define the quantity index as

$$Q(p^1, x^1, p^0, x^0) \equiv \frac{p^1 \cdot x^1}{p^0 \cdot x^0} \frac{h(p^0)}{h(p^1)}. \qquad (3.102)$$

But this function will in general not satisfy the identity axiom **A3'**. It must be concluded that there is an inherent conflict between the identity axioms, the circularity test, the product test, and/or the factor reversal test. These requirements cannot be satisfied by functions $P(.)$ and $Q(.)$ simultaneously. The economic theory of price and quantity indices sheds more light on these impossibility results.

3.6 Characterizations of Price and Quantity Indices

In section 3.3 we observed that the set of all the positive functions which satisfy the functional equations **A1, A2, A3, A4, A5** or **A1, A4, A5, A6** is rather large. In section 3.5 we learned that for certain combinations of functional equations the set of all positive functions satisfying them is empty. An interesting line of research is to look for those combinations of (independent) functional equations such that the set of all positive functions satisfying them contains precisely one element. If this element is a price index we say that we have obtained a *characterization* of that price index. It is also possible to look for a characterization of a price index and a quantity index simultaneously. In this section all characterizations known to the author will be reviewed. For convenience' sake the discussion will in general be limited to price indices. By obvious transformations, however, any characterization of a price index becomes a characterization of a quantity index.

3.6.1 The Fisher Indices

The first set of characterizations concerns the Fisher price index. They are presented in the order of discovery. The first characterization was obtained by Van IJzeren (1952). It makes use of what later came to be called the value dependence test. The name is due to Funke and Voeller (1984).

T5. Value dependence test. There exists a function $f : \mathfrak{R}_{++}^4 \to \mathfrak{R}_{++}$ such that $P(p, x, p', x') = f(p \cdot x, p \cdot x', p' \cdot x, p' \cdot x')$.

T5'. Value dependence test. There exists a function $g : \mathfrak{R}_{++}^4 \to \mathfrak{R}_{++}$ such that $Q(p, x, p', x') = g(p \cdot x, p \cdot x', p' \cdot x, p' \cdot x')$.

Thus the value dependence test requires that the price index and the quantity index have a particular functional form. Notice that, if the price index $P(.)$ satisfies **T5**, then the implicit quantity index $p \cdot x / p' \cdot x' P(.)$ satisfies **T5'**. And, if the quantity index $Q(.)$ satisfies **T5'**, then the implicit price index $p \cdot x / p' \cdot x' Q(.)$ satisfies **T5**.

Theorem 3.3 *A function $P(.)$ satisfies the linear homogeneity axiom* **A2**, *the factor reversal test* **T4**, *and the value dependence test* **T5** *if and only if* $P(p^1, x^1, p^0, x^0) = P^F(p^1, x^1, p^0, x^0)$.

Proof: The original proof of Van IJzeren (1952) was by contradiction. The method of Balk's (1985) proof was borrowed from Funke and Voeller (1984). See Balk (1995).   QED

The next characterization is also due to Van IJzeren (1958), but was redis-covered by Eichhorn and Voeller (1976, p. 42).

Theorem 3.4 *The functions* $P(.), Q(.)$ *satisfy the product test* **T3** *and the following functional equation*

$$\frac{P(p^1, x^1, p^0, x^0)}{P^L(p^1, x^1, p^0, x^0)} = \frac{Q(p^1, x^1, p^0, x^0)}{Q^L(p^1, x^1, p^0, x^0)} \tag{3.103}$$

if and only if $P(p^1, x^1, p^0, x^0) = P^F(p^1, x^1, p^0, x^0)$ *and* $Q(p^1, x^1, p^0, x^0) = Q^F(p^1, x^1, p^0, x^0)$.

Proof: The product test **T3** tells us that $Q(p^1, x^1, p^0, x^0) = p^1 \cdot x^1 / p^0 \cdot x^0 P(p^1, x^1, p^0, x^0)$. By substituting this into the functional equation (3.103) we obtain

$$\frac{P(p^1, x^1, p^0, x^0)}{P^L(p^1, x^1, p^0, x^0)} = \frac{p^1 \cdot x^1 / p^0 \cdot x^0}{P(p^1, x^1, p^0, x^0) Q^L(p^1, x^1, p^0, x^0)}. \tag{3.104}$$

This can be rearranged to

$$[P(p^1, x^1, p^0, x^0)]^2 = \frac{(p^1 \cdot x^1 / p^0 \cdot x^0) P^L(p^1, x^1, p^0, x^0)}{Q^L(p^1, x^1, p^0, x^0)} \tag{3.105}$$

$$= P^L(p^1, x^1, p^0, x^0) P^P(p^1, x^1, p^0, x^0), \tag{3.106}$$

by using relation (3.72). Now taking the positive root, we obtain the result that $P(p^1, x^1, p^0, x^0) = P^F(p^1, x^1, p^0, x^0)$. In the same way, or by using relation (3.74), one obtains $Q(p^1, x^1, p^0, x^0) = Q^F(p^1, x^1, p^0, x^0)$. The other direction of the proof is trivial.   QED

The functional equation (3.103) can also be written in the following way,

$$\frac{P(p^1, x^1, p^0, x^0)}{Q(p^1, x^1, p^0, x^0)} = \frac{P^L(p^1, x^1, p^0, x^0)}{Q^L(p^1, x^1, p^0, x^0)}, \tag{3.107}$$

saying that the ratio of any price index and quantity index must be equal to the ratio of the Laspeyres price index and quantity index.

Theorem 3.5 *A function* $P(.)$ *satisfies the time reversal test* **T2**, *the factor reversal test* **T4**, *and the functional equation*

$$P(p^1, x^1, p^0, x^0) = P(p^1, x^0, p^0, x^1) \tag{3.108}$$

if and only if $P(p^1, x^1, p^0, x^0) = P^F(p^1, x^1, p^0, x^0)$.

Proof: (Funke and Voeller 1978) Interchanging p^1 and p^0 in **T4**, we obtain

$$P(p^0, x^1, p^1, x^0)P(x^1, p^0, x^0, p^1) = p^0 \cdot x^1 / p^1 \cdot x^0. \quad (3.109)$$

Applying the functional equation (3.108), the last expression becomes

$$P(p^0, x^0, p^1, x^1)P(x^1, p^1, x^0, p^0) = p^0 \cdot x^1 / p^1 \cdot x^0. \quad (3.110)$$

Dividing **T4** by this expression, we obtain

$$P(p^1, x^1, p^0, x^0)/P(p^0, x^0, p^1, x^1) = [P^F(p^1, x^1, p^0, x^0)]^2. \quad (3.111)$$

Using **T2**, this expression transforms into

$$[P(p^1, x^1, p^0, x^0)]^2 = [P^F(p^1, x^1, p^0, x^0)]^2. \quad (3.112)$$

The other direction of the proof is trivial.   QED

The functional equation in Theorem 3.5 means that the price index is invariant to interchanging base period and comparison period quantities. Expression (3.108) is therefore called the quantity reversal test, going back to Funke and Voeller (1978). The next characterization is a slight modification of the former. Now base period and comparison period prices are interchanged.

Theorem 3.6 *A function $P(.)$ satisfies the time reversal test* **T2**, *the factor reversal test* **T4**, *and the functional equation*

$$P(p^1, x^1, p^0, x^0) = 1/P(p^0, x^1, p^1, x^0) \quad (3.113)$$

if and only if $P(p^1, x^1, p^0, x^0) = P^F(p^1, x^1, p^0, x^0)$.

Proof: (Funke and Voeller 1979) Interchanging x^1 and x^0 in the functional equation (3.113), we obtain

$$P(p^1, x^0, p^0, x^1) = 1/P(p^0, x^0, p^1, x^1). \quad (3.114)$$

Combined with **T2** this gives

$$P(p^1, x^0, p^0, x^1) = P(p^1, x^1, p^0, x^0). \quad (3.115)$$

We can now apply the previous theorem. The other direction of the proof is trivial.   QED

The next characterization uses a functional equation which, loosely formulated, says that replacing comparison period quantities by base period

quantities in the price index has the same effect as replacing comparison
period prices by base period prices in the associated quantity index.

Theorem 3.7 *A function* $P(.)$ *satisfies the identity axiom* **A3**, *the factor reversal test* **T4**, *and the functional equation*

$$\frac{P(p^1, x^1, p^0, x^0)}{P(p^1, x^0, p^0, x^0)} = \frac{P(x^1, p^1, x^0, p^0)}{P(x^1, p^0, x^0, p^0)} \qquad (3.116)$$

if and only if $P(p^1, x^1, p^0, x^0) = P^F(p^1, x^1, p^0, x^0)$.

Proof: (Hacker 1979, pp. 82–4) Substituting the functional equation (3.116)
into **T4**, we obtain

$$\frac{[P(p^1, x^1, p^0, x^0)]^2 \, P(x^1, p^0, x^0, p^0)}{P(p^1, x^0, p^0, x^0)} = \frac{p^1 \cdot x^1}{p^0 \cdot x^0}. \qquad (3.117)$$

From **T4** follows

$$P(x^1, p^0, x^0, p^0) P(p^0, x^1, p^0, x^0) = \frac{p^0 \cdot x^1}{p^0 \cdot x^0}. \qquad (3.118)$$

From **A3** follows

$$P(p^0, x^1, p^0, x^0) = 1, \qquad (3.119)$$

hence

$$P(x^1, p^0, x^0, p^0) = \frac{p^0 \cdot x^1}{p^0 \cdot x^0}. \qquad (3.120)$$

Similarly from **T4**

$$P(p^1, x^0, p^0, x^0) P(x^0, p^1, x^0, p^0) = \frac{p^1 \cdot x^0}{p^0 \cdot x^0}, \qquad (3.121)$$

and from **A3**

$$P(x^0, p^1, x^0, p^0) = 1, \qquad (3.122)$$

hence

$$P(p^1, x^0, p^0, x^0) = \frac{p^1 \cdot x^0}{p^0 \cdot x^0}. \qquad (3.123)$$

Substituting expressions (3.120) and (3.123) into (3.117) and taking the
positive root yields the desired result. The other direction of the proof is
trivial.   QED

The next theorem can be seen as a modification of Theorem 3.6. The factor reversal test is replaced by the weaker product test and an analogous functional equation for the quantity index is added.

Theorem 3.8 *The functions* $P(.), Q(.)$ *satisfy the time reversal test* **T2**, *the product test* **T3**, *and the functional equations*

$$P(p^1, x^1, p^0, x^0) = 1/P(p^0, x^1, p^1, x^0) \qquad (3.124)$$

$$Q(p^1, x^1, p^0, x^0) = 1/Q(p^1, x^0, p^0, x^1) \qquad (3.125)$$

if and only if $P(p^1, x^1, p^0, x^0) = P^F(p^1, x^1, p^0, x^0)$ *and* $Q(p^1, x^1, p^0, x^0) = Q^F(p^1, x^1, p^0, x^0)$.

Proof: (Funke and Voeller 1984) From **T3** we have

$$P(p^1, x^0, p^0, x^1) Q(p^1, x^0, p^0, x^1) = \frac{p^1 \cdot x^0}{p^0 \cdot x^1}. \qquad (3.126)$$

Using expression (3.125), we obtain

$$\frac{P(p^1, x^0, p^0, x^1)}{Q(p^1, x^1, p^0, x^0)} = \frac{p^1 \cdot x^0}{p^0 \cdot x^1}. \qquad (3.127)$$

Multiplying this equation by **T3**, we obtain

$$P(p^1, x^1, p^0, x^0) P(p^1, x^0, p^0, x^1) = \frac{p^1 \cdot x^0}{p^0 \cdot x^0} \frac{p^1 \cdot x^1}{p^0 \cdot x^1}. \qquad (3.128)$$

Using expression (3.124) and **T2** subsequently, we obtain

$$P(p^1, x^0, p^0, x^1) = 1/P(p^0, x^0, p^1, x^1) = P(p^1, x^1, p^0, x^0). \qquad (3.129)$$

Substituting this result into expression (3.128) and taking the positive root, we obtain $P(p^1, x^1, p^0, x^0) = P^F(p^1, x^1, p^0, x^0)$. Using **T3** again we find $Q(p^1, x^1, p^0, x^0) = Q^F(p^1, x^1, p^0, x^0)$. The other direction of the proof is trivial. QED

The following theorem is a modification of Theorem 3.3. The factor reversal test is replaced by the weaker product test. This is counterbalanced by the addition of the time reversal test and a linear homogeneity axiom.

Theorem 3.9 *The functions* $P(.), Q(.)$ *satisfy the linear homogeneity axioms* **A2**, **A2′**, *the time reversal test* **T2**, *the product test* **T3**, *and the value dependence test* **T5** *if and only if* $P(p^1, x^1, p^0, x^0) = P^F(p^1, x^1, p^0, x^0)$ *and* $Q(p^1, x^1, p^0, x^0) = Q^F(p^1, x^1, p^0, x^0)$.

Proof: Funke and Voeller (1984); see Balk (1995).   QED

The following characterization of the Fisher price index is essentially a modification of Theorem 3.5.

Theorem 3.10 *A function $P(.)$ satisfies the time reversal test* **T2** *and the following two functional equations (respectively called quantity reversal test and price reversal test),*

$$P(p^1, x^1, p^0, x^0) = P(p^1, x^0, p^0, x^1) \qquad (3.130)$$

$$\frac{p^1 \cdot x^1}{p^0 \cdot x^0 P(p^1, x^1, p^0, x^0)} = \frac{p^0 \cdot x^1}{p^1 \cdot x^0 P(p^0, x^1, p^1, x^0)}, \qquad (3.131)$$

if and only if $P(p^1, x^1, p^0, x^0) = P^F(p^1, x^1, p^0, x^0)$.

Proof: (Diewert 1992) Rewriting expression (3.131) gives

$$\frac{p^1 \cdot x^1}{p^0 \cdot x^0} \frac{p^1 \cdot x^0}{p^0 \cdot x^1} = \frac{P(p^1, x^1, p^0, x^0)}{P(p^0, x^1, p^1, x^0)}$$

$$= \frac{P(p^1, x^1, p^0, x^0)}{P(p^0, x^0, p^1, x^1)}$$

$$= [P(p^1, x^1, p^0, x^0)]^2,$$

where (3.130) and **T2**, respectively, were applied. Taking the positive root yields the desired result. The other direction of the proof is trivial.   QED

It is interesting to compare Theorem 3.10 to Theorem 3.5. We see that the factor reversal test **T4** is replaced by the functional equation (3.131). Note that if $P(p^1, x^1, p^0, x^0)$ is a price index, then $p^1 \cdot x^1 / p^0 \cdot x^0 P(p^1, x^1, p^0, x^0)$ is the implicit quantity index. Equation (3.130) says that interchanging comparison period and base period quantities does not matter for the price index. Then (3.131) says analogously that interchanging comparison period and base period prices does not matter for the implicit quantity index. This so-called price reversal test was introduced by Diewert (1992).

The final characterization of the Fisher price index is due to Diewert (1997). It says that the Fisher price index is the only linearly homogeneous function of Laspeyres and Paasche price indices that satisfies the time reversal test.

Theorem 3.11 *A function $P(.)$ satisfies the time reversal test* **T2** *and the functional equation*

$$P(p^1, x^1, p^0, x^0) = m(P^L(p^1, x^1, p^0, x^0), P^P(p^1, x^1, p^0, x^0)), \quad (3.132)$$

where $m : \Re_{++}^2 \to \Re_{++}$ is such that $m(\lambda a, \lambda b) = \lambda m(a, b)$ $(\lambda > 0)$, if and only if $P(p^1, x^1, p^0, x^0) = P^F(p^1, x^1, p^0, x^0)$.

Proof: (Diewert 1997) By substituting the various definitions into the time reversal test we conclude that $m(.)$ must satisfy

$$
\begin{aligned}
1 &= m(a, b)m(b^{-1}, a^{-1}) \\
&= am(1, b/a)a^{-1}m(a/b, 1) \\
&= m(1, b/a)(a/b)m(1, b/a),
\end{aligned}
$$

which implies that $m(1, b/a) = (b/a)^{1/2}$. Then $m(a, b) = am(1, b/a) = (ab)^{1/2}$, by which we are finished since the reverse direction of the proof is trivial. QED

3.6.2 The Cobb-Douglas Indices

The following characterization was obtained by Funke, Hacker, and Voeller (1979) and concerns the so-called Cobb-Douglas (1928) price index.

Theorem 3.12 *A function $P(.)$ satisfies the axioms* **A1, A2, A3, A5** *and the circularity test* **T1** *if and only if $P(p^1, x^1, p^0, x^0) = \prod_{n=1}^{N}(p_n^1/p_n^0)^{\alpha_n}$ with $\alpha_n > 0$ $(n = 1, \dots, N)$ and $\sum_{n=1}^{N} \alpha_n = 1$.*

Proof: (This proof replaces the original one by Funke, Hacker, and Voeller 1979) Rewriting **T1** we have

$$P(p^2, x^2, p^1, x^1) = P(p^2, x^2, p^0, x^0)/P(p^1, x^1, p^0, x^0). \quad (3.133)$$

For an arbitrary but fixed value of (p^0, x^0) one defines $P(p, x, p^0, x^0) \equiv g(p, x)$. Thus we can write

$$P(p^2, x^2, p^1, x^1) = g(p^2, x^2)/g(p^1, x^1). \quad (3.134)$$

Applying **A3** to this equation we find

$$g(p^1, x^2) = g(p^1, x^1) \quad (3.135)$$

for all x^1, $x^2 \in \Re_{++}^N$. Thus $g(p, x)$ does not depend on x, and we can write $g(p, x) = g(p)$. Applying **A5** to expression (3.134) we obtain

$$g(p^2 \Lambda)/g(p^1 \Lambda) = g(p^2)/g(p^1) \qquad (3.136)$$

for all diagonal matrices Λ with elements of $\Re_{++}$. In particular

$$g(p^2/p^1)/g(1_N) = g(p^2)/g(p^1) \qquad (3.137)$$

where $p^2/p^1 \equiv (p_1^2/p_1^1, \ldots, p_N^2/p_N^1)$ and $1_N \equiv (1, \ldots, 1)$. We conclude from expression (3.137) that the function $h(p) \equiv g(p)/g(1_N)$ is multiplicative. By **A1**, $h(p)$ must be strictly increasing. Using a result of Aczél (1966) on multiplicative functions,[20] we obtain

$$h(p) = \prod_{n=1}^{N} p_n^{\alpha_n} \qquad (3.138)$$

with all $\alpha_n > 0$. Axiom **A2** then implies that $\sum_{n=1}^{N} \alpha_n = 1$. The other direction of the proof is trivial.   QED

Remark: The Cobb-Douglas price index also satisfies axiom **A4**. In general it can be shown that the linear homogeneity axiom **A2** and the circularity test **T1** imply the homogeneity-of-degree-0 axiom **A4**.

Proof: (Funke, Hacker, and Voeller 1979) From **T1**

$$
\begin{aligned}
P(p^2, x^2, p^0, x^0) &= P(p^2, x^2, \lambda p^1, x^1) P(\lambda p^1, x^1, p^0, x^0) \ (\lambda > 0) \\
&= \lambda P(p^2, x^2, \lambda p^1, x^1) P(p^1, x^1, p^0, x^0) \ [\text{by } \mathbf{A2}] \\
&= P(\lambda p^2, x^2, \lambda p^1, x^1) P(p^1, x^1, p^0, x^0) \ [\text{by } \mathbf{A2}].
\end{aligned}
$$

But also by **T1**

$$P(p^2, x^2, p^0, x^0) = P(p^2, x^2, p^1, x^1) P(p^1, x^1, p^0, x^0). \qquad (3.139)$$

Hence

$$P(\lambda p^2, x^2, \lambda p^1, x^1) = P(p^2, x^2, p^1, x^1), \qquad (3.140)$$

which means that $P(.)$ satisfies **A4**.   QED

Thus Theorem 3.12 tells us that a function $P(.)$ that satisfies our five axioms **A1**, ..., **A5**, and in addition satisfies the circularity test, is necessarily of the Cobb-Douglas form. Notice that this form only contains the price variables.

---

[20] See also Aczél (1990).

From the proof of Theorem 3.12 it is clear that we can replace axiom **A5** by the condition

$$P(p^0 \Lambda, x^1, p^0, x^0) = P(p^1 \Lambda, x^1, p^1, x^0) \qquad (3.141)$$

for any diagonal matrix Λ with elements of $\Re_{++}$. Moreover, the linear homogeneity axiom **A2** and the identity axiom **A3** can be replaced by the proportionality axiom **A6**. The independence of the monotonicity axiom **A1**, the proportionality axiom **A6**, condition (3.141), and the circularity test **T1** was proved by Eichhorn and Voeller (1983). It is easy to see that condition (3.141) implies that the price index, in addition to the comparison period and base period quantities, depends only on the N price relatives p_n^1/p_n^0.

Notice that the Geometric Laspeyres, Geometric Paasche, Törnqvist, and Sato-Vartia price indices can be considered as special cases of the Cobb-Douglas price index.

3.6.3 The Stuvel Indices

The next characterization concerns the generalized Stuvel indices. These indices can be derived in various ways, as appears from publications by Stuvel (1957), Banerjee (1959), Stuvel (1989), and Balk (1996b). The simplest approach is to return to Theorem 3.4 and consider the additive counterpart to functional equation (3.103):

$$a[P(p^1, x^1, p^0, x^0) - P^L(p^1, x^1, p^0, x^0)]$$
$$= b[Q(p^1, x^1, p^0, x^0) - Q^L(p^1, x^1, p^0, x^0)] \qquad (3.142)$$

where a and b are positive scalars. Now, suppppose that $P(.)$ and $Q(.)$ satisfy the product test **T3**. Then $Q(p^1, x^1, p^0, x^0) = p^1 \cdot x^1 / p^0 \cdot x^0 P(p^1, x^1, p^0, x^0)$. By substituting this into equation (3.142) we obtain

$$a P(.) - a P^L(.) + b Q^L(.) - b \frac{p^1 \cdot x^1 / p^0 \cdot x^0}{P(.)} = 0, \qquad (3.143)$$

or

$$a[P(.)]^2 - [a P^L(.) - b Q^L(.)] P(.) - b \frac{p^1 \cdot x^1}{p^0 \cdot x^0} = 0. \qquad (3.144)$$

By taking the positive root of this quadratic equation, we obtain

$$P(.) = P^{S(a,b)}(.) \equiv (P^L(.) - (b/a)Q^L(.))/2 + [(P^L(.) - (b/a)Q^L(.))^2/4$$
$$+ (b/a)p^1 \cdot x^1 / p^0 \cdot x^0]^{1/2}. \qquad (3.145)$$

In the same way, by substituting $P(.) = p^1 \cdot x^1/p^0 \cdot x^0 Q(.)$ into equation (3.142) and solving the resulting quadratic equation, we obtain

$$Q(.) = Q^{S(a,b)}(.) \equiv (Q^L(.) - (a/b)P^L(.))/2 + [(Q^L(.) - (a/b)P^L(.))^2/4$$
$$+ (a/b)p^1 \cdot x^1/p^0 \cdot x^0]^{1/2}. \qquad (3.146)$$

The functions $P^{S(a,b)}(.)$ and $Q^{S(a,b)}(.)$ are called generalized Stuvel indices. They are functions of the Laspeyres price index $P^L(p^1, x^1, p^0, x^0) \equiv p^1 \cdot x^0/p^0 \cdot x^0$, the Laspeyres quantity index $Q^L(p^1, x^1, p^0, x^0) \equiv p^0 \cdot x^1/p^0 \cdot x^0$, and the value ratio $p^1 \cdot x^1/p^0 \cdot x^0$. For $a = b$, $P^{S(a,b)}(.)$ and $Q^{S(a,b)}(.)$ reduce to the original indices of Stuvel (1957).[21]

The reader is invited to check that the generalized Stuvel price and quantity indices satisfy the axioms **A1**, **A4–A6** and **A1′**, **A4′–A6′**, respectively, but fail **A2** and **A2′**. Moreover, notice that $P^{S(a,a)}(.)$ and $Q^{S(a,a)}(.)$ are ideal indices. A numerical comparison with the other three pairs of ideal indices, those of Fisher, Sato-Vartia, and Montgomery-Vartia, was made in Tables 3.12 and 3.13. We return to the Stuvel indices in section 3.7, where we will see that they play a remarkable role.

For future reference, the foregoing is summarized as follows:

Theorem 3.13 *The functions $P(.)$, $Q(.)$ satisfy the product test* **T3** *and the functional equation*

$$a[P(p^1, x^1, p^0, x^0) - P^L(p^1, x^1, p^0, x^0)]$$
$$= b[Q(p^1, x^1, p^0, x^0) - Q^L(p^1, x^1, p^0, x^0)] \ (a, b > 0) \quad (3.147)$$

if and only if $P(p^1, x^1, p^0, x^0) = P^{S(a,b)}(p^1, x^1, p^0, x^0)$ *and* $Q(p^1, x^1, p^0, x^0) = Q^{S(a,b)}(p^1, x^1, p^0, x^0)$.

This theorem can be extended with the cases $a = 0$, $b > 0$ and $a > 0$, $b = 0$. In the first case we find $Q(p^1, x^1, p^0, x^0) = Q^L(p^1, x^1, p^0, x^0) = p^0 \cdot x^1/p^0 \cdot x^0 \equiv Q^{S(0,b)}(p^1, x^1, p^0, x^0)$. Then, by **T3**, $P(p^1, x^1, p^0, x^0) = p^1 \cdot x^1/p^0 \cdot x^1 \equiv P^P(p^1, x^1, p^0, x^0)$, which is the Paasche price index. Thus we define $P^{S(0,b)}(p^1, x^1, p^0, x^0) \equiv p^1 \cdot x^1/p^0 \cdot x^1$. Similarly, in the second case we find $P(p^1, x^1, p^0, x^0) = P^L(p^1, x^1, p^0, x^0) = p^1 \cdot x^0/p^0 \cdot x^0 \equiv P^{S(a,0)}(p^1, x^1, p^0, x^0)$. Then, by **T3**, $Q(p^1, x^1, p^0, x^0) = p^1 \cdot x^1/p^1 \cdot x^0 \equiv Q^P(p^1, x^1, p^0, x^0)$, which is the Paasche quantity index. Thus we define $Q^{S(a,0)}(p^1, x^1, p^0, x^0) \equiv p^1 \cdot x^1/p^1 \cdot x^0$.

---

[21] These indices also materialize as a special case in the "factorial approach"; see Banerjee (1980).

For $a = b$, Theorem 3.13 was proved by Van IJzeren (1958) and independently by Vogt (1981).

3.6.4 Linear Indices

Funke (1988) considered the class of linear price indices, that is, functions of the form

$$P^{LIN}(p^1, x^1, p^0, x^0) \equiv \frac{p^1 \cdot \bar{x}}{p^0 \cdot \bar{x}} \tag{3.148}$$

where $\bar{x}_n \equiv m_n(x^0, x^1)$ and $m_n : \mathfrak{R}^{2N}_{++} \to \mathfrak{R}_{++}$ ($n = 1, \ldots, N$). Thus each component of the quantity vector $\bar{x}$ is supposed to be a (possibly different) function of the vectors of base period and comparison period quantities. For this class of price indices Funke obtained the following characterization.

Theorem 3.14 A function $P(.)$ satisfies the identity axiom **A3** and the functional equations

$$P(p^1 + p^2, x^1, p^0, x^0) = P(p^1, x^1, p^0, x^0) + P(p^2, x^1, p^0, x^0) \tag{3.149}$$

$$1/P(p^1, x^1, p^0 + p^2, x^0) = 1/P(p^1, x^1, p^0, x^0) + 1/P(p^1, x^1, p^2, x^0) \tag{3.150}$$

if and only if $P(p^1, x^1, p^0, x^0) = P^{LIN}(p^1, x^1, p^0, x^0)$.

Proof: Consider $P(p^1, x^1, p^0, x^0)$ as a function of p^1 and p^0 and apply the results of Aczél and Eichhorn (1974a, 1974b; see Eichhorn and Voeller 1976, pp. 17–21).   QED

Condition (3.149) means that $P(.)$ is additive in comparison period prices, and condition (3.150) means that $P(.)$ is "harmonic additive" in base period prices. It is easy to see that $P^{LIN}(p^1, x^1, p^0, x^0)$ satisfies **A1**, **A2**, **A3**, and **A4**, but not necessarily **A5**. Additional results on linear price indices can be found in Funke (1988).

An important subclass of the class of linear price indices is obtained when we specify $\bar{x}_n \equiv m(x^0_n, x^1_n)$ ($n = 1, \ldots, N$) where $m : \mathfrak{R}^2_{++} \to \mathfrak{R}_{++}$. Thus each component of the quantity vector $\bar{x}$ is now supposed to be the same function of the corresponding base period and comparison period quantities. When we further specify the function $m(.)$ to be the arithmetic mean, that is $m(a, b) = (a + b)/2$, we get the Marshall-Edgeworth price index.

This index was defined by expression (3.19). In the literature the following characterization can be found.

Theorem 3.15 *A function $P(.)$ satisfies the linear homogeneity axiom* **A2**, *the homogeneity-of-degree-0 axiom* **A4**, *the value dependence test* **T5** *(where the function $f(.)$ is assumed to be continuously differentiable) and the following conditions:*

(i) $P(p^0\Pi, x^0\Pi, p^0, x^0) = 1$ for any permutation matrix Π;
(ii) if $P(p^1, x^1, p^0, x^0) = p_n^1/p_n^0$ for a certain commodity n, then

$$P(p^1, x_1^1, \ldots, x_{n-1}^1, t^1 x_n^1, x_{n+1}^1, \ldots, x_N^1, p^0, x_1^0, \ldots, x_{n-1}^0,$$
$$t^0 x_n^0, x_{n+1}^0, \ldots, x_N^0) = p_n^1/p_n^0 \text{ for all } t^1, t^0 > 1;$$

if and only if $P(p^1, x^1, p^0, x^0) = P^{ME}(p^1, x^1, p^0, x^0)$.

Condition (i), which is also called the permutation test, means that if the comparison period prices and quantities are a permutation of the base period prices and quantities, then the price index should deliver the value 1. Condition (ii) means that if the price index happens to be equal to a particular price relative p_n^1/p_n^0, then the price index remains equal to this price relative if we let the corresponding quantities x_n^0 and x_n^1 tend to infinity. The reader is referred to Krtscha (1979, pp. 104–9) or Krtscha (1984) for the very complicated proof. Krtscha (1979) contains another characterization of $P^{ME}(p^1, x^1, p^0, x^0)$, but also with a very long and complicated proof. For more results related to the permutation test the reader is referred to von Auer (2002a).

When the function $m(.)$ is specified as the geometric mean, that is, $m(a, b) = (ab)^{1/2}$, we get the Walsh-1 price index (3.21). Diewert (2001) obtained the following characterization for this index.

Theorem 3.16 *A function $P^{LIN}(.)$ with $\bar{x}_n \equiv m(x_n^0, x_n^1)$ $(n = 1, \ldots, N)$, where $m : \mathfrak{R}_{++}^2 \to \mathfrak{R}_{++}$ is a continuous function such that $m(a, a) = a$, satisfies the time reversal test* **T2** *and is invariant to proportional changes of the comparison period quantities, i.e. satisfies functional equation (3.70), if and only if* $P^{LIN}(p^1, x^1, p^0, x^0) = P^{W1}(p^1, x^1, p^0, x^0)$.

Proof: (Diewert 2001) For this proof the domain of definition of $P^{LIN}(.)$ must be extended to $p, p' \in \mathfrak{R}_+^N$. In the first place we notice that the time reversal test implies that the function $m(.)$ must be symmetric, that is

$m(a, b) = m(b, a)$. Secondly, inserting the definition of $P^{LIN}(.)$ into the functional equation (3.70), we obtain

$$\frac{\sum_{n=1}^{N} p_n^1 m(x_n^0, \lambda x_n^1)}{\sum_{n=1}^{N} p_n^0 m(x_n^0, \lambda x_n^1)} = \frac{\sum_{n=1}^{N} p_n^1 m(x_n^0, x_n^1)}{\sum_{n=1}^{N} p_n^0 m(x_n^0, x_n^1)} \quad (\lambda > 0). \quad (3.151)$$

For $p^1 = (1, 0, \ldots, 0)$ and $p^0 = (0, 1, 0, \ldots, 0)$ expression (3.151) reduces to

$$\frac{m(x_1^0, \lambda x_1^1)}{m(x_2^0, \lambda x_2^1)} = \frac{m(x_1^0, x_1^1)}{m(x_2^0, x_2^1)} \quad (\lambda > 0), \quad (3.152)$$

or

$$\frac{m(x_1^0, \lambda x_1^1)}{m(x_1^0, x_1^1)} = \frac{m(x_2^0, \lambda x_2^1)}{m(x_2^0, x_2^1)} \quad (\lambda > 0). \quad (3.153)$$

Since this equation must hold for all $x_1^0, x_2^0, x_1^1, x_2^1$, the function $m(.)$ must be such that

$$\frac{m(a, \lambda b)}{m(a, b)} = f(\lambda) \ (a, b, \lambda > 0) \quad (3.154)$$

for a certain function $f(.)$. Since $m(1, 1) = 1$, it follows that $m(1, \lambda) = f(\lambda)$. Then

$$\begin{aligned} f(\lambda b) &= m(1, \lambda b) \\ &= f(\lambda)m(1, b) \\ &= f(\lambda)f(b), \end{aligned} \quad (3.155)$$

which means that $f(.)$ is a (continuous) multiplicative function. Expression (3.155) is one of Cauchy's functional equations (see Aczél 1966), the solution being $f(\lambda) = \lambda^c$ for some $c \neq 0$. Then

$$\begin{aligned} m(a, b) &= f(b)m(a, 1) \\ &= f(b)m(1, a) \text{ by symmetry} \\ &= f(b)f(a) \\ &= (ab)^c. \end{aligned} \quad (3.156)$$

Since $m(a, a) = a^{2c} = a$, we see that $c = 1/2$. The reverse direction of the proof is trivial.   QED

3.6.5 The Törnqvist Indices

Let us finally consider the class of aggregated price relatives defined by

$$P^{AGG}(p^1, x^1, p^0, x^0) \equiv \prod_{n=1}^{N}(p_n^1/p_n^0)^{m_n(s_n^0, s_n^1)}, \qquad (3.157)$$

where the functions $m_n : [0, 1] \times [0, 1] \to \mathfrak{R}_+$ are such that $m(0, 0) = 0$ ($n = 1, \dots, N$). Thus, $P^{AGG}(.)$ is a weighted product of the individual price relatives, whereby each weight is a (possibly different) function of the base period and comparison period value shares of the corresponding commodity. For $m_n(a, b) \equiv (a + b)/2$ ($n = 1, \dots, N$) we obtain the Törnqvist price index (3.53). This index can be characterized as follows.

Theorem 3.17 *A function* $P^{AGG}(.)$ *satisfies the linear homogeneity axiom* **A2** *and the time reversal test* **T2** *if and only if* $P^{AGG}(p^1, x^1, p^0, x^0) = P^T(p^1, x^1, p^0, x^0)$.

Proof: (Balk and Diewert 2001) Recall that by definition $\sum_{n=1}^{N} s_n^t = 1$ ($t = 0, 1$). The requirement of linear homogeneity implies that $\sum_{n=1}^{N} m_n(s_n^0, s_n^1) = 1$. The general solution of this system of functional equations appears to be

$$m_n(a, b) = \alpha_0 a + \alpha_1 b, \quad \alpha_0 + \alpha_1 = 1, \quad \alpha_0, \alpha_1 \geq 0; \qquad (3.158)$$

that is, the functions $m_n(.)$ are identical linear functions with positive coefficients adding up to 1 (see Aczél 1987, Chapter 1, Theorem 2). The time reversal test obviously implies that the functions $m_n(.)$ must be symmetric, which in this case implies that $\alpha_0 = \alpha_1 = 1/2$. The reverse direction of the proof is trivial.   QED

3.7 Consistency-in-Aggregation and Additivity

3.7.1 Two-Stage Indices

Given price and quantity data for base and comparison period, a price index $P(.)$ or quantity index $Q(.)$ enables us to compute a price index number or quantity index number for an aggregate, in one step. Now the aggregates considered in official statistics usually consist of hundreds or thousands of commodities. It is therefore operationally efficient to divide such an aggregate into subaggregates and to use this structure for a stepwise calculation.

For example, the aggregate that forms the scope of a Consumer Price Index usually consists of a number of subaggregates (commodity groups) such as "food and alcohol-free beverages," "clothing and footwear," and "housing." In turn each of such subaggregates is built up from subsubaggregates, for example "food and alcohol-free beverages" from "food" and "alcohol-free beverages." Again, "food" consists of a large number of commodity groups such as "bread" and "fruit."

In productivity measurement, the commodities at the input side of an industry are frequently grouped together into subaggregates called capital (K), labour (L), energy (E), materials (M), and services (S). And each of these groups in turn consists of a number of subgroups.

Such structures can easily contain four or five levels. At the lowest level of the hierarchy we are then dealing with subaggregates consisting of individual commodities. Also, in addition to the structure given in official publications one could consider different decompositions of an aggregate. For example, one could want to partition "household consumption" into the subaggregates "energy" and "other commodities."

In all such situations an important requirement is that price and quantity indices be consistent-in-aggregation.[22] What does this mean?

Let us call the aggregate under consideration A, and let A be partitioned arbitrarily into K subaggregates A_k,

$$A = \cup_{k=1}^{K} A_k, \quad A_k \cap A_l = \emptyset \ (k \neq l). \tag{3.159}$$

Each subaggregate consists of a number of commodities. Let $N_k \geq 1$ denote the number of commodities contained in A_k ($k = 1, \ldots, K$). Obviously $N = \sum_{k=1}^{K} N_k$. Let $(p_k^1, x_k^1, p_k^0, x_k^0)$ be the subvector of (p^1, x^1, p^0, x^0) corresponding to the subaggregate A_k. Recall that $v_n^t \equiv p_n^t x_n^t$ is the value of commodity n at period t. Then $V_k^t \equiv \sum_{n \in A_k} v_n^t$ ($k = 1, \ldots, K$) is the value of subaggregate A_k at period t, and $V^t \equiv \sum_{n \in A} v_n^t = \sum_{k=1}^{K} V_k^t$ is the value of aggregate A at period t.

Consider a price index for the aggregate A, $P_N(p, x, p', x')$, where the subscript N is added to the function symbol to show explicitly the dimension of the price and quantity vectors involved. If the dimension N is reduced to N_k, $P_{N_k}(p, x, p', x')$ is a price index for the subaggregate A_k ($k = 1, \ldots, K$) which has the same functional form as $P_N(p, x, p', x')$. Similarly, $Q_{N_k}(p, x, p', x')$ and $Q_N(p, x, p', x')$ share the same functional form.

---

[22] See for instance Al, Balk, de Boer, and den Bakker (1986).

It is assumed that the dimensional invariance axioms **A5** and **A5'** are satisfied. As shown in section 3.2, this is equivalent to assuming that the price index $P_N(p, x, p', x')$ is a function of price relatives p_n/p'_n and commodity values $v'_n = p'_n x'_n$ and $v_n = p_n x_n$ ($n = 1, \ldots, N$), and the quantity index $Q_N(p, x, p', x')$ is a function of quantity relatives x_n/x'_n and commodity values v'_n and v_n ($n = 1, \ldots, N$). Then, in particular, $P_1(p, x, p', x')$ is a function of p/p', v' and v; and $Q_1(p, x, p', x')$ is a function of x/x', v' and v. Now it is also assumed that $P_1(p, x, p', x') = p/p'$ and $Q_1(p, x, p', x') = x/x'$. Put otherwise, for single-commodity aggregates the indices reduce to price or quantity relatives.

The structure given by (3.159) then leads naturally to the definition of two-stage indices. Let $P_K(.)$, $P_{N_1}(.)$, $\ldots$, $P_{N_K}(.)$ be price indices of dimension K, $N_1, \ldots, N_K$ respectively, not necessarily of the same functional form, that satisfy the axioms **A1**, ..., **A5**. Then the price index defined by

$$P_N^*(p^1, y^1, p^0, y^0) \equiv P_K(P_{N_k}(p_k^1, y_k^1, p_k^0, y_k^0), V_k^0, V_k^1; k = 1, \ldots, K)$$

$$(3.160)$$

is of dimension N and also satisfies the axioms **A1**, ..., **A5**. The index $P_N^*(.)$ is called a two-stage index. The first stage refers to the indices $P_{N_k}(.)$ for the subaggregates A_k ($k = 1, \ldots, K$). The second stage refers to the index $P_K(.)$ which is applied to the subaggregate indices $P_{N_k}(.)$ ($k = 1, \ldots, K$). A two-stage index such as defined by expression (3.160) closely corresponds to the calculation practice at statistical agencies. All the subaggregate indices are then usually of the same functional form, say Laspeyres or Paasche indices. The aggregate, second-stage index may or may not be of the same functional form. This could be, for instance, a Fisher index. If the functional forms of the subaggregate indices $P_{N_k}(.)$ ($k = 1, \ldots, K$) and the aggregate index $P_K(.)$ are the same, then $P_N^*(.)$ is called a two-stage $P_N(.)$-index.

By way of example we consider the Laspeyres price index, defined by expression (3.3). As shown in expression (3.4), the index for the aggregate can also be written as a function of price relatives and (base period) commodity values,

$$P_N^L(p^1, x^1, p^0, x^0) = \sum_{n=1}^{N} v_n^0(p_n^1/p_n^0) / \sum_{n=1}^{N} v_n^0.$$

$$(3.161)$$

The two-stage Laspeyres price index then reads

$$P_N^{*L}(p^1, y^1, p^0, y^0) \equiv \sum_{k=1}^{K} V_k^0 P_{N_k}^L(p_k^1, y_k^1, p_k^0, y_k^0) / \sum_{k=1}^{K} V_k^0, \quad (3.162)$$

Table 3.14. *Single- and Two-Stage Price Index Numbers*

Period t	F	*F	T	*T
1	1.0000	1.0000	1.0000	1.0000
2	1.4011	1.4004	1.4052	1.4052
3	1.2721	1.2789	1.2890	1.2872
4	1.1762	1.2019	1.2268	1.2243
5	1.0712	1.1286	1.2477	1.2441

which is a Laspeyres index of Laspeyres subaggregate indices $P_{N_k}^L(p_k^1, y_k^1, p_k^0, y_k^0)$ ($k = 1, \ldots, K$), and one simply checks that the two-stage Laspeyres index in expression (3.162) coincides with the single-stage Laspeyres index in expression (3.161). Similarly, the single-stage Paasche price index for the aggregate, defined by expression (3.7) or (3.9), can be written as a function of price relatives and (comparison period) commodity values,

$$P_N^P(p^1, x^1, p^0, x^0) = \left(\sum_{n=1}^{N} v_n^1 (p_n^1/p_n^0)^{-1} / \sum_{n=1}^{N} v_n^1\right)^{-1}, \quad (3.163)$$

whereas the two-stage Paasche price index reads

$$P_N^{*P}(p^1, x^1, p^0, x^0) \equiv \left(\sum_{k=1}^{K} V_k^1 (P_{N_k}^P(p_k^1, y_k^1, p_k^0, y_k^0))^{-1} / \sum_{k=1}^{K} V_k^1\right)^{-1}. \quad (3.164)$$

Again, it is straightforward to check that the two price indices coincide, that is, $P_N^{*P}(p^1, x^1, p^0, x^0) = P_N^P(p^1, x^1, p^0, x^0)$. However, the identity of Laspeyres and Paasche single-stage and two-stage indices is the exception rather than the rule. For most indices, single-stage and two-stage variants do not coincide. Put otherwise, most price indices are not consistent-in-aggregation.

To illustrate the difference between single-stage and two-stage price indices we return to our numerical example. We divide the six commodities into two subaggregates: the first is "goods," consisting of commodities 1–4, and the second is "services," consisting of commodities 5 and 6. Table 3.14 contains some outcomes. The columns headed F and T contain the single-stage Fisher and Törnqvist price index numbers, defined by expressions (3.27) and (3.53), respectively, and thus repeat the corresponding columns of Table 3.6. The two-stage Fisher price index is defined by

$$P_N^{*F}(p^1, x^1, p^0, x^0) \equiv \left(\frac{\sum_{k=1}^K V_k^0 P_{N_k}^F(p_k^1, y_k^1, p_k^0, y_k^0) / \sum_{k=1}^K V_k^0}{\sum_{k=1}^K V_k^1 (P_{N_k}^F(p_k^1, y_k^1, p_k^0, y_k^0))^{-1} / \sum_{k=1}^K V_k^1} \right)^{1/2},$$

$$(3.165)$$

and the two-stage Törnqvist price index is defined by

$$P_N^{*T}(p^1, x^1, p^0, x^0) \equiv \prod_{k=1}^K \left(P_{N_k}^T(p_k^1, y_k^1, p_k^0, y_k^0) \right)^{(V_k^0 / \sum_{k=1}^K V_k^0 + V_k^1 / \sum_{k=1}^K V_k^1)/2}.$$

$$(3.166)$$

The two-stage Fisher and Törnqvist price index numbers are in columns
*F and *T, respectively. As one sees, the difference between the Fisher index
numbers appears to be larger than the difference between the Törnqvist
index numbers.

Before proceeding to the formal definition of consistency-in-aggregation we must also define two-stage quantity indices. Thus, let $Q_K(.)$,
$Q_{N_1}(.), \ldots, Q_{N_K}(.)$ be quantity indices of dimension $K, N_1, \ldots, N_K$, respectively, that satisfy the axioms **A1′, . . . , A5′**. Then the quantity index
defined by

$$Q_N^*(p^1, y^1, p^0, y^0) \equiv Q_K(Q_{N_k}(p_k^1, y_k^1, p_k^0, y_k^0), V_k^0, V_k^1; k = 1, \ldots, K)$$

$$(3.167)$$

is of dimension N and also satisfies the axioms **A1′, . . . , A5′**. The index
$Q_N^*(.)$ is called a two-stage index. If the functional forms of the subaggregate
indices $Q_{N_k}(.)$ $(k = 1, \ldots, K)$ and the aggregate index $Q_K(.)$ are the same,
then $Q_N^*(.)$ is called a two-stage $Q_N(.)$-index.

3.7.2 Two Tests

As may be clear from the Laspeyres and Paasche examples, consistency-in-
aggregation means that there must exist a certain relation between the price
(quantity) index number for the aggregate and the price (quantity) index
numbers for the subaggregates. This relation can be described in words as
follows[23]:

   (i) the index number for the aggregate, which is defined as the outcome
       of a single-stage index, can also be computed in two stages, namely

---

[23] Von Auer (2002b) calls this strict consistency.

by first computing the index numbers for the subaggregates and
from these the index number for the aggregate;

(ii) the indices used in the single-stage computation and those used in
the first-stage computation have the same functional form (except
for the dimension of the variables);

(iii) the formula used in the second-stage computation has the same
functional form (except possibly for the dimension of the variables)
as the indices used in the single and in the first stage after the following transformation has been applied: commodity price or quantity
relatives are replaced by subaggregate indices and commodity values
are replaced by subaggregate values.

Extending the work of previous authors, Balk (1995 and 1996b) proposed
to formalize this as follows:

T6. Consistency-in-aggregation test. For any partition (3.159) of an aggregate A the following relation holds between aggregate and subaggregate
price indices:

$$\psi(P_N(p^1, x^1, p^0, x^0), V^0, V^1) = \sum_{k=1}^{K} \psi(P_{N_k}(p_k^1, x_k^1, p_k^0, x_k^0), V_k^0, V_k^1)$$

(3.168)

where $\psi : \mathfrak{R}_{++}^3 \rightarrow R_{++}$ is continuous and strictly monotonic in its first
argument.

T6'. Consistency-in-aggregation test. For any partition (3.159) of an aggregate A the following relation holds between aggregate and subaggregate
quantity indices:

$$\zeta(Q_N(p^1, x^1, p^0, x^0), V^0, V^1) = \sum_{k=1}^{K} \zeta(Q_{N_k}(p_k^1, x_k^1, p_k^0, x_k^0), V_k^0, V_k^1)$$

(3.169)

where $\zeta : \mathfrak{R}_{++}^3 \rightarrow R_{++}$ is continuous and strictly monotonic in its first
argument.

The monotonicity condition implies that a unique solution for $P_N(.)$ and
$Q_N(.)$ exists. A price (quantity) index is called *consistent-in-aggregation* if
the index satisfies **T6** (**T6'**).

Remark: For price and quantity indices which satisfy the product test **T3**
the tests **T6** and **T6'** are equivalent. This is simple to verify. Suppose that **T6**

holds. The product test **T3** tells us that $P_N(p^1, x^1, p^0, x^0) = p^1 \cdot x^1 / p^0 \cdot x^0 Q_N(p^1, x^1, p^0, x^0)$. Substituting this into **T6** delivers

$$\psi\left(\frac{p^1 \cdot x^1 / p^0 \cdot x^0}{Q_N(p^1, x^1, p^0, x^0)}, V^0, V^1\right) = \sum_{k=1}^{K} \psi\left(\frac{p_k^1 \cdot x_k^1 / p_k^0 \cdot x_k^0}{Q_{N_k}(p_k^1, x_k^1, p_k^0, x_k^0)}, V_k^0, V_k^1\right).$$

(3.170)

By setting $\zeta(\alpha, \beta, \gamma) \equiv \psi(\gamma/\beta\alpha, \beta, \gamma)$, this equation reduces to **T6′**. A similar substitution leads from **T6′** to **T6**.

The concept of consistency-in-aggregation, that is, conditions (i)–(iii), was developed by Vartia (1974, 1976). A more formal definition was proposed by Blackorby and Primont (1980). However, they overlooked the important requirement (iii). If this requirement is satisfied, one can compute the index number for the aggregate from the index numbers for the subaggregates, using only the base period and comparison period values *of these subaggregates* (as emphasized by Stuvel 1989, p. 36). In section 3.10 more light will be shed on the somewhat peculiar form of expressions (3.168) and (3.169).

To get some feeling for the consistency-in-aggregation tests let us turn to a number of examples. As we have seen, the two-stage Laspeyres price index is identical to the single-stage index. Thus, by rearranging expression (3.162) somewhat, we obtain

$$V^0 P_N^L(p^1, y^1, p^0, y^0) = \sum_{k=1}^{K} V_k^0 P_{N_k}^L(p_k^1, y_k^1, p_k^0, y_k^0), \quad (3.171)$$

which is a special case of expression (3.168), namely with $\psi(\alpha, \beta, \gamma) = \alpha\beta$. Similarly, by rearranging expression (3.164), we obtain for the Paasche price index

$$V^1(P_N^P(p^1, x^1, p^0, x^0))^{-1} = \sum_{k=1}^{K} V_k^1(P_{N_k}^P(p_k^1, y_k^1, p_k^0, y_k^0))^{-1}, \quad (3.172)$$

which is also a special case of expression (3.168), but with $\psi(\alpha, \beta, \gamma) = \gamma/\alpha$. The reader may check, however, that the Fisher price index cannot be written in the form of expression (3.168).

Another example of a price index that is not consistent-in-aggregation is the Walsh-2 price index, defined as

$$\ln P^{W2}(p^1, x^1, p^0, x^0) \equiv \frac{\sum_{n=1}^{N}(v_n^0 v_n^1)^{1/2} \ln(p_n^1/p_n^0)}{\sum_{n=1}^{N}(v_n^0 v_n^1)^{1/2}}. \quad (3.173)$$

Indeed, by rewriting this expression we obtain

$$\left(\sum_{k=1}^{K}\sum_{n\in A_k}(v_n^0 v_n^1)^{1/2}\right)\ln P_N^{W2}(p^1, x^1, p^0, x^0)$$

$$=\sum_{k=1}^{K}\sum_{n\in A_k}(v_n^0 v_n^1)^{1/2}\ln(p_n^1/p_n^0)$$

$$=\sum_{k=1}^{K}\left(\sum_{n\in A_k}(v_n^0 v_n^1)^{1/2}\right)\ln P_{N_k}^{W2}(p_k^1, x_k^1, p_k^0, x_k^0). \qquad (3.174)$$

It is easy to see that the requirements (i) and (ii) are satisfied. However, requirement (iii) will in general be violated, because $\sum_{n\in A_k}(v_n^0 v_n^1)^{1/2} \neq (V_k^0 V_k^1)^{1/2}$ ($k = 1, \ldots, K$). The aggregate index number cannot be calculated from the subaggregate index numbers by using only subaggregate values. One still needs the individual commodity values.[24]

Let us finally consider the Montgomery-Vartia price index. It is straightforward to check that this index does satisfy the consistency-in-aggregation test **T6**, because by rewriting its definition (3.86) one obtains

$$L(V^0, V^1)\ln P_N^{MV}(p^1, x^1, p^0, x^0)$$

$$=\sum_{k=1}^{K}\sum_{n\in A_k}L(v_n^0, v_n^1)\ln(p_n^1/p_n^0)$$

$$=\sum_{k=1}^{K}L(V_k^0, V_k^1)\ln P_{N_k}^{MV}(p_k^1, x_k^1, p_k^0, x_k^0). \qquad (3.175)$$

We see that in the second-stage computation knowledge of the subaggregate values is sufficient to compute the aggregate index number. Notice that for the Montgomery-Vartia price index the function $\psi(.)$ takes the form $\psi(\alpha, \beta, \gamma) \equiv L(\beta, \gamma)\ln\alpha$.

When an aggregate consists of subaggregates a second requirement, relating aggregate and subaggregate index numbers, is of great importance.

T7. Equality test. If $P_{N_k}(p_k^1, x_k^1, p_k^0, x_k^0) = \lambda$ for all $k = 1, \ldots, K$, then $P_N(p^1, x^1, p^0, x^0) = \lambda$.

T7'. Equality test. If $Q_{N_k}(p_k^1, x_k^1, p_k^0, x_k^0) = \lambda$ for all $k = 1, \ldots, K$, then $Q_N(p^1, x^1, p^0, x^0) = \lambda$.

---

[24] In a similar way it can be shown that the Törnqvist price index (3.53) is not consistent-in-aggregation.

These tests are due to Stuvel (1989) but had already been suggested by Van IJzeren (1958). Notice that the proportionality axiom **A6** (**A6′**) is a consequence of **T7** (**T7′**), namely for the particular case of subaggregates consisting of single commodities. The reverse, however, does not hold. For instance, the Fisher price index satisfies axiom **A6** but does not satisfy **T7**, as was pointed out by Stuvel (1989, p. 39). A simple demonstration is based on the difference between single- and two-stage Fisher price indices. Using the consistency-in-aggregation property of the Laspeyres and Paasche indices, the single-stage Fisher price index for an aggregate can be written as

$$
P_N^F(p^1, x^1, p^0, x^0) = \left(\frac{\sum_{k=1}^K V_k^0 P_{N_k}^L(p_k^1, y_k^1, p_k^0, y_k^0) / \sum_{k=1}^K V_k^0}{\sum_{k=1}^K V_k^1 (P_{N_k}^P(p_k^1, y_k^1, p_k^0, y_k^0))^{-1} / \sum_{k=1}^K V_k^1} \right)^{1/2}.
$$
$$(3.176)$$

The two-stage Fisher price index, however, reads

$$
P_N^{*F}(p^1, x^1, p^0, x^0) \equiv \left(\frac{\sum_{k=1}^K V_k^0 P_{N_k}^F(p_k^1, y_k^1, p_k^0, y_k^0) / \sum_{k=1}^K V_k^0}{\sum_{k=1}^K V_k^1 (P_{N_k}^F(p_k^1, y_k^1, p_k^0, y_k^0))^{-1} / \sum_{k=1}^K V_k^1} \right)^{1/2}.
$$
$$(3.177)$$

Now the premise of **T7** requires that $P_{N_k}^F(p_k^1, x_k^1, p_k^0, x_k^0) = \lambda$ for all $k = 1, \ldots, K$. This evidently implies that $P_N^{*F}(p^1, x^1, p^0, x^0) = \lambda$, but does not imply that $P_N^F(p^1, x^1, p^0, x^0) = \lambda$ unless the Laspeyres, Paasche, and Fisher price index numbers for the subaggregates are the same. We will return to this topic in section 4.2.4.

Remark: If a price index $P_N(p, x, p', x')$ (or quantity index $Q_N(p, x, p', x')$) satisfies the consistency-in-aggregation test **T6** (**T6′**) and the proportionality axiom **A6** (**A6′**), then it satisfies the equality test **T7** (**T7′**).

Proof: (N. Ivanov 1995[25]) Choose an arbitrary price vector $\hat{p}^0 \equiv (\hat{p}_1^0, \ldots, \hat{p}_K^0)$ and define $\hat{x}^0 \equiv (V_1^0 / \hat{p}_1^0, \ldots, V_K^0 / \hat{p}_K^0)$, $\hat{p}^1 \equiv \lambda \hat{p}^0$ (for an arbitrary $\lambda > 0$) and $\hat{x}^1 \equiv (V_1^1 / \hat{p}_1^1, \ldots, V_K^1 / \hat{p}_K^1)$. Then, by **A6**, $P_K(\hat{p}^1, \hat{x}^1, \hat{p}^0, \hat{x}^0) = \lambda = \hat{p}_k^1 / \hat{p}_k^0 = P_1(\hat{p}_k^1, \hat{x}_k^1, \hat{p}_k^0, \hat{x}_k^0)$ for $k = 1, \ldots, K$. Substituting this in the consistency-in-aggregation relation (3.168) (for $N = K$ and $N_k = 1$ for $k = 1, \ldots, K$) leads to the conclusion that $\psi(\lambda, V^0, V^1) = \sum_{k=1}^K \psi(\lambda, V_k^0, V_k^1)$ for all $\lambda > 0$. But this implies that **T7** holds. QED

---

[25] Personal communication.

One verifies immediately from expression (3.174) that the Walsh-2 price index satisfies **T7**. However, the Montgomery-Vartia price index $P^{MV}(.)$ does not satisfy the equality test **T7**. Setting $P_{N_k}^{MV}(p_k^1, x_k^1, p_k^0, x_k^0) = \lambda$ ($k = 1, \ldots, K$) in expression (3.175), we do not obtain $P_N^{MV}(p^1, x^1, p^0, x^0) = \lambda$, since in general $L(V^0, V^1) \neq \sum_{k=1}^K L(V_k^0, V_k^1)$. Hence, the tests **T6** and **T7** (**T6′** and **T7′**) are independent.

3.7.3 An Important Theorem

There are, infinitely many, functional forms for price (or quantity) indices that satisfy the tests **T6** and **T7** (or **T6′** and **T7′**). By way of example, the reader is invited to consider the set of generalized mean price indices

$$P^{GM(\rho)}(p^1, x^1, p^0, x^0) \equiv \left(\sum_{n=1}^N (v_n^0/V^0)(p_n^1/p_n^0)^\rho \right)^{1/\rho} \quad (\rho \neq 0),$$

(3.178)

or the set of generalized mean quantity indices

$$Q^{GM(\rho)}(p^1, x^1, p^0, x^0) \equiv \left(\sum_{n=1}^N (v_n^0/V^0)(x_n^1/x_n^0)^\rho \right)^{1/\rho} \quad (\rho \neq 0).$$

(3.179)

Notice that the Laspeyres price and quantity indices are special cases: for $\rho = 1$, $P^{GM(1)}(.) = P^L(.)$ and $Q^{GM(1)}(.) = Q^L(.)$.

However, imposing a number of other basic requirements dramatically reduces the number of admissible indices, as the next theorems show. Quite surprisingly, the generalized Stuvel indices materialize here.

Theorem 3.18 *The functions $P(.)$, $Q(.)$ satisfy the product test **T3**, the equality tests **T7** and **T7′**, and the consistency-in-aggregation test **T6** or **T6′** if and only if $P(p^1, x^1, p^0, x^0) = P^{S(a,b)}(p^1, x^1, p^0, x^0)$ and $Q(p^1, x^1, p^0, x^0) = Q^{S(a,b)}(p^1, x^1, p^0, x^0)$.*

Proof: For the sufficiency part we recall the characterization of the generalized Stuvel indices in Theorem 3.13:

$$a[P^{S(a,b)}(.) - P^L(.)] = b[Q^{S(a,b)}(.) - Q^L(.)] \quad (a, b \geq 0). \quad (3.180)$$

Inserting the definitions of $P^L(.)$ and $Q^L(.)$, and multiplying both sides of the equation by V^0, we obtain

$$a V^0 P^{S(a,b)}(.) - b V^0 Q^{S(a,b)}(.) = \sum_{n=1}^{N} a p_n^1 x_n^0 - \sum_{n=1}^{N} b p_n^0 x_n^1. \quad (3.181)$$

Since the generalized Stuvel indices satisfy **T3**, this equation can be rewritten as

$$a V^0 P^{S(a,b)}(.) - b V^1 / P^{S(a,b)}(.) = \sum_{n=1}^{N} [a v_n^0 (p_n^1 / p_n^0) - b v_n^1 (p_n^1 / p_n^0)^{-1}]. \quad (3.182)$$

But this implies that $P^{S(a,b)}(.)$ for $a, b \geq 0$ satisfies the consistency-in-aggregation test **T6** with $\psi(\alpha, \beta, \gamma) \equiv a\beta\alpha - b\gamma/\alpha$. And, by **T3**, also **T6'** holds.

It remains to check that the proportionality tests **A6** and **A6'** hold. Let $p_n^1 / p_n^0 = \lambda$ for $n = 1, \ldots, N$. Then the last equation reduces to

$$\psi(P^{S(a,b)}(.), V^0, V^1) = \psi(\lambda, V^0, V^1). \quad (3.183)$$

Since the function $\psi(.)$ is strictly monotonic in its first argument, the conclusion must be that $P^{S(a,b)} = \lambda$. Similarly one can show that **A6'** holds.

The necessity part of the proof is rather tedious. It is provided by Balk (1995) and goes back to a derivation given by Gorman (1986).   QED

Notice that, by the remark immediately following the definition of the equality test, in this theorem the equality tests **T7** and **T7'** may be replaced by the (weaker) proportionality axioms **A6** and **A6'**.

It is left to the reader to verify from the explicit definitions that the generalized Stuvel price index $P^{S(a,b)}(p^1, x^1, p^0, x^0)$ for $a, b \neq 0$ does not satisfy the linear homogeneity axiom **A2** and that $Q^{S(a,b)}(p^1, x^1, p^0, x^0)$ does not satisfy **A2'**. This leads to an important corollary.

Theorem 3.19 *The functions $P(.), Q(.)$ satisfy the linear homogeneity axioms **A2**, **A2'**, the product test **T3**, the equality tests **T7** and **T7'**, and the consistency-in-aggregation test **T6** or **T6'** if and only if $P(p^1, x^1, p^0, x^0) = P^L(p^1, x^1, p^0, x^0)$ and $Q(p^1, x^1, p^0, x^0) = Q^P(p^1, x^1, p^0, x^0)$ or $P(p^1, x^1, p^0, x^0) = P^P(p^1, x^1, p^0, x^0)$ and $Q(p^1, x^1, p^0, x^0) = Q^L(p^1, x^1, p^0, x^0)$.*

Loosely formulated, this theorem means that, under rather weak assumptions, the only price and quantity indices that are consistent-in-aggregation are those of Laspeyres and Paasche. This result sheds light on the issue of additivity in economic accounting systems, as will be shown next.

Recall that the (nominal) value of aggregate A at period t $(t = 0, 1)$ is $V^t = \sum_{k=1}^{K} V_k^t$, where V_k^t is the value of subaggregate A_k $(k = 1, \ldots, K)$. The *real* value[26] of A at period 1 can be defined in two ways, namely by deflating the comparison period (nominal) value,

$$V^1 / P_N(p^1, x^1, p^0, x^0), \qquad (3.184)$$

or by inflating the base period (nominal) value,

$$V^0 Q_N(p^1, x^1, p^0, x^0). \qquad (3.185)$$

If and only if $P(.)$ and $Q(.)$ satisfy the product test, then these two definitions are identical:

$$\frac{V^1}{P_N(p^1, x^1, p^0, x^0)} = V^0 Q_N(p^1, x^1, p^0, x^0); \qquad (3.186)$$

in fact, this is nothing but a reformulation of **T3**, as the reader can easily check. Similarly, provided that the product test is satisfied, the real value of subaggregate A_k $(k = 1, \ldots, K)$ at period 1 is given by

$$\frac{V_k^1}{P_{N_k}(p_k^1, x_k^1, p_k^0, x_k^0)} = V_k^0 Q_{N_k}(p_k^1, x_k^1, p_k^0, x_k^0). \qquad (3.187)$$

Now, like (nominal) values are additive, one wants real values to be additive; that is, one wants the following relations to hold:

$$\frac{V^1}{P_N(p^1, x^1, p^0, x^0)} = \sum_{k=1}^{K} \frac{V_k^1}{P_{N_k}(p_k^1, x_k^1, p_k^0, x_k^0)}, \qquad (3.188)$$

or

$$V^0 Q_N(p^1, x^1, p^0, x^0) = \sum_{k=1}^{K} V_k^0 Q_{N_k}(p_k^1, x_k^1, p_k^0, x_k^0). \qquad (3.189)$$

It is clear that expression (3.188) is a special case of the consistency-in-aggregation relation (3.168), and that expression (3.189) is a special case of (3.169). Moreover, the two equality tests are satisfied, since expression (3.188) means that the aggregate price index is a weighted harmonic average of the subaggregate price indices, whereas expression (3.189) means that the

---

[26] National accountants usually call this *volume*.

aggregate quantity index is a weighted arithmetic average of the subaggregate quantity indices.

Hence, requiring additivity and adding the basic requirement of linear homogeneity effectively reduces the set of admissible price and quantity indices to those of Laspeyres and Paasche.

3.8 Is There a "King" of Indices?

Since the days of Jevons one has been searching for the ultimate price index (and/or quantity index). This has delivered an amazingly large number of functional forms. The axioms $\{A1, \ldots, A6\}$ (and $\{A1', \ldots, A6'\}$, respectively) could be used as a first sieve. We prefer the system $\{A1, A2, A3, A4, A5\}$ to the system $\{A1, A4, A5, A6\}$, since the last system admits price indices that do not satisfy the linear homogeneity axiom $A2$. A price index which does not satisfy this axiom cannot be interpreted as an economic price index. An economic price index is defined as a ratio of values of a revenue or cost function, which is linearly homogeneous in prices by definition. Hence, it is difficult to give a price index not satisfying axiom $A2$, such as the (generalized) Stuvel index, a welfare-theoretic meaning.

Maintaining the axioms $\{A1, \ldots, A5\}$ still leaves us with a large number of admissible price indices. Adding the circularity test $T1$ reduces this number to one, namely the Cobb-Douglas price index (Theorem 3.12). This price index, however, is a degenerate member of our class of price indices, since it is a function of prices only. Moreover, the implicit quantity index $p^1 \cdot x^1 / p^0 \cdot x^0 \prod_{n=1}^{N} (p_n^1 / p_n^0)^{\alpha_n}$ does not satisfy the linear homogeneity axiom $A2'$. In this way Theorem 3.12 throws additional light on the early result of Wald (Theorem 3.1). The conclusion must be that maintaining the circularity test would lead to a dead end. Fisher (1921) was already convinced of this state of affairs.

Fisher (1922, p. 366) concluded that his ideal price index is "probably the king of all index number formulae." This is certainly true with respect to its score of characterization theorems. However, to be honest one must observe that every characterization of $P^F(.)$ (and $Q^F(.)$) contains at least one functional equation that is not self-evident. Theorems 3.3 and 3.9 restrict the class of admissible price indices by requiring a special functional form (the value dependence test $T5$). The functional equation in Theorem 3.4 can be interpreted as a requirement of unbiasedness with respect to the Laspeyres price and quantity indices. But one could ask why these particular indices should serve as benchmarks. The same applies to Theorem 3.11. Theorems 3.5, 3.6, 3.7, 3.8, and 3.10 each contain a functional equation saying that the price index must be invariant to reversing or changing comparison period and base period quantities. But again it is not clear that such a requirement is at all desirable. Finally, the characterizations of the Fisher price index provide no evidence for preferring this index to another ideal price index mentioned, the Sato-Vartia price index.

In many practical situations the statistician must deal with aggregates that consist of subaggregates, which in turn consist of subsubaggregates, etc., until the level of individual commodities is reached. Think of an aggregate such as consumption of households, or Gross Domestic Product. Three requirements appear to be of vital importance in this context:

(i) Any value ratio must be decomposed into two components, a price index and a quantity index number.

(ii) The price index as well as the quantity index must be consistent-in-aggregation.

(iii) If the (price or quantity) index numbers for all subaggregates at a certain level happen to be equal to each other, then the index number for the aggregate must be equal to this common value.

In section 3.7 it was shown that the only admissible price and quantity index pairs that satisfy these requirements are (Laspeyres, Paasche) and (Paasche, Laspeyres). This remarkable result can be used to legitimize the use of these simple indices in multilayered economic-statistical systems such as the National Accounts.

Implicitly this chapter has already revealed a number of topics for further research. There are, for example, a number of indices waiting for their characterization. Among them is the Sato-Vartia price index. Another point deserving attention is whether the consistency-in-aggregation test as stated here is the only possible formalization of the consistency-in-aggregation concept.[27]

3.9 Direct Indices and Chained Indices

3.9.1 Direct Indices

Usually there are more than two periods involved in a price and/or quantity comparison project, say $0, 1, 2, \ldots, T$, where T may be fixed or moving

---

[27] Pursiainen (2005) proposes a more general definition of consistency-in-aggregation. It is, however, reassuring to see that, when restricted to indices, his definition reduces to the one presented here.

forward. This section discusses the two main strategies for executing such comparisons. Suppose that one has decided on certain functional forms $P(p, x, p', x')$ and $Q(p, x, p', x')$.

The first strategy is to choose a certain period as base period and compute price and quantity index numbers for other periods by comparing each of these periods in turn to the base period. If period 0 was chosen to act as base period, then we would have obtained the following arrays of so-called *direct* index numbers:

$$P(p^0, x^0, p^0, x^0) \quad Q(p^0, x^0, p^0, x^0)$$
$$P(p^1, x^1, p^0, x^0) \quad Q(p^1, x^1, p^0, x^0)$$
$$P(p^2, x^2, p^0, x^0) \quad Q(p^2, x^2, p^0, x^0)$$
$$\cdot \quad \cdot$$

(3.190)

$$\cdot \quad \cdot$$
$$P(p^t, x^t, p^0, x^0) \quad Q(p^t, x^t, p^0, x^0)$$
$$\cdot \quad \cdot$$

Notice that the entries on the first row equal 1 whenever $P(.)$ and $Q(.)$ exhibit the identity property **A3** and **A3'**. In case $P(.)$ and $Q(.)$ do not satisfy the product test **T3**, two columns could be added to (3.190), namely implicit price and quantity index numbers.

This strategy has the virtue of simplicity, but there are obvious drawbacks. With the march of time it becomes less and less meaningful to compare the prices of period t to those of period 0 by means of an index number that in general depends on the period 0 quantities; suppose for instance that as price index $P(.)$ the Laspeyres formula had been selected. This is one of the main reasons why most official statistical agencies update the base period of their CPI and PPI at regular time intervals.

A more serious drawback, however, concerns the comparison of consecutive time periods. Based on (3.190), the price change between periods $t - 1$ and t is measured by

$$P(p^t, x^t, p^0, x^0)/P(p^{t-1}, x^{t-1}, p^0, x^0),$$ (3.191)

and the quantity change by

$$Q(p^t, x^t, p^0, x^0)/Q(p^{t-1}, x^{t-1}, p^0, x^0).$$ (3.192)

Let us now suppose that $P(.)$ satisfies the axioms $\{A1, \ldots, A5\}$. Then one easily checks that the ratio (3.191) as a function of $(p^t, x^t, p^{t-1}, x^{t-1})$ satisfies the axioms **A1, A2, A4**, and **A5**, but not necessarily **A3**. That is, unless the price index $P(p, x, p', x')$ does not depend on quantities x, the ratio

$$P(p^{t-1}, x^t, p^0, x^0)/P(p^{t-1}, x^{t-1}, p^0, x^0) \qquad (3.193)$$

is not necessarily equal to 1. A similar observation applies of course to the measurement of quantity change between consecutive time periods.

An example might be useful in demonstrating the problem we are facing here. Suppose the Paasche price index (3.7) is used in (3.190). The price change going from period $t - 1$ to t is then measured by

$$\frac{P^P(p^t, x^t, p^0, x^0)}{P^P(p^{t-1}, x^{t-1}, p^0, x^0)} = \frac{p^t \cdot x^t/p^{t-1} \cdot x^{t-1}}{p^0 \cdot x^t/p^0 \cdot x^{t-1}}. \qquad (3.194)$$

Letting $p^t = p^{t-1}$, this reduces to

$$\frac{P^P(p^{t-1}, x^t, p^0, x^0)}{P^P(p^{t-1}, x^{t-1}, p^0, x^0)} = \frac{p^{t-1} \cdot x^t/p^{t-1} \cdot x^{t-1}}{p^0 \cdot x^t/p^0 \cdot x^{t-1}}, \qquad (3.195)$$

which is a ratio of two different quantity index numbers, and not necessarily equal to 1.

Can the dependency of the functions (3.191) and/or (3.192) on (p^0, x^0) be removed? Suppose that there exists a function $f(.)$ such that

$$\frac{P(p^t, x^t, p^0, x^0)}{P(p^{t-1}, x^{t-1}, p^0, x^0)} = f(p^t, x^t, p^{t-1}, x^{t-1}). \qquad (3.196)$$

This is supposed to hold for all values of $(p^t, x^t, p^{t-1}, x^{t-1}, p^0, x^0)$ and is called base period independency in the older index number literature. By fixing (p^{t-1}, x^{t-1}) and defining $P(p^{t-1}, x^{t-1}, p, x) \equiv h(p, x)$ and $f(p, x, p^{t-1}, x^{t-1}) \equiv g(p, x)$, it follows that

$$P(p^t, x^t, p^0, x^0) = g(p^t, x^t)h(p^0, x^0). \qquad (3.197)$$

Suppose now that the price index $P(.)$ satisfies the identity axiom **A3**. Then it must be the case that

$$1 = g(p, x^t)h(p, x^0) \qquad (3.198)$$

for all p, x^0, x^t. But this implies that $g(p, x) = g(p)$ is a function of p alone, and $h(p, x) = h(p)$ is also a function of p alone; moreover, $h(p) = 1/g(p)$. Hence, expression (3.197) reduces to

$$P(p^t, x^t, p^0, x^0) = g(p^t)/g(p^0). \qquad (3.199)$$

Put otherwise, the price index $P(.)$ does not depend on quantities. For the price change between periods $t-1$ and t one obtains

$$\frac{P(p^t, x^t, p^0, x^0)}{P(p^{t-1}, x^{t-1}, p^0, x^0)} = \frac{g(p^t)}{g(p^{t-1})} = P(p^t, x^t, p^{t-1}, x^{t-1}). \quad (3.200)$$

Consider now the implicit quantity index for period t relative to period $t-1$; that is,

$$\frac{p^t \cdot x^t / p^{t-1} \cdot x^{t-1}}{P(p^t, x^t, p^{t-1}, x^{t-1})} = \frac{p^t \cdot x^t / p^{t-1} \cdot x^{t-1}}{g(p^t)/g(p^{t-1})}. \quad (3.201)$$

It is clear that this index does not exhibit the identity property **A3′**.

Similarly, if the quantity index $Q(.)$ is such that the ratio $Q(p^t, x^t, p^0, x^0)/ Q(p^{t-1}, x^{t-1}, p^0, x^0)$ is independent of (p^0, x^0), and $Q(.)$ exhibits the identity property **A3′**, then the implicit price index for period t relative to period $t-1$ does not exhibit **A3**.

3.9.2 Linked Indices

A regular updating of the base period of a price or quantity index solves the problem of obsolescence of the quantity or price weights, but not the problem of improper short-term comparisons.

Suppose that in our setting each fifth period is chosen to act as a new base period for the next five periods. Then we obtain the following columns of price index numbers:

$$P(p^0, x^0, p^0, x^0)$$
$$P(p^1, x^1, p^0, x^0)$$
$$P(p^2, x^2, p^0, x^0)$$
$$.$$
$$.$$

$$P(p^5, x^5, p^0, x^0) \quad P(p^5, x^5, p^5, x^5)$$
$$P(p^6, x^6, p^5, x^5) \qquad\qquad (3.202)$$
$$P(p^7, x^7, p^5, x^5)$$
$$.$$
$$.$$

$$P(p^{10}, x^{10}, p^5, x^5) \quad P(p^{10}, x^{10}, p^{10}, x^{10})$$
$$P(p^{11}, x^{11}, p^{10}, x^{10})$$
$$.$$

Notice that each of these columns heads off with the value 1 (provided that the identity property holds), and that it therefore does not make sense to merge the different series. There are purposes for which the information provided by such a scheme is sufficient.

There are also purposes, however, for which one wants a single series of index numbers, comparing the price level of each period to that of the first base period. Departing from scheme (3.202), such a series can be constructed as follows[28]:

$$\tilde{P}(0, 0) \equiv P(p^0, x^0, p^0, x^0)$$
$$\tilde{P}(1, 0) \equiv P(p^1, x^1, p^0, x^0)$$

$$\cdot$$
$$\cdot$$

$$\tilde{P}(5, 0) \equiv P(p^5, x^5, p^0, x^0)$$
$$\tilde{P}(6, 0) \equiv P(p^6, x^6, p^5, x^5) P(p^5, x^5, p^0, x^0) \qquad (3.203)$$

$$\cdot$$
$$\cdot$$

$$\tilde{P}(10, 0) \equiv P(p^{10}, x^{10}, p^5, x^5) P(p^5, x^5, p^0, x^0)$$
$$\tilde{P}(11, 0) \equiv P(p^{11}, x^{11}, p^{10}, x^{10}) P(p^{10}, x^{10}, p^5, x^5) P(p^5, x^5, p^0, x^0)$$

$$\cdot$$
$$\cdot$$

This procedure is called *linking* of index numbers, the linking interval being five periods. There are a number of points to be observed here.

The first is that $\tilde{P}(t, 0)$ for $t \geq 6$ is not a bilateral price index in the sense defined in section 3.2. In particular the identity axiom **A3** will be violated: from $p^t = p^0$ it does not necessarily follow that $\tilde{P}(t, 0) = 1$. Even a weaker requirement will in general be violated: from $p^t = p^0$ and $x^t = x^0$ it does not necessarily follow that $\tilde{P}(t, 0) = 1$.

Second, a drawback of the linking procedure outlined in the scheme above is that each updating of the base period can lead to a discontinuity in the time series of $\tilde{P}(t, 0)$ ($t = 0, 1, \ldots, T$).

Third, this procedure does not solve the problem of improper adjacent-period comparisons. Consider for instance the price change between periods

---

[28] It is assumed that the three series do not overlap. The problem of handling overlapping index number series was discussed by Hill and Fox (1997).

122 Axioms, Tests, and Indices

Table 3.15. *Direct and Chained Price Index Numbers*

Period t	L	cL	cP	P
1	1.0000	1.0000	1.0000	1.0000
2	1.4200	1.4200	1.3823	1.3823
3	1.3450	1.3646	1.2740	1.2031
4	1.3550	1.3351	1.2060	1.0209
5	1.4400	1.3306	1.1234	0.7968

$t-1$ and t. Based on (3.203), this change is measured by

$$\frac{\bar{P}(t,0)}{\bar{P}(t-1,0)} = \frac{P(p^t, x^t, p^{t'}, x^{t'})}{P(p^{t-1}, x^{t-1}, p^{t'}, x^{t'})}, \qquad (3.204)$$

where t' is the highest number that is smaller than t and divisible by 5. But the right-hand side of this expression has the same structure as expression (3.191).

3.9.3 Chained Indices

The second strategy is basically the limiting case of the linking procedure. At every new period, the previous period is chosen to act as base period, and the period-to-period price index numbers are multiplied with each other. Put otherwise, the linking interval is one period. This strategy is called *chaining* of index numbers, and the final index numbers are called *chained index numbers*. They are calculated according to the formula

$$P^c(t,0) \equiv \prod_{\tau=1}^{t} P(p^\tau, x^\tau, p^{\tau-1}, x^{\tau-1}), \qquad (3.205)$$

where $P^c(0,0) \equiv 1$. Notice that $P^c(t,0)$ depends on all the prices and quantities of all the periods involved, $p^t, x^t, p^{t-1}, x^{t-1}, \ldots, p^1, x^1, p^0, x^0$. Again, one easily verifies that $P^c(t,0)$ for $t \geq 2$ does not necessarily exhibit the identity property **A3**.

For illustration, let us return to our numerical example. Table 3.15 compares direct and chained price index numbers. The columns 2 and 5 are copied from Table 3.4. The columns 3 and 4 contain chained Laspeyres and Paasche price index numbers, respectively. Of course, in the first two rows direct and chained price index numbers coincide.

As one sees, for periods 3–5 the (percentage) difference between chained Laspeyres and Paasche index numbers is smaller than between direct Laspeyres and Paasche index numbers. This is a pattern one regularly encounters in empirical material. However, chaining does not necessarily reduce the Paasche-Laspeyres gap or spread, as shown by von der Lippe (2001, pp. 130–3) and Hill (2006a). In particular, one should watch out for cycles, seasonality, and "bouncing" behaviour of the data (see also Szulc 1983). The length of the periods that are involved in the comparison appears to be of crucial importance.

In order to find the beginning of an insight we compare the simple three-period chained Laspeyres price index $P^L(p^1, x^1, p^0, x^0)P^L(p^2, x^2, p^1, x^1)$ to its direct counterpart $P(p^2, x^2, p^0, x^0)$. It is straightforward to verify that the following relation holds, using the shorthand notation introduced earlier,

$$\frac{P^L(1,0)P^L(2,1)}{P^L(2,0)}$$
$$= 1 + \frac{\sum_{n=1}^{N} s_n^{10}\left(\frac{p_n^2}{p_n^1} - P^{Lo}(p^2, p^1; x^0)\right)\left(\frac{x_n^1}{x_n^0} - Q^P(1,0)\right)}{P^{Lo}(p^2, p^1; x^0)Q^P(1,0)}, \qquad (3.206)$$

where $s_n^{10} \equiv p_n^1 x_n^0 / p^1 \cdot x^0$ ($n = 1, \ldots, N$), $P^{Lo}(p^2, p^1; x^0)$ is a Lowe price index for period 2 relative to period 1, and $Q^P(1,0)$ is the Paasche quantity index for period 1 relative to period 0. The term at the right-hand side of this equation is the (hybrid value share weighted) covariance of price changes between periods 1 and 2 and quantity changes between periods 0 and 1. It is clear that nothing can be said with certainty about the sign of this covariance.

Let us, however, consider the consumer side of a market, let the periods be long (say, years), and let the commodities be highly aggregated. Then one will usually discover that the covariance of price changes and quantity changes is negative, even when those changes are not strictly contemporaneous. The reason is that the combination of long periods and highly aggregated commodities gives the price and quantity relatives the character of trends, and trends tend to be more or less persistent through time. In such a case, therefore, the chained Laspeyres price index will drop below the direct index.

Now, let the periods be short (say, weeks), and let the commodities be very detailed. Then price changes between periods 0 and 1 tend to be negatively correlated with price changes between periods 1 and 2. When, further, price changes are negatively correlated with contemporaneous quantity changes, then the net result is a positive correlation between quantity changes from 0 to 1 and price changes from 1 to 2. The chained Laspeyres price index will then exceed the direct index.

Using relation (3.72), the previous equation transforms into

$$
\frac{Q^P(2,0)}{Q^P(1,0)Q^P(2,1)}
$$
$$
= 1 + \frac{\sum_{n=1}^{N} s_n^{10}\left(\frac{p_n^2}{p_n^1} - P^{Lo}(p^2,p^1;x^0)\right)\left(\frac{x_n^1}{x_n^0} - Q^P(1,0)\right)}{P^{Lo}(p^2,p^1;x^0)Q^P(1,0)}. \qquad (3.207)
$$

In the case of chained and direct Paasche price indices it is straightforward to verify that the following relation holds:

$$
\frac{P^P(2,0)}{P^P(1,0)P^P(2,1)} = \frac{Q^L(1,0)Q^L(2,1)}{Q^L(2,0)}
$$
$$
= 1 + \frac{\sum_{n=1}^{N} s_n^{01}\left(\frac{p_n^1}{p_n^0} - P^P(1,0)\right)\left(\frac{x_n^2}{x_n^1} - Q^{Lo}(x^2,x^1;p^0)\right)}{P^P(1,0)Q^{Lo}(x^2,x^1;p^0)},
$$
$$
\qquad (3.208)
$$

where $s_n^{01} \equiv p_n^0 x_n^1 / p^0 \cdot x^1$ ($n = 1, \ldots, N$), $P^P(1,0)$ is the Paasche price index for period 1 relative to period 0, and $Q^{Lo}(x^2,x^1;p^0)$ is a Lowe quantity index for period 2 relative to period 1. The term at the right-hand side of this equation is the (hybrid value share weighted) covariance of price changes between periods 0 and 1 and quantity changes between periods 1 and 2. It is left to the reader to consider the two cases discussed above once more.[29]

The choice between the two strategies, the fixed base strategy with regular updating of the base period and the chaining strategy, is a difficult one. Neither strategy is best for all purposes. Balk (2008) compares the two strategies by considering the main index number problem, namely the decomposition of a value ratio into price and quantity index numbers.

Suppose that $P(.)$ and $Q(.)$ satisfy the product test **T3**. Then for periods $t = 2, \ldots, T$ one can decompose the value ratio as

$$
V^t/V^0 = P(t,0)Q(t,0), \qquad (3.209)
$$

[29] Expression (3.206) is, apart from notation, the same as expression (42) of von Bortkiewicz (1924), whereas expression (3.208) replaces his slightly more complex expression (44), reading

$$
\frac{P^P(1,0)P^P(2,1)}{P^P(2,0)} = 1 - \frac{\sum_{n=1}^{N} s_n^{01}\left(\frac{p_n^1}{p_n^0} - P^P(1,0)\right)\left(\frac{x_n^2}{x_n^1} - Q^{Lo}(x^2,x^1;p^0)\right)}{P^{Lo}(p^1,p^0;x^2)Q^{Lo}(x^2,x^1;p^0)}.
$$

but also as

$$V^t/V^0 = \prod_{\tau=1}^{t} V^\tau/V^{\tau-1} = \prod_{\tau=1}^{t} P(\tau, \tau - 1)Q(\tau, \tau - 1)$$

$$= \prod_{\tau=1}^{t} P(\tau, \tau - 1) \prod_{\tau=1}^{t} Q(\tau, \tau - 1) = P^c(t, 0)Q^c(t, 0), \quad (3.210)$$

with the shorthand notation introduced earlier. These decompositions look really different. However, expression (3.209) can be rewritten as

$$V^t/V^0 = \prod_{\tau=1}^{t} \frac{P(\tau, 0)}{P(\tau - 1, 0)} \prod_{\tau=1}^{t} \frac{Q(\tau, 0)}{Q(\tau - 1, 0)}, \quad (3.211)$$

since $P(0, 0)Q(0, 0) = V^0/V^0 = 1$. The form of this decomposition is the same as the form on the second line of expression (3.210). Identity of the two decompositions requires that the price index $P(.)$ or the quantity index $Q(.)$ satisfy the circularity test **T1** or **T1'**. Then, imposing the identity axiom **A3** on the price index implies violation of **A3'** by the quantity index, and *vice versa*. From this point of view, the question is not so much whether to decompose the value ratio between periods t and 0 by direct or chained index numbers, but whether adjacent periods should be compared by index numbers of the form $< P(\tau, 0)/P(\tau - 1, 0), Q(\tau, 0)/Q(\tau - 1, 0) >$ or $< P(\tau, \tau - 1), Q(\tau, \tau - 1) >$. Thus, according to Balk (2008), there is here a choice between two paradigms.

Official, monthly consumer and producer price index numbers are, based on considerations about practicality and timeliness of results, usually constructed according to the first strategy, whereby the base period is updated at annual, 5-yearly, or 10-yearly frequency.[30] In the framework of the annual National Accounts, however, Al *et al.* (1986) advocated the use of chained index numbers. This strategy was adopted in the *System of National Accounts 1993* and the *European System of Accounts 1995*.[31] In particular SNA

---

[30] Interesting empirical material is here provided by Boldsen Hansen (2007). Within a linking strategy he calculates monthly consumer price index numbers for Denmark over the period 1996–2006 according to formulas which can be considered as approximations of Walsh-1, Marshall-Edgeworth, Fisher, and Törnqvist indices. These index numbers are compared to those delivered by the formulas of Young and Lowe, and variants such as the Geometric Young and Harmonic Young indices.

[31] It is instructive to read Young (1992) on the motives of the U. S. Bureau of Economic Analysis to introduce chained index numbers in their annual accounting system. The French system used chained index numbers already since the late 1950s; see Vanoli (2005), chapter 9.

(1993, chapter XVI) as well as ESA (1995, chapter 10) advised chained Fisher indices. An early and strong advocate of chaining was Mudgett (1951). A strongly opposing view was voiced by von der Lippe (2001).[32]

An intermediate way between linking at fixed time intervals and (annual or quarterly) chaining was developed by Ehemann (2005b): the optimal linking interval is chosen by minimizing a loss function that is based on the weighted variance of the price changes. The obvious disadvantage of this procedure is its dependence on the data under consideration.

3.10 Indicators

3.10.1 Axioms and Tests

What in the literature is called the "index number problem" can be formulated as the problem of finding a price index and a quantity index that satisfy the product test **T3**. If so, we obtain a decomposition of the aggregate value ratio in two parts,

$$\frac{V^1}{V^0} = \frac{p^1 \cdot x^1}{p^0 \cdot x^0} = P(p^1, x^1, p^0, x^0)Q(p^1, x^1, p^0, x^0), \quad (3.212)$$

of which the first part, $P(p^1, x^1, p^0, x^0)$, measures the effect of differing prices and the second part, $Q(p^1, x^1, p^0, x^0)$, the effect of differing quantities. Price as well as quantity indices map the prices and quantities of the two periods into unitless scalars.

Traditionally, value change is measured as a *ratio*. Measurement of change may, however, also proceed by way of a *difference*. Hence, the alternative problem is to decompose the aggregate value difference into two parts,

$$V^1 - V^0 = p^1 \cdot x^1 - p^0 \cdot x^0 = \mathcal{P}(p^1, x^1, p^0, x^0) + \mathcal{Q}(p^1, x^1, p^0, x^0),$$
$$(3.213)$$

of which the first term, $\mathcal{P}(p^1, x^1, p^0, x^0)$, is supposed to measure the part of the value difference that is due to differing prices and the second term, $\mathcal{Q}(p^1, x^1, p^0, x^0)$, is the part of the value difference that is due to differing quantities. Both functions operate on the price and quantity vectors of the two periods and map these into money amounts.[33] Provided that

---

[32] Von der Lippe (2005) argued for the use of a direct Lowe price index, $P^{Lo}(p^t, p^0; p^b)$, where b is some third (fixed) period. Essentially the same argument would lead to $Q^{Lo}(x^t, x^0; x^b)$ as a direct quantity index. Unfortunately these two indices do not satisfy the product test **T3**.

[33] It is presupposed that adding, subtracting, or averaging values from different periods makes sense. If not, then all the values must first be deflated by some general inflation measure.

certain reasonable requirements are satisfied, the continuous functions $\mathcal{P}(p, x, p', x') : \mathfrak{R}_{++}^{4N} \to \mathfrak{R}$ and $\mathcal{Q}(p, x, p', x') : \mathfrak{R}_{++}^{4N} \to \mathfrak{R}$ will be called *price indicator* and *quantity indicator*, respectively. Notice that these functions may take on negative or zero values.

What are those reasonable requirements? Diewert (2005a) listed a number of them. They appear to correspond closely to the axioms formulated for indices. The basic requirements are:

AA1. Monotonicity in prices. $\mathcal{P}(p, x^1, p^0, x^0)$ is increasing in comparison period prices p_n and $\mathcal{P}(p^1, x^1, p, x^0)$ is decreasing in base period prices p_n $(n = 1, \ldots, N)$.

AA1′. Monotonicity in quantities. $\mathcal{Q}(p^1, x, p^0, x^0)$ is increasing in comparison period quantities x_n and $\mathcal{Q}(p^1, x^1, p^0, x)$ is decreasing in base period quantities x_n $(n = 1, \ldots, N)$.

AA3. Identity property. If all the comparison period prices are equal to the corresponding base period prices, then the price indicator must deliver the outcome 0: $\mathcal{P}(p^0, x^1, p^0, x^0) = 0$.

AA3′. Identity property. If all the comparison period quantities are equal to the corresponding base period quantities, then the quantity indicator must deliver the outcome 0: $Q(p^1, x^0, p^0, x^0) = 0$.

AA4. Homogeneity of degree 1 in prices. Multiplication of all comparison and base period prices by a common factor changes the price indicator outcome by this factor; that is, $\mathcal{P}(\lambda p^1, x^1, \lambda p^0, x^0) = \lambda \mathcal{P}(p^1, x^1, p^0, x^0)$ $(\lambda > 0)$.

AA4′. Homogeneity of degree 1 in quantities. Multiplication of all comparison period and base period quantities by a common factor changes the quantity indicator outcome by this factor; that is, $\mathcal{Q}(p^1, \lambda x^1, p^0, \lambda x^0) = \lambda \mathcal{Q}(p^1, x^1, p^0, x^0)$ $(\lambda > 0)$.

AA5. Dimensional invariance. The price indicator is invariant to changes in the units of measurement of the commodities: let Λ be a diagonal matrix with elements of $\mathfrak{R}_{++}$, then $\mathcal{P}(p^1\Lambda, x^1\Lambda^{-1}, p^0\Lambda, x^0\Lambda^{-1}) = \mathcal{P}(p^1, x^1, p^0, x^0)$.

AA5′. Dimensional invariance. The quantity indicator is invariant to changes in the units of measurement of the commodities: let Λ be a diagonal matrix with elements of $\mathfrak{R}_{++}$, then $\mathcal{Q}(p^1\Lambda, x^1\Lambda^{-1}, p^0\Lambda, x^0\Lambda^{-1}) = \mathcal{Q}(p^1, x^1, p^0, x^0)$.

Notice that the indicator axioms **AA1**, **AA1′**, **AA5**, and **AA5′** are the same as the index axioms **A1**, **A1′**, **A5**, and **A5′**, respectively. The axioms **AA3–AA4** and **AA3′–AA4′** serve to give $\mathcal{P}(.)$ and $\mathcal{Q}(.)$, respectively, the character of difference-type measures of change. There is no analogue to the index axioms **A2** and **A2′**.

The analogue to the time reversal test reads

TT2. Time reversal test. The price indicator for period 1 relative to period 0 is identically equal to the negative of the price indicator for period 0 relative to period 1; that is, $\mathcal{P}(p^1, x^1, p^0, x^0) = -\mathcal{P}(p^0, x^0, p^1, x^1)$.

TT2′. Time reversal test. The quantity indicator for period 1 relative to period 0 is identically equal to the negative of the quantity indicator for period 0 relative to period 1; that is, $\mathcal{Q}(p^1, x^1, p^0, x^0) = -\mathcal{Q}(p^0, x^0, p^1, x^1)$.

The analogue to the product test has been stated already in expression (3.213), whereas the factor reversal test for indicators requires that (3.213) be satisfied while $\mathcal{Q}(p^1, x^1, p^0, x^0) = \mathcal{P}(x^1, p^1, x^0, p^0)$; that is, price indicator and quantity indicator have the same functional form except that prices and quantities have been interchanged. An indicator is called *ideal* if it satisfies the factor reversal test.

There is a simple link between additive and multiplicative decompositions of the value change. In order to see this, we make use of the simple but powerful tool of the logarithmic mean. Thus, starting with a multiplicative decomposition of the value ratio (3.212), one takes the logarithm at both sides, so that

$$\ln\left(\frac{V^1}{V^0}\right) = \ln P(p^1, x^1, p^0, x^0) + \ln Q(p^1, x^1, p^0, x^0), \quad (3.214)$$

which can be written, using the definition of the logarithmic mean, as

$$\frac{V^1 - V^0}{L(V^1, V^0)} = \ln P(p^1, x^1, p^0, x^0) + \ln Q(p^1, x^1, p^0, x^0). \quad (3.215)$$

But this can be rearranged as

$$V^1 - V^0 = L(V^1, V^0)\ln P(p^1, x^1, p^0, x^0) + L(V^1, V^0)\ln Q(p^1, x^1, p^0, x^0), \quad (3.216)$$

which is an additive decomposition of the value difference into a price indicator and a quantity indicator. Recall that $L(V^1, V^0)$ is an average of the comparison period value V^1 and the base period value V^0, and notice that

$\ln P(.)$ and $\ln Q(.)$ are approximately equal to the percentage of aggregate price and quantity change, respectively.

Reversely, starting with an additive decomposition of the value difference (3.213), the logarithmic mean can be applied to its left-hand side to obtain

$$L(V^1, V^0)\ln\left(\frac{V^1}{V^0}\right) = \mathcal{P}(p^1, x^1, p^0, x^0) + \mathcal{Q}(p^1, x^1, p^0, x^0). \quad (3.217)$$

This can be rearranged as

$$\ln\left(\frac{V^1}{V^0}\right) = \frac{\mathcal{P}(p^1, x^1, p^0, x^0)}{L(V^1, V^0)} + \frac{\mathcal{Q}(p^1, x^1, p^0, x^0)}{L(V^1, V^0)}, \quad (3.218)$$

and this in turn as

$$\frac{V^1}{V^0} = \exp\left\{\frac{\mathcal{P}(p^1, x^1, p^0, x^0)}{L(V^1, V^0)}\right\}\exp\left\{\frac{\mathcal{Q}(p^1, x^1, p^0, x^0)}{L(V^1, V^0)}\right\}, \quad (3.219)$$

which clearly is a multiplicative decomposition of the value ratio into a price index and a quantity index.

Hence, any multiplicative decomposition of the aggregate value ratio can be turned into an additive decomposition of the aggregate value difference, and *vice versa*. However, notice that their properties do not automatically carry over. One checks easily that if $P(.)$ satisfies the index axioms **A1–A5**, then $L(V^1, V^0)\ln P(.)$ satisfies **AA3–AA5**, but not necessarily **AA1**. Also, if $\mathcal{P}(.)$ satisfies the indicator axioms **AA1, AA3–AA5**, then $\exp\{\mathcal{P}(.)/L(V^1, V^0)\}$ satisfies **A3–A5**, but not necessarily **A1** and **A2**. Similar observations, of course, apply to the quantity part of the two decompositions.

3.10.2 The Main Indicators

Let us consider some examples of additive decompositions. The first is the analogue to the first part of expression (3.72):

$$\begin{aligned}V^1 - V^0 &= (p^1 - p^0)\cdot x^0 + p^1\cdot(x^1 - x^0)\\ &\equiv \mathcal{P}^L(p^1, x^1, p^0, x^0) + \mathcal{Q}^P(p^1, x^1, p^0, x^0). \quad (3.220)\end{aligned}$$

The first term at the right-hand side may be called the Laspeyres price indicator, and the second term the Paasche quantity indicator. The second example is the obvious alternative,

$$\begin{aligned}V^1 - V^0 &= (p^1 - p^0)\cdot x^1 + p^0\cdot(x^1 - x^0)\\ &\equiv \mathcal{P}^P(p^1, x^1, p^0, x^0) + \mathcal{Q}^L(p^1, x^1, p^0, x^0). \quad (3.221)\end{aligned}$$

The first term at the right-hand side will be called the Paasche price indicator, and the second term the Laspeyres quantity indicator. Bennet's (1920) solution to the (difference type) index number problem was

$$V^1 - V^0 = \frac{1}{2}(x^0 + x^1) \cdot (p^1 - p^0) + \frac{1}{2}(p^0 + p^1) \cdot (x^1 - x^0)$$

$$= \sum_{n=1}^{N} \frac{x_n^0 + x_n^1}{2}(p_n^1 - p_n^0) + \sum_{n=1}^{N} \frac{p_n^0 + p_n^1}{2}(x_n^1 - x_n^0)$$

$$\equiv \mathcal{P}^B(p^1, x^1, p^0, x^0) + \mathcal{Q}^B(p^1, x^1, p^0, x^0). \qquad (3.222)$$

It can be seen by comparing the previous three expressions that

$$\mathcal{P}^B(p^1, x^1, p^0, x^0) = \frac{1}{2}(\mathcal{P}^L(p^1, x^1, p^0, x^0) + \mathcal{P}^P(p^1, x^1, p^0, x^0))$$

$$\mathcal{Q}^B(p^1, x^1, p^0, x^0) = \frac{1}{2}(\mathcal{Q}^L(p^1, x^1, p^0, x^0) + \mathcal{Q}^P(p^1, x^1, p^0, x^0));$$

$$(3.223)$$

that is, Bennet's indicators are the additive counterparts to Fisher's indices, and the additive decomposition (3.222) mirrors the multiplicative decomposition (3.74). At the same time the Bennet price and quantity indicators can be conceived as analogous to the Walsh-1 price and quantity indices, as defined by the expressions (3.21) and (3.22), or as analogous to the Marshall-Edgeworth price and quantity indices (see expressions (3.19) and (3.20)). The Bennet indicators exhibit all of the basic properties, plus the time reversal test, and the factor reversal test, as already shown by Diewert (2005a).

Notice that the multiplicative counterparts of the Bennet indicators, defined as $\exp\{\mathcal{P}^B(.)/L(V^1, V^0)\}$ and $\exp\{\mathcal{Q}^B(.)/L(V^1, V^0)\}$, constitute another pair of ideal indices.

An interesting relation between the Bennet price indicator and the Marshall-Edgeworth price index was discovered by Hillinger (2002). One can easily check that

$$\mathcal{P}^B(p^1/P^{ME}(p^1, x^1, p^0, x^0), x^1, p^0, x^0) = 0, \qquad (3.224)$$

or, equivalently,

$$V^1/P^{ME}(p^1, x^1, p^0, x^0) - V^0 = \mathcal{Q}^B(p^1/P^{ME}(p^1, x^1, p^0, x^0), x^1, p^0, x^0). \qquad (3.225)$$

The last equation means that deflation of nominal values by Marshall-Edgeworth price index numbers leads to real value differences that can be interpreted as outcomes of the Bennet quantity indicator.

The final example is due to Montgomery and the indicators will be labelled accordingly. By using the logarithmic mean repeatedly, one obtains

$$V^1 - V^0 = \sum_{n=1}^{N}(v_n^1 - v_n^0)$$

$$= \sum_{n=1}^{N} L(v_n^1, v_n^0) \ln(v_n^1/v_n^0)$$

$$= \sum_{n=1}^{N} L(v_n^1, v_n^0) \ln(p_n^1/p_n^0) + \sum_{n=1}^{N} L(v_n^1, v_n^0) \ln(x_n^1/x_n^0)$$

$$= \sum_{n=1}^{N} \frac{L(v_n^1, v_n^0)}{L(p_n^1, p_n^0)}(p_n^1 - p_n^0) + \sum_{n=1}^{N} \frac{L(v_n^1, v_n^0)}{L(x_n^1, x_n^0)}(x_n^1 - x_n^0)$$

$$\equiv \mathcal{P}^M(p^1, x^1, p^0, x^0) + \mathcal{Q}^M(p^1, x^1, p^0, x^0). \qquad (3.226)$$

The expression on the third line of (3.226) is the decomposition that was actually obtained by Montgomery (1929, p. 14; 1937, p. 34). The Montgomery indicators satisfy the time reversal test as well as the factor reversal test. Of the basic properties, they only fail to exhibit monotonicity globally, but, as argued in appendix 2 (drawn from Balk 2003), this problem is unlikely to be of much practical importance.

It is straightforward to check that the multiplicative counterparts of the Montgomery indicators are identical to the Montgomery-Vartia indices; that is,

$$\exp\left\{\mathcal{P}^M(p^1, x^1, p^0, x^0)/L(V^1, V^0)\right\} = P^{MV}(p^1, x^1, p^0, x^0)$$
$$\exp\left\{\mathcal{Q}^M(p^1, x^1, p^0, x^0)/L(V^1, V^0)\right\} = Q^{MV}(p^1, x^1, p^0, x^0). \qquad (3.227)$$

The weights $L(v_n^1, v_n^0)/L(p_n^1, p_n^0)$, occurring in the Montgomery price indicator, might look peculiar, yet their interpretation is straightforward. The numerator is the logarithmic mean of commodity n's base and comparison period value, whereas the denominator is the logarithmic mean of commodity n's base and comparison period price. The ratio can therefore be interpreted as a mean quantity, which implies that Montgomery's price indicator has basically the same structure as Bennet's price indicator. Likewise the weights $L(v_n^1, v_n^0)/L(x_n^1, x_n^0)$ in the Montgomery quantity indicator can be interpreted as mean prices.

Returning to our numerical example, it is simple to calculate the various price and quantity indicator values. However, for comparison with

Table 3.16. *Price Indicator Based Index Numbers*

Period t	L	P	B	M
1	1.0000	1.0000	1.0000	1.0000
2	1.4219	1.3866	1.4041	1.4024
3	1.3192	1.2302	1.2739	1.2907
4	1.3026	1.0272	1.1567	1.2392
5	1.3566	0.7022	0.9760	1.2678

the index numbers in previous tables it is better to present the outcomes of the multiplicative counterparts of the indicators; that is, $\exp\{\mathcal{P}(p^t, x^t, p^1, x^1)/L(V^t, V^1)\}$ and $\exp\{\mathcal{Q}(p^t, x^t, p^1, x^1)/L(V^t, V^1)\}$ for $t = 1, \ldots, 5$. Table 3.16 contains the price indicator based index numbers, and Table 3.17 the quantity indicator based index numbers. According to expression (3.227) the columns headed M in these tables are identical to the columns headed MV in Tables 3.12 and 3.13.

It is interesting to compare the first of these two tables to Tables 3.4, 3.6, and 3.12, and the second to Tables 3.5, 3.7, and 3.13. The conclusion is left to the reader.

3.10.3 Consistency-in-Aggregation Again

The decompositions discussed in the previous subsection share the basic feature that

$$\mathcal{P}_N(p^1, x^1, p^0, x^0) = \sum_{n=1}^{N} \mathcal{P}_1(p_n^1, x_n^1, p_n^0, x_n^0) \qquad (3.228)$$

$$\mathcal{Q}_N(p^1, x^1, p^0, x^0) = \sum_{n=1}^{N} \mathcal{Q}_1(p_n^1, x_n^1, p_n^0, x_n^0), \qquad (3.229)$$

where a subscript is added to the function symbol to indicate the dimension of the price and quantity vectors. This is due to the fact that

Table 3.17. *Quantity Indicator Based Index Numbers*

Period t	L	P	B	M
1	1.0000	1.0000	1.0000	1.0000
2	1.0169	0.9917	1.0042	1.0054
3	1.2491	1.1583	1.1995	1.1839
4	1.7095	1.3480	1.5181	1.4170
5	2.8481	1.4743	2.0491	1.5776

$V^1 - V^0 = \sum_{n=1}^{N}(v_n^1 - v_n^0)$. Now the axioms **AA5** and **AA5$'$** imply that

$$\mathcal{P}_1(p_n^1, x_n^1, p_n^0, x_n^0) = \psi(p_n^1/p_n^0, v_n^0, v_n^1) \tag{3.230}$$

$$\mathcal{Q}_1(p_n^1, x_n^1, p_n^0, x_n^0) = \zeta(x_n^1/x_n^0, v_n^0, v_n^1) \tag{3.231}$$

for certain functions $\psi(.)$ and $\zeta(.)$. Hence, the canonical form of price and quantity indicators appears to be

$$\mathcal{P}_N(p^1, x^1, p^0, x^0) = \sum_{n=1}^{N} \psi(p_n^1/p_n^0, v_n^0, v_n^1) \tag{3.232}$$

$$\mathcal{Q}_N(p^1, x^1, p^0, x^0) = \sum_{n=1}^{N} \zeta(x_n^1/x_n^0, v_n^0, v_n^1). \tag{3.233}$$

Now, let $P_N(p^1/p^0, v^0, v^1)$ be the solution P of the equation

$$\mathcal{P}_N(p^1, x^1, p^0, x^0) = \psi(P, V^0, V^1). \tag{3.234}$$

This equation is just another way of stating test **T6**. Put otherwise, the price index $P_N(p^1/p^0, v^0, v^1)$ is consistent-in-aggregation. Similarly, let $Q_N(p^1/p^0, v^0, v^1)$ be the solution Q of the equation

$$\mathcal{Q}_N(p^1, x^1, p^0, x^0) = \zeta(Q, V^0, V^1). \tag{3.235}$$

Then we have obtained test **T6$'$**, and the quantity index $Q_N(p^1/p^0, v^0, v^1)$ is consistent-in-aggregation. This insight is due to Pursiainen (2005, chapter 6).

By way of example we consider the Bennet price indicator. One easily checks that

$$\mathcal{P}^B(p^1, x^1, p^0, x^0) = \sum_{n=1}^{N} \psi(p_n^1/p_n^0, v_n^0, v_n^1), \tag{3.236}$$

where $\psi(\alpha, \beta, \gamma) \equiv [\beta(\alpha - 1) + \gamma(1 - 1/\alpha)]/2$. On the other hand, the Bennet price indicator can be expressed as

$$\mathcal{P}^B(p^1, x^1, p^0, x^0) = [V^0(P^L(1, 0) - 1) + V^1(1 - 1/P^P(1, 0))]/2. \tag{3.237}$$

Solving the equation

$$\mathcal{P}^B(p^1, x^1, p^0, x^0) = \psi(P, V^0, V^1) \tag{3.238}$$

delivers $P = P^{S(1/2, 1/2)}(p^1, x^1, p^0, x^0)$, which is the Stuvel price index. Thus there appears to be an intrinsic relation between the Bennet indicators and the Stuvel indices.

3.11 Appendix 1: The Logarithmic Mean

For any two strictly positive real numbers a and b, their logarithmic mean is defined by

$$L(a, b) \equiv \frac{a - b}{\ln(a/b)} \text{ if } a \neq b$$

$$L(a, a) \equiv a. \tag{3.239}$$

The logarithmic mean was introduced in the economics literature by Törnqvist in 1935 in an unpublished memo of the Bank of Finland; see Törnqvist, Vartia and Vartia (1985). Although its outlook is unfamiliar, its genesis is simple to understand, as will be shown.

Recall that for any differentiable function $f(x) : \mathfrak{R}_{++} \to \mathfrak{R}$ the Mean Value Theorem of differential calculus asserts that for $a \neq b$ we have

$$\frac{f(a) - f(b)}{a - b} = df(m)/dx, \tag{3.240}$$

where m is strictly between a and b. Let $f(x) \equiv \ln(x)$; then $m = L(a, b)$.

Let now $f(x) \equiv x^\alpha$, where α is a real number distinct from 0 and 1. Then one easily checks that

$$m = \left[\frac{a^\alpha - b^\alpha}{\alpha(a - b)} \right]^{1/(\alpha-1)} \equiv M(a, b; \alpha). \tag{3.241}$$

This function is called the generalized logarithmic mean.[34] It is straightforward to verify that $M(a, b; -1) = (ab)^{1/2}$, the geometric mean of a and b; that $M(a, b; 2) = (a + b)/2$, the arithmetic mean; and that (by using L'Hospital's Rule) $\lim_{\alpha \to 0} M(a, b; \alpha) = L(a, b)$, the logarithmic mean.

Stolarsky (1975) showed that $M(a, b; \alpha)$ is monotonous in α. His proof rests on the fact that one can write

$$\ln M(a, b; \alpha) = \frac{1}{\alpha - 1} \ln \left[\frac{a^\alpha - b^\alpha}{\alpha(a - b)} \right]$$

$$= \frac{1}{\alpha - 1} \left[\ln \left| \frac{a^\alpha - b^\alpha}{\alpha} \right| - \ln \left| \frac{a - b}{1} \right| \right]$$

$$= \frac{1}{\alpha - 1} \int_1^\alpha \frac{d}{dr} \ln \left| \frac{a^r - b^r}{r} \right| dr, \tag{3.242}$$

---

[34] The logarithmic mean for more than two variables, also called generalized logarithmic mean, was studied by Mustonen (2002).

and that the function $\ln|\frac{a^r-1}{r}|$ is convex in r. The monotonicity of $M(a, b; \alpha)$ combined with the foregoing three relations then leads to

$$(ab)^{1/2} \le L(a, b) \le (a + b)/2, \tag{3.243}$$

where equality applies in case $a = b$. Carlson (1972a) shows that

$$L(a, b) = \frac{1}{3} \left(\frac{a + b}{2} + 2(ab)^{1/2} \right) (1 + \epsilon)^{-1}, \tag{3.244}$$

with $0 \le \epsilon \le \frac{1}{2880}(\frac{a-b}{(ab)^{1/2}})^4$. Thus $L(a, b)$ is closer to the geometric mean than to the arithmetic mean. Based on an algorithm developed by Carlson (1972b) it appears that $\epsilon \approx \frac{1}{32}(\frac{\ln(a/b)}{\pi})^4$.

It is interesting to note that Sato (1974) independently obtained the approximation

$$L(a, b) \approx \frac{1}{3} \left(\frac{a + b}{2} + 2(ab)^{1/2} \right), \tag{3.245}$$

whereas Theil (1973) got

$$L(a, b) \approx \left(\frac{a + b}{2}((ab)^{1/2})^2 \right)^{1/3} = \left(\frac{a + b}{2} ab \right)^{1/3}. \tag{3.246}$$

Since a geometric mean is always less than or equal to an arithmetic mean, Theil's approximation appears to be less than or equal to Sato's approximation.

The generalized logarithmic mean has the following properties:

(1) $\min(a, b) \le M(a, b; \alpha) \le \max(a, b)$.
(2) $M(a, b; \alpha)$ is a continuous function.
(3) $M(a, b; \alpha)$ is linearly homogeneous in (a, b); that is, $M(\lambda a, \lambda b; \alpha) = \lambda M(a, b; \alpha)$ $(\lambda > 0)$. In particular, this implies that $M(a, b; \alpha) = a M(1, b/a; \alpha) = b M(a/b, 1; \alpha)$.
(4) $M(a, b; \alpha)$ is symmetric; that is, $M(a, b; \alpha) = M(b, a; \alpha)$.
(5) $M(a, b; \alpha)$ is strictly increasing in a and b.

Additional material that might be helpful for interpreting the (generalized) logarithmic mean was provided by Lorenzen (1990).

The following results for $L(a, 1)$ $(a \ne 1)$ are useful. Its first-order derivative is

$$\frac{dL(a, 1)}{da} = \frac{1}{\ln a} - \frac{L(a, 1)}{a \ln a}, \tag{3.247}$$

from which it follows that

$$\frac{d \ln L(a, 1)}{d \ln a} = \frac{a}{a - 1} - \frac{1}{\ln a}. \qquad (3.248)$$

Both derivatives are strictly positive. Since $\ln \bar{a} \approx \bar{a} - 1$ whenever $\bar{a} \approx 1$, it follows that

$$\frac{d \ln L(\bar{a}, 1)}{d \ln a} \approx 1 \qquad (3.249)$$

whenever $\bar{a} \approx 1$.

The second-order derivative of $L(a, 1)$ is

$$\frac{d^2 L(a, 1)}{da^2} = 2 \frac{L(a, 1) - (a + 1)/2}{a^2 (\ln a)^2}, \qquad (3.250)$$

which appears to be strictly negative. This means that $L(a, 1)$ is concave.

3.12 Appendix 2: On Monotonicity

3.12.1 The Montgomery-Vartia Price Index

The definition of $P^{MV}(p^1, x^1, p^0, x^0)$ can, by using the linear homogeneity of the logarithmic mean, be rearranged as

$$V^0 L(V^1/V^0, 1) \ln P^{MV}(.) = \sum_{n=1}^{N} v_n^0 L(v_n^1/v_n^0, 1) \ln(p_n^1/p_n^0). \qquad (3.251)$$

Call $r_k \equiv p_k^1/p_k^0$ for a certain $k \in \{1, \dots, N\}$ and consider $\partial \ln P^{MV}(.)/ \partial \ln r_k$. After differentiating expression (3.251) and rearranging, one obtains

$$\frac{\partial \ln P^{MV}(.)}{\partial \ln r_k} = \frac{L(v_k^1, v_k^0)}{L(V^1, V^0)} + \frac{L(v_k^1, v_k^0)}{L(V^1, V^0)} \frac{\partial \ln L(v_k^1/v_k^0, 1)}{\partial \ln r_k} \ln r_k$$

$$- \frac{\partial \ln L(V^1/V^0, 1)}{\partial \ln r_k} \ln P^{MV}(.). \qquad (3.252)$$

Using the fact that $v_k^1/v_k^0 = r_k(x_k^1/x_k^0)$ and $V^1/V^0 = \sum_{n=1}^{N} s_n^0(v_n^1/v_n^0)$, and the chain rule of differentiation, the last equation can be simplified to

$$\frac{\partial \ln P^{MV}(.)}{\partial \ln r_k} = \frac{L(v_k^1, v_k^0)}{L(V^1, V^0)} + \frac{L(v_k^1, v_k^0)}{L(V^1, V^0)} \frac{d \ln L(v_k^1/v_k^0, 1)}{d \ln a} \ln r_k$$

$$- \frac{v_k^1}{V^1} \frac{d \ln L(V^1/V^0, 1)}{d \ln a} \ln P^{MV}(.). \qquad (3.253)$$

The two final terms of this expression exhibit the same structure but are of opposite sign. Whenever v_k^1/v_k^0 and V^1/V^0 are in the neighbourhood of 1, expression (3.253) reduces to

$$\frac{\partial \ln P^{MV}(.)}{\partial \ln r_k} \approx \frac{v_k^1}{V^1}\left[1 + \ln r_k - \ln P^{MV}(.)\right], \qquad (3.254)$$

which in "normal" situations might be expected to be positive. This expression will become negative whenever the relative price change of commodity k, that is $r_k / P^{MV}(.)$, is less than $1/e$, where $e = 2.71828\ldots$ is the base of the natural logarithm.

3.12.2 The Montgomery Price Indicator

From the definition of $\mathcal{P}^M(p^1, x^1, p^0, x^0)$ one obtains immediately that

$$\begin{aligned}
\frac{\partial \mathcal{P}^M(.)}{\partial \ln r_k} &= L(v_k^1, v_k^0) + \frac{\partial L(v_k^1, v_k^0)}{\partial \ln r_k} \ln r_k \\
&= L(v_k^1, v_k^0)\left[1 + \frac{d \ln L(v_k^1/v_k^0, 1)}{d \ln a} \ln r_k\right] \\
&\approx v_k^0 \left[1 + \ln r_k\right]
\end{aligned} \qquad (3.255)$$

whenever v_k^1/v_k^0 is in the neighbourhood of 1. This expression will become negative whenever the price change of commodity k, r_k, is less than $1/e$.

3.12.3 The Sato-Vartia Price Index

The definition of $P^{SV}(p^1, x^1, p^0, x^0)$ can be written as

$$\left(\sum_{n=1}^{N} L(s_n^1, s_n^0)\right) \ln P^{SV}(.) = \sum_{n=1}^{N} L(s_n^1, s_n^0) \ln(p_n^1/p_n^0). \qquad (3.256)$$

After differentiating and rearranging, one obtains

$$\begin{aligned}
\frac{\partial \ln P^{SV}(.)}{\partial \ln r_k} &= \frac{L(s_k^1, s_k^0)}{\sum_{n=1}^{N} L(s_n^1, s_n^0)} + \frac{1}{\sum_{n=1}^{N} L(s_n^1, s_n^0)} \sum_{n=1}^{N} \frac{\partial L(s_n^1, s_n^0)}{\partial \ln r_k} \ln(p_n^1/p_n^0) \\
&\quad - \frac{1}{\sum_{n=1}^{N} L(s_n^1, s_n^0)} \frac{\partial(\sum_{n=1}^{N} L(s_n^1, s_n^0))}{\partial \ln r_k} \ln P^{SV}(.) \\
&= \frac{L(s_k^1, s_k^0)}{\sum_{n=1}^{N} L(s_n^1, s_n^0)} + \frac{1}{\sum_{n=1}^{N} L(s_n^1, s_n^0)} \sum_{n=1}^{N} \frac{\partial L(s_n^1, s_n^0)}{\partial \ln r_k} \\
&\quad \times \left[\ln(p_n^1/p_n^0) - \ln P^{SV}(.)\right].
\end{aligned} \qquad (3.257)$$

Now

$$\frac{\partial L(s_n^1, s_n^0)}{\partial \ln r_k} = L(s_n^1, s_n^0)\frac{d \ln L(s_n^1/s_n^0, 1)}{d \ln a}\frac{\partial \ln(s_n^1/s_n^0)}{\partial \ln r_k}, \qquad (3.258)$$

and straightforward calculations show that

$$\frac{\partial \ln(s_n^1/s_n^0)}{\partial \ln r_k} = s_k^1 \text{ if } n \neq k$$

$$= s_k^1 + 1 \text{ if } n = k. \qquad (3.259)$$

Substituting this into (3.257) yields

$$\frac{\partial \ln P^{SV}(.)}{\partial \ln r_k} = \frac{L(s_k^1, s_k^0)}{\sum_{n=1}^N L(s_n^1, s_n^0)} + \frac{s_k^1}{\sum_{n=1}^N L(s_n^1, s_n^0)}$$

$$\times \sum_{n=1}^N L(s_n^1, s_n^0)\frac{d \ln L(s_n^1/s_n^0, 1)}{d \ln a}[\ln(p_n^1/p_n^0) - \ln P^{SV}(.)]$$

$$+ \frac{1}{\sum_{n=1}^N L(s_n^1, s_n^0)}L(s_k^1, s_k^0)\frac{d \ln L(s_k^1/s_k^0, 1)}{d \ln a}[\ln r_k - \ln P^{SV}(.)]. \qquad (3.260)$$

When $s_n^1/s_n^0 \approx 1$ $(n = 1, \ldots, N)$, then the second term on the right-hand side vanishes and the entire expression reduces to

$$\frac{\partial \ln P^{SV}(.)}{\partial \ln r_k} \approx s_k^0\left[1 + \ln r_k - \ln P^{SV}(.)\right]. \qquad (3.261)$$

The right-hand side of this expression will become negative whenever the relative price change of commodity k, that is $r_k/P^{SV}(.)$, is less than $1/e$. In "normal" situations this is unlikely to happen.

3.12.4 The Geometric Paasche Price Index

The definition of $P^{GP}(p^1, x^1, p^0, x^0)$ can be written as

$$\ln P^{GP}(.) = \sum_{n=1}^N s_n^0(s_n^1/s_n^0) \ln(p_n^1/p_n^0). \qquad (3.262)$$

Differentiation with respect to $\ln r_k$ for $k \in \{1, \ldots, N\}$ delivers

$$\frac{\partial \ln P^{GP}(.)}{\partial \ln r_k} = \sum_{n=1}^{N} s_n^0 \frac{\partial (s_n^1/s_n^0)}{\partial \ln r_k} \ln(p_n^1/p_n^0) + s_k^1$$

$$= \sum_{n=1}^{N} s_n^0 (s_n^1/s_n^0) \frac{\partial \ln(s_n^1/s_n^0)}{\partial \ln r_k} \ln(p_n^1/p_n^0) + s_k^1$$

$$= s_k^1 [1 + \ln r_k + \ln P^{GP}(.)], \qquad (3.263)$$

where (3.259) has been used to obtain the final line. It is clear that under rather exceptional circumstances these derivatives may become negative.

4

Decompositions and Subperiods

4.1 Introduction

In addition to measuring aggregate price or quantity change as such, it is important to be able to judge to what extent the individual commodities or groupings thereof contribute to the change. Put formally: what is the contribution of price relatives p_n^1/p_n^0 or quantity relatives x_n^1/x_n^0 $(n = 1, \ldots, N)$, or groupings of these relatives, to $P(p^1, x^1, p^0, x^0)$ or $Q(p^1, x^1, p^0, x^0)$, respectively? For most indices this question can be answered relatively easily, since they can be expressed as arithmetic or geometric means of price or quantity relatives. Some indices, however, look more or less decomposition-resistant. An important example is the Fisher price or quantity index.[1] Another example is the implicit Walsh-1 price or quantity index. The discussion of this sort of decompositions forms the content of section 4.2.

Also, being able to decompose an index commodity-wise is useful when one wants to compute indices where some commodity or group of commodities is excluded, in a way that is consistent with the original index. An example is the computation of a CPI excluding energy.

Section 4.3 is concerned with the decomposition of time periods into subperiods, and the relation of indices for subperiods to indices for periods. Studies of this issue are, as far as related to the measurement of aggregate price change, usually concerned with the problem of how to deal with so-called seasonal products. As far as is related to the measurement of aggregate quantity change, the issue emerges in the area of Quarterly National Accounts: is it possible to obtain consistency between growth rates

---

[1] For example, von der Lippe's (2001, p. 208) objection to Fisher indices is that "there is neither a weighted mean of relatives, nor a ratio of expenditures interpretation."

derived from quarterly and annual accounts? The purpose of section 4.3 is to present an integrated treatment of these two points of view.

4.2 Decompositions of Indices

4.2.1 Additive and Multiplicative Decompositions

We know that any price index $P(p^1, x^1, p^0, x^0)$ that satisfies axiom **A5** can be written as a function of price relatives p_n^1/p_n^0, comparison period values $v_n^1 = p_n^1 x_n^1$, and base period values $v_n^0 = p_n^0 x_n^0$ $(n = 1, \ldots, N)$. Likewise, any quantity index $Q(p^1, x^1, p^0, x^0)$ that satisfies axiom **A5'** can be written as a function of quantity relatives x_n^1/x_n^0, comparison period values v_n^1, and base period values v_n^0 $(n = 1, \ldots, N)$. The discussion in this section will be cast in terms of price indices. The reader should be able to make the obvious transformation to quantity indices.

As we have seen, a large number of price indices can be expressed as a weighted arithmetic average of price relatives,

$$P(p^1, x^1, p^0, x^0) = \sum_{n=1}^{N} w_n(v^1, v^0)(p_n^1/p_n^0), \qquad (4.1)$$

for some set of positive weights $w_n(v^1, v^0)$ $(n = 1, \ldots, N)$ such that their sum $\sum_{n=1}^{N} w_n(v^1, v^0) = 1$. This will be called an additive decomposition. If such an identity holds, it can be reformulated as

$$P(p^1, x^1, p^0, x^0) - 1 = \sum_{n=1}^{N} w_n(v^1, v^0)(p_n^1/p_n^0 - 1); \qquad (4.2)$$

that is, the percentage change of the price index is a weighted average of the percentage price changes of the individual commodities. However, since percentage changes, when of small magnitude, can be approximated by logarithmic differences, the foregoing expression can be read as saying that

$$\ln P(p^1, x^1, p^0, x^0) \approx \sum_{n=1}^{N} w_n(v^1, v^0) \ln(p_n^1/p_n^0). \qquad (4.3)$$

The question now is, do there exist positive weights σ_n $(n = 1, \ldots, N)$, $\sum_{n=1}^{N} \sigma_n = 1$, such that

$$\ln P(p^1, x^1, p^0, x^0) = \sum_{n=1}^{N} \sigma_n \ln(p_n^1/p_n^0) \qquad (4.4)$$

holds exactly? This will be called a multiplicative decomposition. The answer appears to be affirmative, and the tool thereby used is the logarithmic mean, as will be shown next.

The first step is to rewrite expression (4.1) as

$$\sum_{n=1}^{N} w_n(.)(P(.) - p_n^1/p_n^0) = 0,$$

(4.5)

where the arguments of $P(.)$ and $w_n(.)$ $(n = 1, \ldots, N)$ have been suppressed. Applying the definition of the logarithmic mean (see appendix 1 of chapter 3), one obtains

$$\sum_{n=1}^{N} w_n(.)L(P(.),\, p_n^1/p_n^0) \ln(P(.)p_n^0/p_n^1) = 0.$$

(4.6)

This can be split as

$$\sum_{n=1}^{N} w_n(.)L(P(.),\, p_n^1/p_n^0) \ln P(.) - \sum_{n=1}^{N} w_n(.)L(P(.),\, p_n^1/p_n^0) \ln(p_n^1/p_n^0) = 0,$$

(4.7)

from which it follows that (4.4) holds with

$$\sigma_n(p^1/p^0, v^1, v^0) \equiv \frac{w_n(.)L(P(.),\, p_n^1/p_n^0)}{\sum_{n=1}^{N} w_n(.)L(P(.),\, p_n^1/p_n^0)} \quad (n = 1, \ldots, N),$$

(4.8)

where p^1/p^0 denotes the vector of price relatives p_n^1/p_n^0 $(n = 1, \ldots, N)$. Notice that $\sigma_n(.)$ does not depend only on v^1 and v^0, but also on p^1/p^0.

Does the reverse also hold? As we have seen, a large number of price indices are defined as a weighted geometric average of price relatives,

$$P(p^1, x^1, p^0, x^0) = \prod_{n=1}^{N} (p_n^1/p_n^0)^{\sigma_n(v^1, v^0)},$$

(4.9)

so that this question is also important.

The first step is to rewrite expression (4.9), by taking the logarithm, as

$$\sum_{n=1}^{N} \sigma_n(.) \ln(p_n^1/p_n^0 P(.)) = 0.$$

(4.10)

We now apply the logarithmic mean to get

$$\sum_{n=1}^{N} \sigma_n(.) \frac{p_n^1/p_n^0 - P(.)}{L(p_n^1/p_n^0,\, P(.))} = 0,$$

(4.11)

which can be split as

$$\sum_{n=1}^{N} \frac{\sigma_n(.)}{L(p_n^1/p_n^0, P(.))}(p_n^1/p_n^0) - \sum_{n=1}^{N} \frac{\sigma_n(.)}{L(p_n^1/p_n^0, P(.))}P(.) = 0, \quad (4.12)$$

from which we see that expression (4.1) holds, although with

$$w_n(p^1/p^0, v^1, v^0) \equiv \frac{\sigma_n(.)/L(p_n^1/p_n^0, P(.))}{\sum_{n=1}^{N}\sigma_n(.)/L(p_n^1/p_n^0, P(.))} \quad (n = 1, \ldots, N). \quad (4.13)$$

A variant of the last reasoning leads to the result obtained by Reinsdorf (1996), that a geometric mean price index can be expressed as a basket-type price index. Notice that $w_n(.)$ does not depend only on v^1 and v^0, but also on the price relatives p^1/p^0.

Summarizing, we have seen that any price index that admits an additive decomposition also admits a multiplicative decomposition, and *vice versa*. The issue is important, since users of price statistics want to see decompositions of either of the two forms to get an idea where aggregate price change, as measured by $P(p^1, x^1, p^0, x^0)$, comes from. For most price indices this information can easily be provided. At first sight, however, this does not apply to the Fisher index.

Recall that the Fisher price index, as the geometric mean of the Laspeyres and the Paasche price indices, is defined by

$$P^F(p^1, x^1, p^0, x^0) \equiv [P^L(.)P^P(.)]^{1/2} \equiv \left(\frac{p^1 \cdot x^0}{p^0 \cdot x^0} \frac{p^1 \cdot x^1}{p^0 \cdot x^1}\right)^{1/2}, \quad (4.14)$$

and that the Fisher quantity index is defined by

$$Q^F(p^1, x^1, p^0, x^0) \equiv [Q^L(.)Q^P(.)]^{1/2} \equiv \left(\frac{p^0 \cdot x^1}{p^0 \cdot x^0} \frac{p^1 \cdot x^1}{p^1 \cdot x^0}\right)^{1/2}. \quad (4.15)$$

It has been shown in section 3.3.1 that the constituent parts, $P^L(.)$, $P^P(.)$, $Q^L(.)$, and $Q^P(.)$, can be written as weighted arithmetic means of price or quantity relatives. But does this also apply to the Fisher indices themselves?

In order to economize on notation, in the remainder of this section the vector of arguments (p^1, x^1, p^0, x^0) will be abbreviated by $(1, 0)$. Recall that the Fisher indices satisfy the factor reversal test **T4**; that is,

$$P^F(1, 0)Q^F(1, 0) = \frac{p^1 \cdot x^1}{p^0 \cdot x^0}. \quad (4.16)$$

One also easily checks that

$$\frac{P^F(1,0)}{Q^F(1,0)} = \frac{p^1 \cdot x^0}{p^0 \cdot x^1},$$

(4.17)

which is an important relation to be used in the sequel.

4.2.2 Additive Decompositions of the Fisher Index

The first solution to problem (4.1) was provided by Van IJzeren (1952), unfortunately in an article in a rather obscure publication series of what is now called Statistics Netherlands. Van IJzeren (1983) restated his solution, but now in the context of international price and quantity comparisons. Both publications, however, apparently escaped the attention of the wider statistical community, which has led to a number of rediscoveries.

Van IJzeren's (1952) basic result was the following identity,

$$P^F(1,0) = \frac{p^1 \cdot x^0 + p^1 \cdot x^1/Q^F(1,0)}{p^0 \cdot x^0 + p^0 \cdot x^1/Q^F(1,0)},$$

(4.18)

which can easily be checked by repeated use of the product relation (4.16). In more familiar notation (4.18) reads

$$P^F(1,0) = \frac{\sum_{n=1}^N (x_n^0 + x_n^1/Q^F(1,0)) p_n^1}{\sum_{n=1}^N (x_n^0 + x_n^1/Q^F(1,0)) p_n^0},$$

(4.19)

which has the form of a ratio of values. Note that, apart from the division of comparison period quantities by $Q^F(1,0)$, the right-hand side of this expression is equal to the well-known Marshall-Edgeworth price index, which compares prices by using the average quantities of both periods. If, say, on average, all quantities increase between base and comparison period, then the structure of the vector of average quantities will be dominated by the structure of the quantity vector of the comparison period. This asymmetry of the Marshall-Edgeworth is, so to speak, corrected through "deflating" all comparison period quantities by the quantity index. But the resulting expression turns out to be equivalent to the Fisher price index.

In terms of percentage changes one obtains from (4.18)

$$P^F(1,0) - 1 = \sum_{n=1}^N \left(\frac{p_n^0 x_n^0}{p^0 \cdot x^0 + p^0 \cdot x^1/Q^F(1,0)} \right.$$

$$\left. + \frac{p_n^0 x_n^1/Q^F(1,0)}{p^0 \cdot x^0 + p^0 \cdot x^1/Q^F(1,0)} \right) \left(\frac{p_n^1 - p_n^0}{p_n^0} \right),$$

(4.20)

which, using the definition of value shares,[2] can be simplified to

$$
P^F(1,0) - 1 = \sum_{n=1}^{N} \left(\frac{Q^F(1,0)}{Q^F(1,0)+Q^L(1,0)} s_n^0 \right.
$$
$$
\left. + \frac{Q^L(1,0)}{Q^F(1,0)+Q^L(1,0)} s_n^{01} \right) \left(\frac{p_n^1 - p_n^0}{p_n^0} \right). \quad (4.21)
$$

This is an expression of the desired form (4.2). Note that all the weights are positive and add up to 1. Each weight is a convex combination of s_n^0, which might be called the Laspeyres weight, and s_n^{01}, which might be called the Paasche weight.[3]

Diewert (2002a) and Reinsdorf, Diewert, and Ehemann (2002) obtained, via an economic-theoretic detour, the following identity:

$$
P^F(1,0) - 1 = \frac{(p^1 - p^0) \cdot (x^0 + (P^F(1,0)/Q^F(1,0))x^1)}{p^0 \cdot x^0 + P^F(1,0)\, p^0 \cdot x^0}. \quad (4.22)
$$

This identity can easily be checked by using the relations (4.16) and (4.17). Using more familiar notation, expression (4.22) reads

$$
P^F(1,0) - 1 = \sum_{n=1}^{N} \left(\frac{p_n^0 x_n^0 + (P^F(1,0)/Q^F(1,0))\, p_n^0 x_n^1}{p^0 \cdot x^0 + P^F(1,0)\, p^0 \cdot x^0} \right) \left(\frac{p_n^1 - p_n^0}{p_n^0} \right).
$$
$$
(4.23)
$$

It appears that, by using (4.17), this expression can be simplified to

$$
P^F(1,0) - 1 = \sum_{n=1}^{N} \left(\frac{1}{1 + P^F(1,0)} s_n^0 + \frac{P^L(1,0)}{1 + P^F(1,0)} s_n^{01} \right) \left(\frac{p_n^1 - p_n^0}{p_n^0} \right),
$$
$$
(4.24)
$$

which has the same structure as expression (4.21). The important difference is that the weights in (4.24) do not add up to 1. In particular, they add up to $(1 + P^L(1,0))/(1 + P^F(1,0))$, which is larger (smaller) than 1 if and only if $P^L(1,0)$ is larger (smaller) than $P^F(1,0)$. The weights add up to 1 only in the trivial case when $P^F(1,0) = P^L(1,0)$.

---

[2] Recall that $s_n^t = p_n^t x_n^t / p^t \cdot x^t$ ($n = 1, \ldots, N; t = 0, 1$). Moreover, $s_n^{01} \equiv p_n^0 x_n^1 / p^0 \cdot x^1$ ($n = 1, \ldots, N$).

[3] The corresponding expression for $Q^F(1,0) - 1$ is obtained by interchanging prices and quantities in (4.21). This form appears to be used by the U.S. Bureau of Economic Analysis (see Moulton and Seskin 1999). An alternative, less appealing, derivation was provided by Reinsdorf *et al.* (2002). Also, Dumagan (2002) independently rediscovered (4.21).

By exploiting its property of being linearly homogeneous in comparison period prices, Hallerbach (2005) succeeded in deriving another additive decomposition of the Fisher price index. Unfortunately, in this decomposition the weights also do not add up to 1.

4.2.3 Multiplicative Decompositions of the Fisher Index

The first multiplicative decomposition of the Fisher price index was obtained by Vartia (1974, 1976). Its derivation makes repeated use of the logarithmic mean, as can be seen from the following sequence of expressions, which starts from the logarithmic version of expression (4.14):

$$2 \ln P^F(1,0)$$

$$= \ln \left(\frac{p^1 \cdot x^0}{p^0 \cdot x^0} \right) + \ln \left(\frac{p^1 \cdot x^1}{p^0 \cdot x^1} \right)$$

$$= \frac{p^1 \cdot x^0 - p^0 \cdot x^0}{L(p^1 \cdot x^0, p^0 \cdot x^0)} + \frac{p^1 \cdot x^1 - p^0 \cdot x^1}{L(p^1 \cdot x^1, p^0 \cdot x^1)}$$

$$= \sum_{n=1}^{N} \left(\frac{x_n^0}{L(p^1 \cdot x^0, p^0 \cdot x^0)} + \frac{x_n^1}{L(p^1 \cdot x^1, p^0 \cdot x^1)} \right) (p_n^1 - p_n^0)$$

$$= \sum_{n=1}^{N} \left(\frac{x_n^0}{L(p^1 \cdot x^0, p^0 \cdot x^0)} + \frac{x_n^1}{L(p^1 \cdot x^1, p^0 \cdot x^1)} \right) L(p_n^1, p_n^0) \ln(p_n^1/p_n^0)$$

$$= \sum_{n=1}^{N} \left(\frac{L(p_n^1, p_n^0)x_n^0}{L(p^1 \cdot x^0, p^0 \cdot x^0)} + \frac{L(p_n^1, p_n^0)x_n^1}{L(p^1 \cdot x^1, p^0 \cdot x^1)} \right) \ln(p_n^1/p_n^0). \qquad (4.25)$$

Using the property that the logarithmic mean is linearly homogeneous, one finally obtains

$$\ln P^F(1,0) = (1/2) \sum_{n=1}^{N} \left(\frac{L(p_n^1 x_n^0, p_n^0 x_n^0)}{L(p^1 \cdot x^0, p^0 \cdot x^0)} + \frac{L(p_n^1 x_n^1, p_n^0 x_n^1)}{L(p^1 \cdot x^1, p^0 \cdot x^1)} \right) \ln(p_n^1/p_n^0). \tag{4.26}$$

Again using the property of linear homogeneity, this expression can be rewritten as

$$\ln P^F(1,0) = (1/2) \sum_{n=1}^{N} \left(\frac{L(p_n^1/p_n^0, 1)}{L(P^L(1,0), 1)} s_n^0 + \frac{L(p_n^1/p_n^0, 1)}{L(P^P(1,0), 1)} s_n^{01} \right) \ln(p_n^1/p_n^0), \tag{4.27}$$

or, alternatively, as

$$\ln P^F(1,0) = (1/2) \sum_{n=1}^{N} \left(\frac{L(p_n^1/p_n^0, 1)}{L(P^L(1,0),1)} s_n^0 + \frac{L(p_n^0/p_n^1, 1)}{L(1/P^P(1,0),1)} s_n^1 \right) \ln(p_n^1/p_n^0).$$

$$(4.28)$$

Do the weights in these two expressions add up to 1? Using the fact that $L(a,1)$ is concave (see appendix 1 of chapter 3), and applying the well-known Jensen Inequality, one sees that

$$\sum_{n=1}^{N} s_n^0 L(p_n^1/p_n^0, 1) \leq L \left(\sum_{n=1}^{N} s_n^0 (p_n^1/p_n^0), 1 \right) = L(P^L(1,0),1) \quad (4.29)$$

and

$$\sum_{n=1}^{N} s_n^{01} L(p_n^1/p_n^0, 1) \leq L \left(\sum_{n=1}^{N} s_n^{01} (p_n^1/p_n^0), 1 \right) = L(P^P(1,0),1). \quad (4.30)$$

Hence, the sum of the weights in expressions (4.27) and (4.28) is less than or equal to 1.

A more satisfactory multiplicative decomposition of the Fisher price index, that is, a decomposition of the form (4.9), was obtained by Reinsdorf *et al.* (2002). There are several ways to derive this result. Here is what seems to be the simplest one.

First, recall expressions (3.4) and (3.11), expressing the Laspeyres and Paasche price index as a weighted arithmetic average. Then, applying (4.4)–(4.8), we obtain

$$\ln P^L(1,0) = \sum_{n=1}^{N} \frac{s_n^0 L(p_n^1/p_n^0, P^L(1,0))}{\sum_{n=1}^{N} s_n^0 L(p_n^1/p_n^0, P^L(1,0))} \ln(p_n^1/p_n^0), \quad (4.31)$$

and

$$\ln P^P(1,0) = \sum_{n=1}^{N} \frac{s_n^{01} L(p_n^1/p_n^0, P^P(1,0))}{\sum_{n=1}^{N} s_n^{01} L(p_n^1/p_n^0, P^P(1,0))} \ln(p_n^1/p_n^0). \quad (4.32)$$

Combining the last two expressions, we obtain

$$\ln P^F(1,0) = [\ln P^L(1,0) + \ln P^P(1,0)]/2$$

$$= (1/2) \sum_{n=1}^{N} \left[\frac{s_n^0 L(p_n^1/p_n^0, P^L(1,0))}{\sum_{n=1}^{N} s_n^0 L(p_n^1/p_n^0, P^L(1,0))} \right.$$

$$\left. + \frac{s_n^{01} L(p_n^1/p_n^0, P^P(1,0))}{\sum_{n=1}^{N} s_n^{01} L(p_n^1/p_n^0, P^P(1,0))} \right] \ln(p_n^1/p_n^0). \quad (4.33)$$

This expression resembles (4.27), except that the weights now add up to 1. For alternative expressions the reader is referred to Balk (2004). Using one of these expressions, Ehemann (2005a) considered the ratio of a Fisher to a Törnqvist price index. But one can also use such an expression to compare the Fisher to the Sato-Vartia price index, which is also ideal.

4.2.4 Conclusion on the Fisher Index

The Fisher price index has as such not a "natural" additive or multiplicative decomposition. Nevertheless, it appears that such decompositions can be constructed. A satisfactory additive decomposition is provided by expression (4.21), and a satisfactory multiplicative decomposition is provided by expression (4.33).

In the case of the Fisher quantity index it is interesting to note that Kohli (2002) compared the two decompositions on data concerning U.S. GDP change over the period 1981–2001. It appeared that, whenever the changes were modest, the results exhibited stark similarity. Over longer periods, however, the differences appeared to be not negligible.

Dumagan (2005) argues that the multiplicative decomposition should be preferred when the price and quantity index are considered together. The reason is that, according to expression (4.16),

$$\ln P^F(1,0) + \ln Q^F(1,0) = \ln \left(\frac{p^1 \cdot x^1}{p^0 \cdot x^0} \right), \quad (4.34)$$

whereas

$$(P^F(1,0) - 1) + (Q^F(1,0) - 1) \neq \frac{p^1 \cdot x^1}{p^0 \cdot x^0} - 1. \quad (4.35)$$

Moreover, since $\ln z \leq z - 1$, percentage changes based on a multiplicative decomposition are always smaller than those based on an additive decomposition.

The additive decomposition can also be used to throw more light on the fact that the Fisher indices, though satisfying the proportionality axioms **A6, A6′**, in general do not satisfy the equality tests **T7, T7′**. Let, as in section 3.7.1, the aggregate under consideration be called A, and let A be partitioned arbitrarily into K subaggregates A_k,

$$A = \cup_{k=1}^{K} A_k, \quad A_k \cap A_l = \emptyset \; (k \neq l).$$

Let $N_k \geq 1$ denote the number of commodities contained in A_k ($k = 1, \ldots, K$). Obviously $N = \sum_{k=1}^{K} N_k$. Let $(p_k^1, x_k^1, p_k^0, x_k^0) \equiv (1_k, 0_k)$ be the subvector of $(p^1, x^1, p^0, x^0) \equiv (1, 0)$ corresponding to the subaggregate A_k. Recall that $v_n^t \equiv p_n^t x_n^t$ is the value of commodity n at period t. Then $V_k^t \equiv \sum_{n \in A_k} v_n^t$ ($k = 1, \ldots, K$) is the value of subaggregate A_k at period t, and $V^t \equiv \sum_{n \in A} v_n^t = \sum_{k=1}^{K} V_k^t$ is the value of aggregate A at period t.

Consider the Fisher price index, and rewrite expression (4.21) in the following form:

$$P_N^F(1, 0) = \sum_{n=1}^{N} \left(\frac{Q_N^F(1, 0)}{Q_N^F(1, 0) + Q_N^L(1, 0)} s_n^0 + \frac{Q_N^L(1, 0)}{Q_N^F(1, 0) + Q_N^L(1, 0)} s_n^{01} \right) \left(\frac{p_n^1}{p_n^0} \right).$$

$$(4.36)$$

For each subaggregate A_k ($k = 1, \ldots, K$) the weights and price relatives occurring in this expression can be used to construct a price index of the form

$$P_{N_k}(1_k, 0_k) \equiv \frac{\sum_{n \in A_k} \left(\frac{Q_N^F(1,0)}{Q_N^F(1,0) + Q_N^L(1,0)} s_n^0 + \frac{Q_N^L(1,0)}{Q_N^F(1,0) + Q_N^L(1,0)} s_n^{01} \right) \left(\frac{p_n^1}{p_n^0} \right)}{\sum_{n \in A_k} \left(\frac{Q_N^F(1,0)}{Q_N^F(1,0) + Q_N^L(1,0)} s_n^0 + \frac{Q_N^L(1,0)}{Q_N^F(1,0) + Q_N^L(1,0)} s_n^{01} \right)}. \quad (4.37)$$

One checks easily that, if $P_{N_k}(1_k, 0_k) = \lambda$ for all $k = 1, \ldots, K$, then $P_N^F(1, 0) = \lambda$, the reason being that

$$P_N^F(1, 0) = \sum_{k=1}^{K} \left(\sum_{n \in A_k} \left(\frac{Q_N^F(1, 0)}{Q_N^F(1, 0) + Q_N^L(1, 0)} s_n^0 \right. \right.$$

$$\left. \left. + \frac{Q_N^L(1, 0)}{Q_N^F(1, 0) + Q_N^L(1, 0)} s_n^{01} \right) \right) P_{N_k}(1_k, 0_k), \quad (4.38)$$

in which the weights add up to 1. However, the price indices $P_{N_k}(1_k, 0_k)$ are not identical to the subaggregate Fisher price indices

$$P_{N_k}^F(1_k, 0_k) = \sum_{n \in A_k} \left(\frac{Q_{N_k}^F(1_k, 0_k)}{Q_{N_k}^F(1_k, 0_k) + Q_{N_k}^L(1_k, 0_k)} \frac{v_n^0}{V_k^0} \right.$$

$$\left. + \frac{Q_{N_k}^L(1_k, 0_k)}{Q_{N_k}^F(1_k, 0_k) + Q_{N_k}^L(1_k, 0_k)} \frac{p_n^0 x_n^1}{p_k^0 \cdot x_k^1} \right) \left(\frac{p_n^1}{p_n^0} \right). \quad (4.39)$$

A careful consideration of expression (4.37) reveals that each subaggregate price index $P_{N_k}(1_k, 0_k)$ is not only a function of the prices and quantities of subaggregate A_k but, via its weights, also a function of the prices and quantities of the other subaggregates.

Put otherwise, there is a choice to be made here. Starting from a Fisher price index for the aggregate, price indices for the subaggregates can be constructed by (4.37). This yields an additive system, but the subaggregate price indices are not Fisher indices. The alternative is to compute the subaggregate price indices as Fisher indices, but then the resulting system is not additive.

4.2.5 The Implicit Walsh Index

Not all the price indices can be written in the separable form of expression (4.1). An example is the Walsh-1 price index, which was defined as

$$P^{W1}(1, 0) \equiv \frac{\sum_{n=1}^{N} p_n^1 (x_n^0 x_n^1)^{1/2}}{\sum_{n=1}^{N} p_n^0 (x_n^0 x_n^1)^{1/2}}. \quad (4.40)$$

It is simple to verify that

$$P^{W1}(1, 0) = \sum_{n=1}^{N} w_n(x^1/x^0, v^0)(p_n^1/p_n^0), \quad (4.41)$$

where $w_n(x^1/x^0, v^0) \equiv v_n^0 (x_n^1/x_n^0)^{1/2} / \sum_{n=1}^{N} v_n^0 (x_n^1/x_n^0)^{1/2}$ $(n = 1, \ldots, N)$ and x^1/x^0 denotes the vector of quantity relatives x_n^1/x_n^0 $(n = 1, \ldots, N)$. The implicit Walsh-1 quantity index is defined by

$$\bar{Q}^{W1}(1, 0) \equiv (p^1 \cdot x^1/p^0 \cdot x^0)/P^{W1}(1, 0), \quad (4.42)$$

which can be written as

$$\tilde{Q}^{W1}(1,0) = \frac{\sum_{n=1}^{N} s_n^0 (x_n^1/x_n^0)^{1/2}}{\sum_{n=1}^{N} s_n^1 (x_n^1 x_n^0)^{-1/2}}, \tag{4.43}$$

where, as usual, s_n^t ($n = 1, \ldots, N; t = 0, 1$) denote value shares. The question now is: does $\tilde{Q}^{W1}(1,0) - 1$ admit an additive decomposition? Diewert (2002a) answered this question affirmatively by using an economic-theoretic detour. Here a simple mathematical derivation will be provided.

Consider expression (4.42) with (4.40) substituted, and rewrite this as

$$\frac{\sum_{n=1}^{N} p_n^0 (x_n^0 x_n^1)^{1/2}}{p^0 \cdot x^0} = \frac{\sum_{n=1}^{N} p_n^1 (x_n^0 x_n^1)^{1/2}}{p^1 \cdot x^1} \tilde{Q}^{W1}(1,0). \tag{4.44}$$

Define normalized prices by $w_n^t \equiv p_n^t / p^t \cdot x^t$ ($n = 1, \ldots, N; t = 0, 1$) and notice that $w^t \cdot x^t = 1$ ($t = 0, 1$). Using this definition, and adding $\tilde{Q}^{W1}(1,0) - 1$ to both sides, expression (4.44) can be written as

$$\tilde{Q}^{W1}(1,0) - 1 = \sum_{n=1}^{N} w_n^0 (x_n^0 x_n^1)^{1/2} - \sum_{n=1}^{N} w_n^0 x_n^0 + \sum_{n=1}^{N} w_n^1 x_n^1 \tilde{Q}^{W1}(1,0)$$

$$- \sum_{n=1}^{N} w_n^1 (x_n^0 x_n^1)^{1/2} \tilde{Q}^{W1}(1,0). \tag{4.45}$$

Then it follows that

$$\tilde{Q}^{W1}(1,0) - 1 = \sum_{n=1}^{N} \left(w_n^0 (x_n^0)^{1/2} + w_n^1 (x_n^1)^{1/2} \tilde{Q}^{W1}(1,0) \right) \left((x_n^1)^{1/2} - (x_n^0)^{1/2} \right)$$

$$= \sum_{n=1}^{N} \frac{(w_n^0 (x_n^0)^{1/2} + w_n^1 (x_n^1)^{1/2} \tilde{Q}^{W1}(1,0))}{(x_n^0)^{1/2} + (x_n^1)^{1/2}} (x_n^1 - x_n^0)$$

$$= \sum_{n=1}^{N} \frac{(s_n^0 + s_n^1 (x_n^1/x_n^0)^{-1/2} \tilde{Q}^{W1}(1,0))}{1 + (x_n^1/x_n^0)^{1/2}} \left(\frac{x_n^1 - x_n^0}{x_n^0} \right), \tag{4.46}$$

by observing that $w_n^t x_n^t = s_n^t$ ($n = 1, \ldots, N; t = 0, 1$). It is important to notice, however, that these weights do not add up to 1.

4.3 Indices for Periods and Subperiods

Suppose that every period t consists of M subperiods. Let x_n^{tm} denote the quantity of commodity n ($n = 1, \ldots, N$) consumed or produced during subperiod m ($m = 1, \ldots, M$) of period t, and let p_n^{tm} denote the corresponding unit value. All the prices and quantities are supposed to be positive. The aggregate value at period t is naturally defined as

$$V^t \equiv \sum_{m=1}^{M} \sum_{n=1}^{N} p_n^{tm} x_n^{tm}. \qquad (4.47)$$

This value can be disaggregated in two ways. The first way is to disaggregate according to subperiods. The aggregate value at subperiod tm is naturally defined as

$$V^{tm} \equiv \sum_{n=1}^{N} p_n^{tm} x_n^{tm} \ (m = 1, \dots, M), \qquad (4.48)$$

and we see that

$$V^t = \sum_{m=1}^{M} V^{tm}. \qquad (4.49)$$

Looking at the aggregation process bottom-up, expressions (4.48) and (4.49) mean that one first aggregates over commodities per subperiod and next over subperiods. This procedure reflects the time order according to which data collection usually proceeds.[4,5]

However, the order of aggregation can be reversed. Thus, aggregating per commodity over the subperiods, the natural definition of the period t quantity is

$$x_n^t \equiv \sum_{m=1}^{M} x_n^{tm} \ (n = 1, \dots, N), \qquad (4.50)$$

and the corresponding unit value is obtained as the period t value divided by the period t quantity,

$$p_n^t \equiv \sum_{m=1}^{M} p_n^{tm} x_n^{tm} \Big/ \sum_{m=1}^{M} x_n^{tm} \ (n = 1, \dots, N). \qquad (4.51)$$

[4] In practice, V^t might be estimated from a different source than V^{tm}. For instance, the source that delivers high-frequency data, usually of preliminary nature, can differ from the source that delivers low-frequency data that are moreover considered to be final. In all such cases the high-frequency data must be adjusted, so that the accounting identity (4.49) is satisfied. In general, some sort of reconciliation will be performed in which additional constraints are imposed; for instance, the main developments shown by the preliminary (unadjusted) high-frequency data should be preserved in the adjusted data. This is known as the "benchmarking" of time series. A classic paper in this area was written by Denton (1971).

[5] Recall that it was assumed that the length of the time period t is such that it is considered meaningful to add up subperiod values. If not, then subperiod values must first be deflated.

One simply checks that

$$V^t = \sum_{n=1}^{N} p_n^t x_n^t. \tag{4.52}$$

The notation highlights the fact that, if we had started with period t as the smallest temporal unit of observation, then our basic data would have been p_n^t and x_n^t ($n = 1, \ldots, N$).

Bilateral price and quantity indices can be used to compare any subperiod tm to any other subperiod $t'm'$; any period t to any other period t'; and any subperiod tm to any period t'. Some comparisons, however, are "more natural" than other comparisons. This should be determined case by case by considering the nature of the aggregate involved. For instance, when production or consumption exhibits a seasonal pattern – due to climate and/or custom – the most natural length of period t is a year (which does not necessarily mean that period t should be a calendar year). When over the years the seasonal pattern is relatively stable, the most natural subperiod-subperiod comparisons are those between corresponding subperiods of different periods: that is, between subperiods tm and $t'm$ ($m = 1, \ldots, M$). Whether these subperiods should be months or quarters, however, depends to a large extent on the actual stability of the seasonal pattern; and this is, again, an empirical matter.

Since any period is the union of subperiods, a quite natural requirement is that in some sense subperiod-to-(sub)period indices be consistent with period-to-period indices. There are several approaches here.[6]

4.3.1 The Traditional Approach

The traditional approach, going back to Mudgett (1955) and Stone (1956), conceives the subperiod m in which commodity n is produced or consumed as an (additional) attribute of the commodity. Put otherwise, instead of N, we are dealing with NM commodities. Our vector notation must be extended somewhat to take account of this situation. Let $p^{tm} \equiv (p_1^{tm}, \ldots, p_N^{tm})$ and $x^{tm} \equiv (x_1^{tm}, \ldots, x_N^{tm})$ be the N-vectors of prices and quantities at subperiod m ($m = 1, \ldots, M$) of period t; let $p^t \equiv (p_1^t, \ldots, p_N^t)$ and $x^t \equiv (x_1^t, \ldots, x_N^t)$ be the N-vectors of (average) prices and (total) quantities at period t; and let $\vec{p}^t \equiv (p^{t1}, \ldots, p^{tM})$ and

---

[6] A still very useful, CPI-oriented survey is Baldwin (1990). More recent are the *CPI Manual* and *PPI Manual* chapters by Diewert (2004b).

$\vec{x}^t \equiv (x^{t1}, \ldots, x^{tM})$ denote the NM-vectors of all period t prices and quantities, respectively.

Using this notation one can also write $V^{tm} = p^{tm} \cdot x^{tm}$ $(m = 1, \ldots, M)$ and $V^t = \vec{p}^t \cdot \vec{x}^t = \sum_{m=1}^{M} p^{tm} \cdot x^{tm}$.

Let $P(.)$ and $Q(.)$ be a price index and quantity index, respectively, where as before a subscript will be added to indicate the dimension of the price and quantity vectors involved. Both indices are supposed to satisfy the basic axioms, in particular the linear homogeneity axioms **A2** and **A2′**. It is assumed that $P(.)$ and $Q(.)$ are used for comparing period 1 to period 0, as well as for comparing subperiod $1m$ to subperiod $0m$ $(m = 1, \ldots, M)$.

In particular, aggregate price change between comparison period 1 and base period 0 is measured by $P_{NM}(1, 0) \equiv P_{NM}(\vec{p}^1, \vec{x}^1, \vec{p}^0, \vec{x}^0)$, and aggregate quantity change by $Q_{NM}(1, 0) \equiv Q_{NM}(\vec{p}^1, \vec{x}^1, \vec{p}^0, \vec{x}^0)$. Likewise, aggregate price change between subperiods $1m$ and $0m$ is measured by $P_N(1m, 0m) \equiv P_N(p^{1m}, x^{1m}, p^{0m}, x^{0m})$, and aggregate quantity change by $Q_N(1m, 0m) \equiv Q_N(p^{1m}, x^{1m}, p^{0m}, x^{0m})$ $(m = 1, \ldots, M)$. Which relations does one want to exist?

The first requirement is that the product test **T3** be satisfied for periods as well as subperiods; that is, one requires that

$$V^1 / V^0 = P_{NM}(1, 0) Q_{NM}(1, 0) \tag{4.53}$$

and

$$V^{1m} / V^{0m} = P_N(1m, 0m) Q_N(1m, 0m) \ (m = 1, \ldots, M). \tag{4.54}$$

The second requirement is that the price index and the quantity index be consistent-in-aggregation; that is, the relation between period and subperiod indices must have the same functional form as the indices themselves, provided that commodity relatives and values are replaced by subperiod indices and values. Put formally, it is required that **T6** hold,

$$\psi(P_{NM}(1, 0), V^0, V^1) = \sum_{m=1}^{M} \psi(P_N(1m, 0m), V^{0m}, V^{1m}), \tag{4.55}$$

or that **T6′** hold,

$$\zeta(Q_{NM}(1, 0), V^0, V^1) = \sum_{m=1}^{M} \zeta(Q_N(1m, 0m), V^{0m}, V^{1m}), \tag{4.56}$$

where $\psi(.)$ and $\zeta(.)$ are continuous functions that are strictly monotonic in their first argument.

The third requirement is that the equality tests **T7** and **T7'** be satisfied; that is,

$$\text{if } P_N(1m, 0m) = \lambda \ (m = 1, \ldots, M) \text{ then } P_{NM}(1, 0) = \lambda; \quad (4.57)$$

and

$$\text{if } Q_N(1m, 0m) = \lambda \ (m = 1, \ldots, M) \text{ then } Q_{NM}(1, 0) = \lambda. \quad (4.58)$$

In particular this means that, if there is no price or quantity change between each of the corresponding subperiods then there is no overall price or quantity change, either.

The reader recognizes all these requirements as precisely those occurring in Theorem 3.19. The conclusion therefore is that the only indices satisfying these requirements are the pairs $< P^L(.), Q^P(.) >$ and $< P^P(.), Q^L(.) >$. Indeed, as one verifies easily,

$$
\begin{aligned}
P_{NM}^L(1, 0) &= \frac{\sum_{m=1}^{M} \sum_{n=1}^{N} p_n^{1m} x_n^{0m}}{\sum_{m=1}^{M} \sum_{n=1}^{N} p_n^{0m} x_n^{0m}} \\
&= \sum_{m=1}^{M} \left(\frac{p^{0m} \cdot x^{0m}}{p^0 \cdot x^0} \frac{p^{1m} \cdot x^{0m}}{p^{0m} \cdot x^{0m}} \right) \\
&= \sum_{m=1}^{M} (V^{0m} / V^0) P_N^L(1m, 0m).
\end{aligned}
\quad (4.59)
$$

Here, the period-to-period Laspeyres price index is a weighted arithmetic mean of the subperiod-to-corresponding-subperiod Laspeyres price indices, whereby the weights are equal to the relative aggregate values of the base subperiods. Such subperiod price indices were proposed by Bean and Stine (1924) for the first time (and called "Type D" indices).

By using relation (3.72) one verifies also that

$$
\begin{aligned}
(Q_{NM}^P(1, 0))^{-1} &= \frac{\sum_{m=1}^{M} \sum_{n=1}^{N} p_n^{1m} x_n^{0m}}{\sum_{m=1}^{M} \sum_{n=1}^{N} p_n^{1m} x_n^{1m}} \\
&= \sum_{m=1}^{M} \left(\frac{p^{1m} \cdot x^{1m}}{p^1 \cdot x^1} \frac{p^{1m} \cdot x^{0m}}{p^{1m} \cdot x^{1m}} \right) \\
&= \sum_{m=1}^{M} (V^{1m} / V^1)(Q_N^P(1m, 0m))^{-1}.
\end{aligned}
\quad (4.60)
$$

Here the type of mean is harmonic, and the relative aggregate values are those of the comparison period.

Similarly, it appears that

$$
\begin{aligned}
(P_{NM}^P(1,0))^{-1} &= \frac{\sum_{m=1}^M \sum_{n=1}^N p_n^{0m} x_n^{1m}}{\sum_{m=1}^M \sum_{n=1}^N p_n^{1m} x_n^{1m}} \\
&= \sum_{m=1}^M \left(\frac{p^{1m} \cdot x^{1m}}{p^1 \cdot x^1} \frac{p^{0m} \cdot x^{1m}}{p^{1m} \cdot x^{1m}} \right) \\
&= \sum_{m=1}^M (V^{1m}/V^1)(P_N^P(1m,0m))^{-1},
\end{aligned} \tag{4.61}
$$

$$
\begin{aligned}
Q_{NM}^L(1,0) &= \frac{\sum_{m=1}^M \sum_{n=1}^N p_n^{0m} x_n^{1m}}{\sum_{m=1}^M \sum_{n=1}^N p_n^{0m} x_n^{0m}} \\
&= \sum_{m=1}^M \left(\frac{p^{0m} \cdot x^{0m}}{p^0 \cdot x^0} \frac{p^{0m} \cdot x^{1m}}{p^{0m} \cdot x^{0m}} \right) \\
&= \sum_{m=1}^M (V^{0m}/V^0) Q_N^L(1m,0m).
\end{aligned} \tag{4.62}
$$

The foregoing equations, especially (4.59), constitute the traditional solution to the problem of handling consumer or producer aggregates in which seasonal commodities occur. Notice that these expressions can accommodate commodities for which certain quantities x_n^{lm} are equal to zero. The single requirement is that $x_n^{1m} \neq 0$ whenever $x_n^{0m} \neq 0$, or, what amounts to the same, that p_n^{1m} exist whenever p_n^{0m} exists.

When the seasonal pattern is relatively stable, then the subperiod-to-corresponding-subperiod indices $P_N^L(1m, 0m)$ $(m = 1, \ldots, M)$ are free from seasonal effects. Moreover, due to the fact that each period-to-period index is a mean of all the subperiod-to-corresponding-subperiod indices, the last can be conceived as estimators of the first. For the Laspeyres indices $P_{NM}^L(1,0)$ and $Q_{NM}^L(1,0)$ it is even possible, when time progresses, say, from the first to the last subperiod of period 1, to improve upon the estimator of the period-to-period index by averaging over more and more subperiod-to-corresponding-subperiod indices until the target is reached. Notice, however, that all the means in expressions (4.59)–(4.62) are weighted. Taking unweighted (arithmetic or harmonic) means of the subperiod-to-corresponding-subperiod indices presupposes that $V^{0m}/V^0 = 1/M$ or $V^{1m}/V^1 = 1/M$ $(m = 1, \ldots, M)$, depending on the type of index; that is, all the subperiods are supposed to be equally important.

A disadvantage of the traditional solution is that it does not deliver arbitrary subperiod-to-subperiod comparisons. The reader can check easily that, for example, the ratio $P_N^L(1m, 0m)/P_N^L(1m', 0m')$ $(m \neq m')$ is hard to interpret. The problem is that the comparisons of subperiods $1m$ to $0m$ and $1m'$ to $0m'$ are not connected by a joint element.

Finally, notice that when, per commodity, all the base subperiod quantities are the same, that is, $x_n^{0m}/x_n^0 = 1/M$ $(n = 1, \ldots, N; m = 1, \ldots, M)$, then the subperiod-to-corresponding-subperiod Laspeyres price index reduces to

$$P_N^L(1m, 0m) = \frac{p^{1m} \cdot x^0}{p^{0m} \cdot x^0}. \tag{4.63}$$

This price index compares the prices of subperiod $1m$ to those of the corresponding subperiod $0m$ by using the total (or average) period 0 quantity vector x^0. Bean and Stine (1924) called this a "Type B" index.

Similarly, when all base subperiod prices are the same, that is, $p_n^{0m}/p_n^0 = 1$ $(n = 1, \ldots, N; m = 1, \ldots, M)$, then the subperiod-to-corresponding-subperiod Laspeyres quantity index reduces to

$$Q_N^L(1m, 0m) = \frac{p^0 \cdot x^{1m}}{p^0 \cdot x^{0m}}. \tag{4.64}$$

This quantity index compares the quantities of subperiod $1m$ to those of the corresponding subperiod $0m$ by using the average period 0 price vector x^0. In the framework of Quarterly National Accounts, this is known as the "over-the-year" technique of calculating quarterly rates of volume change (see Bloem, Dippelsman, and Mæhle 2001).

Notice, however, that under any of these two assumptions it need not be the case that $V^{0m}/V^0 = 1/M$ $(m = 1, \ldots, M)$. Put otherwise, the unweighted average of subperiod-to-corresponding-subperiod indices will in general differ from the period-to-period index.

4.3.2 The First Alternative: Rothwell-Type Indices

There are a number of alternatives to the traditional approach, due to the fact that any period t value, V^t, can be expressed in a number of ways. The first alternative emerges when we notice that $V^t = \sum_{m=1}^M \sum_{n=1}^N p_n^t x_n^{tm}$ and consider the value ratio

$$\frac{V^1}{V^0} = \frac{\sum_{m=1}^M \sum_{n=1}^N p_n^{1m} x_n^{1m}}{\sum_{m=1}^M \sum_{n=1}^N p_n^0 x_n^{0m}}. \tag{4.65}$$

This means that we are comparing period 1 with data $(\vec{p}^1, \vec{x}^1)$ to period 0 with data $((p^0, \ldots, p^0), \vec{x}^0)$. Application of the theory of the previous section then delivers the following results: instead of expressions (4.59)–(4.62) we obtain, respectively,

$$
\begin{aligned}
P_{NM}^L(1,0) &= \frac{\sum_{m=1}^M \sum_{n=1}^N p_n^{1m} x_n^{0m}}{\sum_{m=1}^M \sum_{n=1}^N p_n^0 x_n^{0m}} \\
&= \sum_{m=1}^M \left(\frac{p^0 \cdot x^{0m}}{p^0 \cdot x^0} \frac{p^{1m} \cdot x^{0m}}{p^0 \cdot x^{0m}} \right) \\
&= \sum_{m=1}^M (p^0 \cdot x^{0m}/V^0) P_N^L(p^{1m}, x^{1m}, p^0, x^{0m}), \quad (4.66)
\end{aligned}
$$

$$
\begin{aligned}
(Q_{NM}^P(1,0))^{-1} &= \frac{\sum_{m=1}^M \sum_{n=1}^N p_n^{1m} x_n^{0m}}{\sum_{m=1}^M \sum_{n=1}^N p_n^{1m} x_n^{1m}} \\
&= \sum_{m=1}^M \left(\frac{p^{1m} \cdot x^{1m}}{p^1 \cdot x^1} \frac{p^{1m} \cdot x^{0m}}{p^{1m} \cdot x^{1m}} \right) \\
&= \sum_{m=1}^M (V^{1m}/V^1)(Q_N^P(p^{1m}, x^{1m}, p^0, x^{0m}))^{-1}, \quad (4.67)
\end{aligned}
$$

$$
\begin{aligned}
(P_{NM}^P(1,0))^{-1} &= \frac{\sum_{m=1}^M \sum_{n=1}^N p_n^0 x_n^{1m}}{\sum_{m=1}^M \sum_{n=1}^N p_n^{1m} x_n^{1m}} \\
&= \sum_{m=1}^M \left(\frac{p^{1m} \cdot x^{1m}}{p^1 \cdot x^1} \frac{p^0 \cdot x^{1m}}{p^{1m} \cdot x^{1m}} \right) \\
&= \sum_{m=1}^M (V^{1m}/V^1)(P_N^P(p^{1m}, x^{1m}, p^0, x^{0m}))^{-1}, \quad (4.68)
\end{aligned}
$$

$$
\begin{aligned}
Q_{NM}^L(1,0) &= \frac{\sum_{m=1}^M \sum_{n=1}^N p_n^0 x_n^{1m}}{\sum_{m=1}^M \sum_{n=1}^N p_n^0 x_n^{0m}} \\
&= \sum_{m=1}^M \left(\frac{p^0 \cdot x^{0m}}{p^0 \cdot x^0} \frac{p^0 \cdot x^{1m}}{p^0 \cdot x^{0m}} \right) \\
&= \sum_{m=1}^M (p^0 \cdot x^{0m}/V^0) Q_N^L(p^{1m}, x^{1m}, p^0, x^{0m}). \quad (4.69)
\end{aligned}
$$

In expression (4.66), $P_{NM}^L(1, 0)$ is written as a weighted arithmetic mean of Laspeyres price indices $P_N^L(p^{1m}, x^{1m}, p^0, x^{0m})$ $(m = 1, \ldots, M)$. Alternatively, one can view them as Lowe indices $P_N^{Lo}(p^{1m}, p^0; x^{0m})$. Each of these indices compares, per commodity, the price of subperiod $1m$ with the mean price of the whole period 0, using the quantity basket of the corresponding subperiod $0m$. Notice that the subperiod weights differ from the actual relative values V^{0m}/V^0; but they add up to 1. The subperiod-to-period price indices $P_N^L(p^{1m}, x^{1m}, p^0, x^{0m})$ go back to Rothwell (1958) and Bean and Stine (1924) ("Type C").

Notice that these indices can accommodate commodities for which certain quantities x_n^{tm} are equal to zero. The single requirement is that $x_n^{1m} \neq 0$ whenever $x_n^{0m} \neq 0$, or, what amounts to the same, that p_n^{1m} exist whenever p_n^{0m} exists.

Consider the ratio of two of those subperiod price indices. It appears that $P_N^L(p^{1m}, x^{1m}, p^0, x^{0m})/P_N^L(p^{1m'}, x^{1m'}, p^0, x^{0m'})$ $(m \neq m')$, although not a genuine price index for subperiod $1m$ relative to subperiod $1m'$, is better interpretable than in the traditional approach. As one easily checks,

$$\frac{P_N^L(p^{1m}, x^{1m}, p^0, x^{0m})}{P_N^L(p^{1m'}, x^{1m'}, p^0, x^{0m'})} = \frac{p^{1m} \cdot x^{0m}}{p^{1m'} \cdot x^{0m'}} \frac{p^0 \cdot x^{0m'}}{p^0 \cdot x^{0m}}, \tag{4.70}$$

which is a value index divided by a quantity index. Put otherwise, p^{1m} and $p^{1m'}$ are compared to the same base period price vector p^0. On the other hand, this means that these subperiod price indices will display seasonal effects, if any.

Notice that, when, per commodity, all the base subperiod quantities are the same, that is, $x_n^{0m}/x_n^0 = 1/M$ $(n = 1, \ldots, N; m = 1, \ldots, M)$, then the Rothwell price indices $P_N^L(p^{1m}, x^{1m}, p^0, x^{0m})$ reduce to $P_N^L(p^{1m}, x^{1m}, p^0, x^0)$. The last price index compares the prices of subperiod $1m$ to those of the base period by means of the total base period quantity vector x^0.

An interesting offspring was delivered by Mudgett (1955). At subperiod μ $(1 \leq \mu \leq M)$ of period 1 one calculates

$$\sum_{m=1}^{\mu} \frac{p^0 \cdot x^{0m}}{\sum_{m=1}^{\mu} p^0 \cdot x^{0m}} P_N^L(p^{1m}, x^{1m}, p^0, x^{0m}) \tag{4.71}$$

as a cumulative price index for the subperiods 11 to 1μ relative to the base period. At the final subperiod, that is, when $\mu = M$, one obtains the full period index $P_{NM}^L(1, 0)$.

In expression (4.69), the Laspeyres quantity index for period 1 relative to period 0 is seen to be equal to a weighted mean of quantity indices for corresponding subperiods, based on the vector of average period 0 prices p^0. Here we meet again the "over-the-year" technique that is used in the framework of Quarterly National Accounts, this time however without the need of making an additional assumption.

4.3.3 The Second Alternative: Same Subperiod Baskets

The second alternative emerges when we notice that $V^t = \sum_{m=1}^{M} \sum_{n=1}^{N} p_n^t x_n^t / M$, and consider the value ratio

$$\frac{V^1}{V^0} = \frac{\sum_{m=1}^{M} \sum_{n=1}^{N} p_n^{1m} x_n^{1m}}{\sum_{m=1}^{M} \sum_{n=1}^{N} p_n^0 x_n^0 / M}. \tag{4.72}$$

This means that we are comparing period 1 with data $(\vec{p}^1, \vec{x}^1)$ to period 0 with data $((p^0, \ldots, p^0), (x^0/M, \ldots, x^0/M))$. Each base subperiod is given the same price vector (namely, the vector of average prices) and the same quantity vector (namely, the vector of average quantities).

Application of the theory of section 4.3.1 then yields the following results: instead of expressions (4.59)–(4.62) we obtain, respectively,

$$\begin{aligned}
P_{NM}^L(1, 0) &= \frac{\sum_{m=1}^{M} \sum_{n=1}^{N} p_n^{1m} x_n^{0m}}{\sum_{m=1}^{M} \sum_{n=1}^{N} p_n^0 x_n^0 / M} \\
&= \sum_{m=1}^{M} \left(\frac{p^0 \cdot x^0/M}{p^0 \cdot x^0} \frac{p^{1m} \cdot x^0/M}{p^0 \cdot x^0/M} \right) \\
&= \sum_{m=1}^{M} (1/M) P_N^L(p^{1m}, x^{1m}, p^0, x^0/M), \tag{4.73}
\end{aligned}$$

$$\begin{aligned}
(Q_{NM}^P(1, 0))^{-1} &= \frac{\sum_{m=1}^{M} \sum_{n=1}^{N} p_n^{1m} x_n^0 / M}{\sum_{m=1}^{M} \sum_{n=1}^{N} p_n^{1m} x_n^{1m}} \\
&= \sum_{m=1}^{M} \left(\frac{p^{1m} \cdot x^{1m}}{p^1 \cdot x^1} \frac{p^{1m} \cdot x^0/M}{p^{1m} \cdot x^{1m}} \right) \\
&= \sum_{m=1}^{M} (V^{1m}/V^1)(Q_N^P(p^{1m}, x^{1m}, p^0, x^0/M))^{-1}, \tag{4.74}
\end{aligned}$$

$$(P_{NM}^P(1,0))^{-1} = \frac{\sum_{m=1}^M \sum_{n=1}^N p_n^0 x_n^{1m}}{\sum_{m=1}^M \sum_{n=1}^N p_n^{1m} x_n^{1m}}$$

$$= \sum_{m=1}^M \left(\frac{p^{1m} \cdot x^{1m}}{p^1 \cdot x^1} \frac{p^0 \cdot x^{1m}}{p^{1m} \cdot x^{1m}} \right)$$

$$= \sum_{m=1}^M (V^{1m}/V^1)(P_N^P(p^{1m}, x^{1m}, p^0, x^0/M))^{-1}, \quad (4.75)$$

$$Q_{NM}^L(1,0) = \frac{\sum_{m=1}^M \sum_{n=1}^N p_n^0 x_n^{1m}}{\sum_{m=1}^M \sum_{n=1}^N p_n^0 x_n^0/M}$$

$$= \sum_{m=1}^M \left(\frac{p^0 \cdot x^0/M}{p^0 \cdot x^0} \frac{p^0 \cdot x^{1m}}{p^0 \cdot x^0/M} \right)$$

$$= \sum_{m=1}^M (1/M) Q_N^L(p^{1m}, x^{1m}, p^0, x^0/M). \quad (4.76)$$

The first of these expressions, (4.73), shows that the period-to-period Laspeyres price index reduces to an unweighted mean of subperiod-to-period indices $P_N^L(p^{1m}, x^{1m}, p^0, x^0/M)$. These indices can alternatively be viewed as Lowe indices $P_N^{Lo}(p^{1m}, p^0; x^0/M)$. Each of these indices compares the prices of subperiod $1m$ to the average base period prices, by means of the base period (average) quantity vector (basket). In Bean and Stine's (1924) system these indices were classified as "Type A." Taking unweighted means corresponds to the usual practice of calculating, say, an annual consumer or producer price index number as unweighted average of monthly index numbers.

The ratio of two subperiod-to-period indices appears to be equal to

$$\frac{P_N^L(p^{1m}, x^{1m}, p^0, x^0/M)}{P_N^L(p^{1m'}, x^{1m'}, p^0, x^0/M)} = \frac{p^{1m} \cdot x^0}{p^{1m'} \cdot x^0} = P_N^{Lo}(p^{1m}, p^{1m'}; x^0). \quad (4.77)$$

This is a Lowe price index, comparing p^{1m} to $p^{1m'}$ by means of the vector of base period quantities x^0. Since this basket can differ starkly from the subperiod-specific baskets x^{1m} or $x^{1m'}$, this price index can be very uncharacteristic.

Using the same basket for every subperiod-to-period comparison can be viewed as an extreme form of seasonal adjustment on the part of the quantities. The prices, however, are entered unadjusted into the index. The result might be that the subperiod-to-period indices will display exaggerated seasonal behaviour, if any. Moreover, notice that these indices cannot accommodate commodities for which certain quantities x_n^{tm} are equal to zero and, consequentially, prices p_n^{tm} do not exist. In all those cases imputations must be executed; see Balk (1980a) for a discussion of methods.

The last of these expressions, (4.76), likewise shows that the period-to-period Laspeyres quantity index reduces to the unweighted mean of indices that compare the subperiod $1m$ quantity vector to the average period 0 quantity vector, based on average period 0 prices. In the area of Quarterly National Accounts this is known as the "annual overlap" method.

4.3.4 The Third Alternative: Balk-Type Indices

The third alternative basically generalizes the two foregoing ones. Notice that $V^t = \sum_{m=1}^{M} \sum_{n=1}^{N} p_n^t x_n^{t(t'm)}$, where $x_n^{t(t'm)} \equiv x_n^t x_n^{t'm} / x_n^{t'}$ ($m = 1, \ldots, M; n = 1, \ldots, N; t \neq t'$). This definition means that, for each commodity, the total period t quantity x_n^t is distributed over the subperiods according to the period t' proportions $x_n^{t'm} / x_n^{t'}$. Notice that $\sum_{m=1}^{M} x_n^{t(t'm)} = x_n^t$ ($n = 1, \ldots, N$).

Consider now the value ratio

$$\frac{V^1}{V^0} = \frac{\sum_{m=1}^{M} \sum_{n=1}^{N} p_n^{1m} x_n^{1m}}{\sum_{m=1}^{M} \sum_{n=1}^{N} p_n^0 x_n^{0(1m)}}. \tag{4.78}$$

This means that we are comparing period 1 with data $(\vec{p}^1, \vec{x}^1)$ to period 0 with data $((p^0, \ldots, p^0), (x^{0(11)}, \ldots, x^{0(1M)}))$. Application of the theory of section 4.3.1 then yields, instead of (4.59), the following decomposition:

$$
\begin{aligned}
P_{NM}^L(1,0) &= \frac{\sum_{m=1}^{M} \sum_{n=1}^{N} p_n^{1m} x_n^{0(1m)}}{\sum_{m=1}^{M} \sum_{n=1}^{N} p_n^0 x_n^0} \\
&= \sum_{m=1}^{M} \left(\frac{p^0 \cdot x^{0(1m)}}{p^0 \cdot x^0} \frac{p^{1m} \cdot x^{0(1m)}}{p^0 \cdot x^{0(1m)}} \right) \\
&= \sum_{m=1}^{M} (p^0 \cdot x^{0(1m)} / V^0) P_N^L(p^{1m}, x^{1m}, p^0, x^{0(1m)}). \tag{4.79}
\end{aligned}
$$

In this expression the period-to-period Laspeyres price index is written as a weighted mean of Laspeyres price indices $P_N^L(p^{1m}, x^{1m}, p^0, x^{0(1m)})$ ($m = 1, \ldots, M$). These indices can also be viewed as Lowe indices $P_N^{Lo}(p^{1m}, p^0; x^{0(1m)})$. Each of these price indices compares the prices of subperiod $1m$ to those of the entire period 0, by means of artificial quantities $x^{0(1m)}$. Though the subperiod weights differ from the actual relative values V^{0m}/V^0, they add up to 1. The decomposition (4.79) was developed by Balk (1980a, 1980c).

The ratio of two of these subperiod-to-period indices has, as before, the structure of a value index divided by a quantity index,

$$\frac{P_N^L(p^{1m}, x^{1m}, p^0, x^{0(1m)})}{P_N^L(p^{1m'}, x^{1m'}, p^0, x^{0(1m')})} = \frac{p^{1m} \cdot x^{0(1m)}}{p^{1m'} \cdot x^{0(1m')}} \frac{p^0 \cdot x^{0(1m')}}{p^0 \cdot x^{0(1m)}}, \quad (4.80)$$

which enables its interpretation. Put otherwise, both p^{1m} and $p^{1m'}$ are compared to the same base period price vector p^0. Reversely, this implies that these subperiod-to-period indices will display seasonal behaviour, if any.

Further, the decomposition (4.79) has the following interesting property. If for each commodity the comparison subperiod quantities are the same, $x_n^{1m}/x_n^1 = 1/M$, then $x_n^{0(1m)} = x_n^0/M$ $(m = 1, \ldots, M; n = 1, \ldots, N)$, and the decomposition reduces to

$$P_{NM}^L(1, 0) = \sum_{m=1}^{M} \left(\frac{1}{M} \frac{p^{1m} \cdot x^0}{p^0 \cdot x^0} \right). \quad (4.81)$$

Put otherwise, the period-to-period Laspeyres price index reduces to the unweighted mean of subperiod-to-period indices $P_N^L(p^{1m}, x^{1m}, p^0, x^0/M)$.

The advantage of Balk's approach over the other two approaches is that expression (4.79) is based on the comparison period's seasonal pattern. Hence, instability of this pattern through time does not lead to problems of computation and interpretation. Also, there is no need for imputations.[7]

Of course, the disadvantage is that computation of all the comparison subperiod indices must wait until the complete period has expired. As long as this is not the case, the artificial quantities $x^{0(1m)}$ could be replaced by actual quantities x_n^{0m}, which reduces the subperiod indices to those of Rothwell. Put otherwise, the Rothwell subperiod indices could be used as provisional estimators of price change between base period and comparison subperiods, the definitive measures at a later stage being given by $P_N^L(p^{1m}, x^{1m}, p^0, x^{0(1m)})$. Some other suggestions were discussed and illustrated by Balk (1980a, 1991).

It is left to the reader to derive the other three decompositions, namely for $Q_{NM}^P(1, 0)$, $P_{NM}^P(1, 0)$, and $Q_{NM}^L(1, 0)$.

---

[7] Numerical evidence on the devastating effects of unstable seasonal patterns is provided by Finkel, Rakhmilevic, and Roshal (2007).

4.3.5 Rolling Period Indices

The idea of aggregating prices and quantities by means of rolling (or moving) period indices was pioneered by Diewert (1983) (but there called "split year" comparisons).

Consider periods $t = 0, 1, 2, \ldots$ and let period 0 be chosen as base period. Next, consider the time span starting with subperiod $\mu + 1$ of a certain period $t - 1$ to subperiod μ of period t, where μ is some integer between 1 and M and $t \geq 1$. Any such series of M consecutive subperiods can be compared to the base period, provided that corresponding subperiods are compared to each other. In terms of the notation introduced in section 4.3.1 this means that we must compare the price vector $(p^{t1}, \ldots, p^{t\mu}, p^{t-1,\mu+1}, \ldots, p^{t-1,M})$ and its corresponding quantity vector $(x^{t1}, \ldots, x^{t\mu}, x^{t-1,\mu+1}, \ldots, x^{t-1,M})$ to the base period pair $(\vec{p}^0, \vec{x}^0)$. Imposing the same requirements as in section 4.3.1 leads to the following decomposition:

$$
\begin{aligned}
&P^L_{NM}((p^{t1}, \ldots, p^{t\mu}, p^{t-1,\mu+1}, \ldots, p^{t-1,M}), \\
&(x^{t1}, \ldots, x^{t\mu}, x^{t-1,\mu+1}, \ldots, x^{t-1,M}), \vec{p}^0, \vec{x}^0) \\
&= \sum_{m=1}^{\mu} \frac{V^{0m}}{V^0} \frac{p^{tm} \cdot x^{0m}}{p^{0m} \cdot x^{0m}} + \sum_{m=\mu+1}^{M} \frac{V^{0m}}{V^0} \frac{p^{t-1,m} \cdot x^{0m}}{p^{0m} \cdot x^{0m}}.
\end{aligned}
\tag{4.82}
$$

Proceeding through time, this procedure leads, at any subperiod $t\mu$, to a price index that compares the last M subperiods to the entire base period. In particular, at subperiod 1μ one gets

$$
\begin{aligned}
&P^L_{NM}((p^{11}, \ldots, p^{1\mu}, p^{0,\mu+1}, \ldots, p^{0M}), \\
&(x^{11}, \ldots, x^{1\mu}, x^{0,\mu+1}, \ldots, x^{0M}), \vec{p}^0, \vec{x}^0) \\
&= \sum_{m=1}^{\mu} \frac{V^{0m}}{V^0} \frac{p^{1m} \cdot x^{0m}}{p^{0m} \cdot x^{0m}} + \sum_{m=\mu+1}^{M} \frac{V^{0m}}{V^0} 1,
\end{aligned}
\tag{4.83}
$$

and at subperiod $1M$ one gets

$$
\begin{aligned}
&P^L_{NM}((p^{11}, \ldots, p^{1M}), (x^{11}, \ldots, x^{1M}), \vec{p}^0, \vec{x}^0) \\
&= \sum_{m=1}^{M} \frac{V^{0m}}{V^0} \frac{p^{1m} \cdot x^{0m}}{p^{0m} \cdot x^{0m}},
\end{aligned}
\tag{4.84}
$$

which equals expression (4.59), as it should be. It is clear that the series of index numbers so obtained is free from any seasonal effects. On the other hand, the series will exhibit a time lag of $M/2$ subperiods. This is apparent from expresson (4.82): the price index on the left-hand side is a weighted mean of M subperiod-to-corresponding-subperiod price indices, the most recent being that of subperiod $t\mu$, and the least recent that of M subperiods earlier.

This state of affairs led Diewert (2004b) to develop an approximation strategy. From expression (4.82) it is clear that its left-hand side can be approximated by the subperiod price index or indices corresponding to the midpoint of the time span running from subperiod $\mu + 1$ of period $t - 1$ to subperiod μ of period t. Estimating the relation between these two indices on data from the past yields M factors that can be used, given a recent subperiod-to-corresponding-subperiod price index, to predict the outcome of a rolling period index that is centered around this recent subperiod.

The rolling period indices corresponding to expressions (4.60)–(4.62), respectively, are

$$
(Q^P_{NM}((p^{t1}, \ldots, p^{t\mu}, p^{t-1,\mu+1}, \ldots, p^{t-1,M}),
$$
$$
(x^{t1}, \ldots, x^{t\mu}, x^{t-1,\mu+1}, \ldots, x^{t-1,M}), \vec{p}^0, \vec{x}^0))^{-1}
$$
$$
= \sum_{m=1}^{\mu} \frac{V^{tm}}{V^{(t\mu)}} \frac{p^{tm} \cdot x^{0m}}{p^{tm} \cdot x^{tm}} + \sum_{m=\mu+1}^{M} \frac{V^{t-1,m}}{V^{(t\mu)}} \frac{p^{t-1,m} \cdot x^{0m}}{p^{t-1,m} \cdot x^{t-1,m}},
$$
$$
\tag{4.85}
$$
$$
(P^P_{NM}((p^{t1}, \ldots, p^{t\mu}, p^{t-1,\mu+1}, \ldots, p^{t-1,M}),
$$
$$
(x^{t1}, \ldots, x^{t\mu}, x^{t-1,\mu+1}, \ldots, x^{t-1,M}), \vec{p}^0, \vec{x}^0))^{-1}
$$
$$
= \sum_{m=1}^{\mu} \frac{V^{tm}}{V^{(t\mu)}} \frac{p^{0m} \cdot x^{tm}}{p^{tm} \cdot x^{tm}} + \sum_{m=\mu+1}^{M} \frac{V^{t-1,m}}{V^{(t\mu)}} \frac{p^{0m} \cdot x^{t-1,m}}{p^{t-1,m} \cdot x^{t-1,m}},
$$
$$
\tag{4.86}
$$

and

$$
Q^L_{NM}((p^{t1}, \ldots, p^{t\mu}, p^{t-1,\mu+1}, \ldots, p^{t-1,M}),
$$
$$
(x^{t1}, \ldots, x^{t\mu}, x^{t-1,\mu+1}, \ldots, x^{t-1,M}), \vec{p}^0, \vec{x}^0)
$$
$$
= \sum_{m=1}^{\mu} \frac{V^{0m}}{V^0} \frac{p^{0m} \cdot x^{tm}}{p^{0m} \cdot x^{0m}} + \sum_{m=\mu+1}^{M} \frac{V^{0m}}{V^0} \frac{p^{0m} \cdot x^{t-1,m}}{p^{0m} \cdot x^{0m}}
$$
$$
\tag{4.87}
$$

where $V^{(t\mu)} \equiv \sum_{m=1}^{\mu} V^{tm} + \sum_{m=\mu+1}^{M} V^{t-1,m}$. It is straightforward to extend the idea of rolling period indices to the three alternatives discussed in the previous sections. The exploration of this topic is left to the reader.

4.3.6 Concluding Observations

The foregoing was based on the imposition of the product test **T3**, the consistency-in-aggregation test **T6** or **T6′**, and the equality tests **T7** and

T7′. This limited the range of admissible indices to those of Laspeyres and Paasche. There are, however, good reasons to use other indices for the comparison of periods to periods or subperiods to subperiods. But this implies that at least one of the requirements must be sacrificed. Which one?

Since the relation between the value of a whole period and the values of its subperiods is an additive one – see expression (4.49) – a natural starting point is to consider the value difference $V^1 - V^0$ rather than the ratio V^1 / V^0. The value difference can be written as

$$V^1 - V^0 = \sum_{m=1}^{M} (V^{1m} - V^{0m}). \tag{4.88}$$

As we have seen in section 3.10, each of these subperiod value differences can be decomposed in a price and a quantity part by means of indicators – see expression (3.213). Doing this, and using the shorthand notation introduced earlier, one obtains

$$V^1 - V^0 = \sum_{m=1}^{M} \mathcal{P}_N(1m, 0m) + \sum_{m=1}^{M} \mathcal{Q}_N(1m, 0m). \tag{4.89}$$

Using next the logarithmic mean to switch to ratios, one obtains the following decomposition of the value ratio:

$$\ln(V^1 / V^0) = \frac{\sum_{m=1}^{M} \mathcal{P}_N(1m, 0m)}{L(V^1, V^0)} + \frac{\sum_{m=1}^{M} \mathcal{Q}_N(1m, 0m)}{L(V^1, V^0)}. \tag{4.90}$$

This leads naturally to the following definitions for the price and quantity indices for period 1 relative to period 0:

$$\ln P_{NM}(1, 0) \equiv \frac{\sum_{m=1}^{M} \mathcal{P}_N(1m, 0m)}{L(V^1, V^0)} \tag{4.91}$$

$$\ln Q_{NM}(1, 0) \equiv \frac{\sum_{m=1}^{M} \mathcal{Q}_N(1m, 0m)}{L(V^1, V^0)}. \tag{4.92}$$

If the subperiod-to-corresponding-subperiod price and quantity indices are defined, respectively, by

$$\ln P_N(1m, 0m) \equiv \frac{\mathcal{P}_N(1m, 0m)}{L(V^{1m}, V^{0m})} \tag{4.93}$$

$$\ln Q_N(1m, 0m) \equiv \frac{\mathcal{Q}_N(1m, 0m)}{L(V^{1m}, V^{0m})}, \tag{4.94}$$

then the following relation between period and subperiod indices is obtained:

$$P_{NM}(1, 0) = \prod_{m=1}^{M} (P_N(1m, 0m))^{\phi(1m, 0m)} \tag{4.95}$$

$$Q_{NM}(1, 0) = \prod_{m=1}^{M} (Q_N(1m, 0m))^{\phi(1m, 0m)}, \tag{4.96}$$

where $\phi(1m, 0m) \equiv L(V^{1m}, V^{0m})/L(V^1, V^0)$ measures the mean relative value of the corresponding subperiods $0m$ and $1m$ ($m = 1, \ldots, M$). Specific expressions are obtained by chosing for the price and/or quantity indicators $P_N(1m, 0m)$ and $Q_N(1m, 0m)$ for instance those named after Laspeyres, Paasche, Bennet, or Montgomery, all of them introduced in section 3.10.

Notice that the product test **T3** is satisfied by definition, as well as the consistency-in-aggregation tests **T6** and **T6′**. The equality tests **T7** and **T7′** are, however, not satisfied, the reason being that in general the coefficients $\phi(1m, 0m)$ do not add up to 1. Also, it should be noticed that the indices $P_N(1m, 0m)$ and $Q_N(1m, 0m)$ do not necessarily satisfy the basic axioms **A1, A2, A1′, A2′**.

The last problem can be overcome by applying the logarithmic mean directly to expression (4.88), resulting in

$$V^1 - V^0 = \sum_{m=1}^{M} L(V^{1m}, V^{0m}) \ln(V^{1m}/V^{0m}). \tag{4.97}$$

Each of these subperiod value ratios can then be decomposed, by using appropriate functional forms, into a price and a quantity index number,

$$V^1 - V^0 = \sum_{m=1}^{M} L(V^{1m}, V^{0m}) \ln P_N(1m, 0m)$$

$$+ \sum_{m=1}^{M} L(V^{1m}, V^{0m}) \ln Q_N(1m, 0m), \tag{4.98}$$

which, after again applying the logarithmic mean transformation, results in

$$\ln(V^1/V^0) = \sum_{m=1}^{M} \left(\frac{L(V^{1m}, V^{0m})}{L(V^1, V^0)} \ln P_N(1m, 0m) \right)$$

$$+ \sum_{m=1}^{M} \left(\frac{L(V^{1m}, V^{0m})}{L(V^1, V^0)} \ln Q_N(1m, 0m) \right). \tag{4.99}$$

This suggests the following definition for the price index and quantity index, respectively, for period 1 relative to period 0:

$$P_{NM}(1, 0) \equiv \prod_{m=1}^{M} (P_N(1m, 0m))^{\phi(1m, 0m)} \qquad (4.100)$$

$$Q_{NM}(1, 0) \equiv \prod_{m=1}^{M} (Q_N(1m, 0m))^{\phi(1m, 0m)}. \qquad (4.101)$$

Specific expressions are obtained by chosing for the subperiod-to-corresponding subperiod indices $P_N(1m, 0m)$ and/or $Q_N(1m, 0m)$ specific functional forms.

Again, we have obtained indices that satisfy the product test **T3** and the consistency-in-aggregation tests **T6** and **T6′**. The coefficients $\phi(1m, 0m)$ are the same as defined earlier. Recall that they do not add up to 1. This, again, implies that the equality tests **T7** and **T7′** will in general be violated.

The foregoing two pairs of relations, (4.95)–(4.96) and (4.100)–(4.101), basically exhaust all mathematical possibilities.[8] The general conclusion is that, starting with arbitrary functional forms for indicators or indices at the level of subperiod-to-corresponding-subperiod comparisons, it is possible to define in a consistent way indices for period-to-period comparisons. The important equality tests, however, will thereby in general be violated.

Let us finally consider, for instance, what happens when Fisher indices are used for the comparison both of periods to periods and of subperiods to corresponding subperiods. Starting from $P_N^F(1m, 0m)$ ($m = 1, \ldots, M$), the consistent period-to-period price index is given by expression (4.100), being

$$P_{NM}(1, 0) \equiv \prod_{m=1}^{M} (P_N^F(1m, 0m))^{\phi(1m, 0m)}$$

$$= \left[\prod_{m=1}^{M} (P_N^L(1m, 0m))^{\phi(1m, 0m)} \prod_{m=1}^{M} (P_N^P(1m, 0m))^{\phi(1m, 0m)} \right]^{1/2}. \qquad (4.102)$$

---

[8] Additional decompositions can be obtained by writing the aggregate value difference $V^1 - V^0$ in forms analogous to the ratios (4.65), (4.72), or (4.78), but this does not lead to new insights.

On the other hand, by combining expressions (4.59) and (4.61), one obtains for the period-to-period price index

$$P_{NM}^F(1,0) = [P_{NM}^L(1,0)\,P_{NM}^P(1,0)]^{1/2}$$

$$= \left(\frac{\sum_{m=1}^{M}(V^{0m}/V^0)\,P_N^L(1m,0m)}{\sum_{m=1}^{M}(V^{1m}/V^1)(P_N^P(1m,0m))^{-1}} \right)^{1/2}. \qquad (4.103)$$

It is mathematically impossible to reconcile those two expressions. Of course, one expression might be a good approximation of the other. But this is by and large an empirical matter.

5

Price Indices for Elementary Aggregates

5.1 Introduction

The theory presented so far applies to aggregates consisting of a finite set of commodities. Two basic assumptions are that the set of commodities does not change between the two time periods compared, and that all the price and quantity data which are necessary for the computation of an index are available. In this chapter we are concerned with what to do when the second of these assumptions is not or cannot be fulfilled. There are, of course, various kinds of unavailability of data. The situation we will consider in particular in this chapter is that we have only data for a *sample* of commodities. These data might consist of prices and quantities, but more often only prices are available.

Since such a situation materializes at the very first stage of the computation of any official price index, such as a consumer price index (CPI) or a producer price index (PPI), we are dealing here with an issue of great practical significance.

The usual approach to the problem of unavailable quantity data is to consider price indices that are functions of prices only. The main formulas discussed in the literature and used in practice are

- the ratio of arithmetic average prices; that is, the formula of Dutot; see expression (1.1);
- the arithmetic average of price relatives; that is, the formula of Carli; see expression (1.2);
- the geometric average of price relatives = the ratio of geometric average prices; that is, the formula of Jevons; see expression (1.5).

In the literature, the suitability of these formulas has been studied by various methods. Following the early contribution of Eichhorn and Voeller (1976),

Dalén (1992) and Diewert (1995a) studied the properties of these three formulas from an axiomatic point of view. Additional insights were obtained by deriving (approximate) numerical relations between these formulas, and by combining these relations with more or less intuitive economic reasoning. The approach of Balk (1994) was to see which assumptions would validate these formulas as estimators of true but unknown population price indices, which by definition are functions of prices and quantities.

This chapter develops the sampling approach. In section 5.2 it is argued that, although not known to the statistician, all the detailed price and quantity data of the commodities pertaining to the aggregate under consideration exist in the real world. Section 5.3 then argues that the first task faced by the statistician is to decide on the nature of the aggregate (homogeneous or heterogeneous), and on the target price index (the unit value index or some other price index). Next the sampling design comes into the picture. With help of these two pieces of information, one can judge the various estimators with respect to their performance. This is the topic of section 5.4, which deals with homogeneous aggregates, and section 5.5, which deals with heterogeneous aggregates and a number of important target and sample price indices. This is by far the largest part of the chapter. Section 5.5 continues with some microeconomic considerations on the choice of a sample price index and closes with a discussion of the not-unimportant case where, for operational reasons, a Lowe price index has been chosen as target. Section 5.6 surveys the behaviour of the various sample price indices with respect to the time reversal test and reviews the (approximate) numerical relations between them. Section 5.7 summarizes the key results and concludes with some practical advice.

5.2 Setting the Stage

The aggregates covered by a price index such as a CPI or a PPI are usually arranged in the form of a tree-like hierarchy (according to some international commodity classification such as COICOP or NACE). Any aggregate is a set of economic transactions pertaining to a set of commodities. Commodities can be goods or services. Every economic transaction relates to the change of ownership (in the case of a good) or the delivery (in the case of a service) of a specific, well-defined commodity at a particular place and date, and comes with a quantity and a price. The price index for an aggregate is calculated as a weighted average of the price indices for the subaggregates, the (expenditure or sales) weights and the type of average being determined by the index formula. Descending in such a hierarchy is possible as far as available information permits the weights to be decomposed. The lowest level aggregates are called elementary aggregates. They are basically of two types:

- those for which all detailed price and quantity information is available;
- those for which the statistician, considering the operational cost and/or the response burden of getting detailed price and quantity information about all the transactions, decides to make use of a representative sample of commodities and/or respondents.

Any actual CPI or PPI, considered as a function that transforms sample survey data into an index number, can be considered as a stochastic variable, the expectation of which ideally is equal to the population counterpart. The elementary aggregates then serve as strata for the sampling procedure.[1] We are of course particularly interested in strata of the second type.

The practical relevance of studying this topic is great. Since the elementary aggregates form the building blocks of a CPI or a PPI, the choice of an inappropriate formula at this level can have a big impact higher up in the aggregation tree.

The detailed price and quantity data, although not available to the statistician, nevertheless – at least in principle – exist in the outside world. It is thereby frequently the case that at the respondent level (outlet or firm) already some aggregation of the basic transaction information has been executed, usually in a form that suits the respondents financial and/or logistic information system. This could be called the basic information level. This is, however, in no way a naturally given level. One could always ask the respondent to provide more disaggregated information. For instance, instead of monthly data one could ask for weekly data; whenever appropriate, one could ask for regional instead of global data; or, one could ask for data according to a finer commodity classification. The only natural barrier to further disaggregation is the individual transaction level.[2]

Thus, conceptually, for all well-defined commodities belonging to a certain elementary aggregate and all relevant respondents, there exists information on both the quantity sold and the associated average price (unit value) over a certain time period. Let us formalize this. The basic information – which in principle exists in the outside world – is of the form $\{(p_n^t, x_n^t); n = 1, \ldots, N\}$, where t denotes a time period; the elements of the population of (nonvoid) pairs of well-defined commodities and

---

[1] This point of view goes back to Adelman (1958).
[2] This approach goes back to Balk (1994).

respondents, henceforth called elements, are labelled from 1 to N; p_n^t denotes the price, and x_n^t denotes the quantity of element n at time period t. It may be clear that N usually is a very large number, since even at very low levels of aggregation there can be thousands of elements involved. Recall that it will be assumed that the population does not change between the time periods considered. Of course, in reality any population changes more or less continuously. It is, however, important to study the properties of the price index estimators in an artificially stable environment.

It is assumed that we must compare a later period 1 to an earlier period 0. As usual, the later period will be called the comparison period and the earlier period the base period. The conceptual problem is to split the value change multiplicatively into a price index and a quantity index,

$$\frac{V^1}{V^0} = \frac{\sum_{n=1}^N v_n^1}{\sum_{n=1}^N v_n^0} = \frac{p^1 \cdot x^1}{p^0 \cdot x^0} = P(p^1, x^1, p^0, x^0)Q(p^1, x^1, p^0, x^0), \quad (5.1)$$

where $p^t \equiv (p_1^t, \ldots, p_N^t)$ and $x^t \equiv (x_1^t, \ldots, x_N^t)$ $(t = 0, 1)$. This is traditionally called the index number problem. The two indices depend on the prices and quantities of both periods. In this chapter we concentrate on the estimation of a price index. To economize on notation, in the remainder of this chapter the vector of variables (p^1, x^1, p^0, x^0) is abbreviated by $(1, 0)$.

5.3 Homogeneity or Heterogeneity

To start with, there is an important choice to be made. In the statistician's parlance this is known as the homogeneity or heterogeneity issue. Although in the literature many words have been devoted to this issue, at the end of the day the whole problem can be reduced to a rather simple-looking operational question.

- Basic question: Does it make (economic) sense to add up the quantities x_n^t of the elements $n = 1, \ldots, N$?

If the answer to this question is "yes," then the elementary aggregate is called *homogeneous*. The elementary aggregate can then be considered as a single commodity. The appropriate, also called target, price index is the unit value index, defined earlier by expression (3.55) and repeated here,

$$P^U(1, 0) \equiv \frac{p^1 \cdot x^1 / 1_N \cdot x^1}{p^0 \cdot x^0 / 1_N \cdot x^0}; \quad (5.2)$$

that is, the average comparison period price divided by the average base period price. Recall that the unit value index satisfies the basic axioms for a price index, except the dimensional invariance axiom and the proportionality axiom. However, when the elements are commensurate, the dimensional invariance axiom reduces to $P(p^1\lambda, x^1\lambda^{-1}, p^0\lambda, x^0\lambda^{-1}) = P(p^1, x^1, p^0, x^0)$ $(\lambda > 0)$, which clearly is satisfied.

When the quantities are additive, we are obviously dealing with a situation where the same commodity during a time period is sold or bought at different places and/or at different subperiods at different prices. Put otherwise, we are dealing with pure price differences. These can be caused by market imperfections, such as price discrimination, consumer ignorance, or rationing. Economic theory seems to preclude this possibility because it is stated that in equilibrium "the law of one price" must hold. In reality, however, market imperfections are the rule rather than the exception. But physical restrictions can also play a role. Though, for instance, a "representative" consumer is assumed to be fully informed about all the prices and to have immediate and costless access to all the outlets throughout a country, the sheer physical distance between the outlets precludes real consumers from exploiting this magical possibility. Thus price differences exist where they, according to a representative-agent-based theory, are not supposed to exist.

If the answer the basic question is "no" – which in practice will generally be the case – then the elementary aggregate is called *heterogeneous* and there are various options available for the target price index. We will consider a number of options. The first is the Törnqvist price index, defined earlier by expression (3.53),

$$P^T(1, 0) \equiv \prod_{n=1}^{N} (p_n^1 / p_n^0)^{(s_n^0 + s_n^1)/2},\qquad(5.3)$$

where $s_n^t \equiv v_n^t / V^t$ $(n = 1, \ldots, N; t = 0, 1)$. This price index is a weighted geometric average of the price relatives, the weights being the mean of the value shares of base and comparison period. The second price index considered is the Fisher index, defined earlier by expression (3.27),

$$P^F(1, 0) \equiv [P^L(1, 0) P^P(1, 0)]^{1/2}$$
$$= \left[\frac{p^1 \cdot x^0}{p^0 \cdot x^0} \frac{p^1 \cdot x^1}{p^0 \cdot x^1} \right]^{1/2},\qquad(5.4)$$

which is the geometric mean of the Laspeyres and the Paasche price indices. The third price index considered is the Walsh-1 index, defined earlier by expression (3.21),

$$P^{W1}(1, 0) \equiv \frac{p^1 \cdot (x^0 x^1)^{1/2}}{p^0 \cdot (x^0 x^1)^{1/2}}. \tag{5.5}$$

The Walsh-1 price index is a member of the class of so-called basket price indices: that is, price indices that compare the cost of a certain basket of quantities in the comparison period to the cost of this basket in the base period. The Laspeyres and Paasche price indices are typical examples: the first employs the base period basket and the second the comparison period basket. The basket of the Walsh-1 price index is an artificial one, namely consisting of the geometric means of the quantities of the two periods.

These three price indices are functions of price and quantity data of the two periods compared. Many statistical offices, however, for obvious operational reasons, appear to define either implicitly or explicitly a simpler price index as target. In general their target appears to have the form of a Lowe price index, defined earlier by expression (3.34),

$$P^{Lo}(1, 0; x^b) \equiv p^1 \cdot x^b / p^0 \cdot x^b, \tag{5.6}$$

where b denotes some period prior to the base period.

It could be that the statistician is unable to decide between a simple yes or no reply to the basic question; that is, he or she finds that for certain subsets of the elementary aggregate $\{1, \ldots, N\}$ it makes sense to add up the quantities, whereas for the remainder this does not make sense. In such a case the aggregate should be split into subsets to which either the yes or the no answer applies. If this splitting appears not to be feasible, then the no answer should take precedence over the yes answer. Thus, conceptually, we have to deal with only two cases.[3]

Having defined the target price (and quantity) index, the statistician must face the basic problem that not all the information on the prices and quantities of the elements is available. The best he or she can obtain is information $\{p_n^0, x_n^0, p_n^1, x_n^1; n \in S\}$ for a sample $S \subset \{1, \ldots, N\}$. More realistic, however, is the situation where the information set has the form $\{p_n^0, p_n^1; n \in S\}$;

---

[3] This decision is, however, not always simple. Silver and Webb (2002) provide considerations and empirical evidence on the so-called unit value bias. This bias emerges when a heterogeneous aggregate is treated as being homogeneous.

that is, only a matched sample of prices is available. From this sample information the population price index (or quantity index) must be estimated. This is the point where the theory of finite population sampling will appear to be helpful for obtaining insight into the properties of the various estimators.

At the outset one must notice that in practice the way in which the sample S is drawn usually remains hidden in a sort of darkness. The main problem is that there is no such thing as a sampling frame. Knowledge about the composition of the elementary aggregate, in the form of an exhaustive listing of all its elements, is usually absent. There is only, more or less *ad hoc*, evidence available about particular elements belonging or not belonging to this aggregate. In order to use the theory of finite population sampling, however, we must make certain simplifying assumptions about the sampling design.

In the remainder of this chapter we consider two scenarios. Each of these is believed to be more or less representative of actual statistical practice. The first scenario assumes that S is drawn as a simple random sample without replacement. This means that each element of the population has the same probability of being included in the sample. This so-called (first order) inclusion probability is $\Pr(n \in S) = \zeta(S)/N$, where $\zeta(S)$ denotes the (prespecified) sample size.

In the second scenario the more important elements of the population have a correspondingly larger probability of being included in the sample than the less important elements. This is formalized by assuming that the elements of S were drawn with probability proportional to size (pps) and without replacement, where size denotes some measure of importance. If the size of element n is denoted by a positive scalar a_n ($n = 1, \ldots, N$), then the probability that element n is included in the sample S is $\Pr(n \in S) = \zeta(S)a_n / \sum_{n=1}^{N} a_n$. Without loss of generality, it can be assumed that $\Pr(n \in S) < 1$ ($n = 1, \ldots, N$).[4] Notice that in both scenarios it is the case that $\sum_{n=1}^{N} \Pr(n \in S) = \zeta(S)$.

Usually the sample S has been drawn at some period prior to the base period, say period b. In particular this means that in the case of pps sampling the size measure, which is based on either relative quantities (for homogeneous aggregates) or relative values (for heterogeneous aggregates), refers to period b. Now consider the target indices $P^U(1, 0)$, $P^T(1, 0)$, $P^F(1, 0)$, and $P^{W1}(1, 0)$. All these indices are based on population price and quantity data

---

[4] Elements for which initially this probability would turn out to be greater than or equal to 1 are selected with certainty and from the remaining set of elements a sample is drawn.

of the two periods 0 and 1. This implies immediately that any estimator that is based on sample data of the form $\{p_n^0, x_n^0, p_n^1; n \in S\}$ or $\{p_n^0, p_n^1; n \in S\}$ must be biased, since the two sampling designs do not compensate for the missing quantity data. Put otherwise, to obtain (approximately) unbiased estimators of the target indices we must either work with estimators based on sample data $\{p_n^0, x_n^0, p_n^1, x_n^1; n \in S\}$ or relax the requirement that the size measure used in pps sampling refer to the prior period b. The last alternative leads, of course, to sampling designs that look unrealistic from a practical point of view. The reader should be aware of this. However, it is considered important to study the behaviour of index estimators in somewhat idealized circumstances, to get at least an idea about their behaviour in more realistic situations.

5.4 Homogeneous Aggregates

Suppose we deal with a homogeneous aggregate. Then the target (or population) price index is the unit value index $P^U(1, 0)$. If the total base period value V^0 as well as the total comparison period value V^1 is known, the obvious route to take – see expression (5.2) – is to estimate the Dutot quantity index $1_N \cdot x^1 / 1_N \cdot x^0$. A likely candidate is its sample counterpart

$$Q^D(\underline{x}^1, \underline{x}^0) \equiv \frac{\sum_{n \in S} x_n^1}{\sum_{n \in S} x_n^0}. \tag{5.7}$$

Suppose that S is a simple random sample. The expected value of $Q^D(\underline{x}^1, \underline{x}^0)$ under this sampling design appears to be approximately equal to its population counterpart; that is (see the detailed proof in the appendix, section 5.8),

$$E[Q^D(\underline{x}^1, \underline{x}^0)] \approx \frac{\sum_{n=1}^N x_n^1}{\sum_{n=1}^N x_n^0}. \tag{5.8}$$

Put otherwise, the sample Dutot quantity index is an approximately unbiased estimator of the population Dutot quantity index. The bias tends to zero when the sample size increases.

Consider next the sample Carli quantity index, defined as

$$Q^C(\underline{x}^1, \underline{x}^0) \equiv \frac{1}{\zeta(S)} \sum_{n \in S} \frac{x_n^1}{x_n^0}. \tag{5.9}$$

Assume that the elements were drawn with probability proportional to size, whereby the size of element n is defined as its base period quantity share $x_n^0 / \sum_{n=1}^N x_n^0$ ($n = 1, \ldots, N$). Hence, the probability that element n is included in the sample is equal to $\Pr(n \in S) = \zeta(S) x_n^0 / \sum_{n=1}^N x_n^0$. Then the expected value of the sample Carli quantity index is equal to

$$E[Q^C(\underline{x}^1, \underline{x}^0)] = \frac{1}{\zeta(S)} \sum_{n=1}^N \frac{x_n^1}{x_n^0} \Pr(n \in S) = \sum_{n=1}^N \frac{x_n^1}{x_n^0} \frac{x_n^0}{\sum_{n=1}^N x_n^0} = \frac{\sum_{n=1}^N x_n^1}{\sum_{n=1}^N x_n^0}. \tag{5.10}$$

Put otherwise, under this sampling design, the sample Carli quantity index is an unbiased estimator of the population Dutot quantity index.

Let the total comparison period value V^1 now be unknown to the statistician and consider the sample unit value index

$$P^U(\underline{p}^1, \underline{x}^1, \underline{p}^0, \underline{x}^0) \equiv \frac{\sum_{n \in S} v_n^1 / \sum_{n \in S} x_n^1}{\sum_{n \in S} v_n^0 / \sum_{n \in S} x_n^0}. \tag{5.11}$$

This presupposes that the sample is of the form $\{(v_n^t, x_n^t); t = 0, 1; n \in S\}$; that is, for every sampled element one knows its value and quantity in the two periods.[5] Then one can show, in much the same way as was done in the case of expression (5.8), that under simple random sampling the sample unit value index is an approximately unbiased estimator of the target unit value index . Likewise, by mimicking the proof of (5.8), one can show that

$$V^0 \frac{\sum_{n \in S} v_n^1}{\sum_{n \in S} v_n^0} \tag{5.12}$$

is an approximately unbiased estimator of the aggregate comparison period value V^1. Notice that (5.12) has the well-known form of a ratio estimator.

Suppose next that only sample prices are available, that is, the sample is of the form $\{p_n^0, p_n^1; n \in S\}$, and consider the sample Dutot price index, defined as

$$P^D(\underline{p}^1, \underline{p}^0) \equiv \frac{\sum_{n \in S} p_n^1}{\sum_{n \in S} p_n^0} = \frac{\frac{1}{\zeta(S)} \sum_{n \in S} p_n^1}{\frac{1}{\zeta(S)} \sum_{n \in S} p_n^0}. \tag{5.13}$$

The second part of this expression reflects the familiar interpretation of the sample Dutot price index as a ratio of unweighted average sample prices. Clearly, taking the average of prices is the counterpart of the adding-up

---

[5] This situation will typically occur when one has access to electronic transaction data (so-called scanner data).

of quantities; that is, the first makes sense if and only if the second does. Under pps sampling, whereby again the size of element n is defined as its base period quantity share, it can be shown (detailed in the appendix) that, apart from a nonlinearity bias which tends to zero when the sample size increases,

$$E[P^D(\underline{p}^1, \underline{p}^0)] \approx \frac{p^1 \cdot x^0/1_N \cdot x^0}{p^0 \cdot x^0/1_N \cdot x^0}. \tag{5.14}$$

The denominator of the right-hand side ratio is the same as the denominator of the unit value index $P^U(1, 0)$. The numerators, however, are different: the target index uses comparison period quantity shares as weights, whereas $E[P^D(\underline{p}^1, \underline{p}^0)]$ yields base period quantity shares as weights. Thus the sample Dutot price index will in general be a biased estimator of the unit value index. The relative bias amounts to

$$\frac{E[P^D(\underline{p}^1, \underline{p}^0)]}{P^U(1, 0)} \approx \frac{p^1 \cdot x^0/1_N \cdot x^0}{p^1 \cdot x^1/1_N \cdot x^1}. \tag{5.15}$$

The relative bias of the sample Dutot price index thus consists of two components: a technical part that vanishes as the sample size gets larger and a structural part that is independent of the sample size. This structural part is given by the right-hand side of expression (5.15). It vanishes if the (relative) quantities in the comparison period are the same as those in the base period, which is unlikely to happen in practice. The result, expressed by (5.14), goes back to Balk (1994, p. 139) and can also be found in Diewert (2002b, section 7.4).

5.5 Heterogeneous Aggregates

5.5.1 Using a Sample of Matched Prices and Quantities (or Values)

Let us now turn to the more important situation where one deals with a heterogeneous aggregate. Suppose that the Törnqvist price index (5.3) is chosen to be the target and consider its sample analogue

$$P^T(\underline{p}^1, \underline{x}^1, \underline{p}^0, \underline{x}^0) \equiv \prod_{n \in S}(p_n^1/p_n^0)^{(\underline{s}_n^0 + \underline{s}_n^1)/2}, \tag{5.16}$$

where $\underline{s}_n^t \equiv v_n^t/\sum_{n \in S} v_n^t$ ($t = 0, 1$) is element n's sample value share. It is clear that the sample must be of the form $\{(v_n^t, p_n^t); t = 0, 1; n \in S\}$; that is, for each sample element one must know its value and its price in the two periods. Under the assumption of simple random sampling it can be shown that

$$E[\ln P^T(\underline{p}^1, \underline{x}^1, \underline{p}^0, \underline{x}^0)]$$

$$= \frac{1}{2} E \left[\frac{\sum_{n \in S} v_n^0 \ln(p_n^1/p_n^0)}{\sum_{n \in S} v_n^0} + \frac{\sum_{n \in S} v_n^1 \ln(p_n^1/p_n^0)}{\sum_{n \in S} v_n^1} \right]$$

$$\approx \frac{1}{2} \left[\frac{E[\frac{1}{\zeta(S)} \sum_{n \in S} v_n^0 \ln(p_n^1/p_n^0)]}{E[\frac{1}{\zeta(S)} \sum_{n \in S} v_n^0]} + \frac{E[\frac{1}{\zeta(S)} \sum_{n \in S} v_n^1 \ln(p_n^1/p_n^0)]}{E[\frac{1}{\zeta(S)} \sum_{n \in S} v_n^1]} \right]$$

$$= \frac{1}{2} \left[\frac{\frac{1}{N} \sum_{n=1}^N v_n^0 \ln(p_n^1/p_n^0)}{\frac{1}{N} \sum_{n=1}^N v_n^0} + \frac{\frac{1}{N} \sum_{n=1}^N v_n^1 \ln(p_n^1/p_n^0)}{\frac{1}{N} \sum_{n=1}^N v_n^1} \right]$$

$$= \ln P^T(1, 0). \tag{5.17}$$

This means that $\ln P^T(\underline{p}^1, \underline{x}^1, \underline{p}^0, \underline{x}^0)$ is an approximately unbiased estimator of $\ln P^T(1, 0)$. But what can be said about the estimator $P^T(\underline{p}^1, \underline{x}^1, \underline{p}^0, \underline{x}^0)$ itself? Using the Taylor series expansion of $f(x) = \exp\{x\}$, one obtains

$$E[P^T(\underline{p}^1, \underline{x}^1, \underline{p}^0, \underline{x}^0)] = E[\exp\{\ln P^T(\underline{p}^1, \underline{x}^1, \underline{p}^0, \underline{x}^0)\}]$$

$$= \exp\{E[\ln P^T(\underline{p}^1, \underline{x}^1, \underline{p}^0, \underline{x}^0)]\}(1 + R). \tag{5.18}$$

The leading term of the remainder R appears to be equal to

$$\frac{1}{2} E[\ln P^T(\underline{p}^1, \underline{x}^1, \underline{p}^0, \underline{x}^0) - E[\ln P^T(\underline{p}^1, \underline{x}^1, \underline{p}^0, \underline{x}^0)]]^2.$$

This term is positive[6] but can be shown to tend to zero when the sample size increases towards N. Combining (5.17) and (5.18), one obtains

$$E[P^T(\underline{p}^1, \underline{x}^1, \underline{p}^0, \underline{x}^0)] \approx P^T(1, 0) \exp\{R_1\}(1 + R), \tag{5.19}$$

where R_1 denotes the bias that corresponds to (5.17). It is difficult to predict the direction of the entire bias of the sample Törnqvist price index. However, in any case the bias tends to zero for increasing sample size.

Suppose that instead of the Törnqvist price index one has decided that the Fisher price index (5.4) should be the target. As before, our sample information consists of matched prices and quantities. The sample

---

[6] Expression (5.18) is an instance of Jensen's Inequality, which says that $E[f(x)] \geq f(E[x])$ when $f(x)$ is convex and the expectation $E[x]$ exists.

analogue of the population Fisher price index is

$$
P^F(\underline{p}^1, \underline{x}^1, \underline{p}^0, \underline{x}^0) \equiv \left(\frac{\sum_{n \in S} p_n^1 x_n^0 \sum_{n \in S} p_n^1 x_n^1}{\sum_{n \in S} p_n^0 x_n^0 \sum_{n \in S} p_n^0 x_n^1} \right)^{1/2}
$$

$$
= \left(\frac{\frac{1}{\zeta(S)} \sum_{n \in S} p_n^1 x_n^0 \, \frac{1}{\zeta(S)} \sum_{n \in S} p_n^1 x_n^1}{\frac{1}{\zeta(S)} \sum_{n \in S} p_n^0 x_n^0 \, \frac{1}{\zeta(S)} \sum_{n \in S} p_n^0 x_n^1} \right)^{1/2}. \tag{5.20}
$$

Then one can show (detailed in the appendix) that, under simple random sampling,

$$
E[\ln P^F(\underline{p}^1, \underline{x}^1, \underline{p}^0, \underline{x}^0)] \approx \ln P^F(1, 0). \tag{5.21}
$$

By repeating the argument around expressions (5.18) and (5.19), one may then also conclude that the sample Fisher price index itself is an approximately unbiased estimator of its population counterpart. The bias tends to zero when the sample size increases.[7]

Suppose finally that the Walsh-1 price index (5.5) was chosen to be the target. Its sample analogue is

$$
P^{W1}(\underline{p}^1, \underline{x}^1, \underline{p}^0, \underline{x}^0) \equiv \frac{\sum_{n \in S} p_n^1 (x_n^0 x_n^1)^{1/2}}{\sum_{n \in S} p_n^0 (x_n^0 x_n^1)^{1/2}}. \tag{5.22}
$$

Let S again be a simple random sample. Then we find, in the same way as detailed earlier, that

$$
\begin{aligned}
E[P^{W1}(\underline{p}^1, \underline{x}^1, \underline{p}^0, \underline{x}^0)] &= E\left[\frac{\frac{1}{\zeta(S)} \sum_{n \in S} p_n^1 (x_n^0 x_n^1)^{1/2}}{\frac{1}{\zeta(S)} \sum_{n \in S} p_n^0 (x_n^0 x_n^1)^{1/2}} \right] \\
&\approx \frac{E\left[\frac{1}{\zeta(S)} \sum_{n \in S} p_n^1 (x_n^0 x_n^1)^{1/2} \right]}{E\left[\frac{1}{\zeta(S)} \sum_{n \in S} p_n^0 (x_n^0 x_n^1)^{1/2} \right]} \\
&= \frac{\frac{1}{N} \sum_{n=1}^N p_n^1 (x_n^0 x_n^1)^{1/2}}{\frac{1}{N} \sum_{n=1}^N p_n^0 (x_n^0 x_n^1)^{1/2}} \\
&= P^{W1}(1, 0), \tag{5.23}
\end{aligned}
$$

which means that the sample Walsh-1 price index is an approximately unbiased estimator of the population Walsh-1 price index.

---

[7] The use of a sample Fisher price index to deflate a value ratio was already recommended by Pigou (1932, part I, chapter VI, par. 17).

5.5.2 Using a Sample of Matched Prices

The previous results critically depend on the availability of sample quantity or value information. In this subsection it will be assumed that the sample is of the form $\{p_n^0, p_n^1; n \in S\}$; that is, only a set of matched prices is available. The behaviour of a number of price index estimators under various sampling designs will be studied.

5.5.2.1 The Sample Jevons Price Index

The first index to consider is the sample Jevons price index[8]

$$P^J(\underline{p}^1, \underline{p}^0) \equiv \prod_{n \in S} (p_n^1/p_n^0)^{1/\zeta(S)}. \tag{5.24}$$

Under pps sampling, whereby the size of element n is defined as its base period value share s_n^0, resulting in $\Pr(n \in S) = \zeta(S)s_n^0$, it is easily seen that

$$
\begin{aligned}
E[\ln P^J(\underline{p}^1, \underline{p}^0)] &= E\left[\frac{1}{\zeta(S)} \sum_{n \in S} \ln(p_n^1/p_n^0)\right] \\
&= \sum_{n=1}^{N} s_n^0 \ln(p_n^1/p_n^0) \\
&= \ln\left(\prod_{n=1}^{N} (p_n^1/p_n^0)^{s_n^0}\right),
\end{aligned}
\tag{5.25}
$$

which is the logarithm of the Geometric Laspeyres price index $P^{GL}(1,0)$ as defined in expression (3.40). By employing (5.18), with $P^T(\underline{p}^1, \underline{x}^1, \underline{p}^0, \underline{x}^0)$ substituted by $P^J(\underline{p}^1, \underline{p}^0)$, we obtain as result

$$E[P^J(\underline{p}^1, \underline{p}^0)] = P^{GL}(1,0)(1+R). \tag{5.26}$$

Thus, apart from the remainder term, we have obtained the Geometric Laspeyres population price index. In general this index differs from the Törnqvist population price index. The relative bias of the sample Jevons price index with respect to the Törnqvist population price index is

$$\frac{E[P^J(\underline{p}^1, \underline{p}^0)]}{P^T(1,0)} = \prod_{n=1}^{N} (p_n^1/p_n^0)^{(s_n^0 - s_n^1)/2}(1+R). \tag{5.27}$$

---

[8] See also Bradley (2001).

The right-hand side of this expression consists of two components, a technical part that vanishes as the sample size gets larger and a structural part that is independent of the sample size. The structural part, that is, the first term on the right-hand side of expression (5.27), is equal to $[P^{GL}(1, 0)/P^{GP}(1, 0)]^{1/2}$. Table 3.4 suggests that this term is less than 1. The term vanishes when base period and comparison period value shares are equal, which is unlikely to occur in practice.

Instead of defining the size of element n as its base period value share, s_n^0, one could as well define its size as being the arithmetic mean of its base and comparison period value share, $(s_n^0 + s_n^1)/2$. Then we obtain, instead of (5.26),

$$E[P^J(\underline{p}^1, \underline{p}^0)] = P^T(1, 0)(1 + R), \qquad (5.28)$$

and instead of (5.27),

$$\frac{E[P^J(\underline{p}^1, \underline{p}^0)]}{P^T(1, 0)} = (1 + R); \qquad (5.29)$$

that is, the sample Jevons price index is an approximately unbiased estimator of the population Törnqvist price index. The bias will vanish when the sample size gets larger. This result goes back to Diewert (2002b, section 7.4).

5.5.2.2 The Sample Carli Price Index

One of the work horses at statistical agencies is the sample Carli price index,

$$P^C(\underline{p}^1, \underline{p}^0) \equiv \frac{1}{\zeta(S)} \sum_{n \in S} p_n^1 / p_n^0. \qquad (5.30)$$

Under pps sampling, whereby the size of element n is defined as its base period value share s_n^0, we immediately see that

$$E[P^C(\underline{p}^1, \underline{p}^0)] = \sum_{n=1}^{N} s_n^0 (p_n^1 / p_n^0) = P^L(1, 0). \qquad (5.31)$$

Thus the expected value of the sample Carli price index appears to be equal to the population Laspeyres price index. This result goes back to Adelman (1958) and was rediscovered by Balk (1994); see also Diewert (2002b, section 7.4).

The relative bias of the sample Carli price index with respect to the population Fisher price index follows immediately from (5.31) and appears to be

$$\frac{E[P^C(\underline{p}^1, \underline{p}^0)]}{P^F(1, 0)} = \frac{P^L(1, 0)}{P^F(1, 0)} = \left(\frac{P^L(1, 0)}{P^P(1, 0)}\right)^{1/2}, \quad (5.32)$$

which is the square root of the ratio of the population Laspeyres price index and the population Paasche price index. Notice that this bias is of structural nature; that is, it will not disappear when the sample size gets larger. Table 3.4 suggests that the bias is larger than 1. Is it possible to do better?

5.5.2.3 The Sample CSWD Price Index

The population Fisher price index can also be written as

$$P^F(1, 0) = \left(\sum_{n=1}^{N} s_n^0 p_n^1/p_n^0\right)^{1/2} \left(\sum_{n=1}^{N} s_n^1 (p_n^1/p_n^0)^{-1}\right)^{-1/2}. \quad (5.33)$$

We now consider whether, following a suggestion of Fisher (1922, p. 472, formula 101) and von Bortkiewicz (1924, p. 247), the Carruthers-Sellwood-Ward (1980) – Dalén (1992) sample price index

$$P^{CSWD}(\underline{p}^1, \underline{p}^0) \equiv \left(\frac{1}{\zeta(S)} \sum_{n\in S} p_n^1/p_n^0\right)^{1/2} \left(\frac{1}{\zeta(S)} \sum_{n\in S} (p_n^1/p_n^0)^{-1}\right)^{-1/2} \quad (5.34)$$

under some sampling design might be a suitable estimator of the population Fisher price index. The CSWD sample price index is the geometric average of the sample Carli price index (5.30) and the sample Harmonic (or Coggeshall) price index, defined earlier by expression (1.12),

$$P^{Co}(\underline{p}^1, \underline{p}^0) \equiv \left(\frac{1}{\zeta(S)} \sum_{n\in S} (p_n^1/p_n^0)^{-1}\right)^{-1}. \quad (5.35)$$

Thus, consider

$$\ln P^{CSWD}(\underline{p}^1, \underline{p}^0) = (1/2)\ln P^C(\underline{p}^1, \underline{p}^0) + (1/2)\ln P^{Co}(\underline{p}^1, \underline{p}^0). \quad (5.36)$$

Under pps sampling, whereby the size of element n is defined as its base period value share s_n^0, and again using the Taylor series expansion of $f(x) = \ln x$, we find that

$$E[\ln P^C(\underline{p}^1, \underline{p}^0)] = \ln P^L(1, 0) + R_1, \quad (5.37)$$

and

$$E[\ln P^{Co}(\underline{p}^1, \underline{p}^0)] = \ln P^{HL}(1, 0) - R_2, \qquad (5.38)$$

where $P^{HL}(1, 0)$ is the population Harmonic Laspeyres price index as defined in expression (3.15). Combining the last three expressions, one obtains

$$E[\ln P^{CSWD}(\underline{p}^1, \underline{p}^0)] = \ln[P^L(1, 0)P^{HL}(1, 0)]^{1/2} + (R_1 - R_2)/2. \qquad (5.39)$$

The leading term of $(R_1 - R_2)/2$ is

$$-(1/4)\left(\mathrm{cv}[P^C(\underline{p}^1, \underline{p}^0)]\right)^{1/2} + (1/4)\left(\mathrm{cv}[(P^{Co}(\underline{p}^1, \underline{p}^0))^{-1}]\right)^{1/2}, \qquad (5.40)$$

where $\mathrm{cv}[.]$ denotes the coefficient of variation. Both parts of this expression tend to zero when the sample size increases. Thus, $\ln P^{CSWD}(\underline{p}^1, \underline{p}^0)$ is an approximately unbiased estimator of $\ln[P^L(1, 0)P^{HL}(1, 0)]^{1/2}$, and, repeating a by-now-familiar argument,

$$E[P^{CSWD}(\underline{p}^1, \underline{p}^0)] = [P^L(1, 0)P^{HL}(1, 0)]^{1/2} \exp\{(R_1 - R_2)/2\}(1 + R), \qquad (5.41)$$

where R also tends to zero when the sample size increases. The main right-hand-side term clearly differs from the population Fisher price index. The relative bias of the CSWD sample price index with respect to the population Fisher price index is

$$\frac{E[P^{CSWD}(\underline{p}^1, \underline{p}^0)]}{P^F(1, 0)} = \left(\frac{P^{HL}(1, 0)}{P^P(1, 0)}\right)^{1/2} \exp\{(R_1 - R_2)/2\}(1 + R). \qquad (5.42)$$

Notice that the relative bias consists of two components, a technical component that vanishes as the sample size gets larger and a structural component that is independent of the sample size. The empirical evidence in Table 3.4 suggests that the structural component, $[P^{HL}(1, 0)/P^P(1, 0)]^{1/2}$, is less than 1.

Instead of defining the size of element n as its base period value share s_n^0, one could as well define its size as being $(s_n^0 + s_n^1)/2$, the arithmetic mean of its base and comparison period value share. Then we obtain, instead of (5.37),

$$E[\ln P^C(\underline{p}^1, \underline{p}^0)] = \ln((P^L(1, 0) + P^{Pa}(1, 0))/2) + R_1, \qquad (5.43)$$

where $P^{Pa}(1,0)$ is the population Palgrave price index, as defined by expression (3.12). Similarly, instead of (5.38) we obtain

$$E[\ln P^{Co}(\underline{p}^1, \underline{p}^0)] = -\ln((1/P^{HL}(1,0) + 1/P^P(1,0))/2) - R_2.$$
(5.44)

Combining these two expressions with (5.36), we obtain

$$E[\ln P^{CSWD}(\underline{p}^1, \underline{p}^0)] = \ln \left(\frac{P^L(1,0) + P^{Pa}(1,0)}{1/P^{HL}(1,0) + 1/P^P(1,0)} \right)^{1/2} + (R_1 - R_2)/2$$
(5.45)

with, again, a remainder term that tends to zero when the sample size increases. And, finally,

$$
\begin{aligned}
E[P^{CSWD}(\underline{p}^1, \underline{p}^0)] \\
= \left(\frac{P^L(1,0) + P^{Pa}(1,0)}{1/P^{HL}(1,0) + 1/P^P(1,0)} \right)^{1/2} \exp\{(R_1 - R_2)/2\}(1 + R) \\
= P^F(1,0) \left(\frac{1 + P^{Pa}(1,0)/P^L(1,0)}{1 + P^P(1,0)/P^{HL}(1,0)} \right)^{1/2} \exp\{(R_1 - R_2)/2\}(1 + R).
\end{aligned}
$$
(5.46)

Recall that $P^{Pa}(1,0) \geq P^P(1,0)$ and $1/P^L(1,0) \leq 1/P^{HL}(1,0)$ (see expressions (3.13) and (3.16), respectively). The empirical example of Table 3.4 suggests, however, that the ratio between big brackets in the last line of expression (5.46) is less than 1. Thus, even under the pps sampling design defined at the beginning of this paragraph, the CSWD sample price index might not be an approximately unbiased estimator of the population Fisher price index.

Let us finally consider the following modification of the CSWD sample price index:

$$
\begin{aligned}
P^{CSWDB}(\underline{p}^1, \underline{x}^1, \underline{p}^0, \underline{x}^0) \\
\equiv \left(\frac{1}{\varsigma(S)} \sum_{n \in S} p_n^1/p_n^0 \right)^{1/2} \left(\frac{1}{\varsigma(S)} \sum_{n \in S} x_n^1/x_n^0 \right)^{-1/2} \left(\frac{1}{\varsigma(S)} \sum_{n \in S} v_n^1/v_n^0 \right)^{1/2}.
\end{aligned}
$$
(5.47)

This is the product of a sample Carli price index, the reciprocal of a sample Carli quantity index, and a sample Carli value index. It is straightforward to check, using the same reasoning as in the previous paragraphs, that under pps sampling, whereby the size of element n is defined as its base period value share s_n^0,

$$E[\ln P^{CSWDB}(\underline{p}^1, \underline{x}^1, \underline{p}^0, \underline{x}^0)]$$
$$= (\ln P^L(1, 0) - \ln Q^L(1, 0) + \ln(V^1/V^0))/2 = \ln P^F(1, 0), \quad (5.48)$$

and thus

$$E[P^{CSWDB}(\underline{p}^1, \underline{x}^1, \underline{p}^0, \underline{x}^0)] \approx P^F(1, 0), \quad (5.49)$$

where the bias tends to zero for increasing sample size. However, it is clear that the computation of $P^{CSWDB}(.)$ requires more information than the computation of $P^{CSWD}(.)$, namely all sample quantity relatives. If one has access to electronic transaction data, however, this should not be much of a problem.

5.5.2.4 The Sample Balk-Walsh Price Index

The population Walsh-1 price index can be written as a quadratic mean of order 1 index,

$$P^{W1}(1, 0) = \frac{\sum_{n=1}^{N}(s_n^0 s_n^1)^{1/2}(p_n^1/p_n^0)^{1/2}}{\sum_{n=1}^{N}(s_n^0 s_n^1)^{1/2}(p_n^1/p_n^0)^{-1/2}}, \quad (5.50)$$

which suggests the following sample price index:

$$P^{BW}(\underline{p}^1, \underline{p}^0) \equiv \frac{\sum_{n\in S}(p_n^1/p_n^0)^{1/2}}{\sum_{n\in S}(p_n^1/p_n^0)^{-1/2}}. \quad (5.51)$$

Since in the literature there appears to be no name attached to this formula, expression (5.51) is baptized as the Balk-Walsh sample price index. Under a pps sampling design, whereby the size of element n is defined as $(s_n^0 s_n^1)^{1/2}$, which is the geometric mean of its base and comparison period value share, we find that

$$E[P^{BW}(\underline{p}^1, \underline{p}^0)] = E\left[\frac{\frac{1}{\zeta(S)}\sum_{n\in S}(p_n^1/p_n^0)^{1/2}}{\frac{1}{\zeta(S)}\sum_{n\in S}(p_n^1/p_n^0)^{-1/2}}\right]$$
$$\approx \frac{E\left[\frac{1}{\zeta(S)}\sum_{n\in S}(p_n^1/p_n^0)^{1/2}\right]}{E\left[\frac{1}{\zeta(S)}\sum_{n\in S}(p_n^1/p_n^0)^{-1/2}\right]}$$
$$= \frac{\frac{1}{N}\sum_{n=1}^{N}(s_n^0 s_n^1)^{1/2}(p_n^1/p_n^0)^{1/2}}{\frac{1}{N}\sum_{n=1}^{N}(s_n^0 s_n^1)^{1/2}(p_n^1/p_n^0)^{-1/2}}$$
$$= P^{W1}(1, 0). \quad (5.52)$$

Thus, under this sampling design, the Balk-Walsh sample price index appears to be an approximately unbiased estimator of the population Walsh-1 price index. The bias will approach zero when the sample size increases. It is easy to demonstrate that, if the size of element n were defined as its base period value share, s_n^0, the expectation of the Balk-Walsh sample price index would be unequal to the population Walsh-1 price index.

5.5.3 Considerations on the Choice of the Sample Price Index

The previous subsection demonstrated that, when nothing but sample prices are available and the sampling design is restricted to one that uses only base period value share information, it is impossible to estimate unbiasedly any of the Törnqvist, Fisher, or Walsh-1 population price indices. Basically, there remain a number of second-best alternatives, namely the sample Jevons (5.24), Carli (5.30), Harmonic (5.35), Carruthers-Sellwood-Ward-Dalén (5.34), and Balk-Walsh (5.51) price indices. Is anyone of these to be preferred?

To assist with the choice, let us consider the sample Generalized Mean (GM) price index, which is here defined as

$$P^{GM}(\underline{p}^1, \underline{p}^0; \sigma) \equiv \left(\frac{1}{\zeta(S)} \sum_{n \in S} (p_n^1/p_n^0)^{1-\sigma} \right)^{1/(1-\sigma)} \quad (\sigma \neq 1)$$

$$P^{GM}(\underline{p}^1, \underline{p}^0; 1) \equiv \prod_{n \in S} (p_n^1/p_n^0)^{1/\zeta(S)}. \tag{5.53}$$

This is a function of sample prices and a parameter σ. One verifies immediately that $P^J(.) = P^{GM}(.; 1)$, $P^C(.) = P^{GM}(.; 0)$, $P^{Co}(.) = P^{GM}(.; 2)$, $P^{CSWD}(.) = [P^{GM}(.; 0) P^{GM}(.; 2)]^{1/2}$ and, finally, $P^{BW}(.) = [P^{GM}(.; 1/2) \, P^{GM}(.; 3/2)]^{1/2}$. However, since the GM price index is a monotonic function of σ, it appears that, to the second order, $P^{CSWD}(.) \approx P^{BW}(.) \approx P^{GM}(.; 1)$ (see also section 5.6). Thus these five sample price indices are all members of the same family.

Under pps sampling, whereby the size of element n is defined as its base period value share s_n^0, one obtains that

$$E[(P^{GM}(\underline{p}^1, \underline{p}^0; \sigma))^{1-\sigma}] = \sum_{n=1}^{N} s_n^0 (p_n^1/p_n^0)^{1-\sigma}. \tag{5.54}$$

To apply Jensen's Inequality, a distinction must be made between two cases. If $\sigma \leq 0$, we obtain

$$E[P^{GM}(\underline{p}^1, \underline{p}^0; \sigma)] \leq \left(\sum_{n=1}^{N} s_n^0 (p_n^1 / p_n^0)^{1-\sigma} \right)^{1/(1-\sigma)} \equiv P^{LM}(1, 0; \sigma),$$

(5.55)

whereas if $\sigma \geq 0$, we obtain

$$E[P^{GM}(\underline{p}^1, \underline{p}^0; \sigma)] \geq \left(\sum_{n=1}^{N} s_n^0 (p_n^1 / p_n^0)^{1-\sigma} \right)^{1/(1-\sigma)} \equiv P^{LM}(1, 0; \sigma) \ (\sigma \neq 1)$$

$$E[P^{GM}(\underline{p}^1, \underline{p}^0; 1)] \geq \prod_{n=1}^{N} (p_n^1 / p_n^0)^{s_n^0} \equiv P^{LM}(1, 0; 1),$$

(5.56)

where $P^{LM}(1, 0; \sigma)$ is the so-called Lloyd-Moulton (LM) population price index. Thus, for $\sigma \leq 0$ the sample GM price index has a negative bias, and for $\sigma \geq 0$ a positive. This bias tends to zero when the sample size increases.

Economic theory teaches us that the LM index is exact for a Constant Elasticity of Substitution (partial) revenue function (for the producer's output side) or (partial) cost function (for the producer's input side or the consumer; see Balk 2000 and Melser 2006). The parameter σ is thereby to be interpreted as the (average) elasticity of substitution within the aggregate. At their output side, producers are supposed to maximize revenue, which implies a nonpositive elasticity of substitution. Producers at their input side and consumers, however, are supposed to minimize cost, which implies a non-negative elasticity of substitution.

In particular, the conclusion must be that, under the pps sampling design here assumed, the sample Jevons, Harmonic, CSWD, and Balk-Walsh price indexes are inadmissible for the producer output side since the expected value of each of these indexes would exhibit a positive substitution elasticity. The sample Carli price index is admissible, even unbiased, but would imply a zero substitution elasticity.

5.5.4 The Lowe Price Index as Target

Let us now turn to the more realistic case where the Lowe price index (5.6) is defined to be the target. The population Lowe price index can be written as a ratio of two Laspeyres price indices,

$$P^{Lo}(1, 0; x^b) = \frac{\sum_{n=1}^{N} p_n^1 x_n^b / \sum_{n=1}^{N} p_n^b x_n^b}{\sum_{n=1}^{N} p_n^0 x_n^b / \sum_{n=1}^{N} p_n^b x_n^b} = \frac{\sum_{n=1}^{N} s_n^b (p_n^1 / p_n^b)}{\sum_{n=1}^{N} s_n^b (p_n^0 / p_n^b)}, \quad (5.57)$$

where s_n^b is element n's value share in period b ($n = 1, \ldots, N$), which is assumed to be some period prior to the base period. This suggests the sample price index[9]

$$P^{Lo}(\underline{p}^1, \underline{p}^0; \underline{p}^b) \equiv \frac{\sum_{n \in S} p_n^1 / p_n^b}{\sum_{n \in S} p_n^0 / p_n^b}, \quad (5.58)$$

which is the ratio of two sample Carli price indices. Indeed, under a pps sampling design, whereby the size of element n is defined as s_n^b, that is, its period b value share, it is straightforward to verify that

$$\begin{aligned} E[P^{Lo}(\underline{p}^1, \underline{p}^0; \underline{p}^b)] &= E\left[\frac{\frac{1}{\zeta(S)} \sum_{n \in S} p_n^1 / p_n^b}{\frac{1}{\zeta(S)} \sum_{n \in S} p_n^0 / p_n^b}\right] \\ &\approx \frac{E[\frac{1}{\zeta(S)} \sum_{n \in S} p_n^1 / p_n^b]}{E[\frac{1}{\zeta(S)} \sum_{n \in S} p_n^0 / p_n^b]} \\ &= \frac{(1/N) \sum_{n=1}^{N} s_n^b (p_n^1 / p_n^b)}{(1/N) \sum_{n=1}^{N} s_n^b (p_n^0 / p_n^b)} \\ &= P^{Lo}(1, 0; x^b). \end{aligned} \quad (5.59)$$

The bias tends to zero when the sample size increases.

Alternatively, and perhaps more consistently with practice, one could consider the hybrid or so-called price-updated period b value shares, defined as

$$s_n^{0b} \equiv \frac{s_n^b (p_n^0 / p_n^b)}{\sum_{n=1}^{N} s_n^b (p_n^0 / p_n^b)} = \frac{p_n^0 x_n^b}{\sum_{n=1}^{N} p_n^0 x_n^b} \quad (n = 1, \ldots, N). \quad (5.60)$$

Under a pps sampling design, whereby the size of element n is now defined as s_n^{0b}, that is, its price-updated period b value share, it is immediately seen that

$$E[P^C(\underline{p}^1, \underline{p}^0)] = \sum_{n=1}^{N} s_n^{0b} (p_n^1 / p_n^0) = P^{Lo}(1, 0; x^b); \quad (5.61)$$

---

[9] See also Bradley (2001, p. 377), but note that he uses the name *modified Laspeyres index* instead of *Lowe index*.

that is, the sample Carli price index is an unbiased estimator of the population Lowe price index. However, if the size of element n was defined as s_n^b, that is, its period b value share itself, one would have obtained

$$E[P^C(\underline{p}^1, \underline{p}^0)] = \sum_{n=1}^{N} s_n^b(p_n^1/p_n^0) = P^Y(\underline{p}^1/\underline{p}^0; \underline{s}^b). \qquad (5.62)$$

This is a Young price index, which, unless the prices have not changed between the periods b and 0, differs from the population Lowe price index.

5.6 The Time Reversal Test and Some Numerical Relations

When there is nothing but sample price information available, that is, the sample has the form $\{p_n^0, p_n^1; n \in S\}$, then the menu of sample price indices appears to be limited. For a *homogeneous* aggregate, only the sample Dutot price index (5.13) is available. Note that this index, like the population unit value index, satisfies the time reversal test; that is,

$$P^D(\underline{p}^1, \underline{p}^0)P^D(\underline{p}^0, \underline{p}^1) = 1. \qquad (5.63)$$

However, as has been shown, under a not-unreasonable sampling design, the sample Dutot price index is a biased estimator of the target unit value index.

For a *heterogeneous* aggregate one has, depending on the definition of the target price index, the choice among the sample Jevons (5.24), Carli (5.30), Harmonic (5.35), Carruthers-Sellwood-Ward-Dalén (5.34), Balk-Walsh (5.51), and Lowe (5.58) price indices. The first three indexes are special cases of the sample GM price index (5.53) for $\sigma = 1, 0, 2$, respectively. Since the GM price index is monotonicly increasing in $1 - \sigma$, we obtain the general result that

$$P^{GM}(\underline{p}^1, \underline{p}^0; \sigma)P^{GM}(\underline{p}^0, \underline{p}^1; \sigma) \geq 1 \text{ for } \sigma < 1$$
$$P^{GM}(\underline{p}^1, \underline{p}^0; \sigma)P^{GM}(\underline{p}^0, \underline{p}^1; \sigma) \leq 1 \text{ for } \sigma > 1, \qquad (5.64)$$

which means that the GM price index fails the time reversal test. In particular, the Carli price index and the Harmonic price index fail the time reversal test, that is,

$$P^C(\underline{p}^1, \underline{p}^0)P^C(\underline{p}^0, \underline{p}^1) \geq 1, \qquad (5.65)$$

and

$$P^{Co}(\underline{p}^1, \underline{p}^0)P^{Co}(\underline{p}^0, \underline{p}^1) \leq 1. \qquad (5.66)$$

The Jevons price index, as well as the CSWD price index and the Balk-Walsh price index, satisfies the time reversal test, as one verifies immediately. As has been shown in subsection 5.5.3, under a not-unreasonable sampling design, these three sample price indexes are (approximately) unbiased estimators of the LM population price index with $\sigma = 1$. The sample Lowe price index also satisfies the time reversal test. This index is, under a not-unreasonable sampling design, an (approximately) unbiased estimator of the population Lowe price index.

Let us now turn to the numerical relations between all these indices. It is well known that

$$P^{Co}(\underline{p}^1, \underline{p}^0) \leq P^J(\underline{p}^1, \underline{p}^0) \leq P^C(\underline{p}^1, \underline{p}^0), \qquad (5.67)$$

and thus we might expect that $P^{CSWD}(.) = [P^{Co}(.)P^C(.)]^{1/2}$ will be close to $P^J(.)$. The magnitudes of the differences between all these indices depend on the variance of the price relatives p_n^1/p_n^0 $(n \in S)$. When all the price relatives are equal, the inequalities (5.67) reduce to equalities. In fact, Dalén (1992) and Diewert (1995a) showed that, to the second order, the following approximations hold[10]:

$$P^J(\underline{p}^1, \underline{p}^0) \approx P^C(\underline{p}^1, \underline{p}^0)(1 - (1/2)\text{var}(\varepsilon))$$
$$P^{Co}(\underline{p}^1, \underline{p}^0) \approx P^C(\underline{p}^1, \underline{p}^0)(1 - \text{var}(\varepsilon)) \qquad (5.68)$$
$$P^{CSWD}(\underline{p}^1, \underline{p}^0) \approx P^C(\underline{p}^1, \underline{p}^0)(1 - (1/2)\text{var}(\varepsilon)),$$

where $\text{var}(\varepsilon) \equiv \frac{1}{\zeta(S)} \sum_{n \in S} \varepsilon_n^2$ and $\varepsilon_n \equiv (p_n^1/p_n^0 - P^C(.))/P^C(.)$ $(n \in S)$. In the same way one can show that[11]

$$P^{BW}(\underline{p}^1, \underline{p}^0) \approx P^C(\underline{p}^1, \underline{p}^0)(1 - (1/2)\text{var}(\varepsilon)). \qquad (5.69)$$

Hence, the sample Jevons price index, the sample CSWD price index, and the sample Balk-Walsh price index approximate each other to the second order. From the point of view of simplicity, the sample Jevons price index obviously qualifies for the highest score.

To obtain some insight into the relation between the sample Lowe price index (5.58) and the sample Carli price index (5.30), notice that the first

---

[10] Only their main results are presented here. An additional result was obtained by Reinsdorf (1994).

[11] The method of proof is to write the ratio of $P^{BW}(.)$ to $P^C(.)$ as a function $f(\varepsilon)$ and expand this function as a Taylor series around 0. Notice thereby that $\sum_{n \in S} \varepsilon_n = 0$.

can be written as

$$P^{Lo}(\underline{p}^1, \underline{p}^0; \underline{p}^b) = \frac{\sum_{n \in S}(p_n^0/p_n^b)(p_n^1/p_n^0)}{\sum_{n \in S}(p_n^0/p_n^b)}. \quad (5.70)$$

Consider now the difference $P^{Lo}(.) - P^C(.)$. By straightforward manipulation of this expression one can show that

$$P^{Lo}(\underline{p}^1, \underline{p}^0; \underline{p}^b) = P^C(\underline{p}^1, \underline{p}^0)(1 + \text{cov}(\delta, \varepsilon)), \quad (5.71)$$

where $\text{cov}(\delta, \varepsilon) \equiv \frac{1}{\zeta(S)} \sum_{n \in S} \delta_n \varepsilon_n$, $\delta_n \equiv (p_n^0/p_n^b - P^C(\underline{p}^0, \underline{p}^b))/P^C(\underline{p}^0, \underline{p}^b)$, and $\varepsilon_n \equiv (p_n^1/p_n^0 - P^C(\underline{p}^1, \underline{p}^0))/P^C(\underline{p}^1, \underline{p}^0)$ ($n \in S$). Thus the difference between these two sample price indices depends on the covariance of the relative price changes between the periods b and 0 and those between the periods 0 and 1. Whether this difference is positive or negative, large or small, is an empirical matter.

Although it was argued that the (sample) Dutot price index makes sense only in the case of homogeneous aggregates, it appears that this index is rather frequently used for more or less heterogeneous aggregates as well. Therefore, it might be of some interest to discuss the relation between this index and the sample Jevons index. The first is a ratio of arithmetic average prices whereas the second can be considered as a ratio of geometric average prices. In order to see their relation, the Jevons index is written as

$$\ln P^J(\underline{p}^1, \underline{p}^0) = \sum_{n \in S} \frac{1}{\zeta(S)} \ln(p_n^1/p_n^0), \quad (5.72)$$

and the Dutot index as

$$\ln P^D(\underline{p}^1, \underline{p}^0) = \sum_{n \in S} \left(\frac{L(p_n^0/\bar{p}^0, p_n^1/\bar{p}^1)}{\sum_{n \in S} L(p_n^0/\bar{p}^0, p_n^1/\bar{p}^1)} \right) \ln(p_n^1/p_n^0), \quad (5.73)$$

where $\bar{p}^t \equiv \frac{1}{\zeta(S)} \sum_{n \in S} p_n^t$ is the (arithmetic) average price at period t ($t = 0, 1$), and $L(.)$ denotes the logarithmic mean. Hence, $L(p_n^0/\bar{p}^0, p_n^1/\bar{p}^1)$ is the mean relative price of element n over the two periods. Then,

$$\ln P^D(\underline{p}^1, \underline{p}^0) - \ln P^J(\underline{p}^1, \underline{p}^0)$$

$$= \sum_{n \in S} \left(\frac{L(p_n^0/\bar{p}^0, p_n^1/\bar{p}^1)}{\sum_{n \in S} L(p_n^0/\bar{p}^0, p_n^1/\bar{p}^1)} - \frac{1}{\zeta(S)} \right) \ln(p_n^1/p_n^0)$$

$$= \frac{1}{\zeta(S)} \sum_{n \in S} \left(\frac{L(p_n^0/\bar{p}^0, p_n^1/\bar{p}^1)}{\frac{1}{\zeta(S)} \sum_{n \in S} L(p_n^0/\bar{p}^0, p_n^1/\bar{p}^1)} - 1 \right)$$

$$\times \left(\ln(p_n^1/p_n^0) - \ln P^J(\underline{p}^1, \underline{p}^0) \right), \quad (5.74)$$

which means that the (sign of the) difference between the Dutot and the Jevons index depends on the (sign of the) covariance between relative prices and price relatives. Whether this difference is positive or negative, large or small, is an empirical matter.[12]

5.7 Conclusion

In this chapter we considered for elementary aggregates the relation between the target index, the sample index, and the sampling design. Although the viewpoint was by and large theoretical, the arguments advanced in the previous sections led to certain practical advice. The advice, to be practical, concerns simple random sampling, sampling with probability proportional to base period quantity shares (in the case of a homogeneous aggregate), and sampling with probability proportional to base period or (price-updated) earlier period value shares (in the case of a heterogeneous aggregate). Sampling in practice may take two stages: first the sampling of respondents (outlets or firms), and then that of commodities. The discussion in this chapter was kept for simplicity in terms of single-stage sampling. Often purposive sampling and/or sampling with cutoff rules is used at either stage. In such circumstances there are implicit sampling frames and selection rules, and some judgement will be necessary as to which theoretical sampling design most closely corresponds to the method used, and what the implications are for the choice of the sample index.[13]

In the first place, the results shown in this chapter indicate that respondents should be encouraged to provide timely data on comparison and base period values and prices (or quantities). Providing a full set of electronic transaction data would even be more helpful. Of course, in some areas this is more feasible than in others. In such cases sample indices that mirror their population counterparts should be used, and respondent-commodity pairs should be sampled using simple random sampling, since each sample index would then be an (approximately) unbiased estimator of the corresponding population one.

---

[12] An approximate relationship between $P^D(.)$ and $P^J(.)$, based on a second-order Taylor series expansion, was derived by Carruthers, Sellwood, and Ward (1980). Using a stochastic model for the prices, Silver and Heravi (2007b) also derived a relationship between the Dutot and Jevons indices and explored with a hedonic model the influence of heterogeneity on the difference between $P^D(.)$ and $P^J(.)$. In their empirical material this influence appeared to be large. Closely related to Silver and Heravi's approach is Beer's (2006) development of a theory of hedonic elementary aggregate price indices.

[13] See Dorfman, Lent, Leaver, and Wegman (2006) for a comparison of two sampling designs, one pps and the other based on purposive/cutoff selection.

When this approach is not feasible and the best one can obtain is a sample of (matched) prices, the sampling design should be such that important elements have a higher probability of inclusion in the sample than unimportant elements. With respect to the sample price index to be used:

- For a homogeneous aggregate, that is, an aggregate for which the quantities of the elements can be meaningfully added up, one must use the sample Dutot price index. Unfortunately, under pps sampling relative to base period quantity shares this index will exhibit bias, the magnitude of which depends on the dispersion of the elementary quantity changes between the two periods compared.
- For a heterogeneous aggregate, not being at the producer's output side, one could use the sample Jevons price index. Under pps sampling relative to base period value shares, its expected value will approximate the Geometric Laspeyres price index, which is identical to the Lloyd-Moulton price index with $\sigma = 1$.
- For a heterogeneous aggregate at the producer's output side one could use a sample Generalized Mean price index with appropriately chosen parameter $\sigma \leq 0$. Under pps sampling relative to base period value shares the expected value of such a price index will approximate a Lloyd-Moulton price index.[14]
- When the target is a Lowe price index, the sample Lowe and Carli price indices exhibit, dependent on the sampling design (pps sampling relative to earlier period (price-updated) value shares), appropriate behaviour.

In any case the time span between the two periods compared should not become too long, because the magnitude of the bias will in general grow with the length of the time span. That is, at regular time intervals one should undertake a base period change.

There remains the practical issue as to how to decide whether an aggregate is homogeneous or not. Recall our basic question:

- Basic question: Does it make (economic) sense to add up the quantities x_n^t of the elements $n = 1, \ldots, N$?

---

[14] The limiting case ($\sigma = 0$) is the sample Carli price index. As shown above, under pps sampling relative to base period value shares this index is an unbiased estimator of the Laspeyres price index, which corresponds to zero substitution. If this index is chosen to be the target, then the sample Carli index is appropriate. One should notice that the *PPI Manual* (2004, par. 20.83)'s usage of the word *bias* refers to the fact that the Carli index does not satisfy the Time Reversal Test.

For example, if the aggregate consists of consumption of 14-inch television sets, the answer must presumably be "no." Brand differences, additional facilities such as stereo, wide screens, and much more account for significant variations in price. Tins of a specific brand and type of food of different sizes similarly lack homogeneity, since much of the price variation will be due to tin size. Homogeneity is lacking when the item itself varies according to identifiable price-determining characteristics. In principle the conditions of sale need to be taken into account, since an item sold by one manufacturer may command a price premium based on better delivery, warranties, or other such features. The prices to be sampled at subsequent periods should correspond to the same specified conditions of sale, but there may be elements of trust in the buyer-seller relationship that are difficult to identify. Nonetheless, for practical purposes items sold by different establishments for the same product are practically treated as homogeneous unless there are clearly identifiable differences in the terms and conditions surrounding the sale.

5.8 Appendix: Proofs

Proof of (5.8): Let S be a simple random sample without replacement and recall that the inclusion probabilities are $\Pr(n \in S) = \zeta(S)/N$, where $\zeta(S)$ denotes the sample size. For the expected value of the (modified) numerator and denominator of expression (5.7) we obtain

$$E\left[\frac{1}{\zeta(S)} \sum_{n \in S} x_n^t\right] = \frac{1}{\zeta(S)} \sum_{n=1}^{N} x_n^t \Pr(n \in S) = \frac{1}{N} \sum_{n=1}^{N} x_n^t \equiv \bar{x}^t \ (t = 0, 1);$$

$$(5.75)$$

that is, the expectation of the sample mean is equal to the population mean. The sample Dutot index itself is, however, a nonlinear function. Expanding $Q^D(\underline{x}^1, \underline{x}^0)$ as a Taylor series at $(\bar{x}^1, \bar{x}^0)$ and taking the expectation, one obtains

$$E[Q^D(\underline{x}^1, \underline{x}^0)] = Q^D(1, 0) + R, \qquad (5.76)$$

where R is the remainder. The leading term thereof is of the second order and has the form

$$\frac{\bar{x}^1}{(\bar{x}^0)^3} E\left[\frac{1}{\zeta(S)} \sum_{n \in S} x_n^0 - \bar{x}^0\right]^2 - \frac{1}{(\bar{x}^0)^2} E\left[\left[\frac{1}{\zeta(S)} \sum_{n \in S} x_n^0 - \bar{x}^0\right]\right.$$
$$\left. \times \left[\frac{1}{\zeta(S)} \sum_{n \in S} x_n^1 - \bar{x}^1\right]\right]. \qquad (5.77)$$

Using classical finite population sampling theory, it is easy to show (see, for instance, Knottnerus 2003, p. 19) that the variance of the sample mean, in the first part of expression (5.77), equals

$$E\left[\frac{1}{\zeta(S)}\sum_{n\in S}x_n^0 - \bar{x}^0\right]^2 = \left(\frac{1}{\zeta(S)} - \frac{1}{N}\right)\frac{1}{N-1}\sum_{n=1}^{N}(x_n^0 - \bar{x}^0)^2.$$

$$(5.78)$$

It is clear that this term approaches zero when the sample size increases towards N. Similar considerations apply to the covariance term in (5.77). The entire bias R is known as small sample nonlinearity bias; empirically this bias appears to be already negligible for samples of moderate size. Expression (5.76) will be abbreviated as

$$E[Q^D(\underline{x}^1, \underline{x}^0)] \approx Q^D(1, 0). \qquad (5.79)$$

We say that $Q^D(\underline{x}^1, \underline{x}^0)$ is an approximately unbiased estimator of $Q^D(1, 0)$.

Proof of (5.14): The proof proceeds in the same way as the previous one, except that now pps sampling is assumed. We find that

$$E\left[\frac{1}{\zeta(S)}\sum_{n\in S}p_n^t\right] = \frac{1}{\zeta(S)}\sum_{n=1}^{N}p_n^t \Pr(n\in S) = \frac{\sum_{n=1}^{N}p_n^t x_n^0}{\sum_{n=1}^{N}x_n^0} \equiv \bar{p}^t \ (t=0,1);$$

$$(5.80)$$

that is, the expectation of the unweighted sample mean is equal to the weighted population mean. Further,

$$E[P^D(\underline{p}^1, \underline{p}^0)] = \bar{p}^1/\bar{p}^0 + R. \qquad (5.81)$$

The leading term of R is of the second order and has the form

$$\frac{\bar{p}^1}{(\bar{p}^0)^3}E\left[\frac{1}{\zeta(S)}\sum_{n\in S}p_n^0 - \bar{p}^0\right]^2 - \frac{1}{(\bar{p}^0)^2}E\left[\left[\frac{1}{\zeta(S)}\sum_{n\in S}p_n^0 - \bar{p}^0\right]\right.$$

$$\left.\times\left[\frac{1}{\zeta(S)}\sum_{n\in S}p_n^1 - \bar{p}^1\right]\right].$$

$$(5.82)$$

Knottnerus (2003, p. 71) shows that, under pps sampling without replacement,

$$E[\frac{1}{\zeta(S)} \sum_{n \in S} p_n^0 - \bar{p}^0]^2 = \frac{1 + (\zeta(S) - 1)\rho}{\zeta(S)} \frac{\sum_{n=1}^{N}(p_n^0 - \bar{p}^0)^2 x_n^0}{\sum_{n=1}^{N} x_n^0},$$

(5.83)

where ρ is the sampling autocorrelation coefficient. This coefficient depends on both the population and the actual sampling design (in particular the second-order inclusion probabilities). For common sampling designs ρ appears to be of the order $1/N$. Then the factor $(1 + (\zeta(S) - 1)\rho)/\zeta(S)$ tends to 0 when $\zeta(S)$ and N tend to infinity. Similar considerations apply to the covariance term in (5.82).

Proof of (5.21): The logarithm of the sample Fisher price index is

$$\ln P^F(\underline{p}^1, \underline{x}^1, \underline{p}^0, \underline{x}^0)$$

$$= \frac{1}{2}\left[\ln\left(\frac{1}{\zeta(S)} \sum_{n \in S} p_n^1 x_n^0\right) - \ln\left(\frac{1}{\zeta(S)} \sum_{n \in S} p_n^0 x_n^0\right)\right.$$

$$\left. + \ln\left(\frac{1}{\zeta(S)} \sum_{n \in S} p_n^1 x_n^1\right) - \ln\left(\frac{1}{\zeta(S)} \sum_{n \in S} p_n^0 x_n^1\right)\right].$$

(5.84)

Using the Taylor series expansion of $f(x) = \ln x$, and assuming simple random sampling, one obtains

$$E\left[\ln\left(\frac{1}{\zeta(S)} \sum_{n \in S} p_n^1 x_n^0\right)\right] = \ln\left(\frac{1}{N} \sum_{n=1}^{N} p_n^1 x_n^0\right) + R,$$

(5.85)

in which the leading term of R has the form

$$-(1/2)\left(\text{cv}(\frac{1}{\zeta(S)} \sum_{n \in S} p_n^1 x_n^0)\right)^2,$$

(5.86)

where cv(.) denotes the sample coefficient of variation. Similar expressions hold for the other three parts of the right-hand side of expression (5.84). Hence,

$$E[\ln P^F(\underline{p}^1, \underline{x}^1, \underline{p}^0, \underline{x}^0)] = \ln P^F(1, 0) + R,$$

(5.87)

where the leading term of R has the form

$$-(1/2)\left(\mathrm{cv}(\frac{1}{\zeta(S)}\sum_{n\in S}p_n^1 x_n^0)\right)^2 + (1/2)\left(\mathrm{cv}(\frac{1}{\zeta(S)}\sum_{n\in S}p_n^0 x_n^0)\right)^2$$

$$-(1/2)\left(\mathrm{cv}(\frac{1}{\zeta(S)}\sum_{n\in S}p_n^1 x_n^1)\right)^2 + (1/2)\left(\mathrm{cv}(\frac{1}{\zeta(S)}\sum_{n\in S}p_n^0 x_n^1)\right)^2. \quad (5.88)$$

If all the prices change proportionally, that is, $p_n^1 = \alpha p_n^0$ for $n = 1, \ldots, N$ and a certain $\alpha > 0$, then one easily verifies that the four parts of expression (5.88) cancel. Moreover, for each separate part it holds that it approaches zero when the sample size increases towards N.

6

Divisia and Montgomery Indices

6.1 Introduction

The quest for measures that adequately show the aggregate development of prices and quantities through time, as well as what precisely should be understood by "adequate" started in the middle of the 19th century. Well known among the various indices are those proposed by Laspeyres in 1871, Paasche in 1874, and Fisher in 1922. Likewise well known is the principle, advocated by Lehr (1885) and Marshall (1887), of multiplying index numbers comparing adjacent periods to obtain measures covering longer time spans. At the beginning of the 20th century literally dozens of formulas were available, together with a number of criteria, also called tests, for choosing between them. All this was codified in Fisher's 1922 book *The Making of Index Numbers.*

Three years after the publication of this book the French economist Divisia (1925) presented a novel solution to the problem of splitting a value change into two parts, a part due to prices and a part due to quantities. He came up with two indices, an "indice monétaire," which was a price index, and an "indice activité," which was a quantity index. Both indices were defined as line integrals.

Up till this invention all price and quantity indices considered were essentially of the bilateral type; that is, they compared two time periods, employing price and quantity data pertaining to these two periods only. Chained indices are nothing but composites of bilateral indices. The novelty of Divisia's indices was that, as functions of *continuous* time, they take into account the prices and quantities of all, infinitely many, intermediate periods. Thus a Divisia index number not only is dependent on the initial and final points of the time interval considered, but will as a rule depend on the entire path that the prices and quantities belonging to an economic aggregate under consideration have taken.

Because Roy (1927) and Frisch (1936) paid some attention to them, the Divisia indices soon came to be more widely known. As a general tool they came to be used in studies of consumer and producer behaviour.

The decade surrounding Divisia's proposal also witnessed the birth of the economic approach to the measurement of price and quantity change. Nataf and Roy (1948) were the first to discuss the relationship of Divisia's price index to the cost of living index concept in consumer theory. A nice summary was given by Wold (1952, section 8.3).

Usually the Divisia price and quantity indices are conceived as providing a theoretical justification for the procedure of chaining bilateral indices; that is, chained indices are seen as approximations to Divisia indices. Von Hofsten (1952) was an early representative of this position. Further documentation can be found in the encyclopedia article by Jazairi (1983). An extensive discussion, focussed at statistical practice, was furnished by Forsyth and Fowler (1981).[1]

A fundamental property of the Divisia indices, which they share with chained indices, is their so-called path-dependency. Over the years this property has led to conflicting views among economists. On the one hand, by a minority this intriguing, almost "magical," property was considered as a virtue. It was thought that the Divisia indices somehow track economic reality better than (simple) bilateral indices. On the other hand, quite a number of economists have wrestled with this property as a problem and sought after conditions under which the indices may exhibit path *in*dependency. The first contribution to this issue was the singular paper by Ville (1946). The most important later publications are those by Richter (1966), Hillinger (1970), Hulten (1973), Samuelson and Swamy (1974), and Usher (1980). Gorman's (1970) interesting lecture notes were unfortunately not published until 1995. Sato (1981, 314–26) summarized the key results.

The conditions for path-independency appear to be extremely restrictive. Assuming that there is a (virtual) agent which is continuously engaged in optimizing behaviour, the necessary and sufficient condition for

---

[1] In the framework of the National Accounts the use of chained indices was advocated by Al, Balk, de Boer, and den Bakker (1986). These authors were of the opinion that "the chain approach would appear to be clearly preferable since users ... are primarily interested in the way in which the changes in the aggregate came about." The *System of National Accounts 1993* now recommends the chaining of bilateral indices comparing adjacent years.

path-independency is that the aggregator (utility or production) function be homothetic.

From an axiomatic point of view the properties of the Divisia indices were studied by Krtscha (1979) and Mundlos (1982). Vogt (1977, 1978a, 1979, 1980a) computed the indices for various paths. Banerjee (1979a, 1979b) considered the relation between the indices and some equations arising from the "factorial approach."[2]

Solow (1957) introduced the Divisia quantity index into the area of productivity measurement.[3] Working in a two-input single-output framework, he provided a nice economic interpretation for the total factor productivity index. The generalization of this approach to a multiple-input multiple-output framework was undertaken by Richter (1966) and Jorgenson and Griliches (1967). Later developments in this area were briefly reviewed by Diewert (1980, pp. 443–6).

The purpose of this chapter is to provide a survey of the theory of line integral indices. The main assumption thereby is that prices and quantities as functions of continuous time are considered as being given, without assuming any behavioural relationship. Put otherwise, the statistical and not the economic theory will be discussed.

The line integral indices will be formally introduced in section 6.2. It appears that there are basically two types, corresponding to the fact that a value change can be measured by a ratio as well as by a difference. The first type is the well-known Divisia line integral index; the second type was independently developed by Montgomery (1929). Section 6.3 contains an exploration of the path-(in)dependency issue. The properties of the two types of indices will be discussed extensively in section 6.4.

The next sections treat the question how to approximate the line integral indices when only data at certain discrete points of time are available. This problem can be approached from two angles. First, one can look for an approximation in the numerical mathematics sense. This is the topic of section 6.5. Second, one can specify hypothetical curves in the space of prices and quantities and evaluate the line integral indices along such curves. This is the topic of section 6.6. In addition to some familiar results, a couple of new results will be presented, of which perhaps the most noteworthy is that

---

[2] In the factorial approach the inner (cross) products of the vectors of prices and quantities of the initial and final time periods are considered as outcomes of a 2×2 factorial experiment.

[3] Divisia (1952, pp. 53–4) seems to have suggested this already.

Fisher's indices can be seen as Divisia line integral indices evaluated along a particular curve. Eventually it appears possible to conceive every bilateral index in this way. Thus the concept of a line integral index provides a sort of unifying conceptual framework.

Section 6.7 argues that, although from the statistical point of view the concept of a line integral index rationalizes the practice of chaining bilateral indices, this rationalization itself should have a solid foundation in economic theory to be useful. Section 6.8 concludes.

6.2 Divisia and Montgomery Indices

We consider a certain economic aggregate consisting of N commodities (that is, sets of transactions), labelled $1, \ldots, N$, which are available through a certain time interval, say $[0, T] \subset \mathfrak{R}$. For any $t \in [0, T]$ the vectors of unit prices and corresponding quantities will be denoted by $p^t \equiv (p_1^t, \ldots, p_N^t)$ and $x^t \equiv (x_1^t, \ldots, x_N^t)$, respectively. The basic assumption is that t is a continuous variable rather than a label and that all prices p_n^t and quantities x_n^t are realizations of certain functions of t, so that $p_n^t = p_n(t)$ and $x_n^t = x_n(t)$ $(n = 1, \ldots, N)$.[4] Accordingly, p^t and x^t are realizations of vector-valued functions, $p^t = p(t)$ and $x^t = x(t)$. All these functions are assumed to be strictly positive and sectionally smooth: that is, continuous and piecewise differentiable. Thus, if t traverses the time interval $[0, T]$, the vector of prices and quantities $(p(t), x(t))$ describes a certain curve or path in $\mathfrak{R}_{++}^N \times \mathfrak{R}_{++}^N$.

Where useful, the inner product of the price vector $p(t)$ and the quantity vector $x(t)$ will be denoted by $V(t) \equiv p(t) \cdot x(t) = \sum_{n=1}^N p_n(t)x_n(t)$. This is the value of the aggregate at time period t. Commodity n's value at time period t will be denoted by $v_n(t) \equiv p_n(t)x_n(t)$ $(n = 1, \ldots, N)$. Commodity n's value share at time period t will be denoted by $s_n(t) \equiv v_n(t)/V(t)$ $(n = 1, \ldots, N)$.

6.2.1 Divisia Indices

The starting point for the approach discussed in this section is to consider (the logarithm of) the value *ratio* for a certain comparison period t relative

---

[4] This assumption must of course be conceived as a mathematical idealization. Prices and quantities are attributes of economic transactions, which as a rule take place irregularly. The limit in disaggregating time periods is achieved when all the individual transactions are recorded.

to a certain base period t' (t', $t \in [0, T]$; without loss of generality it can be assumed that $t' < t$); that is,

$$\ln\left(\frac{p(t) \cdot x(t)}{p(t') \cdot x(t')}\right) = \ln(p(t) \cdot x(t)) - \ln(p(t') \cdot x(t')). \qquad (6.1)$$

The right-hand side of this expression can be seen as the outcome of a line integral,

$$\ln(p(t) \cdot x(t)) - \ln(p(t') \cdot x(t')) = \int_{t'}^{t} \frac{d\ln(p(\tau) \cdot x(\tau))}{d\tau} d\tau, \qquad (6.2)$$

where τ is employed as generic time variable. Working out the integrand, we obtain

$$\frac{d\ln(p(\tau) \cdot x(\tau))}{d\tau} = \frac{\sum_{n=1}^{N} p_n(\tau) dx_n(\tau)/d\tau}{p(\tau) \cdot x(\tau)} + \frac{\sum_{n=1}^{N} x_n(\tau) dp_n(\tau)/d\tau}{p(\tau) \cdot x(\tau)}$$

$$= \sum_{n=1}^{N} s_n(\tau)\frac{d\ln x_n(\tau)}{d\tau} + \sum_{n=1}^{N} s_n(\tau)\frac{d\ln p_n(\tau)}{d\tau}, \qquad (6.3)$$

where $s_n(\tau)$ is the value share of commodity n at time period τ ($n = 1, \ldots, N$). Now the following definitions suggest themselves:

$$\ln P^{Div}(t, t') \equiv \int_{t'}^{t} \sum_{n=1}^{N} s_n(\tau)\frac{d\ln p_n(\tau)}{d\tau} d\tau \qquad (6.4)$$

$$\ln Q^{Div}(t, t') \equiv \int_{t'}^{t} \sum_{n=1}^{N} s_n(\tau)\frac{d\ln x_n(\tau)}{d\tau} d\tau. \qquad (6.5)$$

Combining the foregoing expressions delivers, finally,

$$\ln\left(\frac{p(t) \cdot x(t)}{p(t') \cdot x(t')}\right) = \ln P^{Div}(t, t') + \ln Q^{Div}(t, t'), \qquad (6.6)$$

or

$$V(t)/V(t') = P^{Div}(t, t')Q^{Div}(t, t'). \qquad (6.7)$$

This derivation essentially corresponds to the original one of Divisia (1925, p. 1000) within the framework of the quantity theory of money. He called (6.4) the "indice monétaire" and (6.5) the "indice activité." However, we will designate $P^{Div}(t, t')$ and $Q^{Div}(t, t')$ as the Divisia line integral price index and quantity index, respectively, for time period t relative to time period t'.

By a fundamental property of integrals, (6.4) yields

$$\frac{d \ln P^{Div}(t, t')}{dt} = \sum_{n=1}^{N} s_n(t) \frac{d \ln p_n(t)}{dt}. \tag{6.8}$$

Thus the growth rate of the Divisia price index $P^{Div}(t, t')$ at period t is a weighted average of the growth rates of the prices $p_n(t)$ $(n = 1, \ldots, N)$. This is sometimes expressed by saying that the Divisia price index is a log-change price index. In particular (6.8) implies that the growth rate of the Divisia price index lies between the largest and the smallest of the growth rates of the individual prices. *Mutatis mutandis*, the same applies to the Divisia quantity index.

An alternative, but instructive, derivation of the Divisia indices, which is essentially due to Malaney (1996, chapter 1), proceeds as follows. To ease the interpretation, we concentrate on the quantity index problem. The basic issue is how to compare the period t quantity vector, $x(t)$, to the earlier period t' quantity vector, $x(t')$, so that a single scalar index number results.

To begin with, consider a period $\tau \in [t', t]$ and an infinitesimal later period $\tau + d\tau$, and project the later-period quantity vector onto (the direction given by) the earlier-period quantity vector. Letting $\Lambda(\tau)$ be a positive, continuously differentiable, real-valued function of time, this can be expressed by

$$x(\tau + d\tau) = \frac{\Lambda(\tau + d\tau)}{\Lambda(\tau)} x(\tau) + \text{remainder.} \tag{6.9}$$

If the remainder happens to vanish, that is, if the later period quantity vector is a proportional (radial) expansion or contraction of the earlier period quantity vector, our problem is solved: over the infinitesimal time interval considered, the index number sought is obviously equal to the factor of proportionality $\Lambda(\tau + d\tau)/\Lambda(\tau)$. It is important to see that a certain notion of equivalence is at play here. The later period quantity vector is equivalent to its projection on the earlier period quantity vector. In fact, the notion of equivalence used here is simple equality.

In reality, things are complicated by the fact that $x(\tau)$ does not move through time according to a certain direction; that is, the remainder will in general *not* vanish. The way out is to define equivalence by placing a certain restriction on the remainder. In particular, $x(\tau + d\tau)$ and its projection on

$x(\tau)$ are considered equivalent when the remainder is costless: that is, when

$$p(\tau) \cdot \left(x(\tau + d\tau) - \frac{\Lambda(\tau + d\tau)}{\Lambda(\tau)} x(\tau) \right) = 0. \tag{6.10}$$

Using infinitesimals, that is, expressing $x(\tau + d\tau)$ as[5] $x(\tau) + dx(\tau)$ and $\Lambda(\tau + d\tau)$ as $\Lambda(\tau) + d\Lambda(\tau)$, it is straightforward to see that expression (6.10) can be rewritten as

$$d \ln \Lambda(\tau) = \frac{\sum_{n=1}^{N} p_n(\tau) dx_n(\tau)}{p(\tau) \cdot x(\tau)}, \tag{6.11}$$

which upon integration over $[t', t]$, and using definition (6.5), results in the Divisia quantity index:

$$\ln \Lambda(t) - \ln \Lambda(t') = \ln Q^{Div}(t, t'). \tag{6.12}$$

The corresponding price index is then obtained by employing relation (6.3).

Thus, the Divisia indices appear to be generated by a certain condition of equivalence, namely (6.10), saying that the remainder after projecting any quantity vector on the infinitesimally preceding one is costless. It is straightforward to verify that the corresponding condition, saying that the remainder after projecting any price vector on its infinitesimal predecessor is costless, will perform the same job.[6]

6.2.2 Montgomery Indices

For the derivation of the second type of line integral indices we return to expression (6.1). However, instead of the value ratio we now consider the value *difference*. Proceeding in the same way as above, we obtain

$$p(t) \cdot x(t) - p(t') \cdot x(t')$$
$$= \int_{t'}^{t} \frac{d(p(\tau) \cdot x(\tau))}{d\tau} d\tau$$
$$= \int_{t'}^{t} \sum_{n=1}^{N} p_n(\tau) \frac{dx_n(\tau)}{d\tau} d\tau + \int_{t'}^{t} \sum_{n=1}^{N} x_n(\tau) \frac{dp_n(\tau)}{d\tau} d\tau$$
$$= \int_{t'}^{t} \sum_{n=1}^{N} v_n(\tau) \frac{d \ln x_n(\tau)}{d\tau} d\tau + \int_{t'}^{t} \sum_{n=1}^{N} v_n(\tau) \frac{d \ln p_n(\tau)}{d\tau} d\tau. \tag{6.13}$$

---

[5] Notation: $dx(\tau) \equiv (dx_1(\tau), \ldots, dx_N(\tau))$.

[6] Notice that condition (6.10) makes the projection unique and invariant to the units of measurement. Expressed in the more complex setting of differential geometry, this condition says that the covariant derivative of $x(\tau)$ is costless. It is also said that $x(\tau)$ is subjected to a parallel translation.

We see that the value difference can be split into two parts, to be called respectively the Divisia quantity indicator and the Divisia price indicator.

The link between ratio and difference, and between multiplicative and additive decompositions, is provided by the logarithmic mean, which as a function of two strictly positive real numbers a and b is defined by $L(a, b) \equiv (a - b)/\ln(a/b)$ if $a \neq b$ and $L(a, a) \equiv a$. Thus, in particular,

$$\ln\left(\frac{p(t) \cdot x(t)}{p(t') \cdot x(t')}\right) = \frac{p(t) \cdot x(t) - p(t') \cdot x(t')}{L(p(t) \cdot x(t), p(t') \cdot x(t'))}. \tag{6.14}$$

Substituting (6.13) into (6.14) suggests the following definitions:

$$\ln P^M(t, t') \equiv \frac{\int_{t'}^{t} \sum_{n=1}^{N} v_n(\tau) \frac{d\ln p_n(\tau)}{d\tau} d\tau}{L(V(t), V(t'))} \tag{6.15}$$

$$\ln Q^M(t, t') \equiv \frac{\int_{t'}^{t} \sum_{n=1}^{N} v_n(\tau) \frac{d\ln x_n(\tau)}{d\tau} d\tau}{L(V(t), V(t'))}. \tag{6.16}$$

Combining the various pieces delivers, finally,

$$\ln\left(\frac{p(t) \cdot x(t)}{p(t') \cdot x(t')}\right) = \ln P^M(t, t') + \ln Q^M(t, t'), \tag{6.17}$$

or

$$V(t)/V(t') = P^M(t, t')Q^M(t, t'). \tag{6.18}$$

This derivation, albeit without the formal use of the logarithmic mean, can be found in Montgomery's 1929 and 1937 publications. For a long time these publications obviously did not get the attention of index number theorists. We will designate $P^M(t, t')$ and $Q^M(t, t')$ as the Montgomery line integral price index and quantity index respectively, for time period t relative to time period t'. As can be expected from their definitions, simple relationships such as expression (6.8) do not hold. In fact, by straightforward calculation one obtains

$$\frac{d\ln P^M(t, t')}{dt} = \frac{\sum_{n=1}^{N} v_n(t) \frac{d\ln p_n(t)}{dt}}{L(V(t), V(t'))}$$
$$- \frac{V(t) - L(V(t), V(t'))}{V(t) - V(t')} \frac{d\ln V(t)}{dt} \ln P^M(t, t'), \tag{6.19}$$

where we recall that $V(\tau)$ is the value of the aggregate at time period τ.

The difference between Divisia's and Montgomery's approach is that, whereas Divisia decomposed the (logarithm of the) value ratio, Montgomery decomposed the value difference. By employing the logarithmic mean, the value difference is then transformed into a ratio. Of course, by using the same tool, the multiplicative decomposition obtained by Divisia can be transformed into an additive one.

6.3 The Path-(In)dependency Issue

As noted, the integrals occurring in the definitions of the Divisia and Montgomery indices are essentially line integrals. That is, in general their outcome depends not only on the prices and quantities of the initial and terminal periods t' and t, but on the entire curve of $(p(\tau), x(\tau))$ between those periods. In this respect they differ from the integrals occurring in expression (6.2) and in the first line of (6.13). These two integrals have integrands that are total differentials, and therefore the outcome of these integrals does depend only on the prices and quantities of the periods t' and t. Thus, whereas $P^{Div}(t, t')$ and $Q^{Div}(t, t')$, and $P^M(t, t')$ and $Q^M(t, t')$, are path-dependent, their respective products are not. The property of path-dependency is crucial to a correct understanding of the Divisia and Montgomery indices. Divisia (1925, p. 1004) himself was very well aware of this property.[7]

In this section this topic will be explored a bit further, starting with the Divisia indices.

First, the foregoing leads us to conclude that, since their product is always path-independent, $P^{Div}(t, t')$ is path-independent if and only if $Q^{Div}(t, t')$ is path-independent.

Second, the main theorem on line integrals (see for instance Courant 1936) informs us that $P^{Div}(t, t')$ is path-independent[8] if and only if there exists a function $\phi(p)$ such that

$$s_n(\tau) = \partial \ln \phi(p(\tau))/\partial \ln p_n \ (n = 1, \ldots, N), \qquad (6.20)$$

in which case one obtains that

$$\ln P^{Div}(t, t') = \ln \left(\frac{\phi(p(t))}{\phi(p(t'))} \right). \qquad (6.21)$$

A similar result holds, of course, for $Q^{Div}(t, t')$.

---

[7] Samuelson and Swamy (1974, p. 579) mistakenly stated that "already in Divisia's original work in the 1920's ... the problem [of lack of path invariance] is ignored." Frisch (1936), however, did ignore the path-dependency problem.

[8] A line integral along a curve connecting t' and t is called path-independent if for all such curves the value of the integral depends only on the endpoints. A line integral is said to satisfy the closed cycle condition if along any closed curve – which in our case means that prices and quantities at t are the same as at t' – the value of the integral is equal to zero. These two definitions are equivalent.

Combining these two results, we conclude that if $P^{Div}(t, t')$ and $Q^{Div}(t, t')$ are path-independent then there exist functions $\phi(p)$ and $\psi(x)$ such that

$$\ln\left(\frac{V(t)}{V(t')}\right) = \ln\left(\frac{\phi(p(t))}{\phi(p(t'))}\right) + \ln\left(\frac{\psi(x(t))}{\psi(x(t'))}\right). \tag{6.22}$$

Since this must hold for any two periods t', t, the necessary condition (6.22) can be replaced by

$$V(\tau) = \phi(p(\tau))\psi(x(\tau)), \tag{6.23}$$

where the functions $\phi(p)$ and $\psi(x)$ must be linearly homogeneous in view of the fact that $V(\tau) = p(\tau) \cdot x(\tau)$. This condition, saying that at any period the value of the aggregate can be decomposed multiplicatively into two parts – the one aggregating prices and the other aggregating quantities – appears to be very restrictive.

Turning to the Montgomery indices, by a completely analogous reasoning we find that a necessary condition for $P^M(t, t')$ and $Q^M(t, t')$ to be path-independent is that there exist functions $\phi(p)$ and $\psi(x)$ such that

$$V(\tau) = \phi(p(\tau)) + \psi(x(\tau)). \tag{6.24}$$

It is clear, however, that this condition cannot be satisfied at all, because of the requirement of linear homogeneity. Thus, there is hardly any reason to expect the Montgomery indices to be path-independent.

This is the appropriate place to devote some attention to Reich's (2004) approach to obtain path-independency for the Divisia price index. In this approach it is, first, assumed – in the spirit of the stochastic approach – that individual price changes can be thought of as consisting of a general and a specific component,

$$d \ln p_n(\tau) = d \ln p(\tau) + d \ln \epsilon_n(\tau) \; (n = 1, \ldots, N), \tag{6.25}$$

respectively called purchasing power change and real price change. Second, it is assumed that

$$\sum_{n=1}^{N} s_n(\tau) d \ln \epsilon_n(\tau) = 0, \tag{6.26}$$

the left-hand side of which can be interpreted as the expected value of a stochastic variable $d \ln \epsilon(\tau)$. It follows that under these two assumptions

$$\ln P^{Div}(t, t') = \int_{t'}^{t} d \ln p(\tau) = \ln(p(t)/p(t')); \qquad (6.27)$$

or, in Reich's words, "Path dependence has become time dependence." On closer scrutiny, however, it appears that this approach is nothing but a repackaging of Malaney's derivation, discussed in the previous section. Put otherwise, path-independency is not attained, because the general component $p(t)/p(t')$ is not given, but must be estimated by $\ln P^{Div}(t, t')$, which is path-dependent.

6.4 Properties of the Indices

One should have noted that the functions $P^{Div}(t, t')$ and $Q^{Div}(t, t')$, and $P^{M}(t, t')$ and $Q^{M}(t, t')$, were called price and quantity indices, following common practice. The task now at hand is to check whether this terminology is warranted. It may be clear that the axioms and other properties accruing to bilateral indices[9] cannot be used right away, because of the specific nature of the Divisia and Montgomery line integral indices. We therefore have to look at their meaning, rather than at their formulation. The discussion will be cast in terms of price indices and will follow the order in which the axioms and properties were discussed in chapter 3.

The meaning of the *monotonicity axiom* is that, when all prices are non-decreasing, then the price index, too, is nondecreasing. Hence, assume that between periods t' and t the growth rates of the prices are non-negative; that is, $d \ln p_n(\tau)/d\tau \geq 0$ ($n = 1, \ldots, N$). Now, applying the mean value theorem of the integral calculus to (6.4), we obtain

$$\ln P^{Div}(t, t') = \sum_{n=1}^{N} s_n(t_n^*) \ln(p_n(t)/p_n(t')), \qquad (6.28)$$

where $t_n^* \in [t', t]$ for $n = 1, \ldots, N$. Hence, the logarithm of the Divisia price index is a linear combination of the logarithms of the individual price relatives. The weights in (6.28) are value shares $s_n(t_n^*)$, but it is important to notice that in general the intermediate points t_n^* will differ from each other; that is, $t_n^* \neq t_{n'}^*$ when $n \neq n'$. Thus in general these weights will not add up

[9] A bilateral price or quantity index is a function of initial and final period prices and quantities only.

to 1. It is, however, clear that if between t' and t the prices do not decrease, then the Divisia price index is greater than or equal to 1.

A similar application of the mean value theorem to (6.15) yields

$$\ln P^M(t, t') = \frac{\sum_{n=1}^{N} v_n(t_n^*) \ln(p_n(t)/p_n(t'))}{L(V(t), V(t'))}, \qquad (6.29)$$

which is obviously greater than or equal to 0. Thus the Montgomery price index is greater than or equal to 1. Notice that also in this case it is likely that $t_n^* \neq t_{n'}^*$ when $n \neq n'$. Thus in general the values $v_n(t_n^*)$ $(n = 1, \ldots, N)$ do not add up to anything observable.

A specific case is obtained when all the growth rates of the individual prices are zero, that is $d \ln p_n(\tau)/d\tau = 0$ $(n = 1, \ldots, N)$. Then the Divisia as well as the Montgomery price index takes on the value 1.

Evidently, the linear homogeneity axiom from bilateral index theory does not make much sense in the present context. The essence of the *proportionality property*, however, can be captured by assuming that all the individual growth rates are non-negative and that the price development happens to be such that $p(t) = \lambda p(t')$ for some $\lambda \geq 1$; that is, comparison period prices are λ times base period prices. Then it follows immediately from (6.28) and (6.29) that neither the Divisia nor the Montgomery price index will generally take on the value λ.[10] Thus the proportionality property will in general be violated.[11] In particular, the identity property ($\lambda = 1$) will in general be violated.

The *homogeneity-of-degree-0 axiom* requires a price index to be independent of the actual level of the prices. Hence, what happens when one replaces the price vector $p(\tau)$ by $\lambda p(\tau)$ for some $\lambda > 0$? One can easily check from (6.4) and (6.15) that such a replacement does not influence the value of the Divisia or the Montgomery price index, since

$$\frac{d \ln \lambda p_n(\tau)}{d\tau} = \frac{d \ln p_n(\tau)}{d\tau} \quad (n = 1, \ldots, N), \qquad (6.30)$$

[10] Only under very restrictive conditions such an outcome can occur. For instance, when $p_n(\tau) = p_n(t')(1 + (\tau - t')(\lambda - 1)/(t - t'))$ or $p_n(\tau) = p_n(t') \exp\{((\tau - t')/(t - t')) \ln \lambda\}$ for $\tau \in [t', t]$ and $n = 1, \ldots, N$, that is, the growth rates are constant and the same for all commodities, then one obtains $P^{Div}(t, t') = \lambda$.

[11] If, however, the Divisia price index is path-independent, then the proportionality property obviously holds.

and the logarithmic mean has the property that $L(\lambda a, \lambda b) = \lambda L(a, b)$. Similarly, replacing the quantity vector $x(\tau)$ by $\lambda x(\tau)$ $(\lambda > 0)$ does not influence the value of the Divisia or the Montgomery price index.

It is also easy to verify that the Divisia as well as the Montgomery price index are *dimensionally invariant*: that is, their outcomes do not depend on the units of measurement employed.

A price index is said to exhibit the *mean value property* if its value is always lying between the smallest and the largest of the individual price relatives. Returning to expressions (6.28) and (6.29), we see that there is no guarantee that the Divisia and Montgomery price indices will exhibit this behaviour.

Although for $N = 1$ the Divisia price index exhibits the desired feature that $P^{Div}(t, t') = p(t)/p(t')$, this does not hold for the Montgomery price index. It is clear that (6.15) reduces to

$$\ln P^M(t, t') \equiv \frac{\int_{t'}^{t} V(\tau) \frac{d \ln p(\tau)}{d\tau} d\tau}{L(V(t), V(t'))} \qquad (6.31)$$

which in general will differ from $p(t)/p(t')$.

A fundamental property of line integrals, in combination with the logarithmic mean property that $L(a, b) = L(b, a)$, ensures that the two price indices satisfy the *time reversal test*; that is, $\ln P^{Div}(t, t') = - \ln P^{Div}(t', t)$ and $\ln P^M(t, t') = - \ln P^M(t', t)$. It is here understood that going from t to t' the curve of $(p(\tau), x(\tau))$ is traversed in the opposite direction.

It should be noticed that all the foregoing observations apply *mutatis mutandis* to the Divisia and Montgomery quantity indices. Moreover, by construction, the Divisia price and quantity indices as well as the Montgomery price and quantity indices satisfy the *factor reversal test*; that is, they satisfy the product test,

$$\frac{p(t) \cdot x(t)}{p(t') \cdot x(t')} = P^{Div}(t, t')Q^{Div}(t, t') \qquad (6.32)$$

and

$$\frac{p(t) \cdot x(t)}{p(t') \cdot x(t')} = P^M(t, t')Q^M(t, t'), \qquad (6.33)$$

and the price and quantity indices have the same mathematical form: by interchanging prices and quantities in the price (quantity) index the corresponding quantity (price) index turns up. Put otherwise, Divisia and Montgomery indices belong to the class of ideal indices.

We next discuss the *circularity (transitivity) test*. For any $t'' \in [t', t]$ we obtain, by the familiar property of line integrals, that

$$\ln P^{Div}(t, t') = \ln P^{Div}(t, t'') + \ln P^{Div}(t'', t'), \qquad (6.34)$$

or, in more familiar notation,

$$P^{Div}(t, t') = P^{Div}(t, t'') P^{Div}(t'', t'). \qquad (6.35)$$

Although one easily checks that the Divisia price indicator (see expression (6.13)) is transitive, the Montgomery price index does not exhibit this feature. In this case we obtain the following identity:

$$\ln P^M(t, t') = \frac{L(V(t), V(t''))}{L(V(t), V(t'))} \ln P^M(t, t'')$$
$$+ \frac{L(V(t''), V(t'))}{L(V(t), V(t'))} \ln P^M(t'', t'). \qquad (6.36)$$

For the Divisia and Montgomery quantity indices, of course, similar identities hold.

We finally consider the property of *consistency-in-aggregation*. Suppose that the N commodities are divided into disjunct groups A_k, each consisting of N_k commodities ($k = 1, \ldots, K$). Let $(p_k(\tau), x_k(\tau))$ be the subvector of $(p(\tau), x(\tau))$ corresponding to the kth group. The Divisia price index for the kth group is then, according to (6.4), given by

$$\ln P_k^{Div}(\tau, t') \equiv \int_{t'}^{\tau} \sum_{n \in A_k} \frac{p_n(\tau') x_n(\tau')}{p_k(\tau') \cdot x_k(\tau')} \frac{d \ln p_n(\tau')}{d\tau'} d\tau'. \qquad (6.37)$$

By decomposing (6.4), and using again the fundamental property of integrals expressed by (6.8), we see that

$$\ln P^{Div}(t, t') = \int_{t'}^{t} \sum_{k=1}^{K} \frac{p_k(\tau) \cdot x_k(\tau)}{p(\tau) \cdot x(\tau)} \sum_{n \in A_k} \frac{p_n(\tau) x_n(\tau)}{p_k(\tau) \cdot x_k(\tau)} \frac{d \ln p_n(\tau)}{d\tau} d\tau$$
$$= \int_{t'}^{t} \sum_{k=1}^{K} \frac{p_k(\tau) \cdot x_k(\tau)}{p(\tau) \cdot x(\tau)} \frac{d \ln P_k^{Div}(\tau, t')}{d\tau} d\tau. \qquad (6.38)$$

The final line has the structure of a Divisia price index, whereby growth rates of Divisia group indices replace commodity price growth rates and group value shares replace commodity value shares. Thus we conclude that the Divisia price index $P^{Div}(t, t')$ satisfies the three criteria discussed in section 3.7 and is therefore consistent-in-aggregation. *Mutatis mutandis,* the same holds for the Divisia quantity index. That the Divisia indices are consistent-in-aggregation was noticed already by Gorman (1970) and Köves (1983, p. 138).

For the Montgomery price index we obtain the following decomposition:

$$
\begin{aligned}
L(V(t),\ V(t'))\ln P^M(t,\ t') \\
&= \int_{t'}^{t} \sum_{k=1}^{K} \sum_{n \in A_k} p_n(\tau) x_n(\tau) \frac{d \ln p_n(\tau)}{d\tau} d\tau \\
&= \int_{t'}^{t} \sum_{k=1}^{K} p_k(\tau) \cdot x_k(\tau) \sum_{n \in A_k} \frac{p_n(\tau) x_n(\tau)}{p_k(\tau) \cdot x_k(\tau)} \frac{d \ln p_n(\tau)}{d\tau} d\tau \\
&= \int_{t'}^{t} \sum_{k=1}^{K} p_k(\tau) \cdot x_k(\tau) \frac{d \ln P_k^{Div}(\tau,\ t')}{d\tau} d\tau.
\end{aligned}
\tag{6.39}
$$

We see here that the overall Montgomery price index $P^M(t,\ t')$ can also be written as a two-stage construction, whereby the first stage consists of Divisia group price indices and the second stage has the structure of a Montgomery price index. Since the functional forms involved in the two stages are different, the Montgomery price index, and *a fortiori* the Montgomery quantity index, is not consistent-in-aggregation.

Summarizing, we have seen that the Divisia and Montgomery line integral indices both provide a decomposition of the aggregate value ratio into two structurally similar parts, the one corresponding to price change and the other to quantity change. Moreover, the properties of the Divisia indices, but to a lesser extent those of the Montgomery indices, resemble those of bilateral indices.

An important exception is the proportionality property, which most bilateral indices do and line integral indices in general do not exhibit. When all comparison period prices (or quantities) happen to be λ times as high as the corresponding base period prices (or quantities), then the Divisia and Montgomery price (or quantity) indices will not necessarily deliver as outcome the proportionality factor λ.[12] This is a direct reflection of their nature as line integrals.

---

[12] This feature was apparently overlooked by Bartholomew (1998, p. 123), when he enthusiastically concluded his review by saying that "There is only one index number that possesses all the desirable properties, and that is the Divisia index."

6.5 Approximations (1): The Numerical-Mathematics Viewpoint

In practice, we do not have knowledge of the vector-valued functions $p(\tau)$ and $x(\tau)$, and actual price and quantity data usually come at discrete time intervals only (for example daily, weekly, monthly, quarterly, or yearly). This raises the question how to approximate the Divisia and Montgomery line integral indices. In this section we will look at this problem from the point of view of numerical mathematics. Because of the structural similarity of the line integral price and quantity indices, the discussion will be restricted to price indices.

Suppose we are concerned with a certain time interval $[t', t]$ and wish to compute $P^{Div}(t, t')$ or $P^{M}(t, t')$ when data are given at the periods $t' = t^{(0)}, t^{(1)}, \ldots, t^{(L)} = t$. The obvious procedure then is to split the interval $[t', t]$ into subintervals and to use the transitivity property (6.35) to calculate the Divisia line integral price index as a chained index

$$P^{Div}(t, t') = \prod_{l=1}^{L} P^{Div}(t^{(l)}, t^{(l-1)}). \qquad (6.40)$$

Similarly, by (6.36) the Montgomery line integral price index can be calculated as a sort of weighted chained index

$$P^{M}(t, t') = \prod_{l=1}^{L} P^{M}(t^{(l)}, t^{(l-1)})^{\psi_l}, \qquad (6.41)$$

where $\psi_l \equiv \frac{L(V(t^{(l)}), V(t^{(l-1)}))}{L(V(t), V(t'))}$ $(l = 1, \ldots, L)$. Notice that these weights do not add up to 1. What remains to see is how to approximate the components at the right-hand side of expressions (6.40) and (6.41).

Hence, without loss of generality, we may ask how to approximate $P^{Div}(t, t')$ or $P^{M}(t, t')$ when only data pertaining to the periods t and t' are given. The obvious approach is to use the trapezoid rule, which says that

$$\ln P^{Div}(t, t') = \int_{t'}^{t} \sum_{n=1}^{N} s_n(\tau) d \ln p_n(\tau)$$

$$= \sum_{n=1}^{N} \frac{\ln p_n(t) - \ln p_n(t')}{2} (s_n(t') + s_n(t))$$

$$\pm \left| \frac{(\ln p_n(t) - \ln p_n(t'))^3}{12} \frac{d^2 s_n(\zeta_n)}{d\tau^2} \right|, \qquad (6.42)$$

for certain $\zeta_n \in [t', t]$ $(n = 1, \ldots, N)$, whenever the mapping $\tau \rightarrow \ln p_n(\tau)$ $(n = 1, \ldots, N)$ is strictly monotonic. The natural approximation thus seems to be

$$P^{Div}(t, t') \approx \prod_{n=1}^{N} (p_n(t)/p_n(t'))^{s_n}, \qquad (6.43)$$

where $s_n \equiv (s_n(t) + s_n(t'))/2$ $(n = 1, \ldots, N)$, which is the Törnqvist price index. This result can alternatively be obtained by assuming that, over the time interval $[t', t]$, the value shares are constant and equal to the arithmetic mean of the initial and final period value shares.

Trivedi (1981) also argues that, from the numerical-mathematics point of view, the Törnqvist price index is the best, because it employs all the available information. The approximation error increases in general with the square of the length of the time interval $[t', t]$. This state of affairs has led many an author to confuse the names Divisia and Törnqvist.

Following Star and Hall (1976), the approximation error made by using the right-hand side of (6.43) can be decomposed as

$$\int_{t'}^{t} \sum_{n=1}^{N} (s_n(\tau) - s_n) \frac{d \ln p_n(\tau)}{d\tau} d\tau$$

$$= \int_{t'}^{t} \sum_{n=1}^{N} (s_n(\tau) - \bar{s}_n) \left(\frac{d \ln p_n(\tau)}{d\tau} - \frac{1}{t - t'} \ln \frac{p_n(t)}{p_n(t')} \right) d\tau$$

$$- \sum_{n=1}^{N} (s_n - \bar{s}_n) \ln \frac{p_n(t)}{p_n(t')}, \qquad (6.44)$$

where $\bar{s}_n \equiv (1/(t - t')) \int_{t'}^{t} s_n(\tau) d\tau$ $(n = 1, \ldots, N)$. This expression contains two covariance-like terms. The first is positive when deviations from the average shares $\bar{s}_n$ are positively correlated with deviations from the average price growth rates, whereas the second is positive when overestimates of the average shares are negatively correlated with the average price growth rates. Without information on the actual time path of the shares $s_n(\tau)$, however, this expression is virtually useless.

For approximating the Montgomery line integral price index, two rather natural approaches suggest themselves. The first is to assume that over the interval $[t', t]$ commodity values are constant, that is $v_n(\tau) = p_n(\tau)x_n(\tau) = v_n$ $(n = 1, \ldots, N)$. Then definition (6.15) leads to the following result:

$$P^M(t, t') \approx \prod_{n=1}^{N}(p_n(t)/p_n(t'))^{v_n/L(V(t), V(t'))}. \tag{6.45}$$

Notice that the weights of the price relatives do not add up to 1. Thus the Montgomery line integral price index is equal to a product of weighted price relatives. It is not a weighted geometric average. Given the data, obvious choices for v_n are $v_n(t')$, $v_n(t)$, or some mean of those values. Choosing the logaritmic mean, that is, $v_n = L(v_n(t), v_n(t'))$ $(n = 1, \ldots, N)$, leads to the Montgomery-Vartia bilateral price index.

The second approach is to assume that over the time interval considered, the quantities are constant, that is $x_n(\tau) = x_n$ $(n = 1, \ldots, N)$. It is then easily seen that (6.15) leads to

$$P^M(t, t') \approx \exp\left\{ \frac{\sum_{n=1}^{N}(p_n(t) - p_n(t'))x_n}{L(V(t), V(t'))} \right\}. \tag{6.46}$$

Given the data, obvious choices for x_n $(n = 1, \ldots, N)$ are the period t' quantities $x_n(t')$, the period t quantities $x_n(t)$, or the arithmetic mean of both periods' quantities $(x_n(t) + x_n(t'))/2$. The last choice will in general provide a better numerical approximation to the Montgomery price index than the other two.

6.6 Approximations (2): The Path-Specification Viewpoint

For discussing the second approximation strategy we explicitly write the Divisia and Montgomery price and quantity indices as line integrals, thus

$$\ln P^{Div}(\mathcal{C}) = \int_{\mathcal{C}} \frac{\sum_{n=1}^{N} x_n dp_n}{p \cdot x} \tag{6.47}$$

$$\ln Q^{Div}(\mathcal{C}) = \int_{\mathcal{C}} \frac{\sum_{n=1}^{N} p_n dx_n}{p \cdot x}, \tag{6.48}$$

and

$$\ln P^M(\mathcal{C}) = \frac{\int_{\mathcal{C}} \sum_{n=1}^{N} x_n dp_n}{L(p^t \cdot x^t, p^{t'} \cdot x^{t'})} \tag{6.49}$$

$$\ln Q^M(\mathcal{C}) = \frac{\int_{\mathcal{C}} \sum_{n=1}^{N} p_n dx_n}{L(p^t \cdot x^t, p^{t'} \cdot x^{t'})}, \tag{6.50}$$

where $\mathcal{C}$ denotes the curve described by $(p(\tau), x(\tau))$ when τ traverses the time interval $[t', t]$. To avoid clumsy notation, in this section we will set $t' = 0$ and $t = 1$. It will again be assumed that only the data (p^0, x^0) and (p^1, x^1) are known. Thus, nothing is known about the curve $\mathcal{C}$, except that it passes through these two data points in $\Re^N_{++} \times \Re^N_{++}$.

The following strategy now suggests itself. One presupposes some hypothetical curve through the two data points given, and evaluates the line integrals along this particular curve. The outcome for a "reasonable" curve can then be taken as approximation to the Divisia or Montgomery line integral index number of period 1 relative to period 0. This is the approach particularly pursued by Vogt (1977, 1978a, 1979, 1980a), Banerjee (1979b), and Van IJzeren (1986). In this section a systematic review of this sort of results, some of which are well known, will be presented.

6.6.1 A Class of Sectionally Smooth Curves

A number of important cases can be subsumed under the following two sectionally smooth curves connecting the initial with the final point:

$$\mathcal{C}(p^*) : (p^0, x^0) \to (p^*, x^0) \to (p^*, x^1) \to (p^1, x^1) \qquad (6.51)$$

$$\mathcal{C}(x^*) : (p^0, x^0) \to (p^0, x^*) \to (p^1, x^*) \to (p^1, x^1). \qquad (6.52)$$

Thus, along the curve $\mathcal{C}(p^*)$, first the quantities are kept fixed at x^0 while we let the prices change from p^0 to some, as yet undetermined, intermediate price vector p^*; next, keeping p^* fixed, we let the quantities change from x^0 to x^1; and finally, keeping the quantities fixed at x^1, we let the prices change from p^* to their final value p^1. The curve $\mathcal{C}(x^*)$ has a similar structure with x^* being an intermediate quantity vector. Figure 6.1 provides a simple graphical illustration of both curves.

The evaluation of the Divisia and Montgomery line integral indices along these two curves is straightforward. Consider, for instance, the Divisia price index (6.47) along $\mathcal{C}(p^*)$. Let us denote the three segments of this curve by $\mathcal{C}'$, $\mathcal{C}''$ and $\mathcal{C}'''$ respectively. Then, since along $\mathcal{C}''$ the prices do not change,

$$
\begin{aligned}
\ln P^{Div}(\mathcal{C}(p^*)) &= \int_{\mathcal{C}(p^*)} \frac{\sum_{n=1}^N x_n dp_n}{p \cdot x} \\
&= \int_{\mathcal{C}'} \frac{\sum_{n=1}^N x_n^0 dp_n}{p \cdot x^0} + \int_{\mathcal{C}'''} \frac{\sum_{n=1}^N x_n^1 dp_n}{p \cdot x^1} \\
&= \int_{\mathcal{C}'} d\ln(p \cdot x^0) + \int_{\mathcal{C}'''} d\ln(p \cdot x^1) \\
&= \ln(p^* \cdot x^0) - \ln(p^0 \cdot x^0) + \ln(p^1 \cdot x^1) - \ln(p^* \cdot x^1),
\end{aligned}
$$
$$(6.53)$$

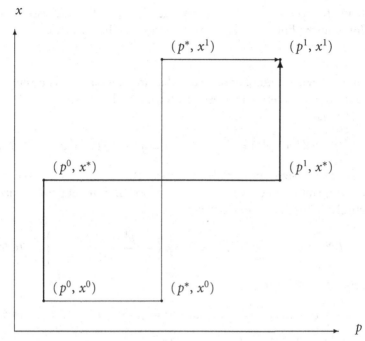

Figure 6.1. Two curves connecting periods 0 and 1

which can also be expressed as

$$P^{Div}(\mathcal{C}(p^*)) = \frac{p^1 \cdot x^1 / p^0 \cdot x^0}{p^* \cdot x^1 / p^* \cdot x^0} = \frac{p^1 \cdot x^1 / p^0 \cdot x^0}{Q^{Div}(\mathcal{C}(p^*))}. \quad (6.54)$$

The right-hand side follows, either by direct evaluation of the Divisia quantity index along $\mathcal{C}(p^*)$ or by employing the fact that the Divisia price and quantity index satisfy the factor reversal test.

A similar derivation applies to the curve $\mathcal{C}(x^*)$, the result being

$$Q^{Div}(\mathcal{C}(x^*)) = \frac{p^1 \cdot x^1 / p^0 \cdot x^0}{p^1 \cdot x^* / p^0 \cdot x^*} = \frac{p^1 \cdot x^1 / p^0 \cdot x^0}{P^{Div}(\mathcal{C}(x^*))}. \quad (6.55)$$

Repeating the calculations, we obtain for the Montgomery line integral price index numbers the following expressions:

$$P^M(\mathcal{C}(p^*)) = \exp\left\{ \frac{p^1 \cdot x^1 - p^0 \cdot x^0 - p^* \cdot (x^1 - x^0)}{L(p^1 \cdot x^1, p^0 \cdot x^0)} \right\} \quad (6.56)$$

and

$$P^M(\mathcal{C}(x^*)) = \exp\left\{ \frac{(p^1 - p^0) \cdot x^*}{L(p^1 \cdot x^1, p^0 \cdot x^0)} \right\}. \quad (6.57)$$

Employing the factor reversal property, the corresponding expressions for the Montgomery line integral quantity index numbers can easily be obtained.

We will now review a number of results that are generated by choosing for p^* and x^* specific intermediate vectors. It is immediately seen from (6.54) and (6.55) that

$$P^{Div}(\mathcal{C}(p^1)) = P^{Div}(\mathcal{C}(x^0)) = p^1 \cdot x^0 / p^0 \cdot x^0, \qquad (6.58)$$

which is the *Laspeyres* price index number. This is the ratio of the initial period quantity vector valued at final period and initial period prices, respectively. It is also easy to see that

$$P^M(\mathcal{C}(p^1)) = P^M(\mathcal{C}(x^0)) = \exp\left\{\frac{(p^1 - p^0) \cdot x^0}{L(p^1 \cdot x^1, \, p^0 \cdot x^0)}\right\}. \qquad (6.59)$$

Similarly, one obtains that

$$P^{Div}(\mathcal{C}(p^0)) = P^{Div}(\mathcal{C}(x^1)) = p^1 \cdot x^1 / p^0 \cdot x^1, \qquad (6.60)$$

which is the *Paasche* price index number, the ratio of the final period quantity vector valued at terminal period and initial period prices, respectively. It is also easy to see that

$$P^M(\mathcal{C}(p^0)) = P^M(\mathcal{C}(x^1)) = \exp\left\{\frac{(p^1 - p^0) \cdot x^1}{L(p^1 \cdot x^1, \, p^0 \cdot x^0)}\right\}. \qquad (6.61)$$

By choosing $p^* = (p^0 + p^1)/2$, one obtains a result that can be expressed as

$$P^{Div}(\mathcal{C}((p^0 + p^1)/2)) = \frac{1 + p^1 \cdot x^0 / p^0 \cdot x^0}{p^0 \cdot x^1 / p^1 \cdot x^1 + 1}, \qquad (6.62)$$

which is known as the true *factorial* price index number (see Banerjee 1980 and Balk 1983). In the numerator we see the Laspeyres price index number and in the denominator the inverse of the Paasche price index number.

Choosing $x^* = (x^0 + x^1)/2$, one obtains

$$P^{Div}(\mathcal{C}((x^0 + x^1)/2)) = \frac{p^1 \cdot (x^0 + x^1)/2}{p^0 \cdot (x^0 + x^1)/2}, \qquad (6.63)$$

which is the *Marshall-Edgeworth* price index number. This is the ratio of the average of initial and final period quantity vectors valued at final period and initial period prices, respectively. Notice that in the last two cases the Montgomery price index numbers are identical, namely

$$P^M(\mathcal{C}((p^0 + p^1)/2)) = P^M(\mathcal{C}((x^0 + x^1)/2))$$
$$= \exp\left\{\frac{(p^1 - p^0) \cdot (x^0 + x^1)/2}{L(p^0 \cdot x^0, p^1 \cdot x^1)}\right\}, \quad (6.64)$$

due to the Bennet (1920) identity, which reads

$$p^1 \cdot x^1 - p^0 \cdot x^0 = \frac{1}{2}(p^1 - p^0) \cdot (x^0 + x^1) + \frac{1}{2}(p^0 + p^1) \cdot (x^1 - x^0). \quad (6.65)$$

Banerjee (1979b) discusses the relations among the three Montgomery line integral price index numbers (6.59), (6.61), and (6.64) and some of the equations that play a role in the "factorial approach."

Instead of taking the arithmetic mean of initial and final period prices or quantities, one could take their geometric mean. Thus, let $(p^0 p^1)^{1/2}$ denote the vector of $(p_n^0 p_n^1)^{1/2}$, and let $(x^0 x^1)^{1/2}$ denote the vector of $(x_n^0 x_n^1)^{1/2}$ ($n = 1, \ldots, N$). One then obtains from (6.54) that

$$P^{Div}(\mathcal{C}((p^0 p^1)^{1/2})) = \frac{p^1 \cdot x^1 / p^0 \cdot x^0}{(p^0 p^1)^{1/2} \cdot x^1 / (p^0 p^1)^{1/2} \cdot x^0}. \quad (6.66)$$

This is the value ratio divided by the *Walsh-1* quantity index number.[13] Some rearrangement results in an alternative expression,

$$P^{Div}(\mathcal{C}((p^0 p^1)^{1/2})) = \frac{\sum_{n=1}^{N} s_n^0 (p_n^1 / p_n^0)^{1/2}}{\sum_{n=1}^{N} s_n^1 (p_n^1 / p_n^0)^{-1/2}}, \quad (6.67)$$

which is a quadratic mean of order 1 price index number. Similarly, we find that

$$P^{Div}(\mathcal{C}((x^0 x^1)^{1/2})) = \frac{p^1 \cdot (x^0 x^1)^{1/2}}{p^0 \cdot (x^0 x^1)^{1/2}}, \quad (6.68)$$

which is the Walsh-1 price index number. This can alternatively be written as the value ratio divided by a quadratic mean of order 1 quantity index number.

Instead of taking unweighted arithmetic means of initial and final period prices or quantities, one could take weighted means. For instance, let p^* be

---

[13] Expression (6.66) can also be conceived as the two-situation instance of the system of multilateral price index numbers proposed by Gerardi (see expression (2.8)).

the vector with elements $(p_n^0 x_n^0 + p_n^1 x_n^1)/(x_n^0 + x_n^1)$ $(n = 1, \ldots, N)$: that is, unit values computed over the initial and final period. Then one obtains for $P^{Div}(C(p^*))$ the price index number of *Lehr* (1885). A dual price index number is obtained as $P^{Div}(C(x^*))$, where x^* is the vector with elements $(p_n^0 x_n^0 + p_n^1 x_n^1)/(p_n^0 + p_n^1)$ $(n = 1, \ldots, N)$.

Let us now return to the case where $p^* = (p^0 + p^1)/2$. Suppose that the prices p^1 are much larger than p^0. Then one finds that $(p_n^0 + p_n^1)/(p_{n'}^0 + p_{n'}^1) \approx p_n^1/p_{n'}^1$ $(n, n' = 1, \ldots, N; n \neq n')$; that is, the relative prices in the average $(p^0 + p^1)/2$ tend to be equal to those of the largest of p^0 and p^1. To cure for this "bias" it is suggested to use instead of the ordinary mean of initial and final period prices a mean of deflated prices, say p^0 and p^1/P^{10}, where P^{10} is some price index number for period 1 relative to period 0.[14]

In particular, let us take $p^* = (p^0 + p^1/P^{Div}(C(p^*)))/2$, and substitute this into (6.54). Solving the resulting equation

$$P^{Div}(C(p^*)) = \frac{p^1 \cdot x^1}{p^0 \cdot x^0} \frac{(p^0 + p^1/P^{Div}(C(p^*))) \cdot x^0}{(p^0 + p^1/P^{Div}(C(p^*))) \cdot x^1}, \qquad (6.69)$$

we find that

$$P^{Div}(C(p^*)) = \left(\frac{p^1 \cdot x^0}{p^0 \cdot x^0} \frac{p^1 \cdot x^1}{p^0 \cdot x^1} \right)^{1/2}, \qquad (6.70)$$

which is the *Fisher* price index number, being the geometric mean of Laspeyres and Paasche price index numbers. One checks easily that also

$$P^{Div}(C(x^*)) = \left(\frac{p^1 \cdot x^0}{p^0 \cdot x^0} \frac{p^1 \cdot x^1}{p^0 \cdot x^1} \right)^{1/2}, \qquad (6.71)$$

where $x^* = (x^0 + x^1/Q^{Div}(C(x^*)))/2$. The vector x^* can be interpreted as a mean of "deflated" quantities. The idea of using this sort of intermediate price or quantity vectors as well as the solution of equation (6.69) can be traced back to an almost unknown article by Van IJzeren (1952), although it was not stated there in the context of Divisia indices. In later years this idea could be generalized to other choices for the intermediate price or quantity vectors, leading to quite a number of interesting results.[15]

To begin with, we observe that taking $p^* = (p^0 p^1/P^{10})^{1/2}$ does not lead to a new result since the factor P^{10} in numerator and denominator

---

[14] Notice that it is allowed that for some commodities $(p_n^0 + p_n^1/P^{10})/2$ falls outside the interval $[p_n^0, p_n^1]$.

[15] See Van IJzeren (1983), where this was done in the context of international comparisons.

of (6.54) cancels. We next set p^* equal to the vector with elements $(v_n^0 + v_n^1 / P^{Div}(\mathcal{C}(p^*)))/(x_n^0 + x_n^1)$, where we recall that $v_n^t = p_n^t x_n^t$ ($n = 1, \dots, N; t = 0, 1$). The elements of this vector can best be interpreted as deflated unit values, computed from the initial and final period data. Substituting this into (6.54) leads to

$$P^{Div}(\mathcal{C}(p^*)) = \frac{p^1 \cdot x^1}{p^0 \cdot x^0} \frac{\sum_{n=1}^N \frac{v_n^0 + v_n^1 / P^{Div}(\mathcal{C}(p^*))}{x_n^0 + x_n^1} x_n^0}{\sum_{n=1}^N \frac{v_n^0 + v_n^1 / P^{Div}(\mathcal{C}(p^*))}{x_n^0 + x_n^1} x_n^1}, \qquad (6.72)$$

which turns out to be a quadratic equation in $P^{Div}(\mathcal{C}(p^*))$. Combining this equation with the identity

$$\left[\sum_{n=1}^N \frac{v_n^0 x_n^0}{x_n^0 + x_n^1} + \sum_{n=1}^N \frac{v_n^0 x_n^1}{x_n^0 + x_n^1} \right] \frac{p^1 \cdot x^1}{p^0 \cdot x^0} = \sum_{n=1}^N \frac{v_n^1 x_n^0}{x_n^0 + x_n^1} + \sum_{n=1}^N \frac{v_n^1 x_n^1}{x_n^0 + x_n^1} \qquad (6.73)$$

delivers as solution

$$P^{Div}(\mathcal{C}(p^*)) = \frac{\sum_{n=1}^N \frac{x_n^0 x_n^1}{x_n^0 + x_n^1} p_n^1}{\sum_{n=1}^N \frac{x_n^0 x_n^1}{x_n^0 + x_n^1} p_n^0}. \qquad (6.74)$$

This is the two-situation instance of the *Geary-Khamis* system of multilateral price index numbers.[16] Notice that the right-hand side of (6.74) could also be obtained as $P^{Div}(\mathcal{C}(x^*))$, where x^* is defined as the vector with elements $2x_n^0 x_n^1/(x_n^0 + x_n^1) = 2((x_n^0)^{-1} + (x_n^1)^{-1})^{-1}$: that is, harmonic means of x_n^0 and x_n^1 ($n = 1, \dots, N$).[17]

A further modification of the vector of intermediate prices is to set

$$p_n^* \equiv \frac{v_n^0 + v_n^1/(V^1/V^0)}{x_n^0 + x_n^1/Q^{Div}(\mathcal{C}(p^*))} \quad (n = 1, \dots, N),$$

where $V^t \equiv p^t \cdot x^t$ ($t = 0, 1$). These prices can best be interpreted as "deflated" unit values, computed from the initial and final period data. In the numerator, the period 1 commodity value is "deflated" by the overall value ratio, and in the denominator the period 1 commodity quantity is "deflated" by the Divisia quantity index number. When we substitute this price vector into (6.54), we obtain an equation which, employing (6.73) where x_n^1 is

---

[16] See section 7.4.1 for details.

[17] The right-hand side of expression (6.74) occurs as formula 3153 in Fisher (1922).

replaced by $x_n^1/Q^{Div}(C(p^*))$ $(n = 1, \ldots, N)$, can be expressed as

$$P^{Div}(C(p^*)) = \frac{\sum_{n=1}^{N} \frac{x_n^0 x_n^1}{x_n^0 Q^{Div}(C(p^*))+x_n^1} p_n^1}{\sum_{n=1}^{N} \frac{x_n^0 x_n^1}{x_n^0 Q^{Div}(C(p^*))+x_n^1} p_n^0}. \tag{6.75}$$

This appears to be the price index number that was proposed by *Iklé* (1972).[18] It is easily checked that equation (6.75) does not admit an explicit solution. A simple proof that this equation has a unique solution, together with a method for finding this solution by numerical iteration, was provided by Van IJzeren (1983). Notice that Iklé's price index number can also be obtained by evaluating $P^{Div}(C(x^*))$, where each x_n^* is defined as the harmonic mean of the initial period quantity x_n^0 and the "deflated" final period quantity $x_n^1/Q^{Div}(C(x^*))$ $(n = 1, \ldots, N)$.

The reader should notice some obvious analogues. Evaluating the Divisia price index along $C(p^*)$, where each p_n^* is defined as the harmonic mean of p_n^0 and p_n^1 $(n = 1, \ldots, N)$, or along $C(x^*)$, where each $x_n^* \equiv (v_n^0 + v_n^1/Q^{Div}(C(x^*)))/(p_n^0 + p_n^1)$ $(n = 1, \ldots, N)$, yields a price index number that can be conceived as dual to the Geary-Khamis price index number (6.74), namely

$$P^{Div}(C(p^*)) = P^{Div}(C(x^*)) = \frac{p^1 \cdot x^1}{p^0 \cdot x^0} \left/ \frac{\sum_{n=1}^{N} \frac{p_n^0 p_n^1}{p_n^0+p_n^1} x_n^1}{\sum_{n=1}^{N} \frac{p_n^0 p_n^1}{p_n^0+p_n^1} x_n^0}\right. . \tag{6.76}$$

Similarly, the Divisia price index along $C(p^*)$, where each p_n^* is defined as the harmonic mean of the initial period price p_n^0 and the deflated final period price $p_n^1/P^{Div}(C(p^*))$ $(n = 1, \ldots, N)$, or along $C(x^*)$, where

$$x_n^* \equiv \frac{v_n^0 + v_n^1/(V^1/V^0)}{p_n^0 + p_n^1/P^{Div}(C(x^*))} \quad (n = 1, \ldots, N),$$

yields a price index number that is dual to Iklé's price index number (6.75), namely

$$P^{Div}(C(p^*)) = P^{Div}(C(x^*)) = \frac{p^1 \cdot x^1}{p^0 \cdot x^0} \left/ \frac{\sum_{n=1}^{N} \frac{p_n^0 p_n^1}{p_n^0 P^{Div}(C(p^*))+p_n^1} x_n^1}{\sum_{n=1}^{N} \frac{p_n^0 p_n^1}{p_n^0 P^{Div}(C(p^*))+p_n^1} x_n^0}\right. . \tag{6.77}$$

It is obvious that the actual value of this index number must be found with help of a suitable numerical procedure.

---

[18] See section 7.4.1 for details.

A final remark concerning curves such as $\mathcal{C}(x^0) : (p^0, x^0) \to (p^1, x^0) \to (p^1, x^1)$ must be made. Recall that

$$P^{Div}(\mathcal{C}(x^0)) = p^1 \cdot x^0 / p^0 \cdot x^0. \tag{6.78}$$

Although it seems that (in the first part of the curve) all prices as well as (in the second part of the curve) all quantities are supposed to change simultaneously, this appears to be not necessary. The various prices and quantities may change in any order without affecting the result. Thus, for example, the curve $\mathcal{C}'(x^0) : (p_1^0, \ldots, p_N^0, x^0) \to (p_1^1, p_2^0, \ldots, p_N^0, x^0) \to (p_1^1, p_2^1, p_3^0, \ldots, p_N^0, x^0) \to \cdots \to (p_1^1, \ldots, p_{N-1}^1, p_N^0, x^0) \to (p^1, x^0) \to (p^1, x^1)$ and the curve $\mathcal{C}''(x^0) : (p_1^0, \ldots, p_N^0, x^0) \to (p_1^0, \ldots, p_{N-1}^0, p_N^1, x^0) \to (p_1^0, \ldots, p_{N-2}^0, p_{N-1}^1, p_N^1, x^0) \to \cdots \to (p_1^0, p_2^1, \ldots, p_N^1, x^0) \to (p^1, x^0) \to (p^1, x^1)$ deliver the same outcome, namely

$$P^{Div}(\mathcal{C}'(x^0)) = P^{Div}(\mathcal{C}''(x^0)) = p^1 \cdot x^0 / p^0 \cdot x^0, \tag{6.79}$$

as the reader may check easily. However, for a curve $\mathcal{C}$ where, starting from (p^0, x^0), first the price of the first commodity changes from p_1^0 to p_1^1, next the quantity of the first commodity changes from x_1^0 to x_1^1, next the price of the second commodity changes from p_2^0 to p_2^1, next the quantity of the second commodity changes from x_2^0 to x_2^1, and so on, the Divisia price index number turns out to be equal to

$$P^{Div}(\mathcal{C}) = \frac{p_1^1 x_1^0 + \sum_{n=2}^N p_n^0 x_n^0}{\sum_{n=1}^N p_n^0 x_n^0} \times \frac{p_1^1 x_1^1 + p_2^1 x_2^0 + \sum_{n=3}^N p_n^0 x_n^0}{p_1^1 x_1^1 + \sum_{n=2}^N p_n^0 x_n^0} \times \cdots. \tag{6.80}$$

This is a chained index number that differs from the Laspeyres price index number for period 1 relative to period 0.

6.6.2 Some Completely Smooth Curves

This section reviews some important examples of completely smooth curves. A rather natural curve connecting (p^0, x^0) with (p^1, x^1) was suggested by Vogt (1977). It is a linear curve $\mathcal{C}$ in $\Re_{++}^N \times \Re_{++}^N$, defined by

$$p_n(\tau) = p_n^0 + \tau(p_n^1 - p_n^0) \ (n = 1, \ldots, N)$$
$$x_n(\tau) = x_n^0 + \tau(x_n^1 - x_n^0) \ (n = 1, \ldots, N) \tag{6.81}$$

where $\tau \in [0, 1]$. Though the curve is simple, the Divisia line integral price index along this curve does not have a simple explicit form. For the details the reader is referred to the various publications by Vogt.

It appears to be much simpler to evaluate the Montgomery line integral price index along the curve defined by expressions (6.81). Doing this, one obtains

$$P^M(\mathcal{C}) = \exp\left\{\frac{(p^1 - p^0) \cdot (x^0 + x^1)/2}{L(p^0 \cdot x^0, p^1 \cdot x^1)}\right\}, \qquad (6.82)$$

which is equal to the right-hand side of expression (6.64).[19]

An interesting, but more complicated variant of (6.81) was considered by Van IJzeren (1986). He specified $\mathcal{C}$ as the curve implicitly defined by

$$p_n(\tau) = (P^{Div}(\mathcal{C}))^\tau [p_n^0 + \tau(p_n^1/P^{Div}(\mathcal{C}) - p_n^0)] \ (n = 1, \ldots, N)$$
$$x_n(\tau) = (Q^{Div}(\mathcal{C}))^\tau [x_n^0 + \tau(x_n^1/Q^{Div}(\mathcal{C}) - x_n^0)] \ (n = 1, \ldots, N) \quad (6.83)$$

where $\tau \in [0, 1]$. We see here that for every commodity the price and quantity development is assumed to consist of a general component which reflects exponential inflation and a specific component which is linear and based on deflated prices or "deflated" quantities. Van IJzeren could then prove that $P^{Div}(\mathcal{C})$ equals the Fisher price index number and $Q^{Div}(\mathcal{C})$ equals the Fisher quantity index number. For the details of this proof the reader is referred to the original article.

Notice that on the curve defined by expressions (6.81) the growth rates of the prices and quantities are not constant. A natural alternative would thus be a curve on which the growth rates are constant. Such a log-linear curve $\mathcal{C}$ is defined by

$$\ln p_n(\tau) = \ln p_n^0 + \tau(\ln p_n^1 - \ln p_n^0) \ (n = 1, \ldots, N)$$
$$\ln x_n(\tau) = \ln x_n^0 + \tau(\ln x_n^1 - \ln x_n^0) \ (n = 1, \ldots, N) \quad (6.84)$$

where $\tau \in [0, 1]$. It is straightforward to check that along this curve

$$\int_{\mathcal{C}} \sum_{n=1}^{N} x_n dp_n = \sum_{n=1}^{N} L(v_n^0, v_n^1) \ln(p_n^1/p_n^0), \qquad (6.85)$$

which implies that the Montgomery line integral price index reduces to the *Montgomery-Vartia* price index.[20] This result was obtained previously by Montgomery (1929, 1937).

---

[19] Diewert (2005a) gives a different but equivalent derivation of this result.
[20] Diewert (2005a) gives a different but equivalent derivation of this result. Recall that the Montgomery-Vartia indices are consistent-in-aggregation.

An explicit formula for the Divisia line integral price index along the curve specified by (6.84) cannot be obtained. One must evaluate

$$\ln P^{Div}(\mathcal{C}) = \int_0^1 \frac{\sum_{n=1}^N v_n^0 (v_n^1/v_n^0)^\tau \ln(p_n^1/p_n^0)}{\sum_{n=1}^N v_n^0 (v_n^1/v_n^0)^\tau} d\tau \qquad (6.86)$$

with help of some numerical procedure. See Vogt (1986, 1989) for details. For $N = 2$ the explicit formula was derived by Fässler and Vogt (1989).

A simple approximation of the right-hand side of expression (6.86) would be to take the arithmetic mean of the integrand values at initial and final periods. One then obtains

$$\ln P^{Div}(\mathcal{C}) \approx \frac{1}{2} \sum_{n=1}^N (s_n^0 + s_n^1) \ln(p_n^1/p_n^0), \qquad (6.87)$$

where $s_n^t = v_n^t / \sum_{n=1}^N v_n^t$ $(n = 1, \ldots, N)$; that is, we again obtained the *Törnqvist* price index.

As a final example we consider the curve $\mathcal{C}$ implicitly defined by[21]

$$x_n(\tau) = b_n p_n(\tau)^{-\sigma} \ (n = 1, \ldots, N), \qquad (6.88)$$

where $\tau \in [0, 1]$, all $p_n(\tau)$ are sectionally smooth functions, and the parameters $b_n > 0$ $(n = 1, \ldots, N)$. Then the value shares have the form

$$s_n(\tau) = \frac{b_n p_n(\tau)^{1-\sigma}}{\sum_{n=1}^N b_n p_n(\tau)^{1-\sigma}} \ (n = 1, \ldots, N). \qquad (6.89)$$

We must now distinguish between two cases. First, let $\sigma = 1$. Then (6.89) reduces to

$$s_n(\tau) = \frac{b_n}{\sum_{n=1}^N b_n} \ (n = 1, \ldots, N); \qquad (6.90)$$

that is, along the curve $\mathcal{C}$ the value shares remain constant. One easily checks that in this case

$$\ln P^{Div}(\mathcal{C}) = \prod_{n=1}^N (p_n(1)/p_n(0))^{b_n/\sum_{n=1}^N b_n}; \qquad (6.91)$$

---

[21] Assuming rational economic behaviour, this curve corresponds to an agent having a time-invariant Constant Elasticity of Substitution preference structure or technology.

that is, a weighted geometric average of price relatives, or a *Cobb-Douglas* price index.[22] Second, let $\sigma \neq 1$. It is straightforward to check that in this case

$$\ln P^{Div}(\mathcal{C}) = \int_0^1 \frac{d \ln \left(\sum_{n=1}^N b_n p_n(\tau)^{1-\sigma} \right)^{1/(1-\sigma)}}{d\tau} d\tau$$

$$= \ln \left(\frac{\sum_{n=1}^N b_n p_n(1)^{1-\sigma}}{\sum_{n=1}^N b_n p_n(0)^{1-\sigma}} \right)^{1/(1-\sigma)}. \tag{6.92}$$

Combining this result with expression (6.89), we obtain as alternative expression

$$\ln P^{Div}(\mathcal{C}) = \ln(p_n(1)/p_n(0)) - \frac{1}{1-\sigma} \ln(s_n(1)/s_n(0)) \ (n = 1, \ldots, N). \tag{6.93}$$

Using the fact that $1/(1-\sigma)$ is a constant scalar, together with the fact that the value shares add up to 1, the following identity results:

$$\sum_{n=1}^N \frac{\ln P^{Div}(\mathcal{C}) - \ln(p_n(1)/p_n(0))}{\ln(s_n(1)/s_n(0))} \left(s_n(1) - s_n(0) \right) = 0, \tag{6.94}$$

which implies that

$$\ln P^{Div}(\mathcal{C}) = \frac{\sum_{n=1}^N L(s_n(1), s_n(0)) \ln(p_n(1)/p_n(0))}{\sum_{n=1}^N L(s_n(1), s_n(0))}, \tag{6.95}$$

where $L(.)$ is the logarithmic mean. The right-hand side of expression (6.95) is known as the *Sato-Vartia* price index. The corresponding quantity index has the same functional form (whereby prices are replaced by quantities). The Sato-Vartia indices belong to the class of ideal indices.

6.7 Direct Indices and Chained Indices

As we have seen, the starting point for the derivation of the Divisia as well as the Montgomery line integral price and quantity indices was the problem of decomposing the value ratio $V(t)/V(t')$ of an economic aggregate into two structurally similar parts, the one accounting for the price changes and the other for the quantity changes. Thus, repeating expression (6.7) and restricting the discussion to Divisia indices, we have

$$V(t)/V(t') = P^{Div}(t, t')Q^{Div}(t, t'). \tag{6.96}$$

---

[22] This result had already been obtained by Roy (1927).

Unfortunately, the actual path that $(p(\tau), x(\tau))$ has taken between periods t' and t is unknown. Therefore, the Divisia indices must be approximated by bilateral indices $P(.)$ and $Q(.)$ that satisfy the product test,

$$P^{Div}(t, t') \approx P(t, t') \qquad (6.97)$$

$$Q^{Div}(t, t') \approx Q(t, t'). \qquad (6.98)$$

As we have seen in the previous sections, each choice of $P(.)$ or $Q(.)$ presupposes a hypothetical path between t' and t.

Suppose now that data are available for the time periods $t' = t^{(0)}$, $t^{(1)}, \ldots, t^{(L)} = t$. Then, as we have seen, the Divisia indices can be decomposed as

$$P^{Div}(t, t') = \prod_{l=1}^{L} P^{Div}(t^{(l)}, t^{(l-1)}) \qquad (6.99)$$

$$Q^{Div}(t, t') = \prod_{l=1}^{L} Q^{Div}(t^{(l)}, t^{(l-1)}). \qquad (6.100)$$

Again using the bilateral indices $P(.)$ and $Q(.)$, we get as alternative approximation to the Divisia indices over the time interval $[t', t]$ a pair of chained indices,

$$P^{Div}(t, t') \approx \prod_{l=1}^{L} P(t^{(l)}, t^{(l-1)}) \qquad (6.101)$$

$$Q^{Div}(t, t') \approx \prod_{l=1}^{L} Q(t^{(l)}, t^{(l-1)}). \qquad (6.102)$$

It is well known that generally it will be the case that the two approximations, the one by direct indices and the other by chained indices, do not coincide.[23] Put otherwise, though expressions (6.99) and (6.100) represent mathematical identities, we usually find that

$$P(t, t') \neq \prod_{l=1}^{L} P(t^{(l)}, t^{(l-1)}) \qquad (6.103)$$

$$Q(t, t') \neq \prod_{l=1}^{L} Q(t^{(l)}, t^{(l-1)}). \qquad (6.104)$$

---

[23] Note that different decompositions of the time interval also lead to different approximations.

Provided that there occur no cycles in the data,[24] the chained indices are better approximations than the direct indices, since (1) the chained indices use all the available data rather than only the initial and final period data, and (2) the hypothetical paths implicitly assumed in the chained indices concern small time segments rather than the entire interval $[t', t]$. Moreover, it is an empirical fact that when the number of data points between t' and t is increased and simultaneously the length of the time span between each pair of adjacent points is decreased, the particular choice of the bilateral indices $P(.)$ and $Q(.)$ matters less and less. This is the sense in which the Divisia indices are said to rationalize chained indices.

For statistical practice, however, this offers no immediate consolation,[25] and one remains with the choice between direct and chained indices. Viewing their difference as a sort of approximation error would only be satisfactory when the limiting concept does afford a clear interpretation. Most direct indices can be given a decent interpretation from the economic-theoretic point of view. The interpretation of chained indices, however, still remains puzzling. That they approximate Divisia line integral indices would only be comforting if we knew that these indices themselves admit a clear interpretation.[26]

6.8 Conclusion

As a rule, the prices and quantities belonging to any economic aggregate change in such a way that the process can be described as being more or less continuous. The basic index number problem is how to decompose the value change between any two time periods into two meaningful parts, a price index number and a quantity index number. There are two paradigms:

(i) Use a pair of bilateral indices for a direct comparison of the two periods. Although perfectly defensible, this leaves us with a multitude of solutions, with numerically differing outcomes as well as with differing interpretations. Bilateral indices can be given an economic-theoretic justification, either by assuming a static preference ordering (or technology) or by conditioning on the preference ordering (or

---

[24] And recall that the data are supposed to be generated by sectionally smooth functions.

[25] The advent of highly disaggregated electronic transaction data, so-called scanner data, however, opens up possibilities for measurement that were hitherto unthought. See for example Allan-Greer, Rao, and O'Donnell (2004). Also, the assumption that data are generated by smooth functions without cycles turns out to be a gross simplification.

[26] Therefore von der Lippe (2000) complained "dass ... es wenig theoretische Fundierung des Kettenindex-Gedanken zu geben scheint."

technology) of a certain period. The longer the time span between the two periods is, the less plausible the assumption of a static preference ordering (or technology).

(ii) If there happen to be intermediate periods, then the price and quantity data of these periods can be used to compute bilateral index numbers for all adjacent periods to obtain chained index numbers covering the entire time interval. This procedure is grounded in the intuition that the time path taken by the aggregate does matter. Although there is still a multitude of solutions (depending on the particular bilateral formulas used), the spread of outcomes will usually be smaller.

Both paradigms are encompassed, albeit in a purely conceptual sense, by the line integral indices of Divisia and Montgomery. Of these two, in view of their properties, the Divisia indices appear to serve the purpose of measurement best.

Viewed from this perspective, and provided that there occur no cycles in the data, any direct or chained index can be conceived as a particular approximation to a line integral index, either in the numerical-mathematical sense or in the sense of presupposing a certain hypothetical time path for the aggregate. The usefulness of this result would be enhanced when the Divisia line integral indices could be given a solid foundation in economic theory. As can be shown, the assumption of a static preference ordering (or technology) fails to provide such a foundation. Balk (2005) has shown, however, that the Divisia line integral indices can be given a satisfactory interpretation once dynamic preference orderings (or technologies) are admitted.

7

International Comparisons:
Transitivity and Additivity

7.1 Introduction

In this era of globalization it is of great importance to have reliable methods that enable one to compare the economic situation of countries or regions. Such a comparison can be directed at (1) the "level" of welfare or some measure of the economic potential of a geographical entity, or (2) its structure of consumption or production. Key statistics which play a role are Gross Domestic Product (and its components), per capita income, industrial production, or (labour) productivity. The comparability of those statistics is to a large extent guaranteed by adherence to international guidelines such as the *System of National Accounts 1993*. The actual comparison, however, is frequently complicated by the fact that the value figures involved read in different currencies. Thus the first task seems to be to convert all those value figures, where necessary, into a single numéraire currency. The instrument that springs to mind here is a set of (market) exchange rates.

The comparison exercise does however not stop here. The second and more important task is to discern to what extent the value differences are "real" or "monetary"; that is, to what extent they are determined by more or less physical factors (different levels of consumption or production) or by different price systems. Put otherwise, the task at hand is to split a value difference, conventionally stated in the form of a value ratio, into a quantity index number (reflecting "real" differences between countries or regions) and a price index number (reflecting "monetary" differences between countries or regions).

Historically seen, the problem of international comparisons is cast in terms of finding appropriate currency convertors: that is, convertors which are regarded as more adequate than exchange rates. As is well known, exchange rates are to a large extent determined by the international flows of financial capital and can exhibit very volatile behaviour. Lurking in the background here is the old idea that each currency has its own "purchasing power."

This wording of the problem, however, is becoming less and less significant in view of the process of monetary unification. Though a large part of Europe now possesses a common currency, the problem of comparing economic aggregates of different countries or regions remains with us. Put otherwise, whether or not the countries involved in a comparison study share a certain currency has become a quite insignificant part of the problem.

During the second half of the 20th century a large number of methods for solving this problem have been developed. When one wishes to compare only two countries at a time (a so-called bilateral comparison), one can simply borrow methods familiar from the field of intertemporal comparisons.[1] However, multilateral comparisons, that is, comparisons in which more than two countries at a time are involved, constitute a subject *sui generis*.

Multilateral international comparisons are not a simple translation of multilateral intertemporal comparisons. Some important differences between the two types of comparisons are:

- Time proceeds continuously, whereas the number of countries involved in a certain comparison study stays fixed.
- Unlike time periods, countries do not exhibit a natural ordering.
- In an intertemporal comparison, the time periods considered are usually of the same size (one compares months with months, years with years, etc.). Countries, however, are by nature not equally "important" (with respect to area, population, economic potential, etc.).
- More than in intertemporal comparisons, there is in international comparisons a strong desire to aggregate the geographical entities and use such aggregates also in comparisons. For example, one wishes to compare the European countries to the European Union as a whole, or the European Union to the United States.

Basically this chapter reviews the progress that has been made over the past decades in understanding the nature of the various methods that have been developed. Some of these are in current use by international organizations.

---

[1] Eichhorn and Voeller (1983) provide a parallel axiomatic treatment of intertemporal and interspatial price and quantity indices.

Hill (1997) developed an interesting and virtually complete taxonomy of multilateral methods for international comparisons. This taxonomy provides insight into the structural similarities and dissimilarities of the various methods. However, a taxonomy as such is not sufficient to discriminate between competing methods. In addition we need a set of criteria, in the spirit of Fisher (1922) called *tests*, which a multilateral method ideally should satisfy. A fairly satisfactory set of tests has been developed for the first time by Diewert (1986). But there are also other points of view possible.

The architecture of this chapter is as follows. After having done with the necessary definitional footwork, section 7.2 discusses an important implication of the requirement of transitivity. Section 7.3 discusses a number of methods, all of which are related by the fact that they can be regarded as generalizations of a bilateral comparison. Section 7.4 is devoted to the class of additive methods. Section 7.5 outlines the test approach and the insights obtained from it. Section 7.6 reviews two recently developed methods which are based on the procedure of chaining. Section 7.7 turns to model-based approaches; that is, approaches based on an assumption concerning the probability distribution of all the individual prices. Section 7.8 concludes.

7.2 The Requirement of Transitivity

It is assumed that we must compare countries[2] $1, \ldots, I$ $(I \geq 3)$ with respect to a well-defined economic aggregate involving commodities which are arbitrarily labelled as $1, \ldots, N$ $(N \geq 2)$. The price vector for country i, expressed in its own currency, will be denoted by $p^i \equiv (p_1^i, \ldots, p_N^i) \in \Re_{++}^N$, and the associated quantity vector will be denoted by $x^i \equiv (x_1^i, \ldots, x_N^i) \in \Re^N$ $(i = 1, \ldots, I)$. Price and quantity vectors are assumed to pertain to the same period of time.[3] Some of the quantities could be negative, for instance in the case of imports. However, it is assumed that $p^i \cdot x^j \equiv \sum_{n=1}^{N} p_n^i x_n^j > 0$ for all i, $j = 1, \ldots, I$. For all $i = 1, \ldots, I$, $p^i \cdot x^i = \sum_{n=1}^{N} p_n^i x_n^i$ represents the value of country i's aggregate.

The price index of country j relative to country i will be denoted by the ratio P^j/P^i, and the quantity index will be denoted by the ratio Q^j/Q^i $(i, j = 1, \ldots, I)$.[4] All P^i and Q^i are supposed to be functions of all the prices

---

[2] The word *country* is used as a shorthand for any kind of geographical entity.

[3] An additional layer of complexity materializes when one takes the time dimension explicitly into account. This leads to the problem of combined interspatial-intertemporal comparisons, considered by Krijnse Locker and Faerber (1984) and, more recently, Hill (2004).

[4] The ratio P^j/P^i is usually called the purchasing power parity (PPP) of country j (or country j's currency) relative to country i (or country i's currency).

and all the quantities, (p^k, x^k) $(k = 1, \ldots, I)$. The notation expresses the requirement that price and quantity indices be transitive.

A second, equally important requirement is that price index and quantity index satisfy the product test; that is, their product must exhaust the value ratio:

$$\frac{P^j}{P^i} \frac{Q^j}{Q^i} = \frac{p^j \cdot x^j}{p^i \cdot x^i} \ (i, j = 1, \ldots, I). \tag{7.1}$$

As indicated, the ultimate purpose of most international comparisons is to compare "real" values of countries. The following definitions serve to make this notion precise. The volume of country i is defined as $p^i \cdot x^i / P^i$ $(i = 1, \ldots, I)$,[5] and the volume share of country i in the aggregate volume of all I countries is defined as

$$Q^i \equiv \frac{p^i \cdot x^i / P^i}{\sum_{k=1}^{I} p^k \cdot x^k / P^k}$$

$$= \left(\sum_{k=1}^{I} (p^k \cdot x^k / p^i \cdot x^i)(P^k / P^i)^{-1} \right)^{-1}$$

$$= \left(\sum_{k=1}^{I} (Q^i / Q^k)^{-1} \right)^{-1} \ (i = 1, \ldots, I). \tag{7.2}$$

The volume shares add up to 1. The second and third lines are added to make clear how volume shares can be calculated from a set of price index numbers or a set of quantity index numbers respectively.

The additive nature of the country-specific volume shares makes it possible to define volume shares for aggregates of countries as well. For example, the volume share of the union of countries i and j is simply given by $Q^i + Q^j$.

The requirement of transitivity appears to have a far-reaching consequence, which can be seen as follows. Suppose that the quantity index Q^j / Q^i does not depend on prices and quantities of countries other than i and j; that is, suppose there exists a function $f(.)$ such that[6]

$$Q^j / Q^i = f(p^j, x^j, p^i, x^i) \ (i, j = 1, \ldots, I). \tag{7.3}$$

---

[5] In practice this is calculated as $p^i \cdot x^i / (P^i / P^k)$ for some choice of the numéraire country k.

[6] The fact that $f(.)$ is assumed to be the same for all pairs of countries reflects the natural but hidden assumption that all countries be treated symmetrically.

In fact, this expression could be regarded as the formalization of the requirement of (maximal) characteristicity, which goes back to Drechsler (1973).[7]
The requirement of transitivity then implies that

$$f(p^j, x^j, p^i, x^i) = \frac{f(p^j, x^j, p^k, x^k)}{f(p^i, x^i, p^k, x^k)} \; (i, j, k = 1, \dots, I). \quad (7.4)$$

Since the left-hand side of this equation does not depend on (p^k, x^k), the
right-hand side cannot depend on it either. But this implies that there exists
a function $g(p, x)$ such that the quantity index can be written as

$$Q^j / Q^i = \frac{g(p^j, x^j)}{g(p^i, x^i)} \; (i, j = 1, \dots, I). \quad (7.5)$$

A very modest, even minimal, requirement on quantity indices is that
whenever all country j quantities are equal to country i quantities, that is,
$x^j = x^i$, then the quantity index Q^j / Q^i takes on the value 1. Put otherwise,
quantity indices are required to satisfy the identity axiom. But this implies
that

$$g(p^j, x^i) = g(p^i, x^i) \; (i, j = 1, \dots, I), \quad (7.6)$$

which means that the function $g(p, x)$ is actually a function $g(x)$. Substituting this into expression (7.5), we must conclude that the quantity index
Q^j / Q^i does not depend on any prices.

This would be an undesirable state of affairs. Hence, if we wish prices
to play a role in the quantity index and if we wish to uphold the requirements of transitivity and identity, then we must sacrifice the requirement
of (maximal) characteristicity.[8] Put otherwise, we must accept that each
quantity index Q^j / Q^i is a function of all the prices and all the quantities,
$p^1, \dots, p^I, x^1, \dots, x^I \; (i, j = 1, \dots, I)$. If Q^j / Q^i is such an index, then,
by relation (7.1), so is P^j / P^i.

---

[7] According to Drechsler (1973), "the characteristicity requirement is satisfied if in the
computation of indices the weights of the given two countries are used. In a Netherlands-
Belgium quantity comparison, for instance, this requirement is completely satisfied if
Dutch prices, Belgian prices or average Dutch-Belgian prices are used as weights. Average
EEC weights are not fully characteristic for a Netherlands-Belgium comparison, and
average European weights even less. To use Indian weights in a Netherlands-Belgium
comparison would be considered wrong by everybody just as if in an Indian-Pakistan
comparison Dutch weights were used. In the latter cases, the weights would be very
uncharacteristic; their use would amount to the same as if in the case of the computation
of a 1971–1970 inter-temporal index 1920 (or 2020) prices were used."

[8] This corresponds to the impossibility theorem of van Veelen (2002), which uses a slightly
more general setting with ordinal rather than cardinal relations.

7.3 Generalizations of a Bilateral Comparison

Let us first consider two countries i and j. The price level of country j relative to country i could be measured by the Laspeyres price index

$$P^L(p^j, x^j, p^i, x^i) \equiv p^j \cdot x^i / p^i \cdot x^i, \tag{7.7}$$

or by the Paasche price index

$$P^P(p^j, x^j, p^i, x^i) \equiv p^j \cdot x^j / p^i \cdot x^j. \tag{7.8}$$

The interpretation of these indices depends of course on the aggregate under study. For instance, when we are studying household consumption, the Laspeyres price index compares the value of country i's household consumption at country j's prices to the value of this consumption at its own prices. Similarly, the Paasche price index compares the value of country j's household consumption at its own prices to the value at country i's prices. When the currencies of the two countries differ, the dimension of both indices is the number of country j currency units per unit of country i's currency.

In general the two price indices (7.7) and (7.8) will deliver different outcomes. Wanting a single outcome, we look for a price index P^j/P^i that lies "between" the Laspeyres and the Paasche price index. In particular we require that

$$P^L(p^j, x^j, p^i, x^i) = t P^j/P^i \text{ and } P^j/P^i = t P^P(p^j, x^j, p^i, x^i) \ (t > 0). \tag{7.9}$$

By employing the relation $1/P^P(p^j, x^j, p^i, x^i) = P^L(p^i, x^i, p^j, x^j)$, these two equations can obviously be reduced to a single equation, one of its versions being

$$P^L(p^j, x^j, p^i, x^i) P^i/P^j = P^L(p^i, x^i, p^j, x^j) P^j/P^i. \tag{7.10}$$

One verifies easily that the solution to (7.10) is the Fisher price index

$$P^j/P^i = P^F(p^j, x^j, p^i, x^i) \equiv [P^L(p^j, x^j, p^i, x^i) P^P(p^j, x^j, p^i, x^i)]^{1/2}, \tag{7.11}$$

the geometric average of the Laspeyres and the Paasche price index. Notice that the Fisher index has the country reversal property[9]: that is,

$$P^F(p^i, x^i, p^j, x^j) = 1/P^F(p^j, x^j, p^i, x^i), \tag{7.12}$$

which reflects the symmetrical position of the two countries i and j.

---

[9] This is the interspatial analogue of the time reversal test.

7.3.1 The GEKS Indices

We now turn to a truly multilateral comparison: that is, a comparison of all the I countries simultaneously. We will assume that we have a set of positive country weights g_i ($i = 1, \ldots, I$). These weights can be regarded as initial measures of country importance. Normalized weights, adding up to 1, are defined by $f_i \equiv g_i / \sum_{i=1}^{I} g_i$ ($i = 1, \ldots, I$).

We proceed by generalizing expression (7.10) in the following way:

$$\prod_{i=1}^{I} [P^L(p^j, x^j, p^i, x^i) P^i / P^j]^{f_i}$$

$$= \prod_{i=1}^{I} [P^L(p^i, x^i, p^j, x^j) P^j / P^i]^{f_i} \ (j = 1, \ldots, I). \quad (7.13)$$

At both sides of these equations we see weighted geometric averages. It is straightforward to check that the solution of this system of equations is

$$\left(\frac{P^j}{P^i}\right)_{GEKS} \equiv \prod_{k=1}^{I} [P^F(p^j, x^j, p^k, x^k) P^F(p^k, x^k, p^i, x^i)]^{f_k}(i, j = 1, \ldots, I). \quad (7.14)$$

If all the weights are the same, which implies that $f_k = 1/I$ ($k = 1, \ldots, I$), then expression (7.14) reduces to the well-known formula that was proposed independently by Elteö and Köves (1964) and Szulc (1964).[10] This formula, however, had already been proposed by Gini (1924).[11] Therefore the subscript GEKS is attached.

Another way of deriving expression (7.14) is by solving the following minimization problem

$$\min_{P^1, \ldots, P^I} \sum_{i=1}^{I} \sum_{j=1}^{I} g_i g_j [\ln P^F(p^j, x^j, p^i, x^i) - \ln(P^j / P^i)]^2. \quad (7.15)$$

Here one seeks to determine transitive, multilateral price indices which approximate as good as possible the intransitive, bilateral Fisher price indices.[12]

---

[10] According to Köves (1999) the EKS formula appeared for the first time in an appendix, written by Elteö, in a 1962 book by L. Drechsler. Actually, Drechsler (1973) introduced the EKS method to the Western world.

[11] This fact was acknowledged by Szulc (1964), who however referred to Gini (1931). On Gini's contributions, see Biggeri, Ferrari, and Lemmi (1987).

[12] Replacing in expression (7.15) the Fisher price index by the Laspeyres or the Paasche price index leads to the same outcome, namely expression (7.14), as shown by Van IJzeren (1987). A more precise name for the indices given by expression (7.14) would be

One could say that the impossible requirement of (maximal) characteristicity is replaced by the objective of obtaining "optimal" characteristicity. This objective is to be attained by minimizing a sum of weighted squared residuals. The weights $g_i g_j$ are used to discriminate between all the pairwise comparisons.[13]

Still another way of interpreting expression (7.14) is to notice that each of the factors $P^F(p^j, x^j, p^k, x^k) P^F(p^k, x^k, p^i, x^i)$ provides a "price index" for country j relative to country i, calculated via a "bridge" country k. Since there are I choices for k, it is rather natural to take an average of all of those factors as the final index.

We notice that, according to expression (7.14), the price indices $(P^j / P^i)_{GEKS}$ depend not only on the prices and quantities of the countries i and j, but also on the prices and quantities of all the other countries involved. Thus if we extend the set of countries, all the price index numbers must be recalculated. This is one of the features distinguishing multilateral price indices from bilateral price indices.

The quantity index associated with $(P^j / P^i)_{GEKS}$ can be obtained easily from expression (7.1) by using the fact that the weights f_k add up to 1, and the factor reversal property of the Fisher price and quantity indices. The index reads

$$\left(\frac{Q^j}{Q^i}\right)_{GEKS} \equiv \prod_{k=1}^{I} [Q^F(p^j, x^j, p^k, x^k) Q^F(p^k, x^k, p^i, x^i)]^{f_k} \quad (i, j = 1, \dots, I),$$

(7.16)

where

$$Q^F(p^j, x^j, p^i, x^i) \equiv [(p^i \cdot x^j / p^i \cdot x^i)(p^j \cdot x^j / p^j \cdot x^i)]^{1/2} \quad (7.17)$$

"GEKS-Fisher" indices. By replacing, in expression (7.15), the Fisher price index by the Törnqvist price index, one obtains the GEKS-Törnqvist indices. An other way of obtaining the last indices is by replacing in expression (7.9) the Laspeyres and Paasche price indices by Geometric Laspeyres and Paasche price indices, $\prod_{n=1}^{N}(p_n^j / p_n^i)^{w_n^i}$ and $\prod_{n=1}^{N}(p_n^j / p_n^i)^{w_n^j}$ respectively. Setting all the weights equal, the GEKS-Törnqvist indices reduce to the multilateral Törnqvist price indices proposed by Caves, Christensen, and Diewert (1982). See also section 7.7.

[13] Rao (2008) considered a generalization of this procedure, whereby the weights $g_i g_j$ are replaced by weights g_{ij}. This implies that there is no explicit solution available. His experiments, based on data from the 1993 OECD survey, suggest that the multilateral price index numbers obtained are not very sensitive to the particular choice of the weights. See also Rao and Timmer (2003), where the weights g_{ij} are indicators of the reliability of the bilateral comparisons. Weights g_{ij} that allow for gaps in the data (due to the fact that not all the commodities exist or are observed in all the countries) were considered by Hill and Timmer (2006).

is the Fisher quantity index. Notice that the GEKS quantity index can also be obtained by interchanging prices and quantities in the GEKS price index (7.14). Thus the GEKS price and quantity indices satisfy the factor reversal test.

7.3.2 Van IJzeren-Type Indices

A second way of generalizing expression (7.10) is by employing arithmetic averages instead of geometric averages. We then obtain, instead of (7.13), the following system of equations:

$$\sum_{i=1}^{I} g_i P^L(p^j, x^j, p^i, x^i) P^i / P^j$$

$$= \sum_{i=1}^{I} g_i P^L(p^i, x^i, p^j, x^j) P^j / P^i (j = 1, \ldots, I). \quad (7.18)$$

One can prove that this system of equations has a unique, positive solution $P_Y^1, \ldots, P_Y^I$, which is determined up to a scalar factor. Thus, although not expressible in explicit form, the price indices P_Y^j / P_Y^i ($i, j = 1, \ldots, I$) are completely determined, as are the quantity indices via expression (7.1). They depend on the prices and quantities of all the I countries. The method defined by expression (7.18) is known as the third, balanced method of Van IJzeren (1955, 1956). The subscript Y will therefore be used.

There are other ways of deriving expression (7.18). In his original publications, Van IJzeren used a so-called tourist model. But he also noticed that the equations (7.18) can be conceived as being the first-order conditions for the following minimization problem:

$$\min_{P^1, \ldots, P^I} \sum_{i=1}^{I} \sum_{j=1}^{I} g_i g_j P^L(p^j, x^j, p^i, x^i) P^i / P^j. \quad (7.19)$$

Notice that $P^L(p^j, x^j, p^i, x^i) P^i / P^j$ is the discrepancy, in the form of a ratio, between the bilateral Laspeyres price index and the desired multilateral price index for country j relative to country i. Thus (7.19) is the same sort of problem as (7.15), the objective function being different.

Still another way of deriving expression (7.18) was provided by Balk (1989a, 1996c). The naming of the method suggests that there are at least two other methods. Being of only historical interest, they will not be discussed here. The genesis of these methods was discussed in section 2.2.

Using relationship (7.1), we find that expression (7.18) can be rewritten as

$$\sum_{i=1}^{I} g_i Q^L(p^j, x^j, p^i, x^i) Q^i / Q^j$$

$$= \sum_{i=1}^{I} g_i Q^L(p^i, x^i, p^j, x^j) Q^j / Q^i \, (j = 1, \ldots, I), \qquad (7.20)$$

where $Q^L(p^j, x^j, p^i, x^i) \equiv p^i \cdot x^j / p^i \cdot x^i$ is the Laspeyres quantity index of country j relative to country i. Notice that expression (7.20) can also be obtained by interchanging prices and quantities in expression (7.18). Thus, although not expressible in explicit form, the Van IJzeren price and quantity indices can be said to satisfy the factor reversal test.

The third way of generalizing expression (7.10) is the polar opposite of the second way, namely by employing harmonic averages. We then obtain

$$\left[\sum_{i=1}^{I} g_i [P^L(p^j, x^j, p^i, x^i) P^i / P^j]^{-1} \right]^{-1}$$

$$= \left[\sum_{i=1}^{I} g_i [P^L(p^i, x^i, p^j, x^j) P^j / P^i]^{-1} \right]^{-1} \, (j = 1, \ldots, I). \qquad (7.21)$$

As one verifies immediately, this system of equations can be written as

$$\sum_{i=1}^{I} g_i P^P(p^j, x^j, p^i, x^i) P^i / P^j$$

$$= \sum_{i=1}^{I} g_i P^P(p^i, x^i, p^j, x^j) P^j / P^i \, (j = 1, \ldots, I). \qquad (7.22)$$

This (relatively unknown) system of equations was proposed by Gerardi (1974). He derived it from a so-called immigrant model, which was a variation of Van IJzeren's "tourist model." The system (7.22) will therefore be called the Gerardi–van IJzeren system. Notice that the equations (7.22) can also be conceived as first-order conditions for the minimization problem

$$\min_{P^1, \ldots, P^I} \sum_{i=1}^{I} \sum_{j=1}^{I} g_i g_j P^P(p^j, x^j, p^i, x^i) P^i / P^j, \qquad (7.23)$$

which differs from (7.19) in that Paasche indices are used instead of Laspeyres indices.

Using relationship (7.1), we find that expression (7.22) can be rewritten as

$$\sum_{i=1}^{I} g_i Q^P(p^j, x^j, p^i, x^i) Q^i / Q^j = \sum_{i=1}^{I} g_i Q^P(p^i, x^i, p^j, x^j) Q^j / Q^i (j = 1, \ldots, I),$$

(7.24)

where $Q^P(p^j, x^j, p^i, x^i) \equiv p^j \cdot x^j / p^j \cdot x^i$ is the Paasche quantity index of country j relative to country i. Thus the price and quantity indices from the Gerardi–Van IJzeren system can be said to satisfy the factor reversal test.

7.3.3 Other Indices

Our next set of generalizations departs from expressions (7.14) and (7.16), which defined the GEKS indices. Using the country reversal property of the Fisher indices, these expressions can be rewritten as

$$\left(\frac{P^j}{P^i}\right)_{GEKS} = \frac{\prod_{k=1}^{I}[P^F(p^j, x^j, p^k, x^k)]^{f_k}}{\prod_{k=1}^{I}[P^F(p^i, x^i, p^k, x^k)]^{f_k}} \quad (i, j = 1, \ldots, I) \quad (7.25)$$

$$\left(\frac{Q^j}{Q^i}\right)_{GEKS} = \frac{\prod_{k=1}^{I}[Q^F(p^j, x^j, p^k, x^k)]^{f_k}}{\prod_{k=1}^{I}[Q^F(p^i, x^i, p^k, x^k)]^{f_k}} \quad (i, j = 1, \ldots, I). \quad (7.26)$$

Two alternatives emerge when we replace in the first expression the geometric averages in numerator and denominator by arithmetic or harmonic averages. The associated quantity indices are then defined residually by (7.1). Two other alternatives emerge when we replace in the second expression the geometric averages by arithmetic or harmonic averages and define the associated price indices residually.

For instance, when we replace in expression (7.25) the geometric averages by arithmetic averages, we obtain

$$\left(\frac{P^j}{P^i}\right)_{WFBS} \equiv \frac{\sum_{k=1}^{I} g_k P^F(p^j, x^j, p^k, x^k)}{\sum_{k=1}^{I} g_k P^F(p^i, x^i, p^k, x^k)} \quad (i, j = 1, \ldots, I), \quad (7.27)$$

where we used the definition of normalized country weights f_k to return to unnormalized weights g_k. This system of multilateral price indices can be said to go back to Fisher (1922). When all the weights are set equal, expression (7.27) reduces to his so-called blended system. Therefore the subscript WFBS (weighted Fisher blended system) will be used.

When we replace in expression (7.26) the geometric averages by harmonic averages, we obtain in the same way

$$
\left(\frac{Q^j}{Q^i}\right)_{WDOS} \equiv \frac{\left(\sum_{k=1}^{I} g_k[Q^F(p^j, x^j, p^k, x^k)]^{-1}\right)^{-1}}{\left(\sum_{k=1}^{I} g_k[Q^F(p^i, x^i, p^k, x^k)]^{-1}\right)^{-1}}
$$

$$
= \frac{\sum_{k=1}^{I} g_k Q^F(p^k, x^k, p^i, x^i)}{\sum_{k=1}^{I} g_k Q^F(p^k, x^k, p^j, x^j)} \quad (i, j = 1, \ldots, I), \quad (7.28)
$$

where the last line was obtained by using the country reversal property of the Fisher quantity indices. Expression (7.28) defines multilateral quantity indices as a generalization of Diewert's (1986) Own Share system (WDOS). Setting all the weights equal, expression (7.28) reduces to the original DOS system.

The two other possible systems have, as far as known, not been discussed in the literature.

Still other methods are those called YKS and Q-YKS (Kurabayashi and Sakuma 1982, 1990). Both are related to the Van IJzeren method, which was defined by expression (7.18) or (7.20). The YKS method was defined by a modification of the first expression, namely by

$$
\sum_{i=1}^{I} g_i P^L(p^j, x^j, p^i, x^i) = \sum_{i=1}^{I} g_i P^L(p^i, x^i, p^j, x^j)(P^j/P^i)^2 (j = 1, \ldots, I),
$$

$$(7.29)$$

whereas the Q-YKS method was defined by a similar modification of the second expression, namely by

$$
\sum_{i=1}^{I} g_i Q^L(p^j, x^j, p^i, x^i) = \sum_{i=1}^{I} g_i Q^L(p^i, x^i, p^j, x^j)(Q^j/Q^i)^2 (j = 1, \ldots, I).
$$

$$(7.30)$$

The existence and uniqueness of a positive solution to these two systems of equations was proved by Balk (1996a).

All the methods discussed in this section effectively provide a mapping from a vector of initial country weights ($f_1, \ldots, f_I$) to a vector of volume shares ($Q^1, \ldots, Q^I$). This is a continuous mapping from the I-dimensional unit simplex into itself. According to Brouwer's Fixed Point Theorem (see Green and Heller 1981) this mapping has a fixed point. Thus in all the formulas one can replace f_k (or g_k) by Q^k ($k = 1, \ldots, I$). The solution vector must of course then be obtained by a suitable numerical iteration method.

7.4 Additive Methods

We now turn our attention to additive methods. A multilateral comparison method is called *additive* when

$$Q^i \propto \pi \cdot x^i \ (i = 1, \ldots, I), \tag{7.31}$$

where $\pi \equiv (\pi_1, \ldots, \pi_N)$ is some price vector. Expression (7.31) says that the volume share of country i is proportional to the aggregate value of this country's quantities at prices π. Since $\sum_{i=1}^{I} Q^i = 1$, this implies that

$$Q^i = \frac{\pi \cdot x^i}{\sum_{i=1}^{I} \pi \cdot x^i} \ (i = 1, \ldots, I). \tag{7.32}$$

Using the product relation (7.1), this in turn implies that

$$P^i \propto \frac{p^i \cdot x^i}{\pi \cdot x^i} \ (i = 1, \ldots, I). \tag{7.33}$$

Thus each purchasing power parity P^i is proportional to a Paasche price index, comparing country i's price vector p^i to the price vector π. When the proportionality factor in the last expression equals 1, the method is called *strongly additive*.

Notice that the quantity index, comparing country j to country i, becomes

$$\frac{Q^j}{Q^i} = \frac{\pi \cdot x^j}{\pi \cdot x^i} \ (i, j = 1, \ldots, I), \tag{7.34}$$

which is a Lowe index. The purchasing power parity of country j relative to country i becomes

$$\frac{P^j}{P^i} = \frac{p^j \cdot x^j}{p^i \cdot x^i} \left[\frac{\pi \cdot x^j}{\pi \cdot x^i} \right]^{-1} \ (i, j = 1, \ldots, I), \tag{7.35}$$

which is the value ratio divided by a Lowe quantity index.

The virtue of an additive method is its simple interpretation, as evidenced by the foregoing expressions. The use of a common price vector enables us to compare the quantity structures of an aggregate across countries in a very straightforward way. The intertemporal analogue is to express the value of an aggregate through time in "constant prices."

The basic problem, of course, is how to pick the price vector π. The symmetric treatment of countries suggests that π must be some average of the country-specific price vectors p^i. Accordingly, π is called a vector of "international prices."

7.4.1 The Geary-Khamis Method

By far the best known member of the class of strongly additive methods was proposed by Geary (1958) and popularized by Khamis (1972). This method consists of the set of definitions

$$\pi_n = \frac{\sum_{i=1}^{I} p_n^i x_n^i / P^i}{\sum_{i=1}^{I} x_n^i} \ (n = 1, \ldots, N)$$

$$P^i = \frac{p^i \cdot x^i}{\pi \cdot x^i} \ (i = 1, \ldots, I), \tag{7.36}$$

which actually is a system of equations that must be solved. Each international price π_n can be regarded as the unit value of commodity n, after having converted the country-specific values $p_n^i x_n^i$ to a common currency. This, however, is old-fashioned language that loses its significance when there are no currency differences between the countries involved in the comparison exercise. It is better to say that each country-specific price p_n^i is deflated by the purchasing power parity P^i, and that a weighted average of the deflated prices p_n^i / P^i is taken, the weights being quantity shares $x_n^i / \sum_{j=1}^{I} x_n^j$. Put otherwise, π is not a vector of average prices, but a vector expressing some average price structure.

Using expression (7.2) we obtain the equivalent system of equations

$$\pi_n = \alpha \frac{\sum_{i=1}^{I} w_n^i Q^i}{\sum_{i=1}^{I} x_n^i} \ (n = 1, \ldots, N)$$

$$\alpha Q^i = \pi \cdot x^i \ (i = 1, \ldots, I), \tag{7.37}$$

where $w_n^i \equiv p_n^i x_n^i / p^i \cdot x^i$ is the value share of commodity n in country i ($n = 1, \ldots, N; i = 1, \ldots, I$), and α is a certain scalar (normalizing) factor. Substituting the first equation of (7.37) into the second, the system of equations can be reduced to

$$\sum_{i=1}^{I} \left(\sum_{n=1}^{N} \left(w_n^i x_n^j / \sum_{i=1}^{I} x_n^i \right) \right) Q^i = Q^j \ (j = 1, \ldots, I). \tag{7.38}$$

Let M be the $I \times I$ matrix with elements $m^{ij} \equiv \sum_{n=1}^{N} (w_n^i x_n^j / \sum_{i=1}^{I} x_n^i)$ and let E be the $I \times I$ unit matrix. Then (7.38) can be written in matrix notation as

$$(Q^1, \ldots, Q^I)(M - E) = (0, \ldots, 0). \tag{7.39}$$

The matrix $M - E$ is singular because $\sum_{j=1}^{I} m^{ij} = 1$ $(i = 1, \ldots, I)$. Following Collier (1999), the constraint $\sum_{i=1}^{I} Q^i = 1$ can be expressed as

$$(Q^1, \ldots, Q^I)R = (1, 0, \ldots, 0), \qquad (7.40)$$

where R is an $I \times I$ matrix the first column of which consists of 1's and the remaining elements are 0. Adding the equations (7.39) and (7.40), we obtain

$$(Q^1, \ldots, Q^I)(M - E + R) = (1, 0, \ldots, 0). \qquad (7.41)$$

The Geary-Khamis (GK) volume shares are thus given by

$$(Q_{GK}^1, \ldots, Q_{GK}^I) = (1, 0, \ldots, 0)(M - E + R)^{-1}; \qquad (7.42)$$

the price indices can be obtained via relation (7.1), and the solution vector π can be obtained via the first equation of (7.37).

The particular definition of the international prices is the point of much criticism directed at the GK method. By virtue of its definition the vector π tends to resemble the price structure of the largest country involved in the comparison exercise,[14] say ℓ. But then, as one verifies easily,

$$\frac{Q_{GK}^i}{Q_{GK}^\ell} = \frac{\pi \cdot x^i}{\pi \cdot x^\ell} \approx \frac{p^\ell \cdot x^i}{p^\ell \cdot x^\ell}, \qquad (7.43)$$

which is the Laspeyres quantity index of country i relative to country ℓ. Depending on the market orientation of the aggregate (producer or consumer), this index is generally felt to be an under- or overestimate of the "true" quantity index. This alleged bias is called the Gerschenkron effect, after its discovery by Gerschenkron (1951). In intertemporal comparisons it finds its parallel in the so-called substitution bias.

Remaining within the framework of additive methods, the obvious remedy is to look for alternative definitions of the international prices. One can generalize the GK definition in the first equation of (7.36) to

$$\pi_n = \sum_{i=1}^{I} \alpha_n^i p_n^i / P^i \ (n = 1, \ldots, N) \qquad (7.44)$$

where the weights α_n^i are positive and $\sum_{i=1}^{I} \alpha_n^i = 1$ $(n = 1, \ldots, N)$. The explicit solution for the volume shares is given by the right-hand side

---

[14] Khamis (1998) denies this: "No country is large enough [with respect to all commodities] to produce such an effect."

of expression (7.42) where M is now the matrix with elements $m^{ij} \equiv \sum_{n=1}^{N}(\alpha_n^i p_n^i x_n^j/(p^i \cdot x^i))$ $(i, j = 1, \ldots, I)$.

Cuthbert (1999) proved that if each α_n^i is a function of all the quantities x_n^i $(n = 1, \ldots, N; i = 1, \ldots, I)$, then α_n^i must necessarily be of the form

$$\alpha_n^i = \beta^i x_n^i / \sum_{i=1}^{I} \beta^i x_n^i \qquad (7.45)$$

where $\beta^i > 0$ $(i = 1, \ldots, I)$. He called the method defined by

$$\pi_n = \frac{\sum_{i=1}^{I} \beta^i p_n^i x_n^i / P^i}{\sum_{i=1}^{I} \beta^i x_n^i} \quad (n = 1, \ldots, N)$$

$$P^i = \frac{p^i \cdot x^i}{\pi \cdot x^i} \quad (i = 1, \ldots, I), \qquad (7.46)$$

the Generalized Geary-Khamis (GGK) method. Indeed, by taking all β^i's to be the same, the GGK method reduces to the GK method.

When $\beta^i = 1/Q^i$ $(i = 1, \ldots, I)$ the GGK method reduces to the Iklé (1972) method.[15] Since the matrix M now becomes a function of all the Q^i's, the existence proof must be expanded by a fixed point argument; see Balk (1996a). The solution, however, is not expressible in an explicit form.

Another method is obtained by specifying the weights α_n^i as

$$\alpha_n^i = w_n^i / \sum_{i=1}^{I} w_n^i. \qquad (7.47)$$

Hill (2000) called this method the "equally weighted GK method" (EWGK). In order to ease the comparison with the GK method (7.36), the complete system of equations defining the EWGK method is stated here:

$$\pi_n = \frac{\sum_{i=1}^{I} w_n^i p_n^i / P^i}{\sum_{i=1}^{I} w_n^i} \quad (n = 1, \ldots, N)$$

$$P^i = \frac{p^i \cdot x^i}{\pi \cdot x^i} \quad (i = 1, \ldots, I). \qquad (7.48)$$

---

[15] Cuthbert (2000) considers $\beta^i = 1/(Q^i)^\alpha$ where $0 \le \alpha \le 1$. The case $\alpha = 0$ corresponds to the GK method while the case $\alpha = 1$ corresponds to the Iklé method. Using price and expenditure data for 199 commodities and 24 countries coming from the 1993 OECD survey, price index numbers and volumes were calculated for various values of α.

As one sees, the difference with the GK method is that quantities x_n^i are replaced by value shares w_n^i.[16] Hill (2000) compared the two methods and found that the EWGK method tends to be less systematically affected by the Gerschenkron effect than the GK method.[17]

7.4.2 Other Additive Methods

Differing from the GK method by its definition of international prices is the KS-S method, proposed by Kurabayashi and Sakuma (1981, 1990). It can be considered as a variant of the GK system (7.37), namely

$$\gamma \pi_n = \sum_{i=1}^{I} (p_n^i / p^i \cdot \iota) Q^i \ (n = 1, \ldots, N)$$

$$\alpha Q^i = \pi \cdot x^i \ (i = 1, \ldots, I), \tag{7.49}$$

where $\iota \equiv (1, \ldots, 1)$ and α and γ are certain positive scalars. The first equation states that each international price π_n is proportional to a weighted mean of country-specific relative prices $p_n^i / \sum_{n=1}^{N} p_n^i$. After substituting the first equation into the second, one obtains

$$\sum_{i=1}^{I} (p^i \cdot x^j / p^i \cdot \iota) Q^i = \alpha \gamma Q^j \ (j = 1, \ldots, I). \tag{7.50}$$

The explicit solution for the volume shares is given by the right-hand side of expression (7.42) where M is now the matrix with elements $m^{ij} \equiv p^i \cdot x^j / p^i \cdot \iota$ $(i, j = 1, \ldots, I)$ and the unit matrix E is replaced by $\alpha \gamma E$.

Recently, however, Sakuma, Rao, and Kurabayashi (2000) developed an interesting variant of this method. The defining system of equations of the new method (called "SRK") is

$$\pi_n = \alpha \sum_{i=1}^{I} (p_n^i / p^i \cdot \sum_{j=1}^{I} x^j) Q^i \ (n = 1, \ldots, N)$$

$$\alpha Q^i = \pi \cdot x^i \ (i = 1, \ldots, I), \tag{7.51}$$

---

[16] Rao (2000) called this method the "size-neutral GK method." He contends that there is no nontrivial solution to the system of equations (7.48). The constraint on the volume shares, however, guarantees a solution.

[17] He used price and expenditure data for 139 commodities and 64 countries coming from the 1985 ICP survey.

or, using price indices rather than volume shares,

$$\pi_n = \sum_{i=1}^{I} (p_n^i/P^i)(p^i \cdot x^i/p^i \cdot \sum_{j=1}^{I} x^j) \, (n = 1, \ldots, N)$$

$$P^i = \frac{p^i \cdot x^i}{\pi \cdot x^i} \, (i = 1, \ldots, I). \tag{7.52}$$

It is interesting to compare this system also to the GK system (7.36). In the GK system the country-specific deflated prices p_n^i/P^i are weighted with commodity-specific quantity shares $x_n^i/\sum_{j=1}^{I} x_n^j$. Using prices p_n^i, these quantity shares can be expressed as value shares $p_n^i x_n^i/p_n^i \sum_{j=1}^{I} x_n^j$. In the SRK system the country-specific deflated prices are weighted with *aggregate* value shares $p^i \cdot x^i/p^i \cdot \sum_{j=1}^{I} x^j$. These weights are the same for every commodity. Each of these weights can be interpreted as the volume share of country i based on its own price vector, or as the Paasche quantity index for country i relative to the aggregate of all countries.

Although empirical evidence is as yet lacking, it could very well be that, since these weights are the same for every commodity, the SRK system is more prone to the Gerschenkron effect than is the GK system.

Again, the explicit solution for the SRK volume shares is given by the right-hand side of expression (7.42), where M is now defined as the matrix with elements $m^{ij} \equiv p^i \cdot x^j/p^i \cdot \sum_{j=1}^{I} x^j$ $(i, j = 1, \ldots, I)$. Notice that $\sum_{j=1}^{I} m^{ij} = 1$ $(i = 1, \ldots, I)$.

It is easily seen that the first equation of (7.52) is an instance of the more general definition

$$\pi_n = \sum_{i=1}^{I} g_i(p_n^i/P^i) \, (n = 1, \ldots, N) \tag{7.53}$$

where g_i $(i = 1, \ldots, I)$ are positive country weights. Expressions (7.31) and (7.53) together define Van IJzeren's second method, alluded to in section 7.3.2. Now, choosing the country weights as being equal to

$$g_i = P^i/p^i \cdot \sum_{j=1}^{I} x^j \, (i = 1, \ldots, I) \tag{7.54}$$

leads us to the (Standardised Structure) method as proposed by Sergeev (2008).[18] It is straightforward to infer that this method leads to volume shares of the form

$$Q_S^i = \frac{\sum_{k=1}^{I} p^k \cdot x^i / p^k \cdot \bar{x}}{\sum_{i=1}^{I} \sum_{k=1}^{I} p^k \cdot x^i / p^k \cdot \bar{x}} \quad (i = 1, \ldots, I) \tag{7.55}$$

where $\bar{x} \equiv \sum_{j=1}^{I} x^j$. Since the unknown P^i's in the numerator of (7.54) and the denominator of (7.53) cancel, there is no need to solve a system of equations, and the concept of international prices becomes superfluous. The corresponding quantity indices can be expressed as

$$\frac{Q_S^i}{Q_S^j} = \frac{\sum_{k=1}^{I} p^k \cdot x^i / p^k \cdot \bar{x}}{\sum_{k=1}^{I} p^k \cdot x^j / p^k \cdot \bar{x}} = \frac{(1/I) \sum_{k=1}^{I} Q^{Lo}(x^i, \bar{x}; p^k)}{(1/I) \sum_{k=1}^{I} Q^{Lo}(x^j, \bar{x}; p^k)} (i, j = 1, \ldots, I). \tag{7.56}$$

The right-hand side of this expression is a ratio of average Lowe quantity index numbers, relating countries i and j, respectively, to the aggregate of all countries, using prices of a third country k.

Until now the international prices were defined as some (weighted) arithmetic average of country-specific deflated prices p_n^i / P^i. Gerardi (1974), however, proposed to define the international prices as unweighted geometric averages

$$\pi_n = \left(\prod_{i=1}^{I} p_n^i / P^i \right)^{1/I} \quad (n = 1, \ldots, N). \tag{7.57}$$

By substituting this into expression (7.31), the quantity index for country j relative to country i becomes

$$\frac{Q^j}{Q^i} = \frac{\sum_{n=1}^{N} (\prod_{k=1}^{I} p_n^k / P^k)^{1/I} x_n^j}{\sum_{n=1}^{N} (\prod_{k=1}^{I} p_n^k / P^k)^{1/I} x_n^i} = \frac{\sum_{n=1}^{N} (\prod_{k=1}^{I} p_n^k)^{1/I} x_n^j}{\sum_{n=1}^{N} (\prod_{k=1}^{I} p_n^k)^{1/I} x_n^i} (i, j = 1, \ldots, I), \tag{7.58}$$

which is a multilateral generalization of the Walsh-1 quantity index. Moreover it is clear that in the definition of the international prices, expression (7.57), the purchasing power parities P^i can be left out.

Let us return to the EWGK method, which was defined by the combination of the expressions (7.31), (7.44), and (7.47). After replacing the

[18] According to the interpretation of Cuthbert in a letter to Sergeev dated 4 October 2000.

arithmetic averages by harmonic averages, that is, replacing (7.44) by

$$\pi_n = \left(\sum_{i=1}^{I} \alpha_n^i (p_n^i / P^i)^{-1} \right)^{-1} \quad (n = 1, \ldots, N), \quad (7.59)$$

we meet again the Iklé (1972) method, as any reader can easily check. A geometric variant of this method was developed by Rao (1990). The defining system of equations is now

$$\pi_n = \prod_{i=1}^{I} (p_n^i / P^i)^{w_n^i / \sum_{i=1}^{I} w_n^i} \quad (n = 1, \ldots, N)$$

$$P^i = \prod_{n=1}^{N} (p_n^i / \pi_n)^{w_n^i} \quad (i = 1, \ldots, I), \quad (7.60)$$

or, using logarithms,

$$\ln \pi_n = \sum_{i=1}^{I} w_n^i \ln(p_n^i / P^i) / \sum_{i=1}^{I} w_n^i \quad (n = 1, \ldots, N)$$

$$\ln P^i = \sum_{n=1}^{N} w_n^i \ln(p_n^i / \pi_n) \quad (i = 1, \ldots, I). \quad (7.61)$$

One can show that this system has a unique (up to a scalar factor), positive solution $P^1, \ldots, P^I$ (see Balk 1996a). We will return to this method in section 7.7.

7.5 A System of Tests

How do we discriminate between all the methods discussed in the last two sections? The classical approach – the landmark in the area of intertemporal comparisons being Fisher (1922) – is to set up a system of tests or desirable properties and find out which method fails which tests. This is the approach followed by Kravis, Kenessey, Heston, and Summers (1975) in their pathbreaking work on international comparisons. The properties they thought most important were (formulated in our jargon) that price and quantity indices be transitive, that these indices satisfy the product test, that all countries be treated symmetrically, and that the method of comparison exhibit additivity.

Now the first two properties are maintained by us from the outset (see section 7.2). Furthermore, a quick perusal of the methods discussed in sections 7.3 and 7.4 leads to the conclusion that in all these methods the countries are indeed treated symmetrically. The fourth property, however, is too vague since there are a number of additive methods, as we have seen in section 7.4.

Diewert (1986, 1987a) more rigidly formulated a set of tests for multilateral comparisons. Balk (1989a) generalized these tests by incorporating country weights. The tests emphasize the fact that the primary purpose of any international comparison is to make volume comparisons. Price indices play only an intermediary role. Consequently, the tests are framed in terms of volume shares, which are here understood to be functions of all the prices, all the quantities, and all the country weights (if any). Thus, formally, $Q^i = Q^i(p^1, \ldots, p^I, x^1, \ldots, x^I, g_1, \ldots, g_I)$ for $i = 1, \ldots, I$.[19]

The tests will now be presented; some explanation follows.

MT1. Positivity and continuity test. The functions Q^i are continuous in all arguments, $Q^i > 0$ ($i = 1, \ldots, I$), and $\sum_{i=1}^{I} Q^i = 1$.

MT2. Weak proportionality test or identity test. If there exists a price vector p and a quantity vector x such that $p^j = \alpha^j p$ and $x^j = \beta^j x$ where $\alpha^j, \beta^j > 0$ ($j = 1, \ldots, I$) and $\sum_{j=1}^{I} \beta^j = 1$, then $Q^i = \beta^i$ ($i = 1, \ldots, I$).

MT3. Proportionality test. Let $\lambda > 0$ and replace for country k the quantity vector x^k by λx^k and the scalar weight g_k by λg_k. Then the relation between the new volume shares $\tilde{Q}^i$ and the old volume shares Q^i is

$$\tilde{Q}^i = \frac{\lambda Q^k}{1 + (\lambda - 1)Q^k} \text{ for } i = k$$

$$= \frac{Q^i}{1 + (\lambda - 1)Q^k} \text{ for } i \neq k.$$

MT4. Monetary unit test or invariance to changes in scale test. Replace p^j by $\alpha^j p^j$ and x^j by βx^j where $\alpha^j, \beta > 0$ ($j = 1, \ldots, I$). Then the new volume shares are identically equal to the old volume shares.

---

[19] Armstrong (2003) pursued a slightly different approach. Instead of quantity vectors x^i he considered vectors of per-household quantities $\bar{x}^i$ and scalar numbers of households h^i ($i = 1, \ldots, I$). Price indices P^j/P^i defined as functions of ($p^j, p^i, \bar{x}^1, \ldots, \bar{x}^I$, $h^1, \ldots, h^I$) were called restricted-domain indices, whereas price indices defined as functions of ($p^1, \ldots, p^I, \bar{x}^1, \ldots, \bar{x}^I, h^1, \ldots, h^I$) were called unrestricted-domain indices. Armstrong devised a set of tests for restricted-domain indices and modified and extended Diewert's (1986) set of tests to apply to unrestricted-domain indices. For a particular class of restricted-domain indices, namely those that are transitive, the two systems of tests turned out to be equivalent.

MT5. Invariance to changes in units of measurement test. The volume shares are invariant to changes in the units of measurement of the commodities.

MT6. Symmetric treatment of countries test. The volume shares are invariant to a permutation of the countries.

MT7. Symmetric treatment of commodities test. The volume shares are invariant to a permutation of the commodities.

MT8. Country partitioning test. Let country k be partitioned into two provinces, denoted by k and $I + 1$, respectively, with the same price vector p^k but quantity vectors λx^k and $(1 - \lambda)x^k$ respectively, and let the scalar country weights be λg_k and $(1 - \lambda)g_k$, respectively ($0 < \lambda < 1$). Then the relation between the new volume shares $\tilde{Q}^i$ and the old volume shares Q^i is

$$\tilde{Q}^i = Q^i \text{ for } i = 1, \ldots, k - 1, k + 1, \ldots, I$$
$$\tilde{Q}^{I+1} = (1 - \lambda)Q^k$$
$$\tilde{Q}^k = \lambda Q^k.$$

MT9. Irrelevance of tiny countries test. Let $\lambda > 0$ and replace for country k the quantity vector x^k by λx^k and the scalar weight g_k by λg_k. Denote the resulting volume shares by $Q^i(\lambda)$ ($i = 1, \ldots, I$). Delete country k and denote the resulting volume shares by $\tilde{Q}^i$ ($i = 1, \ldots, k - 1, k + 1, \ldots, I$). Then

$$\lim_{\lambda \to 0} Q^i(\lambda) = \tilde{Q}^i \ (i = 1, \ldots, k - 1, k + 1, \ldots, I).$$

Here are some explanatory remarks. **MT1** is an obvious test: volume shares must be positive, must add up to 1, and must exhibit continuous behaviour in all the variables. **MT2** suggests that if all the price vectors are proportional to each other and all the quantity vectors are also proportional to each other, then the volume shares are equal to the factors of proportionality of the quantity vectors. A specific case is obtained when all the price vectors are proportional, and all the quantity vectors are equal, that is, $x^1 = \cdots = x^I$. Then all the volume shares must be equal, that is $Q^i = 1/I$ ($i = 1, \ldots, I$). **MT3** suggests that if the prices remain unchanged but country k expands with a certain factor, then the volume shares behave accordingly. **MT4** suggests that differing inflation rates but equal quantity growth rates leave the volume shares invariant. **MT5–MT7** formulate obvious invariance requirements. **MT8** considers the situation where one wants to disaggregate one or more countries and requires then appropriate behaviour of the volume shares. **MT9** stipulates that "small" countries do not influence the volume shares of "large" countries unduly.

Diewert (1999) modified his original system of tests. In particular test **MT2** was split into two separate tests[20]:

MT2x. Proportionality w.r.t. quantities test. If there exists a quantity vector x such that $x^j = \beta^j x$ where $\beta^j > 0$ ($j = 1, \ldots, I$) and $\sum_{j=1}^{I} \beta^j = 1$, then $Q^i = \beta^i$ ($i = 1, \ldots, I$).

MT2p. Proportionality w.r.t. prices test. If there exists a price vector p such that $p^j = \alpha^j p$ where $\alpha^j > 0$ ($j = 1, \ldots, I$), then $Q^i = p \cdot x^i / \sum_{j=1}^{I} p \cdot x^j$ ($i = 1, \ldots, I$).

It is straightforward to check that if **MT2x** or **MT2p** is satisfied, then **MT2** is satisfied. Notice further that all the additive methods, that is, all the methods for which expression (7.31) holds, satisfy **MT2x** (because the volume shares add up to 1).

Balk (1996a) subjected ten methods to the system of tests $\{$**MT1**$, \ldots,$ **MT9**$\}$, namely those of Van IJzeren, YKS, Q-YKS, GEKS, WDOS, GK, Iklé, Gerardi, KS-S, and Rao.[21] It turns out that all these methods, except the Rao method, also satisfy **MT2x** and **MT2p**. The Rao method appears to satisfy **MT2p**, but fails to satisfy **MT2x**.

With respect to the expanded system of tests consisting of **MT1**, **MT2x**, **MT2p**, **MT3–MT9** a number of additional results could be established:

- The Gerardi-Van IJzeren method fails to satisfy only **MT3**.[22]
- The WFBS fails to satisfy only **MT3** and **MT4**.[23]
- The EWGK method fails to satisfy only **MT8** and **MT9**.[24]
- The SRK method fails to satisfy only **MT3**.[25]
- Sergeev's method fails to satisfy **MT3**, **MT8** and **MT9**.[26]

---

[20] The remaining modification of Diewert's original system of tests consists in a generalization of **MT8**, in the sense that country k is partitioned into more than two provinces with price vectors which are proportional instead of identical. Two new tests will be disregarded: the bilateral consistency-in-aggregation test (which is biased towards the bilateral Fisher quantity index) and the additivity test (which would rule out all nonadditive methods).

[21] See Balk (1996a) for (references to) proofs.

[22] The proof is almost a replication of the proof of Balk (1989a) for the Van IJzeren method.

[23] The proof is by straightforward checking.

[24] The proof runs parallel to the proof of Proposition 5 (on the Iklé method) in Balk (1996a).

[25] The proof is a replication, with obvious modifications, of the proof of Proposition 7 (on the KS-S method) in Balk (1996a).

[26] The proof is by straightforward checking.

Table 7.1. *Test Performance of the Various Methods*

Method	Definition	Tests Violated
GEKS	(7.14), (7.16)	MT3, MT8
Van IJzeren	(7.18), (7.20)	MT3
Gerardi-Van IJzeren	(7.22), (7.24)	MT3
WFBS	(7.27)	MT3, MT4
WDOS	(7.28)	MT3, MT8
YKS	(7.29)	MT3, MT4
Q-YKS	(7.30)	MT8, MT9
GK	(7.36), (7.37)	MT3
EWGK	(7.48)	MT8, MT9
KS-S	(7.49)	MT3, MT5
SRK	(7.51), (7.52)	MT3
Sergeev	(7.55)	MT3, MT8, MT9
Gerardi	(7.31)+(7.57)	MT8, MT9
Iklé	(7.31)+(7.47)+(7.59)	MT8, MT9
Rao	(7.60)	MT2x, MT8, MT9

All the results, in the order of discussion of the methods, are summarized in Table 7.1. It appears that there is no method that satisfies all the tests. The methods of Van IJzeren, Gerardi-Van IJzeren, GK, and SRK turn out to violate only the proportionality test **MT3**. Of these methods, the last two are additive.

A novel, quite natural test proposed by Diewert (1999) is:

MT10. Monotonicity test. The functions Q^i are increasing in the components of x^i $(i = 1, \ldots, I)$.

Diewert (1999) was able to show that the Van IJzeren method satisfies this test.[27] By analogy, the Gerardi–Van IJzeren method also satisfies this test. Diewert also showed that, when $I = 2$, the GK method does not satisfy the monotonicity test. However, it remains to be seen what happens when $I \geq 3$. Finally, whether the SRK method satisfies this test is still an open question. Thus the evidence here is, for the time being, inconclusive.[28]

---

[27] He actually proved it for the unweighted case, that is, where $g^i = 1/I$ $(i = 1, \ldots, I)$, but there is no reason to suppose that this proof does not hold in the general case.

[28] Sergeev (2008) provides a numerical comparison of the GEKS, Gerardi, GK, Iklé, Rao, EWGK, and Sergeev methods on Eurostat 2002 data concerning 31 countries and 282 commodities. The results are rather close.

7.6 Methods Based on Chaining

The second, important approach to constructing transitive price and quantity indices is based on the procedure of chaining. The procedure as such is familiar in the realm of intertemporal comparisons. However, as noticed in section 7.1, unlike time periods, countries do not exhibit a natural ordering. Given I countries, there appear to be $I(I-1)/2$ bilateral index numbers (provided that the country reversal test holds) and I^{I-2} possible ways to link the countries together without creating any cycles. Put otherwise, there exist I^{I-2} spanning trees. How could we choose the "optimal" spanning tree?

The natural approach is to use some measure of proximity and order the countries according to this measure. In the time series context this measure is simply given by the length of the time span separating any two periods. Because of the unidirectional flow of time, this leads to a unique ordering, independent of the data. In the spatial context the ideal of data-independency of the ordering must be given up.

Hill (1999a, 1999b) developed two methods that allow the data to determine the "optimal" spanning tree. Multilateral indices are then obtained by linking together bilateral indices as specified by the spanning tree. To give an example, suppose that we are to compare country j to country i. If, according to the spanning tree, the countries appear to be adjacent, then the price index of j relative to i is defined as $P(p^j, x^j, p^i, x^i)$ for some bilateral index satisfying the country reversal test. But if the countries j and i are connected via, say, countries k and l, respectively, then the price index of j relative to i is defined as the chained index $P(p^j, x^j, p^k, x^k)P(p^k, x^k, p^l, x^l)P(p^l, x^l, p^i, x^i)$.

The device used in the two methods for obtaining an "optimal" spanning tree is the so-called Paasche-Laspeyres spread,[29] defined as

$$PLS_{ji} \equiv |\ln P^L(p^j, x^j, p^i, x^i) - \ln P^P(p^j, x^j, p^i, x^i)|$$
$$= |\ln Q^L(p^j, x^j, p^i, x^i) - \ln Q^P(p^j, x^j, p^i, x^i)| \ (i, j = 1, \dots, I).$$
$$(7.62)$$

Its properties are easily checked: $PLS_{ji} \geq 0$, $PLS_{jj} = 0$, and $PLS_{ji} = PLS_{ij}$ $(i, j = 1, \dots, I)$.

The first method is called the shortest path method. It starts with selecting a base country. Then it finds the path between this country and any other country exhibiting the smallest sum of PLS_{ji} values. The union of all

---

[29] Alternative (dis-)similarity measures are considered by Diewert (2008).

these $I - 1$ (bilateral) shortest paths is the spanning tree sought, called the shortest path spanning tree. It is clear that, since every country can be selected to act as base country, there are I shortest path spanning trees available, given the data. So there is no unique solution here.

The second method selects from all possible spanning trees the one with the smallest sum of $I - 1$ PLS_{ji} values, the so-called minimum-spanning tree. Given the data, this provides a unique, truly multilateral solution.[30]

A practical motive for finding and using "optimal" spanning trees is the prospect of economizing on data. Notice that a multilateral method such as GEKS requires knowledge of all the $I(I - 1)/2$ bilateral index numbers. Suppose now that, based on a full data set for a certain period, we have obtained an "optimal" spanning tree. Under the assumption that this structure remains stable over a certain time span, for later periods it is sufficient to compute only the $I - 1$ bilateral index numbers which are required by the spanning tree. This could save on the amount of data as well as lead to an appreciable gain in accuracy of the bilateral comparisons, since the data can be chosen such as to make the bilateral comparisons as accurate as possible without the need of imposing excessive data requirements on "far off" countries.

Examples and robustness results can be found in Hill (1999a, 1999b, 2008). The first publication uses price and expenditure data coming from the ICP 1980 and 1985 surveys, for 30 countries and 151 and 139 commodities, respectively. The second publication uses data coming from the OECD 1990 survey, for 24 countries and 198 commodities. The third publication uses, in addition, data coming from the OECD 1993 and 1996 surveys, for 34 countries and 147 and 162 commodities, respectively.

It appears that although the minimum-spanning trees are not stable over time, they generate similar clusters of countries. It also appears that the multilateral index numbers are less sensitive to the choice of the underlying spanning tree than one might suspect. Similar conclusions were reached by Heston, Summers, and Aten (2001).

7.7 The Stochastic-Model-Based Approach

The approach considered in this section assumes that all the individual prices are generated according to the following (superpopulation) model:

$$\ln p_n^i = \ln P^i + \ln \pi_n + \varepsilon_n^i \ (i = 1, \ldots, I; n = 1, \ldots, N), \quad (7.63)$$

---

[30] In the time series context, using three different sets of annual data, Hill (2001) found that the minimum-spanning tree always closely resembled the chronological order.

where ε_n^i is a residual with expectation 0. The interpretation of this model is rather straightforward: each country-specific price vector p^i is, apart from residual noise, proportional to the international prices vector π, the factor of proportionality being the purchasing power parity P^i. Of course, this model identifies only price indices P^i/P^j; thus a normalization of the purchasing power parities P^i ($i = 1, \ldots, N$) is necessary for estimation. This model was proposed originally by Summers (1973), although in the context of dealing with missing price observations. In the intertemporal context Balk (1980b) used a similar model for dealing with seasonal commodities.[31]

A rather natural way of estimating the price indices P^i/P^j ($i, j = 1, \ldots, N$) and the international prices π_n ($n = 1, \ldots, N$) is by minimizing a sum of weighted squares of residuals,

$$\min_{P^1,\ldots,P^I,\pi_1,\ldots,\pi_N} \sum_{i=1}^{I} \sum_{n=1}^{N} w_n^i (\ln p_n^i - \ln P^i - \ln \pi_n)^2, \qquad (7.64)$$

where the weights w_n^i are the individual commodity value shares. Hence, more important commodities get a larger weight in the sum of squares.[32]

It is straightforward to check that the first-order necessary conditions for a minimum are precisely equal to the equations defining the Rao method (7.60).[33] Thus at first sight it seems that there is nothing new here, apart from being useful in the case of gaps in the data.

The advantage of this approach is, however, that model (7.63) as well as the weights used in (7.64) suggest several potentially useful generalizations. One of these is to extend the model with quality characteristics. Thus the commodities involved in the comparison exercise need not be precisely the same across countries. As long as there is sufficient information on their quality characteristics, the commodities themselves might be different.[34]

Another generalization is given by the fact that estimation of the model via (7.64) is efficient only under the assumption that the covariance matrix of the residuals is proportional to the unit matrix. Relaxing this assumption, by introducing for instance spatial autocorrelation, can lead to markedly different results (see Rao 2008).

---

[31] Both proposals were surveyed by Selvanathan and Rao (1994). Summers' model is known as the Country-Product-Dummy (CPD) method.

[32] Diewert (2005b) considered expression (7.63) for $I = 2$ and alternatives to expression (7.64) and showed that solutions for P^2/P^1 reduced to bilateral indices.

[33] See Rao (2005) for details.

[34] If there is sufficient information on the quality characteristics, then the country-specific samples of commodities for which prices are available need not be matched either. See Silver and Heravi (2005) for an exploratory study.

It is interesting to make another connection between the model (7.63) and the index approach of the previous sections. Subtracting the equation for p_n^j from the equation for p_n^i leads to

$$\ln(p_n^i/p_n^j) = \ln(P^i/P^j) + (\varepsilon_n^i - \varepsilon_n^j)\ (i,\ j = 1, \ldots, I; n = 1, \ldots, N).$$

$$(7.65)$$

Weighting each logarithmic price relative by its average value share $(w_n^i + w_n^j)/2$ and summing across commodities, one obtains

$$\frac{1}{2}\sum_{n=1}^{N}(w_n^i + w_n^j)\ln(p_n^i/p_n^j) = \ln(P^i/P^j)$$

$$+ \frac{1}{2}\sum_{n=1}^{N}(w_n^i + w_n^j)(\varepsilon_n^i - \varepsilon_n^j)\ (i,\ j = 1, \ldots, I). \qquad (7.66)$$

This can be simplified to

$$\ln P^T(p^i, x^i, p^j, x^j) = \ln(P^i/P^j) + \varepsilon^{ij}\ (i,\ j = 1, \ldots, I), \quad (7.67)$$

where $P^T(p^i, x^i, p^j, x^j)$ is the Törnqvist price index of country i relative to country j. Estimating the price indices P^i/P^j via minimization of the sum of squared residuals

$$\min_{P^1, \ldots, P^I} \sum_{i=1}^{I}\sum_{j=1}^{I}(\ln P^T(p^i, x^i, p^j, x^j) - \ln(P^i/P^j))^2 \qquad (7.68)$$

leads to the multilateral Törnqvist price index proposed by Caves, Christensen, and Diewert (1982)[35]:

$$\left(\frac{P^i}{P^j}\right)_{CCD} \equiv \prod_{k=1}^{I}[P^T(p^i, x^i, p^k, x^k)P^T(p^k, x^k, p^j, x^j)]^{1/I}\ (i, j = 1, \ldots, I).$$

$$(7.69)$$

Again, we have obtained a multilateral price index as estimator of the model parameters under fairly simple assumptions on the residuals. Relaxing these assumptions leads us from the realm of indices to the realm of econometrics. See, for example, Selvanathan and Rao (1992).

An interesting feature of the use of superpopulation models such as the example discussed in this section is that they enable us to adjoin index numbers with estimates of their precision.

---

[35] A different derivation, using weighted least squares on equations (7.65), was given by Selvanathan and Rao (1994).

7.8 Conclusion

This chapter has shown that, although we have learned quite a lot about the properties of the various methods, the lessons are not all pointing in the same direction. Put otherwise, there appears to be no unique, award-winning method. However, some methods have better credentials than others. A brief recapitulation may here be sufficient.[36]

The center stage among the methods discussed in section 7.3 was occupied by the GEKS-Fisher price and quantity indices – expressions (7.14) and (7.16), respectively. From the economic viewpoint this pair of indices can be rationalized by assuming identical homothetic preferences across all the countries. Assuming nonhomothetic country-specific preferences that are not "too" different appears to lead to the GEKS-Törnqvist price indices.[37]

However, from the empirical viewpoint it can be expected that the GEKS-Fisher and the GEKS-Törnqvist indices closely approximate each other. Section 7.5 showed that the GEKS-Fisher volume shares only violate the tests **MT3** and **MT8**. However, as documented in section 7.3, the GEKS-Fisher indices are bracketed by the Van IJzeren and the Gerardi–Van IJzeren indices, both of which do satisfy the test **MT8**. Thus, there is reason to expect that the GEKS-Fisher's failure to satisfy **MT8** is not "too" bad. Moreover, as demonstrated by Van IJzeren (1987) on a numerical example, the weights are not particularly influential, so that it is virtually harmless to set all (normalized) weights equal to $1/I$.

Using a data-driven spanning tree as basis for the construction of a system of chained index numbers seems to be an area for further research. Chained Fisher quantity indices can be defended from the economic angle, provided that one is willing to assume identical homothetic preferences.

An international comparison of the structural features of some economic aggregate is best served by employing an additive method. Economically seen, such a method does not allow substitution behaviour. Judged from Table 7.1, the choice seems to be between the GK and SRK methods. The issue here is to find a method that expectedly suffers least from the Gerschenkron effect. As indicated, there is reason to expect that the GK method is to be preferred to the SRK method. Notice that the EWGK method, although shown to be less affected by the Gerschenkron effect than the GK method, exhibits a less trustworthy test performance.

---

[36] Armstrong (2001) compared a large number of aggregation methods on 1990 data for 24 OECD countries and 158 commodities. This interesting exercise once more made it clear that the choice of method really matters.

[37] See Balk (2001, section 8) for a review of the economic-theoretic results.

Bibliography

Aczél, J., 1966, *Lectures on Functional Equations and their Applications* (Academic Press, New York and London).

Aczél, J., 1987, *A Short Course on Functional Equations* (Reidel, Dordrecht).

Aczél, J., 1990, "Determining Merged Relative Scores," Journal of Mathematical Analysis and Applications 150, 20–40.

Aczél, J., and W. Eichhorn, 1974a, "A Note on Additive Indices," Journal of Economic Theory 8, 525–9.

Aczél, J., and W. Eichhorn, 1974b, "Systems of Functional Equations Determining Price and Productivity Indices," Utilitas Mathematica 5, 213–26.

Adelman, I., 1958, "A New Approach to the Construction of Index Numbers," The Review of Economics and Statistics 40, 240–69.

Afriat, S. N., 1972, "The Theory of International Comparisons of Real Income and Prices," in *International Comparisons of Prices and Output*, edited by D. J. Daly (National Bureau of Economic Research, New York). Reprinted in Afriat (2005, appendix 4).

Afriat, S. N., 1977, *The Price Index* (Cambridge University Press). Reprinted in Afriat (2005, Part I).

Afriat, S. N., 2005, *The Price Index and Its Extension; A Chapter in Economic Measurement* (Routledge, London and New York).

Al, P. G., B. M. Balk, S. de Boer, and G. P. den Bakker, 1986, "The Use of Chain Indices for Deflating the National Accounts," Statistical Journal of the United Nations ECE 4, 347–68.

Aldrich, J., 1992, "Probability and Depreciation: A History of the Stochastic Approach to Index Numbers," History of Political Economy 24, 657–87.

Allan-Greer, B., D. S. P. Rao, and C. O'Donnell, 2004, Constructing Divisia Indexes from Retail Scanner Data using Wavelet Methods (School of Economics, University of Queensland, Brisbane).

Allen, R. L., 1993, *Irving Fisher: A Biography* (Blackwell, Oxford).

Armstrong, K. G., 2001, "What Impact Does the Choice of Formula Have on International Comparisons?" Canadian Journal of Economics 34, 697–718.

Armstrong, K. G., 2003, "A Restricted-Domain Multilateral Test Approach to the Theory of International Comparisons," International Economic Review 44, 31–86.

Auer, L. von, 2002a, "Spurious Inflation: The Legacy of Laspeyres and Others," The Quarterly Review of Economics and Finance 42, 529–42.

Auer, L. von, 2002b, Inconsistency of Multi Stage Price Aggregation Procedures (Otto-von-Guericke-Universität Magdeburg, Germany).

Baldwin, A., 1990, "Seasonal Baskets in Consumer Price Indexes," Journal of Official Statistics 6, 251–73.

Balk, B. M., 1980a, Seasonal Products in Agriculture and Horticulture and Methods for Computing Price Indices, Statistical Studies No. 24 (Netherlands Central Bureau of Statistics, Voorburg; Staatsuitgeverij, The Hague).

Balk, B. M., 1980b, "A Method for Constructing Price Indices for Seasonal Commodities," Journal of the Royal Statistical Society A 143, 68–75.

Balk, B. M., 1980c, "Seasonal Commodities and the Construction of Annual and Monthly Price Indexes," Statistische Hefte/Statistical Papers 21, 110–16.

Balk, B. M., 1983, "A Note on the True Factorial Price Index," Statistische Hefte/Statistical Papers 24, 69–72.

Balk, B. M., 1985, "A Simple Characterization of Fisher's Price Index," Statistische Hefte/Statistical Papers 26, 59–63.

Balk, B. M., 1989a, "On Van IJzeren's Approach to International Comparisons and Its Properties," Statistical Papers/Statistische Hefte 30, 295–315.

Balk, B. M., 1989b, "A Note on the IP Procedure," Joint Meeting of the Working Parties Price Statistics and National Accounts, Eurostat, Luxembourg, 15 November.

Balk, B. M., 1991, "Consumer Price Indices and the Problem of Seasonality," Nordic Workshop on Methodologies of Economic Indices, Helsinki, April 9–11, 1991, Tekniske Rapporter 55 (Nordisk Statistisk Secretariat, Copenhagen).

Balk, B. M., 1994, "On the First Step in the Calculation of a Consumer Price Index," Papers and Final Report of the First Meeting of the International Working Group on Price Indices Statistics Canada, Ottawa.

Balk, B. M., 1995, "Axiomatic Price Index Theory: A Survey," International Statistical Review 63, 69–93.

Balk, B. M., 1996a, "A Comparison of Ten Methods for Multilateral International Price and Volume Comparison," Journal of Official Statistics 12, 199–222.

Balk, B. M., 1996b, "Consistency-in-Aggregation and Stuvel Indices," The Review of Income and Wealth 42, 353–63.

Balk, B. M., 1996c, "Van IJzeren's Method of International Price and Volume Comparison: An Exposition," in *International Comparisons of Prices, Output, and Productivity*, edited by D. S. P. Rao and J. Salazar-Carrillo (North-Holland, Amsterdam).

Balk, B. M., 1998a, "On the Use of Unit Value Indices as Consumer Price Subindices," in Proceedings of the Fourth Meeting of the International Working Group on Price Indices, edited by W. Lane (U. S. Bureau of Labor Statistics, Washington, DC); earlier version in *Improving the Quality of Price Indices*, Proceedings of an International Seminar, Florence, 18–20 December 1995 (Office for Official Publications of the European Communities, Luxembourg, 1996).

Balk, B. M., 1998b, *Industrial Price, Quantity, and Productivity Indices: The Micro–Economic Theory and an Application* (Kluwer Academic Publishers, Boston/Dordrecht/London).

Balk, B. M., 2000, "On Curing the CPIs Substitution and New Goods Bias," Research Paper No. 0005 (Department of Statistical Methods, Statistics Netherlands). Presented at the 5th meeting of the International Working Group on Price Indices, Reykjavik, 25–27 August 1999 (www.ottawagroup.org).

Balk, B. M., 2001, "Aggregation Methods in International Comparisons: What Have We Learned?" Report (Erasmus Research Institute of Management, Erasmus University Rotterdam).

Balk, B. M., 2003, "Ideal Indices and Indicators for Two or More Factors," Journal of Economic and Social Measurement 28, 203–17.

Balk, B. M., 2004, "Decompositions of Fisher Indexes," Economics Letters 82, 107–13.

Balk, B. M., 2005, "Divisia Price and Quantity Indices: 80 Years After," Statistica Neerlandica 59, 119–58.

Balk, B. M., 2008, "Direct and Chained Indices: A Review of Two Paradigms," in *Price and Productivity Measurement*, Volume 6, edited by W. E. Diewert, B. M. Balk, D. Fixler, K. J. Fox, and A. O. Nakamura (Trafford Press, www.trafford.com).

Balk, B. M. and W. E. Diewert, 2001, "A Characterization of the Törnqvist Price Index," Economics Letters 72, 279–81.

Balk, B. M., G. J. van Driel, and C. van Ravenzwaaij, 1978, *Inflatie in Nederland van 1952 tot 1975* (Inflation in The Netherlands from 1952 to 1975), CBS Statistische Onderzoekingen M4 (Staatsuitgeverij, Den Haag).

Bamberg, G., and K. Spremann, 1985, "Least-Squares Index Numbers," in *Contributions to Econometrics and Statistics Today*, edited by H. Schneeweiss and H. Strecker (Springer-Verlag, Berlin).

Banerjee, K. S., 1956, "A Comment on the Construction of Price Index Numbers," Applied Statistics 5, 207–10. Reprinted as Appendix B in Banerjee (1975).

Banerjee, K. S., 1975, *Cost of Living Index Numbers: Practice, Precision, and Theory* (Marcel Dekker, New York).

Banerjee, K. S., 1959, "A Generalization of Stuvel's Index Number Formulae," Econometrica 27, 676–8.

Banerjee, K. S., 1979a, "A Note on the Divisia Indices," Statistische Hefte 20, 172–5.

Banerjee, K. S., 1979b, "An Interpretation of the Factorial Indexes in the Light of Divisia Integral Indexes," Statistische Hefte 20, 261–9.

Banerjee, K. S., 1980, *On the Factorial Approach Providing the True Index of Cost of Living*, 2nd enlarged edition (Vandenhoeck & Ruprecht, Göttingen).

Banerjee, K. S., 1983, "On the Existence of Infinitely Many Ideal Log-Change Index Numbers Associated with the CES Preference Ordering," Statistische Hefte 24, 141–8.

Banerjee, K. S., 1986, "Some Observations on the Törnqvist-Vartia-Vartia Article on the Measurement of Relative Changes," The American Statistician 40, 181.

Banerjee, K. S., 1989, *On the Multidimensional, Multilateral and Multidimensional-Multilateral Index Number Systems, Based on the Factorial Approach* (Statistical Publishing Society, Calcutta).

Banzhaf, H. S., 2001, "Quantifying the Qualitative: Quality-Adjusted Price Indexes in the United States, 1915–1961," in *The Age of Economic Measurement*, edited by J. L. Klein and M. S. Morgan, History of Political Economy 33, Annual Supplement, 345–70.

Banzhaf, H. S., 2004, "The Form and Function of Price Indexes: A Historical Accounting," History of Political Economy 36, 589–616.

Bartholomew, D. J., 1998, *The Statistical Approach to Social Measurement* (Academic Press, San Diego).

Bean, L. H., and O. C. Stine, 1924, "Four Types of Index Numbers of Farm Prices," Journal of the American Statistical Association 19, 30–5.

Beer, M., 2006, "Hedonic Elementary Price Indices; Axiomatic Foundation and Estimation Techniques," Ph.D. Thesis, Faculty of Economics and Social Sciences, University of Fribourg, Switzerland.

Bennet, T. L., 1920, "The Theory of Measurement of Changes in Cost of Living," Journal of the Royal Statistical Society 83, 455–62.

Biggeri, L., G. Ferrari, and A. Lemmi, 1987, "The Contribution of Italian Statisticians to the Theory of Price Index Numbers," in *Italian Contributions to the Methodology of Statistics*, edited by A. Naddeo (Società Italiana di Statistica and Cleup, Padova).

BIS, 1999, "Measures of Underlying Inflation and Their Role in the Conduct of Monetary Policy," Proceedings of a Workshop of Central Bank Model Builders Held at the BIS on 18–19 February 1999, BIS Paper (Bank for International Settlements, Basel, www.bis.org).

Blackorby, C., and D. Primont, 1980, "Index Numbers and Consistency in Aggregation," Journal of Economic Theory 22, 87–98.

Bloem, A. M., R. J. Dippelsman, and N. Ø. Mæhle, 2001, *Quarterly National Accounts Manual; Concepts, Data Sources, and Compilation* (International Monetary Fund, Washington, DC).

Boldsen Hansen, C., 2007, "Recalculations of the Danish CPI 1996–2006." Presented at the 10th Meeting of the Ottawa Group (International Working Group on Price Indices), Ottawa, 9–12 October 2007.

Bortkiewicz, L. von, 1923, 1924, "Zweck und Struktur einer Preisindexzahl," Nordisk Statistisk Tidsskrift 2, 369–408; 3, 208–51; 3, 494–516.

Bos, F., 2006, "The Development of the Dutch National Accounts as a Tool for Analysis and Policy," Statistica Neerlandica 60, 225–58.

Boskin, M. J., E. R. Dulberger, R. J. Gordon, Z. Griliches, and D. Jorgenson, 1996, *Toward a More Accurate Measure of the Cost of Living*, Final Report to the (U. S.) Senate Finance Committee, Washington, DC.

Boumans, M., 2001, "Fisher's Instrumental Approach to Index Numbers," in *The Age of Economic Measurement*, edited by J. L. Klein and M. S. Morgan, History of Political Economy 33, Annual Supplement, 313–44.

Bowley, A. L., 1899, "Wages, Nominal and Real," in *Dictionary of Political Economy*, Volume 3, edited by R. H. I. Palgrave (Macmillan, London).

Bowley, A. L., 1901, *Elements of Statistics* (P. S. King & Son, London).

Bowley, A. L., 1920, "Cost of Living and Wage Determination," The Economic Journal 30, 114–17.

Bowley, A. L., 1928, "Notes on Index Numbers," The Economic Journal 38, 216–37.

Bradley, R., 2001, "Finite Sample Effects in the Estimation of Substitution Bias in the Consumer Price Index," Journal of Official Statistics 17, 369–90.

Bradley, R., 2005, "Pitfalls of Using Unit Values as a Price Measure or Price Index," Journal of Economic and Social Measurement 30, 39–61.

Bryan, M. F., and S. G. Cecchetti, 1993, "The Consumer Price Index as a Measure of Inflation," Federal Reserve Bank of Cleveland Economic Review, April 1993, 16–25.

Bryan, M. F., and S. G. Cecchetti, 1994, "Measuring Core Inflation," in *Monetary Policy*, edited by N. G. Mankiw, Studies in Business Cycles Volume 29 (The University of Chicago Press, Chicago and London).

Bureau of Statistics of the European Communities (BSEC), 1960, Preise, Verbrauchergeldparitäten und Realeinkommen in den Ländern der EGKS 1954–1958, Statistische Informationen, Sozialstatistiek nr. 2.

Bureau of Statistics of the European Communities (BSEC), 1973, Enquete naar de Kleinhandelsprijzen en Koopkrachtpariteiten – 1972, Luxembourg.

Butter, F. A. G. den, 2007, "National Accounts and Indicators," in *Measurement in Economics: A Handbook*, edited by M. Boumans (Elsevier/Academic Press, Amsterdam).

Carli, G. R., 1764, *Del Valore e della Proporzione de' Metalli Monetati*, in Scrittori Classici Italiani di Economia Politica, Parte Moderna, XIII, 297–366.

Carlson, B. C., 1972a, "The Logarithmic Mean," The American Mathematical Monthly 79, 615–18.

Carlson, B. C., 1972b, "An Algorithm for Computing Logarithms and Arctangents," Mathematics of Computation 26, 543–9.

Carruthers, A. G., D. J., Sellwood, and P. W., Ward, 1980, "Recent Developments in the Retail Prices Index," The Statistician 29, 1–32.

Caves, D. W., L. R. Christensen, and W. E. Diewert, 1982, "Multilateral Comparisons of Output, Input, and Productivity using Superlative Index Numbers," The Economic Journal 92, 73–86.

Chance, W. A., 1966, "A Note on the Origins of Index Numbers," The Review of Economics and Statistics 48, 108–10.

Chardon, G., 1962, "Application de l'Analyse Factorielle à l'Étude d'Indices de Prix," Bulletin of the International Statistical Institute 1962 (4), 471–5.

Clements, K. W., and H. Y. Izan, 1981, "A Note on Estimating Divisia Index Numbers," International Economic Review 22, 745–7. Corrigendum at 23, 499.

Clements, K. W., and H. Y. Izan, 1987, "The Measurement of Inflation: A Stochastic Approach," Journal of Business and Economic Statistics 5, 339–50.

Clements, K. W., H. Y. Izan, and E. A. Selvanathan, 2006, "Stochastic index Numbers; A Review," International Statistical Review 74, 235–70.

Cobb, C., and P. H. Douglas, 1928, "A Theory of Production," The American Economic Review 18, 39–165.

Coggeshall, F., 1886, "The Arithmetic, Geometric, and Harmonic Means," The Quarterly Journal of Economics 1, 83–6.

Collier, I. L., 1999, "Comment," in *International and Interarea Comparisons of Income, Output, and Prices*, edited by A. Heston and R. E. Lipsey, Studies in Income and Wealth, Volume 61 (University of Chicago Press, Chicago and London).

Courant, R., 1936, *Differential and Integral Calculus*, Volume II (Blackie & Son Limited, London and Glasgow).

Court, A. T., 1939, "Hedonic Price Indexes with Automotive Examples," in *The Dynamics of Automobile Demand* (General Motors Corporation, New York).

CPI Manual, 2004, *Consumer Price Index Manual: Theory and Practice* (Published for ILO, IMF, OECD, UN, Eurostat, The World Bank by ILO, Geneva).

Cuthbert, J. R., 1999, "Categorisation of Additive Purchasing Power Parities," The Review of Income and Wealth 45, 235–49.

Cuthbert, J. R., 2000, "Theoretical and Practical Issues in Purchasing Power Parities Illustrated with Reference to the 1993 Organization for Economic Co-operation and Development Data," Journal of the Royal Statistical Society A, 163, 421–44.

Dalén, J., 1992, "Computing Elementary Aggregates in the Swedish Consumer Price Index," Journal of Official Statistics 8, 129–47.

Denton, F. T., 1971, "Adjustment of Monthly or Quarterly Series to Annual Totals: An Approach Based on Quadratic Minimization," Journal of the American Statistical Association 66, 99–102.

Diehl, H., 1976, "Die Berechnung von Kaufkraftparitäten für Private Verbraucher durch das Statistische Amt der Europäischen Gemeinschaften," in *Messung der Kaufkraft des Geldes*, edited by Gerhard Fürst (Vandenhoeck und Ruprecht, Göttingen).

Diewert, W. E., 1976, "Exact and Superlative Index Numbers," Journal of Econometrics 4, 115–45. Reprinted in Diewert and Nakamura (1993).

Diewert, W. E., 1978, "Superlative Index Numbers and Consistency in Aggregation," Econometrica 46, 883–900. Reprinted in Diewert and Nakamura (1993).

Diewert, W. E., 1980, "Aggregation Problems in the Measurement of Capital," in *The Measurement of Capital*, edited by D. Usher (University of Chicago Press, Chicago and London).

Diewert, W. E., 1981, "The Economic Theory of Index Numbers: A Survey," in *Essays in the Theory and Measurement of Consumer Behaviour in Honour of Sir Richard Stone*, edited by A. Deaton (Cambridge University Press, Cambridge). Reprinted in Diewert and Nakamura (1993).

Diewert, W. E., 1983, "The Treatment of Seasonality in the Cost of Living Index," in *Price Level Measurement*, edited by W. E. Diewert and C. Montmarquette (Statistics Canada, Ottawa).

Diewert, W. E., 1986, "Microeconomic Approaches to the Theory of International Comparisons," Technical Working Paper No. 53, Cambridge MA: National Bureau of Economic Research. Abridged version, entitled "Test Approaches to International Comparisons," in Diewert and Nakamura (1993).

Diewert, W. E., 1987a, "Index Numbers," in *The New Palgrave: A Dictionary of Economics*, Volume 2, edited by J. Eatwell *et al.*, London: Macmillan. Reprinted in Diewert and Nakamura (1993).

Diewert, W. E., 1987b, "Laspeyres, Ernst Louis Etienne," in *The New Palgrave: A Dictionary of Economics*, Volume 3, edited by J. Eatwell, M. Milgate, and P. Newman (Macmillan, London). Reprinted in Diewert and Nakamura (1993).

Diewert, W. E., 1987c, "Konüs, Alexander Alexandrovich" in *The New Palgrave: A Dictionary of Economics*, Volume 3, edited by J. Eatwell, M. Milgate, and P. Newman (Macmillan, London). Reprinted in Diewert and Nakamura (1993).

Diewert, W. E., 1988, "The Early History of Price Index Research," in Diewert and Nakamura (1993). Originally published as NBER Discussion Paper No. 2713.

Diewert, W. E., 1992, "Fisher Ideal Output, Input and Productivity Indexes Revisited," Journal of Productivity Analysis 3, 211–48. Reprinted in Diewert and Nakamura (1993).

Diewert, W. E., 1993, "Overview of Volume I," in Diewert and Nakamura (1993).

Diewert, W. E., 1995a, "Axiomatic and Economic Approaches to Elementary Price Indexes," Discussion Paper No. 95–01 (Department of Economics, University of British Columbia, Vancouver).

Diewert, W. E., 1995b, "On the Stochastic Approach to Index Numbers," Discussion Paper No. 95–31 (Department of Economics, University of British Columbia, Vancouver).

Diewert, W. E., 1997, "Commentary," Review of the Federal Reserve Bank of St. Louis 79(3), 127–38.

Diewert, W. E., 1999, "Axiomatic and Economic Approaches to International Comparisons," in *International and Interarea Comparisons of Income, Output, and Prices*, edited by A. Heston and R. E. Lipsey, Studies in Income and Wealth, Volume 61 (University of Chicago Press, Chicago and London).

Diewert, W. E., 2001, "The Consumer Price Index and Index Number Purpose," Journal of Economic and Social Measurement 27, 167–248.

Diewert, W. E., 2002a, "The Quadratic Approximation Lemma and Decompositions of Superlative Indexes," Journal of Economic and Social Measurement 28, 63–88.

Diewert, W. E., 2002b, "Harmonized Indexes of Consumer Prices: Their Conceptual Foundations," Swiss Journal of Economics and Statistics 138, 547–637.

Diewert, W. E., 2004a, "The Axiomatic and Stochastic Approaches to Index Number Theory," in *CPI Manual* (2004) and *PPI Manual* (2004).

Diewert, W. E., 2004b, "The Treatment of Seasonal Products," in *CPI Manual* (2004) and *PPI Manual* (2004).

Diewert, W. E., 2004c, "Price Indices Using an Artificial Data Set," in *CPI Manual* (2004) and *PPI Manual* (2004).

Diewert, W. E., 2005a, "Index Number Theory Using Differences Rather Than Ratios," in Dimand and Geanakoplos (2005).

Diewert, W. E., 2005b, "Weighted Country Product Dummy Variable Regressions and Index Number Formulae," The Review of Income and Wealth 51, 561–70.

Diewert, W. E., 2008, "Similarity Indexes and Criteria for Spatial Linking," in *Purchasing Power Parities of Currencies. Recent Advances in Methods and Applications*, edited by D. S. P. Rao (Edward Elgar, Cheltenham UK/Northampton MA).

Diewert, W. E., and A. O. Nakamura (editors), 1993, *Essays in Index Number Theory*, Volume 1 (North-Holland, Amsterdam).

Dimand, R. W., and J. Geanakoplos (editors), 2005, *Celebrating Irving Fisher: The Legacy of a Great Economist*, The American Journal of Economics and Sociology 64(2) (Blackwell Publishing).

Divisia, F., 1925, "L' Indice Monétaire et la Theorie de la Monnaie," Revue d' Economie Politique 39, 842–61, 980–1008, 1121–51.

Divisia, F., 1952, *Exposés d'Économique*, Volume 1 (Dunod, Paris).

Dorfman, A. H., J. Lent, S. G. Leaver, and E. Wegman, 2006, "On Sample Survey Designs for Consumer Price Indexes," Survey Methodology 32(2), 197–216.

Drechsler, L., 1973, "Weighting of Index Numbers in Multilateral International Comparisons," The Review of Income and Wealth 19, 17–34.

Drobisch, M. W., 1871, "Ueber die Berechnung der Veränderung der Waarenpreise und des Geldwertes," Jahrbücher für Nationalökonomie und Statistik 16, 416–27.

Dumagan, J. C., 2002, "Comparing the Superlative Törnqvist and Fisher Ideal Indexes," Economics Letters 76, 251–8.

Dumagan, J. C., 2005, "Factor Reversal Tests and Fisher Index Decompositions," Mimeo (Economics and Statistics Administration, U.S. Department of Commerce, Washington, DC).

Dutot, C. F., 1738, *Réflections Politiques sur les Finances et le Commerce*, Volume 1 (Les Frères Vaillant and N. Prevost, The Hague). Édition intégrale publiée pour la première fois par Paul Harsin, Paris-Liège 1935 (Bibliothèque de Faculté de Philosophie et Lettres de l'Université de Liège, Fascicule LXVII).

Economic Commission for Latin America and the Caribbean (ECLAC), 1978, "Series Históricas del Crecimiento de América Latina," Cuadernos Estadisticos de la CEPAL 3 (Santiago de Chile).

Edgeworth, F. Y., 1888, "Some New Methods of Measuring Variation in General Prices," Journal of the Royal Statistical Society 51, 346–68.

Edgeworth, F. Y., 1896, "A Defence of Index-Numbers," The Economic Journal 6, 132–42.

Edgeworth, F. Y., 1923a, "The Doctrine of Index-Numbers According to Mr. Correa Walsh," The Economic Journal 33, 343–51.

Edgeworth, F. Y., 1923b, "Mr. Correa Walsh on the Calculation of Index-Numbers," Journal of the Royal Statistical Society 86, 570–90.

Edgeworth, F. Y., 1925a, "The Plurality of Index Numbers," The Economic Journal 35, 379–88.

Edgeworth, F. Y., 1925b, *Papers Relating to Political Economy*, Volume I (MacMillan, London).

Edgeworth, F. Y. 1925c, "Index Numbers," in *Palgrave's Dictionary of Political Economy*, Volume 2, edited by H. Higgins (Macmillan, London).

Ehemann, C., 2005a, "Chain Drift in Leading Superlative Indexes," Working Paper 2005–09 (Bureau of Economic Analysis, U.S. Department of Commerce, Washington, DC).

Ehemann, C., 2005b, "Evaluating and Adjusting for Chain Drift in National Economic Accounts," Working Paper 2005–10 (Bureau of Economic Analysis, U.S. Department of Commerce, Washington, DC).

Eichhorn, W., 1973, "Zur Axiomatischen Theorie des Preisindex," Demonstratio Mathematica 6, 561–73.

Eichhorn, W., 1976, "Fisher's Tests Revisited," Econometrica 44, 247–56.

Eichhorn, W., 1978, *Functional Equations in Economics* (Addison-Wesley, Reading, MA).

Eichhorn, W., and J. Voeller, 1976, *Theory of the Price Index*, Lecture Notes in Economics and Mathematical Systems 140 (Springer-Verlag, Berlin).

Eichhorn, W., and J. Voeller, 1983, "Axiomatic Foundation of Price Indexes and Purchasing Power Parities," in *Price Level Measurement*, edited by W. E. Diewert and C. Montmarquette (Statistics Canada, Ottawa); also reprinted in *Price Level Measurement*, edited by W. E. Diewert (North-Holland, Amsterdam, 1990).

Eltetö, Ö., and P. Köves, 1964, "On an Index Computation Problem in International Comparisons" (in Hungarian), Statiztikai Szemle 42, 507–18.

ESA 1995, *European System of Accounts* (Eurostat, Luxembourg).

Europäische Gemeinschaft für Kohle und Stahl (ECSC), 1956, Die Arbeitereinkommen der Industrien der Gemeinschaft im Realvergleich, Eine Statistische Analyse, Luxembourg.

Europäische Gemeinschaft für Kohle und Stahl (ECSC), 1957, Die Verbrauchergeldparitäten in den Ländern der Gemeinschaft 1954, Eine Methodologische Studie, Statistische Informationen 4, nr. 4.

Eurostat (Bureau of Statistics of the European Communities), 1976, Enquete inzake de Consumentenprijzen en de Koopkrachtpariteiten – 1975, Luxembourg.

Eurostat, 1977, *Comparison in Real Values of the Aggregates of ESA – 1975* (Statistical Office of the European Communities, Luxembourg).

Eurostat, 1983, *Comparison in Real Values of the Aggregates of ESA – 1980* (Statistical Office of the European Communities, Luxembourg).

Eurostat, 1988, *Purchasing Power Parities and Gross Domestic Product in Real Terms, Results 1985* (Statistical Office of the European Communities, Luxembourg).

Eurostat, 1994, *Comparison in Real Terms of the Aggregates of ESA, Results for 1990 and 1991* (Statistical Office of the European Communities, Luxembourg).

Fase, M. M. G., 1992, "Pierson over Indexcijfers en Prijsstabiliteit," in *Van Amsterdam naar Tilburg en toch weer terug,* edited by J. F. E. Bläsing and H. H. Vleesenbeek (Nijhoff, Leiden/Antwerpen).

Fase, M. M. G., 1998, Pierson on Scarcity of Gold and Changes in the General Price Level, DNB Staff Reports (De Nederlandsche Bank NV, Amsterdam).

Fässler, A., and A. Vogt, 1989, "Analytic Integration of the Divisia Price Index on the Exponential Path for Two Commodities," Communications in Statistics – Part A: Theory and Methods 18, 3473–6.

Ferger, W. F., 1946, "Historical Note on the Purchasing Power Concept, and Index Numbers," Journal of the American Statistical Association 41, 53–7.

Finkel, Y., A. Rakhmilevich, and V. Roshal, 2007, "Different Approaches to the Treatment of Seasonal Products: Tests on the Israeli CPI." Presented at the 10th Meeting of the Ottawa Group (International Working Group on Price Indices), Ottawa, 9–12 October 2007.

Fisher, I., 1911, *The Purchasing Power of Money. Its Determination and Relation to Credit, Interest and Crisis* (Macmillan, New York).

Fisher, I., 1921, "The Best Form of Index Number (with Discussion)," Quarterly Publication of the American Statistical Association, New Series 17, 533–51.

Fisher, I., 1922, *The Making of Index Numbers. A Study of Their Varieties, Tests, and Reliability* (Houghton Mifflin Company, Boston and New York).

Fisher, I., 1927, "The 'Total Value Criterion': A New Principle in Index Number Construction," Journal of the American Statistical Association, New Series 22, 419–41.

Fisher, W. C., 1913, "The Tabular Standard in Massachusetts History," Quarterly Journal of Economics 27, 417–56.

Fisk, P. R., 1977, "Some Approximations to an 'Ideal' Index Number," Journal of the Royal Statistical Society A 140, 217–31.

Fitzpatrick, P. J., 1960, "Leading British Statisticians of the Nineteenth Century," Journal of the American Statistical Association 55, 38–70.

Fleetwood, W., 1704, *Chronicon Preciosum: or, an Account of English Money, the Price of Corn and other Commodities for the Last Six Hundred Years – in a Letter to a Student in the University of Oxford* (London).

Forsyth, F. G., and R. F. Fowler, 1981, "The Theory and Practice of Chain Price Index Numbers," Journal of the Royal Statistical Society A 144, 224–46.

Frisch, R., 1930, "Necessary and Sufficient Conditions Regarding the Form of an Index Number which Shall Meet Certain of Fisher's Tests," Journal of the American Statistical Association 25, 397–406.

Frisch, R., 1936, "Annual Survey of General Economic Theory: The Problem of Index Numbers," Econometrica 4, 1–38.

Fukao, K., D. Ma, and T. Yuan, "International Comparison in Historical Perspective: Reconstructing the 1934–1936 Benchmark Purchasing Power Parity for Japan, Korea, and Taiwan," Explorations in Economic History 43, 280–308.

Funke, H., 1988, "Mean Value Properties of the Weights of Linear Price Indices," in *Measurement in Economics*, edited by W. Eichhorn (Physica-Verlag, Heidelberg).

Funke, H., and J. Voeller, 1978, "A Note on the Characterization of Fisher's 'Ideal Index,'" in *Theory and Applications of Economic Indices*, edited by W. Eichhorn *et al.* (Physica Verlag, Würzburg).

Funke, H., and J. Voeller, 1979, "Characterization of Fisher's 'Ideal Index' by Three Reversal Tests," Statistische Hefte 20, 54–60.

Funke, H., and J. Voeller, 1984, "Price and Quantity Index Characterizations Using the Product Test," Methods of Operations Research 48, 83–96 (Athenäum/Hain/Hanstein, Königstein).

Funke, H., G. Hacker, and J. Voeller, 1979, "Fisher's Circular Test Reconsidered," Schweizerische Zeitschrift für Volkswirtschaft und Statistik 115, 677–687.

Geary, R. C., 1958, "A Note on the Comparison of Exchange Rates and Purchasing Power between Countries," Journal of the Royal Statistical Society A 121, 97–99.

Gerardi, D., 1974, Sul Problema della Comparazione dei Poteri d'Aquisto della Valute (Istituto di Statistica, Universita degli Studi di Padova).

Gerardi, D., 1982a, "Selected Problems of Inter-Country Comparisons on the Basis of the Experiences of the EEC," The Review of Income and Wealth 28, 381–405.

Gerardi, D., 1982b, Contribution to the Definition of a Common Methodology in the Framework of the International Comparison Project with Particular Reference to the Aggregation Formula for Volume Comparisons, Paper presented at the Special Conference on PPP's, International Association for Research in Income and Wealth, 21–24 September, Luxembourg.

Gerschenkron, A., 1951, *A Dollar Index of Soviet Machinery Output, 1927–28 to 1937* (Rand Corporation, Santa Monica CA).

Gilbert, M., and I. B. Kravis, 1954, *An International Comparison of National Products and the Purchasing Power of Currencies. A Study of the United States, the United Kingdom, France, Germany and Italy* (OEEC, Paris).

Gilbert, M., and associates, 1958, *Comparative National Products and Price Levels. A Study of Western Europe and the United States* (OEEC, Paris).

Gini, C., 1924, "Quelques Considérations au Sujet de la Construction des Nombres Indices des Prix et des Questions Analogues," Metron 4, 3–162.

Gini, C., 1926, "The Contribution of Italy to Modern Statistical Methods," Journal of the Royal Statistical Society 89, 703–24.

Gini, C., 1931, "On the Circular Test of Index Numbers," International Review of Statistics 9, no. 2, 3–25.

Gleissner, W., 1990, "A Characterization of the Price Indices Satisfying the Eichhorn-Voeller Axioms," Statistical Papers/Statistische Hefte 31, 241–50.

Gleissner, W., 1992, "A Parameterisation of the Price Indices Characterized by the Eichhorn-Voeller Axioms," Statistical Papers/Statistische Hefte 33, 75–82.

Gorman, W. M., 1970, "Notes on Divisia Indices," in *Separability and Aggregation. Collected Works of W. M. Gorman*, Volume 1, edited by C. Blackorby and A. F. Shorrocks (Clarendon Press, Oxford, 1995).

Gorman, W. M., 1986, "Compatible Indices," Conference Papers Supplement to the Economic Journal 96, 83–95.

Green, J., and W. P. Heller, 1981, "Mathematical Analysis and Convexity with Applications to Economics," in *Handbook of Mathematical Economics*, Volume 1, edited by K. J. Arrow and M. D. Intriligator (North-Holland, Amsterdam).

Griliches, Z., 1961, "Hedonic Price Indexes for Automobiles: An Econometric Analysis of Quality Change," in *The Price Statistics of the Federal Government* (National Bureau of Economic Research, New York); reprinted in *Price Indexes and Quality Change; Studies in New Methods of Measurement*, edited by Z. Griliches (Harvard University Press, Cambridge MA, 1971).

Haberler, G., 1927, *Der Sinn der Indexzahlen* (J. C. B. Mohr, Tübingen).

Hacker, G., 1979, Theorie der Wirtschaftlichen Kennzahl, Dissertation (Universität Fridericiana, Karlsruhe).

Hallerbach, W. G., 2005, "An Alternative Decomposition of the Fisher Index," Economics Letters 86, 147–52.

Harris, R., D. Laidler, and A. Nakamura, 1996, "A Biographical Sketch of Walter Erwin Diewert," Canadian Journal of Economics 29, S678–95.

Heston, A., R. Summers, and B. Aten, 2001, "Price Structures, the Quality Factor, and Chaining," Statistical Journal of the United Nations ECE 18, 77–101.

Hill, R. J., 1997, "A Taxonomy of Multilateral Methods for Making International Comparisons of Prices and Quantities," The Review of Income and Wealth 43, 49–69.

Hill, R. J., 1999a, "Comparing Price Levels across Countries using Minimum-Spanning Trees," The Review of Economics and Statistics, 81, 135–42.

Hill, R. J., 1999b, "International Comparisons using Spanning Trees," in *International and Interarea Comparisons of Income, Output, and Prices*, edited by A. Heston and R. E. Lipsey, Studies in Income and Wealth, Volume 61, University of Chicago Press, Chicago and London.

Hill, R. J., 2000, "Measuring Substitution Bias in International Comparisons Based on Additive Purchasing Power Parity Methods," European Economic Review 44, 145–62.

Hill, R. J., 2001, "Measuring Inflation and Growth using Spanning Trees," International Economic Review 42, 167–85.

Hill, R. J., 2004, "Constructing Price Indexes across Space and Time: The Case of the European Union," The American Economic Review 94, 1379–410.

Hill, R. J., 2006a, "When Does Chaining Reduce the Paasche-Laspeyres Spread? An Application to Scanner Data," The Review of Income and Wealth 52, 309–25.

Hill, R. J., 2006b, "Superlative Indexes: Not All of Them Are Super," Journal of Econometrics 130, 25–43.

Hill, R. J., 2007, "Convergence or Divergence: How to Get the Answer You Want," Discussion Paper 2007/06 (School of Economics, The University of New South Wales, Sydney).

Hill, R. J., 2008, "Comparing per Capita Income Levels across Countries using Spanning Trees: Robustness, Prior Restrictions, Hybrids and Hierarchies," in *Purchasing Power Parities of Currencies. Recent Advances in Methods and Applications*, edited by D. S. P. Rao (Edward Elgar, Cheltenham UK/Northampton MA).

Hill, R. J., and K. J. Fox, 1997, "Splicing Index Numbers," Journal of Business & Economic Statistics 15, 387–9.

Hill, R. J., and M. P. Timmer, 2006, "Standard Errors as Weights in Multilateral Price Indexes," Journal of Business & Economic Statistics 24, 366–77.

Hill, T. P. (Eurostat), 1982, *Multilateral Measurements of Purchasing Power and Real GDP* (Statistical Office of the EC, Luxembourg).

Hillinger, C., 1970, "Comment on Invariance Axioms and Economic Indexes," Econometrica 38, 773–4.

Hillinger, C., 2002, "Consistent Aggregation and Chaining of Price and Quantity Measures," Journal of Economic and Social Measurement 28, 1–20.

Hofsten, E. von, 1952, *Price Indexes and Quality Changes* (Bokförlaget Forum, Stockholm; George Allen & Unwin, London).

Hulten, C. R., 1973, "Divisia Index Numbers," Econometrica 41, 1017–25.

Iklé, D. M., 1972, "A New Approach to the Index Number Problem," Quarterly Journal of Economics 86, 188–211.

International Statistical Institute, 1956, *Bibliography on Index Numbers* (The Hague).

Jastram, R. W., 1951, "Willard Phillips, A Predecessor of Paasche in Index Number Formulation," Journal of the American Statistical Association 46, 124–6.

Jazairi, N. T., 1971, "An Empirial Study of the Conventional and Statistical Theories of Index Numbers," Bulletin of the Oxford University Institute of Economics and Statistics 33, 181–95.

Jazairi, N. T., 1973, "Maximum Likelihood Estimation of Price and Quantity Index Numbers," Contributed paper for the 39th Session of the International Statistical Institute, Vienna.

Jazairi, N. T., 1983, "Index Numbers," in *Encyclopedia of Statistical Sciences*, Volume 4, edited by S. Kott and N. L. Johnson (Wiley, New York).

Jevons, W. S., 1863, *A Serious Fall in the Value of Gold and its Social Effects Set Forth* (Edward Stanford, London).

Jevons, W. S., 1865, "On the Variation of Prices and the Value of the Currency since 1782," Journal of the Statistical Society of London 28, 294–320.

Jorgenson, D. W., and Z. Griliches, 1967, "The Explanation of Productivity Change," Review of Economic Studies 34, 249–83.

Kendall, M. G., 1969, "Studies in History of Probability and Statistics, XXI. The Early History of Index Numbers," Review of the International Statistical Institute 37, 1–12.

Keynes, J. M., 1930, *A Treatise on Money, Volume I: The Pure Theory of Money* (Macmillan, London).

Khamis, S. H., 1972, "A New System of Index Numbers for National and International Purposes," Journal of the Royal Statistical Society A 135, 96–121.

Khamis, S. H., 1998, "Measurement of Real Product: Some Index Number Aspects," Paper presented at the 25th General Conference of the IARIW, Cambridge UK.

Kloek, T., 1966, *Indexcijfers, Enige Methodologische Aspecten* (Indexnumbers, Some Methodological Aspects) (Pasmans, Den Haag).

Kloek, T., and C. J. van Rees, 1962, "On the Method of 'Deflated' Best Linear Index Numbers," Bulletin of the International Statistical Institute 39, 451–62.

Kloek, T., and G. M. de Wit, 1961, "Best Linear and Best Linear Unbiased Index Numbers," Econometrica 29, 602–16.

Knottnerus, P., 2003, *Sample Survey Theory: Some Pythagorean Perspectives* (Springer-Verlag, New York).

Kohli, U., 2002, "A Multiplicative Decomposition of the Fisher Index of Real GDP," Mimeo (Swiss National Bank, Zurich).

Konüs, A. A., 1924, "The Problem of the True Index of the Cost of Living," translated in Econometrica 7 (1939), 10–29.

Köves, P., 1983, *Index Theory and Economic Reality* (Akadémiai Kiadó, Budapest).

Köves, P., 1999, "EKS Index and International Comparisons," Hungarian Statistical Review (Statisztikai Szemle) 77, 3–14.

Kravis, I. B., Z. Kenessey, A. Heston, and R. Summers, 1975, *A System of International Comparisons of Gross Product and Purchasing Power* (The Johns Hopkins University Press, Baltimore and London).

Krijnse Locker, H., and H. D. Faerber, 1984, "Space and Time Comparisons of Purchasing Power Parities and Real Values," The Review of Income and Wealth 30, 53–83.

Krtscha, M., 1979, "Ueber Preisindizes und deren Axiomatische Characterisierung," Dissertation Universität Fridericiana Karlsruhe.

Krtscha, M., 1984, "A Characterization of the Edgeworth-Marshall Index," Methods of Operations Research 48, 127–35 (Athenäum/Hain/Hanstein, Königstein).

Krtscha, M., 1988, "Axiomatic Characterization of Statistical Price Indices," in *Measurement in Economics*, edited by W. Eichhorn (Physica-Verlag, Heidelberg).

Kula, W., 1986, *Measures and Men*. Translated by R. Szreter (Princeton University Press, Princeton NJ).

Kurabayashi, Y., and I. Sakuma, 1981, "An Alternative Method of Multilateral Comparisons of Real Product Constrained with Matrix Consistency," Paper presented at the 17th General Conference of the IARIW, Gouvieux, France.

Kurabayashi, Y., and I. Sakuma, 1982, "Transitivity, Factor Reversal Test and Matrix Consistency in the International Comparisons of Real Product," Discussion Paper 54, Institute of Economic Research, Hitotsubashi University, Tokyo.

Kurabayashi, Y., and I. Sakuma, 1990, *Studies in International Comparisons of Real Product and Prices*, (Kinokuniya Company, Tokyo, and Oxford University Press, Oxford).

Laspeyres, E., 1864, "Hamburger Waarenpreise 1851–1863 und die Kalifornisch-Australischen Goldentdeckungen seit 1848," Jahrbücher für Nationalökonomie und Statistik 3, 81–118, 209–36.

Laspeyres, E., 1871, "Die Berechnung einer Mittleren Waarenpreissteigerung," Jahrbücher für Nationalökonomie und Statistik 16, 296–314.

Laspeyres, E., 1883, "Preise (Die Bewegungen der Waarenpreise in der zweiten Hälfte des 19. Jahrhunderts)," in *Meyers Konversations-Lexikon*, Volume XX, Third edition (Leipzig).

Lehr, J., 1885, *Beiträge zur Statistik der Preise, Insbesondere des Geldes und des Holzes* (J. D. Sauerländer, Frankfurt am Main).

Leontief, W., 1936, "Composite Commodities and the Problem of Index Numbers," Econometrica 4, 39–59.

Lippe, P. von der, 2000, "Der Unsinn von Kettenindizes," Allgemeines Statistisches Archiv 84, 67–82.

Lippe, P. von der, 2001, *Chain Indices; A Study in Price Index Theory*, Volume 16 of the Publication Series Spectrum of Federal Statistics (Statistisches Bundesamt/Metzler-Poeschel, Wiesbaden/Stuttgart).

Lippe, P. von der, 2005, "Das Ideal des 'reinen Preisvergleichs' (The Principle of 'Pure Price Comparison')," Jahrbücher für Nationalökonomie und Statistik (Journal of Economics and Statistics) 225, 499–509.

Lippe, P. von der, 2006, "Price Indices and Unit Value Indices in German Foreign Trade Statistics," Mimeo (Economics Department, University Duisburg-Essen).

Lorenzen, G., 1990, "Konsistent Addierbare Relative Änderungen," Allgemeines Statistisches Archiv 74, 336–44.

Lowe, J., 1823, *The Present State of England in Regard to Agriculture, Trade and Finance*, 2nd edition (Longman, Hurst, Rees, Orme & Brown, London).

Maas, H. B. J. B., 2001, "Mechanical Reasoning: William Stanly Jevons and the Making of Modern Economics," Ph. D. Thesis, University of Amsterdam.

Malaney, P. N., 1996, "The Index Number Problem: A Differential Geometric Approach," Ph.D. Thesis, Harvard University, Cambridge, MA.

Mann, F. K., 1936, "Dutot und sein Werk," Zeitschrift für Nationalökonomie (Journal of Economics) 7, 98–103.

Marshall, A., 1887, "Remedies for Fluctuations of General Prices," Contemporary Review 51, 355–375. Reprinted in *Memorials of Alfred Marshall*, edited by A. C. Pigou (Macmillan, London, 1925).

Martini, M., 1992a, *I Numeri Indice in un Approccio Assiomatico* (Giuffré Editore, Milano).

Martini, M., 1992b, "A General Function of Axiomatic Index Numbers," Journal of the Italian Statistical Society 3, 359–76.

Meinlschmidt, G., 1985, "Faktorenanalyse als ein Instrument zur Konstruktion von Preisniveauindizes," Statistische Hefte/Statistical Papers 26, 199–210.

Melser, D., 2006, "Accounting for the Effects of New and Disappearing Goods using Scanner Data," The Review of Income and Wealth 52, 547–68.

Messedaglia, A., 1880, "Il Calcolo dei Valore Medii e le sue Applicazioni Statistiche" (The Calculation of Averages and its Statistical Applications), Archivio di Statistica 5, (2) 177–224, (4) 489–528; expanded version, edited by R. Benini, in *Biblioteca dell Economista*, Series V, Volume XIX (1908).

Montgomery, J. K., 1929, *Is There a Theoretically Correct Price Index of a Group of Commodities?* (International Institute of Agriculture, Rome).

Montgomery, J. K., 1937, *The Mathematical Problem of the Price Index* (P.S. King & Son, London).

Morgan, M. S., 2007, "An Analytical History of Measuring Practices: The Case of Velocities of Money," in *Measurement in Economics: A Handbook*, edited by M. Boumans (Elsevier/Academic Press, Amsterdam).

Moulton, B. R., and E. P. Seskin, 1999, "A Preview of the 1999 Comprehensive Revision of the National Income and Product Accounts Statistical Changes," *Survey of Current Business* 79 (10), 6–17.

Mudgett, B. D., 1951, *Index Numbers* (Wiley, New York).

Mudgett, B. D., 1955, "The Measurement of Seasonal Movements in Price and Quantity Indexes," Journal of the American Statistical Association 50, 93–8.

Mundlos, B., 1982, "Eine Axiomatik für Preisindizes in Funktionalform – Gleichzeitig eine Kritik der Kritik an Divisia–Indizes," Statistische Hefte/Statistical Papers 23, 275–90.

Mustonen, S., 2002, "Logarithmic Mean for Several Arguments," Mimeo downloadable from www.survo.fi/papers/logmean.pdf (Department of Statistics, University of Helsinki).

Nataf, A., and R. Roy, 1948, "Remarques et Suggestions Relatives aux Nombres–Indices," Econometrica 16, 330–46.

Neary, J. P., 1997, "R. C. Geary's Contributions to Economic Theory," in *Roy Geary, 1896–1983: Irish Statistician*, edited by D. Conniffe (Oak Tree Press in association with The Economic and Social Research Institute, Dublin).

Okamoto, M., 2001, "Midpoint-Year Basket Index as a Practical Approximation to Superlative Index," Paper presented at the 6th meeting of the International Working Group on Price Indices, Canberra, 2–6 April 2001 (www.ottawagroup.org).

Oker, C. W., 1896, "The Fallacy of Index-Numbers," The Journal of Political Economy 4, 515–22.

Olt, B., 1996, *Axiom und Struktur in der Statistischen Preisindextheorie* (Peter Lang, Frankfurt am Main).

Paasche, H., 1874, "Ueber die Preisentwicklung der Letzten Jahre nach den Hamburger Börsennotierungen," Jahrbücher für Nationalökonomie und Statistik 23, 168–178.

Palgrave, R. H. I., 1886, "Currency and Standard of Value in England, France and India, and the Rates of Exchange Between these Countries." Memorandum for the Royal Commission on Depression of Trade and Industry, Third Report, Appendix B.

Párniczky, G., 1974, "Some Problems of Price Measurement in External Trade Statistics," Acta Oeconomica 12, 229–40.

Persky, J., 1998, "Price Indexes and General Exchange Values," Journal of Economic Perspectives 12, 197–205.

Pfouts, R., 1966, "An Axiomatic Approach to Index Numbers," Review of the International Statistical Institute 34, 174–85.

Phillips, W., 1828, *Manual of Political Economy* (Boston).

Pierson, N. G., 1896, "Further Considerations on Index-Numbers," in *Verspreide Economische Geschriften van Mr. N. G. Pierson* (Collected economic papers of Mr. N. G. Pierson), verzameld door Dr. C. A. Verrijn Stuart (Bohn, Haarlem).

Pierson, N. G., 1894, 1895, 1896, in *Verspreide Economische Geschriften van Mr. N. G. Pierson* (Collected Economic Papers of Mr. N. G. Pierson), verzameld door Dr. C. A. Verrijn Stuart (Bohn, Haarlem).

Pigou, A. C., 1912, *Wealth and Welfare* (Macmillan, London).

Pigou, A. C., 1932, *The Economics of Welfare*, Fourth Edition (Macmillan, London). Downloadable from www.econlib.org.

Pollak, R. A., 1971, The Theory of the Cost of Living Index. Working Paper 11 (U.S. Bureau of Labor Statistics, Washington DC). Revised Version, 1982. Reprinted in *Price Level Measurement*, edited by W. E. Diewert and C. Montmarquette (Statistics Canada, Ottawa, 1983); in *Price Level Measurement*, edited by W. E. Diewert (North-Holland, Amsterdam etc., 1990); and in *The Theory of the Cost-of-Living Index* by R. A. Pollak (Oxford University Press, New York/Oxford, 1989).

PPI Manual, 2004, *Producer Price Index Manual: Theory and Practice* (Published for ILO, IMF, OECD, UN, The World Bank by IMF, Washington, DC).

Pursiainen, H., 2005, "Consistent Aggregation Methods and Index Number Theory," Ph.D. Thesis, Research Report No. 106 (Department of Economics, University of Helsinki).

Rao, D. S. P., 1990, "A System of Log-Change Index Numbers for Multilateral Comparisons," in *Comparisons of Prices and Real Products in Latin America*, edited by J. Salazar-Carrillo and D. S. P. Rao (North-Holland, Amsterdam).

Rao, D. S. P., 2000, "Expenditure Share Weighted Size-Neutral Geary-Khamis Method for International Comparisons: Specification and Properties," Mimeo (School of Economics, University of Queensland, Brisbane).

Rao, D. S. P., 2005, "On the Equivalence of Weighted Country-Product-Dummy (CPD) Method and the Rao-System for Multilateral Price Comparison," The Review of Income and Wealth 51, 571–80.

Rao, D. S. P., 2008, "Generalised Elteto-Koves-Szulc (EKS) and Country-Product-Dummy (CPD) Methods for International Comparisons," in *Purchasing Power Parities of Currencies. Recent Advances in Methods and Applications*, edited by D. S. P. Rao (Edward Elgar, Cheltenham UK/Northampton MA).

Rao, D. S. P., and M. P. Timmer, 2003, "Purchasing Power Parities for Industry Comparisons Using Weighted Elteto-Koves-Szulc (EKS) Methods," The Review of Income and Wealth 49, 491–511.

Reich, U.-P., 2004, "Path Dependence of the General Price Level: A Value-Theoretic Analysis," The Review of Income and Wealth 50, 229–42.

Reinsdorf, M. B., 1994, "Letter to the Editor: A New Functional Form for Price Indexes Elementary Aggregates," Journal of Official Statistics 10, 103–8.

Reinsdorf, M. B., 1996, "Log-change Indexes in Fixed Basket Form." Working Paper 278 (U.S. Bureau of Labor Statistics, Washington, DC).

Reinsdorf, M. B., 2007, "Axiomatic Price Index Theory," in *Measurement in Economics: A Handbook*, edited by M. Boumans (Elsevier/Academic Press, Amsterdam).

Reinsdorf, M. B., W. E. Diewert, and C. Ehemann, 2002, "Additive Decompositions for Fisher, Törnqvist and Geometric Mean Indexes," Journal of Economic and Social Measurement 28, 51–61.

Reinsdorf, M. B., and A. Dorfman, 1999, "The Sato-Vartia Index and the Monotonicity Axiom," Journal of Econometrics 90, 45–61.

Reinsdorf, M. B., and J. E. Triplett, 2008, "A Review of Reviews: Ninety Years of Professional Thinking about the CPI," in *Price Index Concepts and Measurement*, edited by W. E. Diewert, J. Greenlees and C. R. Hulten (University of Chicago Press, Chicago).

Richter, M. K., 1966, "Invariance Axioms and Economic Indexes," Econometrica 34, 739–55.

Rinne, H., 1981, "Ernst Louis Etienne Laspeyres," Jahrbücher für Nationalökonomie und Statistik 196, 193–237.

Roberts, H., 2000, "Laspeyres and His Index," Mimeo (Department of Economics, University of Illinois at Chicago).

Ronchetti, S., and G. Bertaud, 1974, "Price Comparisons for Calculating Rates of Equivalence in Member States of the EEC, 1954–1970," in *The Role of the Computer in Economic and Social Research in Latin America*, edited by Nancy D. Ruggles (National Bureau of Economic Research, New York).

Rothwell, D. P., 1958, "Use of Varying Seasonal Weights in Price Index Construction," Journal of the American Statistical Association 53, 66–77.

Roy, R., 1927, "Les Indexes Economiques," Revue d'Economie Politique 41, 1251–91.

Ruderman, A. P., 1954, "A Neglected Point in the Construction of Price Index Numbers," Applied Statistics 3, 44–7, 126–7, 197–8.

Ruggles, R., 1967, "Price Indexes and International Price Comparisons," in *Ten Economic Studies in the Tradition of Irving Fisher*, edited by W. J. Fellner *et al.* (Wiley, New York).

Sakuma, I., D. S. P. Rao, and Y. Kurabayashi, 2000, "Additivity, Matrix Consistency and a New Method for International Comparisons of Real Income and Purchasing Power Parities," Paper presented at the 26th General Conference of the IARIW, Cracow, Poland. Revised version in *Purchasing Power Parities of Currencies. Recent Advances in Methods and Applications*, edited by D. S. P. Rao (Edward Elgar, Cheltenham UK/Northampton MA, 2008).

Samuelson, P. A., 1974, "Remembrances of Frisch," European Economic Review 5, 7–23.

Samuelson, P. A., 1996, "Gottfried Haberler (1900–1995)," The Economic Journal 106, 1679–87.

Samuelson, P. A., and S. Swamy, 1974, "Invariant Economic Index Numbers and Canonical Duality: Survey and Synthesis," American Economic Review 64, 566–93.

Sato, K., 1974, "Ideal Index Numbers That Almost Satisfy the Factor Reversal Test," The Review of Economics and Statistics 56, 549–54.

Sato, K., 1976, "The Ideal Log-Change Index Number," The Review of Economics and Statistics 58, 223–8.

Sato, R., 1981, *Theory of Technical Change and Economic Invariance; Application of Lie Groups* (Reprinted with amendments by Edward Elgar, Cheltenham UK/ Northampton MA, 1999).

Sauerbeck, A., 1886, "Prices of Commodities and the Precious Metals," Journal of the Statistical Society of London 49, 581–648.

Sauerbeck, A., 1893, "Prices of Commodities During the Last Seven Years (with Discussion)," Journal of the Royal Statistical Society 56, 215–54.

Sauerbeck, A., 1895, "Index Numbers of Prices," The Economic Journal 5, 161–74.

Schoch, H., and M. Wagener, 1984, "Price Index Paradoxa," Methods of Operations Research 48, 113–25 (Athenäum/Hain/Hanstein, Königstein).

Scrope, G. P., 1833, *Principles of Political Economy, Deduced from the Natural Laws of Social Welfare and Applied to the Present State of Britain* (Longman, Rees, Orme, Brown, Green and Longman, London).

Selvanathan, E. A., and D. S. P. Rao, 1992, "An Econometric Approach to the Construction of Generalized Theil-Törnqvist Indices for Multilateral Comparisons," Journal of Econometrics 54, 335–46.

Selvanathan, E. A., and D. S. P. Rao, 1994, *Index Numbers: A Stochastic Approach* (The University of Michigan Press, Ann Arbor; Macmillan, Basingstoke and London).

Sergeev, S., 2008, "Aggregation Methods on the Basis of Structural International Prices," in *Purchasing Power Parities of Currencies. Recent Advances in Methods and Applications*, edited by D. S. P. Rao (Edward Elgar, Cheltenham UK/Northampton MA).

Silver, M., 2006, "Core Inflation Measures and Statistical Issues in Choosing among Them," Working Paper No. 06/97 (International Monetary Fund, Washington, DC).

Silver, M., 2007, "Do Unit Value Export, Import, and Terms of Trade Indices Represent or Misrepresent Price Indices?" Working Paper No. 07/121 (International Monetary Fund, Washington, DC).

Silver, M., and S. Heravi, 2005, "Purchasing Power Parity Measurement and Bias from Loose Item Specifications in Matched Samples: An Analytical Model and Empirical Study," Journal of Official Statistics 21, 463–87.

Silver, M., and S. Heravi, 2007a, "The Difference between Hedonic Imputation Indexes and Time Dummy Hedonic Indexes," Journal of Business & Economic Statistics 25, 239–46.

Silver, M., and S. Heravi, 2007b, "Why Elementary Price Index Number Formulas Differ: Evidence on Price Dispersion," Journal of Econometrics 140, 874–83.

Silver, M., and Webb, B., 2002, "The Measurement of Inflation: Aggregation at the Basic Level," Journal of Economic and Social Measurement 28, 21–35.

SNA, 1993, *System of National Accounts 1993* (Commission of the European Communities, International Monetary Fund, Organisation for Economic Co-operation and Development, United Nations, World Bank).

Solow, R. M., 1957, "Technical Change and the Aggregate Production Function," The Review of Economics and Statistics 39, 312–20.

Star, S., and R. E. Hall, 1976, "An Approximate Divisia Index of Total Factor Productivity," Econometrica 44, 257–63.

Stolarsky, K. B., 1975, "Generalizations of the Logarithmic Mean," Mathematics Magazine 48, 87–92.

Stone, R., 1956, *Quantity and Price Indexes in National Accounts* (OEEC, Paris).

Stuvel, G., 1957, "A New Index Number Formula," Econometrica 26, 123–31.

Stuvel, G., 1989, *The Index-number Problem and Its Solution* (Macmillan, Basingstoke and London).

Summers, R., 1973, "International Price Comparisons Based upon Incomplete Data," The Review of Income and Wealth 19, 1–16.

Summers, R., and A. Heston, 1991, "The Penn World Table (Mark 5): An Expanded Set of International Comparisons, 1950–1988," The Quarterly Journal of Economics 106, 327–68.

Swamy, S., 1965, "Consistency of Fisher's Tests," Econometrica 33, 619–23.

Szulc, B., 1964, "Index Numbers of Multilateral Regional Comparisons" (in Polish), Przeglad Statystyczny 3, 239–54.

Szulc, B., 1983, "Linking Price Index Numbers," in *Price Level Measurement*, edited by W. E. Diewert and C. Montmarquette (Statistics Canada, Ottawa).

Szulc, B., 1998, "Effects of Using Various Macro-Index Formulae in Longitudinal Price and Volume Comparisons," Paper presented at the 4th meeting of the International Working Group on Price Indices, Washington, DC, 22–24 April 1998 (www.ottawagroup.org).

Theil, H., 1960, "Best Linear Index Numbers of Prices and Quantities," Econometrica 28, 464–80.

Theil, H., 1973, "A New Index Number Formula," The Review of Economics and Statistics 55, 498–502.

Theil, H., 1974, "More on Log-Change Index Numbers," The Review of Economics and Statistics 56, 549–54.

Törnqvist, L., 1936, "The Bank of Finland's Consumption Price Index," Bank of Finland Monthly Bulletin 16(10), 27–34.

Törnqvist, L., and E. Törnqvist, 1937, "Vilket är Förhållandet Mellan Finska Markens och Svenska Kronans Köpkraft?" Ekonomiska Samfundets Tidskrift 39, 1–39.

Törnqvist, L., P. Vartia, and Y. O. Vartia, 1985, "How Should Relative Changes Be Measured?" The American Statistician 39, 43–6.

Trivedi, P. K., 1981, "Some Discrete Approximations to Divisia Integral Indices," International Economic Review 22, 71–7.

Turvey, R., 1989, *Consumer Price Indices: An ILO Manual* (International Labour Office, Geneva).

Ulmer, M. J., 1946, "On the Economic Theory of Cost of Living Index Numbers," Journal of the American Statistical Association 41, 530–42.

United Nations, 1975, "A System of Quantity and Price Statistics," Document ST/ESA/STA.73 (New York).

Usher, D., 1980, *The Measurement of Economic Growth* (Basil Blackwell, Oxford).

Vanoli, A., 2005, *A History of National Accounting* (IOS Press, Amsterdam). Translation of *Une Histoire de la Comptabilité Nationale* (Editions de la Découverte, Paris, 2002).

Vartia, Y. O., 1974, "Relative Changes and Index Numbers," Licentiate Thesis (University of Helsinki) (The Research Institute of the Finnish Economy, Helsinki, 1976).

Vartia, Y. O., 1976, "Ideal Log-Change Index Numbers," The Scandinavian Journal of Statistics 3, 121–6.

Vartia, Y. O., 1978, "Fishers Five Tined Fork and Other Quantum Theories of Index Numbers," in *Theory and Applications of Economic Indices* edited by W. Eichhorn *et al.* (Physica-Verlag, Würzburg).

Vartia, Y. O., 1985, "Defining Descriptive Price and Quantity Index Numbers: An Axiomatic Approach." Paper presented at Fourth Karlsruhe Seminar on Measurement in Economics.

Vartia, Y. O., and P. L. I. Vartia, 1984, "Descriptive Index Number Theory and the Bank of Finland Currency Index," Scandinavian Journal of Economics 86, 352–64.

Veelen, M. van, 2002, "An Impossibility Theorem Concerning Multilateral International Comparison of Volumes," Econometrica 70, 369–75.

Ville, J., 1946, "The Existence-Conditions of a Total Utility Function," (original French version in) Annales de l'Université de Lyon, Section A, IX, 32–9; (translation in) The Review of Economic Studies 19 (1951–2), 128–32.

Voeller, J., 1974, "Theorie des Preis- und Lebenshaltungskostenindex," Dissertation (Universität Karlsruhe).

Vogt, A., 1977, "Zum Indexproblem: Geometrische Darstellung sowie eine Neue Formel," Schweizerische Zeitschrift für Volkswirtschaft und Statistik 113, 73–88.

Vogt, A., 1978a, "Divisia Indices on Different Paths," in *Theory and Applications of Economic Indices*, edited by W. Eichhorn *et al.* (Physica-Verlag, Würzburg).

Vogt, A., 1978b, "Der Wertindextreue-Test und eine Vereinfachung des Indexproblems," Statistische Hefte 19, 131–9.

Vogt, A., 1979, "Das Statistische Indexproblem im Zwei-Situationen-Fall," Thesis, ETH Zürich.

Vogt, A., 1980a, "Postskriptum zum Natürlichen Index," Schweizerische Zeitschrift für Volkswirtschaft und Statistik 116, 93–7.

Vogt, A., 1980b, "Der Zeitumkehr- und der Faktorumkehrtest als 'finders of tests'," Statistische Hefte 21, 66–71.

Vogt, A., 1981, "Characterizations of Indices, Especially of the Stuvel and the Banerjee Index," Statistische Hefte 22, 241–5.

Vogt, A., 1986, "The Natural Index and the Divisia Index on the Straight Line as well as the Divisia Index on the Exponential Line," Communications in Statistics – Part A: Theory and Methods 15, 3567–82.

Vogt, A., 1989, "Rapide Historique du Problème des Indices et Étude de la Solution de Divisia," Journal de la Société de Statistique de Paris 130(1), 17–35.

Vogt, A., 1992, "Fisher's Test of Proportionality as to Trade and the Value-Index-Preserving Axiom," Diskussionspapier Nr. 66 (Forschungsgemeinschaft für Nationalökonomie an der Hochschule St. Gallen, St. Gallen).

Vogt, A., and J. Barta, 1997, *The Making of Tests for Index Numbers* (Physica-Verlag, Heidelberg).

Wald, A., 1937, "Zur Theorie der Preisindexziffern," Zeitschrift für Nationalökonomie 8, 179–219.

Walsh, C. M., 1901, *The Measurement of General Exchange-Value* (Macmillan, New York).

Walsh, C. M., 1921, *The Problem of Estimation. A Seventeenth-Century Controversy and Its Bearing on Modern Statistical Questions, Especially Index-Numbers* (P. S. King & Son, London).

Walsh, C. M., 1924, "Professor Edgeworth's Views on Index-Numbers," Quarterly Journal of Economics 38, 500–19.

Walsh, C. M., 1932, "Index Numbers," in *Encyclopaedia of the Social Sciences*, Volume 7, edited by E. R. A. Seligman and A. Johnson (The Macmillan Company, New York).

Westergaard, H., 1890, *Die Grundzüge der Theorie der Statistik* (Gustav Fischer, Jena).

Wold, H., 1952, *Demand Analysis* (Almqvist & Wiksell, Stockholm; John Wiley & Sons, New York).

Young, A., 1812, *An Inquiry into the Progressive Value of Money in England as Marked by the Price of Agricultural Products* (Hatchard, Piccadilly).

Young, A. H., 1992, "Alternative Measures of Change in Real Output and Prices," Survey of Current Business 72, 32–48.

IJzeren, J. van, 1952, "Over de Plausibiliteit van Fisher's Ideale Indices" (On the Plausibility of Fisher's Ideal Indices), Statistische en Econometrische Onderzoekingen (C.B.S.), Nieuwe Reeks, 7, 104–15.

IJzeren, J. van, 1955, "Over Verschillende Methoden ter Berekening van Pariteiten ten behoeve van Internationale Koopkrachtvergelijking," Statistische en Econometrische Onderzoekingen (C. B. S.), Nieuwe Reeks 10, 101–32.

IJzeren, J. van, 1956, *Three Methods of Comparing the Purchasing Power of Currencies.* Netherlands Central Bureau of Statistics, Statistical Studies, No. 7 (De Haan, Zeist).

IJzeren, J. van, 1958, "A Note on the Useful Properties of Stuvel's Index Numbers," Econometrica 26, 429–39.

IJzeren, J. van, 1983, *Index Numbers for Binary and Multilateral Comparison; Algebraical and Numerical Aspects*, Statistical Studies 34 (Staatsuitgeverij, 's-Gravenhage).

IJzeren, J. van, 1986, "Fisher's Ideal Index Numbers as Natural Divisia Results," Statistische Hefte/Statistical Papers 27, 89–99; also (in Hungarian) in Statisztikai Szemle 63 (1985), 117–23.

IJzeren, J. van, 1987, "Bias in International Index Numbers: A Mathematical Elucidation," Dissertation, Hungarian Academy of Sciences (Private Edition).

Zalin, G. (editor), 2002, *100 Anniversario della Morte di Angelo Messadaglia*, Studi Villafranchesi No. 14 (Comune di Villafranca di Verona, Assessorato alla Cultura).

Zieschang, K. D., 2004, "The System of Price Statistics," in CPI Manual (2004) and PPI Manual (2004).

Index

Printed in the United States
By Bookmasters